The Dreamer's Path
Twin Peaks and David Lynch the Actor

The Dreamer's Path
Twin Peaks and David Lynch the Actor

Brent Simon

TUCKER

DS

PRESS

Book cover and interior design by Scott Ryan
Edited by David Bushman

Published in the USA by Tucker DS Press
Columbus, Ohio

Contact Information
Email: Tuckerdspress@gmail.com
Website: TuckerDSPress.com
Instagram: @fayettevillemafiapress
Twitter:@fmpbooks

*For my Dad, who could never understand,
and my Mom, who never stopped trying.*

CONTENTS

David Lynch on the set of *Louie*, and in a short called "No One Can Understand David Lynch."

David Lynch, the actor, seen here being directed by Steven Spielberg
in *The Fabelmans* in 2022.

—PROLOGUE—

"For of all sad words of tongue or pen, the saddest
are these: it might have been."
— John Greenleaf Whittier

With the benefit of hindsight, I have come to the realization that *Twin Peaks* very much set me on my way toward becoming a writer, and an arts and entertainment journalist. If I'd already had some interest in writing, the original run of that show was a brain scrambler, in the best possible way, that helped me lean into those instincts.

I was no television historian at my tender age, but I certainly recognized I hadn't ever seen anything else like that on the small screen. It was transportive. The plotting was on a certain level achingly delineated (hey, a murder investigation!) and yet utterly unpredictable. Emotionally, the series was incredibly absorbing and substantively rooted in character, and yet also—with its deeply referential nature—somehow felt like it existed on an elevated plane of coolness. It challenged you even as it entertained.

I could write one hundred thousand words (and very well may have over the course of my professional life) on what *Twin Peaks* means to me. It gave the impression of being beamed in from a world beyond the stars—a world containing multitudes, yes, but also, despite its reputation for "weirdness," innate truths. Some of these larger truths seemed like things actively withheld by adults ("There's a sort of evil out there . . . a darkness, a presence"), but others felt born of and connected to more mystical realms. Things difficult to articulate but powerfully sensed.

Apart from being caught up in the characters and stories, however (and to me there was always more than just who killed Laura Palmer), *Twin Peaks* left me wanting to assay the complexity of feeling attached to such deftly juggled tonalities. How could I laugh at something unnerving, or be so moved by things that evinced such profound uncanniness?

The idea for this book was born in large measure from my enduring love for that show and in particular the way it incorporated and addressed the passage of time between its second and third seasons. The expanded prominence of the character of Gordon Cole was, to me, especially fascinating. While I don't by any means think it's a skeleton key to unlock or solve all the mysteries of the series, it did seem very important—this act of David Lynch, twenty-five years later, stepping back in a very physical way into this world he'd cocreated, the world of his greatest mainstream success. As Cole himself would say: "Now this is really something interesting to think about."

As I kicked the idea around in my head, my thoughts drifted back to *Zelly and Me,* Tina Rathborne's 1988 coming-of-age drama, which predated *Twin Peaks* and featured Lynch in a supporting role opposite his partner at the time, Isabella Rossellini. I thought about his work for his website (and, later, YouTube channel) and various voice cameos that reliably enjoy cyclical viral moments when younger Lynch admirers discover them and various fandoms collide. The manner in which he came to lean into performance seemed interesting—certainly something worth exploring.

• • •

Once you undertake an examination of this sort, you also have to decide on how wide an aperture to indulge.

In this case, multiple efforts were made to contact every living human performer (sorry, Jack Cruz) who shared the screen with Lynch, whether in a substantive dialogue exchange or even a nonspeaking role. For projects in which Lynch either voiced a character or provided voice-over—often recorded separately—the outreach tightened a bit, focusing typically on the writer and/or director, or on occasion other parties who could speak to Lynch's involvement and how it came to enter his orbit.

For short-form videos and other projects generated by Lynch himself (no small amount of material), I connected with numerous former assistants and behind-the-scenes collaborators. I also reached out to a select number of longtime below-the-line collaborators who worked on projects in which Lynch acted. Almost all parties spoke on the record, but some agreed to speak only on background or anonymously.

The idea was always to unpack all of these projects critically, chronicle elements of their production, examine Lynch's role in them, and gather first-person recollections of people who worked with Lynch on them. While these endeavors certainly aren't intended as exhaustive oral histories (especially on something as massive as *Twin Peaks*), my view is that the development and production details of certain works help provide a greater context for Lynch's participation. This is particularly true for projects that weren't self-generated.

Complicating matters, of course, was the timeline in which all this effort was undertaken. This project began in earnest in 2024, and much outreach and a fair number of interviews took place prior to Lynch's passing in January 2025. But many more took place afterward.

Some prospective and even hard commitments to participation fell through, owing either to other projects or simply a change of heart. Other collaborators, still understandably caught up in grief, didn't wish to participate. Some perhaps struggled to make sense of the frame.

Most heartbreaking on a personal level, though, was the fact that prior to his passing, Lynch had confirmed his willingness to sit for an interview discussing his acting work and so many of the projects examined herein. My sorrow, however, was unrelated to the book.

Like so many around the globe, I was crushed by our loss. The world had seemed better and more vibrant just knowing Lynch was out there, cooking up new expressions of art. The realization that the conversation itself—which I think would've been an extraordinarily lively and enjoyable one—would never come to fruition brought a still-lingering sadness.

Having had the incredible fortune to interview Lynch nine times over twenty-plus years (some relevant portions of which are excerpted here), I always felt his sense of humor and playfulness, while fairly widely acknowledged in later years, is still often undersold. Given that a good number of the projects in which he appears or to which he lends his voice could be classified as offbeat or unexpected, and that I wouldn't be asking him calendar-related details, questions about motivation, or other things I knew he couldn't or wouldn't answer, I expected an engaging dialogue that could maybe, just maybe, uncover a trapdoor leading to some special insights.

While that chat regrettably never happened, I'd like to think Lynch was intrigued enough to say yes because he saw some value (and perhaps no small amount of humor) in the oblique nature of my unusual focus.

The resultant work, then, travels a path very much related to but still notably different from the one I originally envisioned—an object lesson if ever there was one that life is so rarely exactly what we plan for or want it to be, but therein lies some beauty if we're willing to accept it. Perhaps there's another timeline or dimension where that imagined version exists. Who knows?

The good news is that there are still interesting perspectives to consider and incredible stories to share about Lynch's acting work—and by extension where and how this lesser-discussed element of his stupendous creative output intersects with his broader embrace of "the art life," and thus his overall artistic legacy.

−CHAPTER 1−

WHAT IS PERFORMANCE?

If you're going to attempt to write a book about David Lynch as an actor, it behooves you to spend some time considering what precisely qualifies in your mind as a performance.

So let's do the definitional thing. IMDb, for example, lists thirty-six credits for Lynch as an actor (though one of those still exists, as of this writing, as in development—a fact we'll get to later). If Wikipedia is your preferred jam, there are twenty-one listed credits as an actor. However, that's not including music videos in which Lynch makes an appearance or a number of short-form video projects from his eponymous website in which he stars or costars.

Does one count voice work and narration in works of fiction? I do, and will here. Lynch's distinctive voice and diction grabbed one's attention—a Midwestern accent, slightly flat and nasal, an emphatic foghorn that could be dialed up and down from benevolent encouragement to ecstatic certitude. Combined with his unironic penchant for old-timey lingo, it could make him seem like, well, a character out of a movie, but also someone connected to a higher level of authenticity and perhaps even knowledge. That it was deployed (and in demand) across a variety of media should come as no surprise.

Does one count documentaries on other topics in which Lynch sits for an interview? Or short films like Richard Beymer's "Behind the Red Curtain" and "I Had Bad Milk in Dehradun," shot on the Red Room set of the third season of *Twin Peaks* and included on its home video release, which are for the most part fly-on-the-wall-captured workplace moments with an unguarded, amongst-friends vibe? Of course not, most people would agree.

But what about something like "Between Two Worlds," a moody home video supplemental extra, written the day of its shooting, that made its debut on the *Entire Mystery* ten-disc Blu-ray release of *Twin Peaks*, in which Lynch serves as a solemn interrogator of the Palmer family? And what about feature-length documentaries focusing entirely on our subject, and for which special and sustained access is granted? Is there, in regard to the latter, a case to be made for such a work eliciting a level of "performance" from Lynch, since there is a perhaps heightened consciousness on his part that he is engaging in image making? If so, might something like *Pretty as a Picture: The Art of David Lynch* or *David Lynch: The Art Life* count?

The latter, which premiered at the 2016 Venice Film Festival, was released theatrically in March 2017. Shot over a period of more than three years, from November 2011 into 2015, it stitches together significant archival material along with images of Lynch working at home, and lays this footage under twenty audio interview recordings in which the filmmaker reflects on his life much more than on specific works from his estimable canon. In one interstitial shot in his open-air workshop, a sharp-eyed viewer can glimpse longhand notes on a yellow legal pad detailing a Parisian sidewalk meeting between Gordon Cole and Monica Bellucci, a scene which would appear in the third season of *Twin Peaks*.

Is this Lynch simply going about his work, evincing comfort with the film's makers? Of course. Is it also a case of the famously secretive Lynch engaging in an act of three-dimensional performance art ("What year is it?"), knowing this documentary would see release before the actual broadcast of *Twin Peaks: The Return* in May 2017? To someone out there, somewhere . . . absolutely.

One could also, if they desired, make a case that talk show appearances constitute a performance. (As a quick personal aside, I would like to lobby for some enterprising entertainment lawyer to tackle the complex rights issues, pro bono, and put together a comprehensive compilation of Will Ferrell's talk show appearances, full of colorful bits, gambits, and characters). While almost all widely known figures have if not a mask then at least a series of various public faces, Lynch's more mainstream television appearances (certainly around the time of *Blue Velvet* and *Twin Peaks*, but also much later) give off the feeling of someone knowingly leaning into a public persona that represents but a sliver of his complete self, or even his most genuine personality.

After over twenty years of interviewing movie stars for a wide variety of publications and across different platforms, I'm well attuned to the performative aspect of certain sit-downs, most especially if time is short and a camera is rolling. For Lynch, particular emotional markers (politeness, geniality) are hallmarks of these TV appearances. And I do not doubt that they are sincere, not merely because they mirror my own experiences in talking with him but also because they occur across decades. And yet more than one thing can be true. There can be value in leaning into a classification of yourself that has brought you a measure of acceptance and adulation.

So when Lynch appears on *The Tonight Show with Jay Leno* in 1993 in advance of a fine art show at the James Corcoran Gallery in Santa Monica, California, and brings a board with individually named bumblebees laid out in four rows of five and then talks about some of the photographs in his exhibition ("Heavy machinery in hospital basements are unbelievably beautiful, I'm not kidding you—it's so unclean, and organic"), it's not, in my view, that he doesn't have a sense of what the studio audience reaction is going to be. It's that he is, in a certain way, leaning into those nervous titters and arched brows, asking people to consider another point of view.

To be clear, I'm not promulgating the theory that Lynch is "posing" or being phony—far from it. I simply think he had enough social and emotional intelligence to recognize at a fairly early point in his career how he was perceived by others. As he then experienced various successes and setbacks, he came to sense how he "fit" within mainstream pop culture (which is to say typically on its edges) and absorb that knowledge into some of his public faces. So is he acting? Maybe a little. But even if so, is that necessarily any different from the social lessons we all learn usually early in life, on playgrounds and in school hallways and buses, and then integrate into our personalities?

As Lynch himself says in *The Art Life*, reflecting on his adolescence and keen desire to maintain partitioned identities: "So you act and speak and think one way in this environment, and then you act and speak and think in this other environment totally different. And then another way of acting and speaking and thinking in the other one."

All these wildly expansive and didactically parsed definitions of "performance" can seem silly of course—and I promise that this won't become (too much of) an academic treatise, truly. But they are somewhat fun to think about, and deeper consideration helps to establish useful parameters. The number of projects in which it could be said that Lynch is delivering a performance, then, maybe has less to do with some website's count and instead really just depends on how obsessive one wishes to be in their tallying. Another, more good-natured way of saying that, perhaps, is how far one wants to disappear up their own posterior.

So what is the actual number of Lynch's performances as an actor? We'll arrive at that answer in due time.

−*CHAPTER 2*−

WHY ACT?

From the outside looking in, the list of things David Lynch did not care about is a long one.

Of course, this isn't to say that he was an uncaring person—decades of tangible evidence assert quite the opposite in fact. But it doesn't take an exhaustive unpacking of his lifestyle or a hard inventory of his living quarters to ascertain his desire to hold at polite arm's length certain things that many other people tend to embrace as defining characteristics of their personalities.

Lynch did not much care about politics, at least by the measuring sticks many today would use. His ethical and moral worldview was, I would argue, evident in a good deal of his work (more on this later) and certainly in his advocacy for Transcendental Meditation, which he saw as a way to grow peace, both inner and outer. But for the majority of his life he was not in the habit of weighing in on current events or social causes or stumping for political candidates. (This changed over the last decade, but his "endorsements" were generally on-brand shared thoughts rather than detailed statements of recommendation.)

Despite his beloved coffee and the twelve-year run of his signature line (and perhaps red wine and, okay, Cheetos), Lynch did not seem to care a great deal about food and drink beyond the requisite sustenance it provided. (Cigarettes, of course, were another matter.) On *The Elephant Man*, he packed a tuna fish sandwich every day for lunch and saved his production per diem to be able to afford a car when he returned to Los Angeles. The stories of his six- or seven-year run of milkshakes and coffee at Bob's Big Boy are legendary, while his later "quinoa phase" spawned a beloved short-form work. When he found places and/or items that he liked, he tended to stick with them, sometimes for quite a while.

In dress, Lynch did not care about high fashion (ironic given numerous luxury brands' pursuit of him for their commercials) or styles of the time—

witness his adoption of and adherence to a standard work uniform of slouchy pants and long-sleeved shirt buttoned up to the neck. Sure, outfits could be a symbol of one's individuality and belief in personal freedom, and his works were meticulously, often gorgeously costumed. But in life, his preferences leaned utilitarian.

Even when hosting a journalist at his home, he did not invest energy in the notion of tidy self-presentation or attempt to dress any other way than he normally dressed or be anyone other than who he normally was. In some interviews, he joked about dressing like a bum most of the time, but in our last in-person conversation, he unself-consciously sported a well-worn shirt ripped open from wrist to elbow. Neither of us mentioned it.

Whenever Lynch lost himself in rhapsodic response or concentration attempting to summon forth a particular detail, he would close his eyes and just continue speaking, fingers fluttering in the air as his mind made its way to its intended resting place.

But Lynch wasn't ascetic. "David liked money. He was not trying to be a monk," said Peggy Reavey, Lynch's first wife and, like him, a lifelong painter. "He liked money, but he just didn't want to make it by doing stuff that didn't interest him."

Ditto *spending* that money on things that didn't interest him, things that weren't connected to his creative passions or family. Despite being born at the front end of a generation that would come to embrace American consumerism unlike any before it, Lynch himself had a far less rapacious appetite than most, it would seem safe to say.

Lynch's divorce from, or deemphasis of, these myriad elements—some literal, practical necessities of life, some luxuries or common hobbies or indulgences—was of course a way to devote more time and energy to the various creative endeavors that fascinated, enlivened, and sustained him. And Lynch was driven by a creativity perhaps as wayward as it was varied.

• • •

After one achieves success in any field, professional advice givers descend, telling you how to capitalize on if not your celebrity, then at least the market forces or trends that helped render some favorable outcome for you. Opportunities for endorsements or ancillary income exist in certain fields more than others, but if you're in the arts, the thrust of advice from any professionally retained representation will almost always be the same—make a version of the same thing you just did, but maybe different by around five degrees. If the success was more niche, the advice will accordingly center on how to pivot and go more "mainstream."

Sometimes, yes, after two or three (lucrative) repetitions, comes the advice to branch out in order to show "range." One thing you will never, ever hear, however, is to go and do something in a totally different field from whatever it was that just won you attention. It takes a lot of intestinal fortitude to remain true to oneself and one's own genuine creative interests in the face of this mostly well-intentioned professional steering, because we all like being told that our vision has merit, that our efforts are laudable.

I imagine for some fans of Lynch's films, there was frustration, especially after *Mulholland Drive*, that he didn't hew more closely to the conventional path of a director (especially an auteur filmmaker), reliably crafting a new film every two or three years, even if in his increasingly handcrafted, downscale-budgeted way. But for a lot of fans of Lynch's work, his refusal to conform to the sensible dictates of forerunners was a big part of the attraction in the first place.

Despite an incredibly fertile midcareer stretch that saw the lensing and release of six feature films plus the *Twin Peaks* pilot over a thirteen-year stretch, Lynch was likely never going to remain that type of guy. Yes, there were some of the typical constrictive market forces at work, plus other exigencies. But the scope of his creative exploration was not something to be fenced in or dictated.

While Lynch always exhibited an exacting craftsmanship in the selection and use of music in his films, here was someone who would take that love even further, branching out into experimental music and releasing collaborations as well as his own albums. Here was someone who would lean into emerging digital technologies in a childlike, let's-see-what-this-can-do manner as well as the community-building possibilities of the nascent Web 1.0. This isn't even including fine art and photography, which were always part of his life.

So why would Lynch add acting to his plate, lending his visage or voice especially to projects other than his own? After all, his pathway into film and cinematic auteurdom was not rooted in writing roles for himself. Why would he even care about performing if it pulled him away from these other endeavors, all of which either had deeper roots for him or were part of an ongoing, state-of-the-art, professional education that could be applied directly to his moviemaking?

Lynch chose to act for several reasons, I imagine.

One reason could be classified very readily as rooted in personal connection—of taking part in a creative endeavor with close friends and/or family and lending his participation to a project he viewed as worthwhile.

A second reason could stem from pure experiential desire. Throughout his life, Lynch exhibited a streak of curiosity born from a refusal to surrender his childhood innocence. When he wanted to learn more about something—

even if that something maybe scared him a bit or made him uneasy—he wasn't afraid to lean into it, to try to figure it out.

Famously, Lynch himself talked about tackling acting to get over a personal sense of panic and anxiety attached to it. "Mainly I did it because I had a fascination to see if I could do it—mainly to overcome this fear of acting, which is phenomenally fearful," said Lynch to David Breskin in *Inner Views.*

Also, while Lynch himself didn't speak of his acting often or deconstruct experiences in such a causal manner, some who knew him did talk about a couple of his earliest forays into acting giving him a stronger awareness of an actor's mindset and thus how to even better communicate with them as a director.

A third reason to act could be found in projects that gave Lynch an opportunity to more readily express his robust sense of humor and thus present a more complete or well-rounded public-facing version of himself.

Appearing on Charlie Rose's eponymous PBS talk show on February 14, 1997, Lynch was asked about comedy and whether he wanted to make one; his answer was a point-blank yes. Asked then whether he could do it, Lynch laughed and blinked hard. "I've made some attempts. I'm very interested in humor," he said. "I'm interested in a humor that can sit next door to horror or fear or something more serious. And an out-and-out comedy, even though I've written them, I somehow keep myself from following through and doing it. . . . Maybe the hardest thing to do is a comedy that works."

Despite ignoring *On the Air,* the dismally received 1992 ABC sitcom that Lynch cocreated with Mark Frost (who then had little to do with the show), these comments are revealing, as there certainly is no small number of Lynch performances that reach intentionally for comedy. Lynch's forays into acting then come into sharper focus as at least partially a way to foreground the rascally side of his eternal child, the same type of child who still lives inside all of us, the child of whom he spoke when he said in a November 28, 1999, BBC Two interview with Mark Cousins, "Inside we are ageless, and when we talk to ourselves, it's the same age of the person we were talking to when we were little."

Finally, a fourth reason for Lynch's interest in performance could be a way to connect with or advance the essential spirit of the art life, in himself as well as others. This certainly seems evident in numerous short-form projects and acting efforts from the last two decades of his life—unsurprising, perhaps, since with age often comes a consideration of and reengagement with the beliefs and principles that most matter to us.

Naturally, projects can check multiple boxes. And these classifications, as deeply considered as they are, aren't necessarily definitive. There's a diversity of opinion on the subject, even from people who knew him for many, many years.

One thing can be stated with certainty, however. Lynch didn't take acting roles for money. If easy paydays were the only aim, there's no doubt he could have very easily traded on his reputation and accrued goodwill among especially the artist class to score an assembly line of light-lift cameos in everything from genre offerings to quirky independent films. Lynch also could have cashed in on his well-known persona and distinctive voice with product endorsements in ad campaigns he helped create and steer. Offers of the latter variety were especially bountiful in his later years—proof of the great truth of the advertising world: when in doubt, try to co-opt cool.

Instead, Lynch made the colorful and interesting performance choices that he did. However essential, collectively and individually, they might have been to him personally, we'll never truly know. We only get to enjoy and contemplate, celebrate and debate.

—CHAPTER 3—

THE YOUNG-ADULT WONDER YEARS (1965-1970)

One of the great underdiscussed realities of life lies in the bracing, unexpected depths of post-high school life, from the end of one's teenage years into their midtwenties. Outright depression or even just choking, deeply rooted ambivalence—call it quarter-life crisis—can strike like a thunderbolt, wholly unexpected. No matter one's relative stability or previous advantages, these years can be tough. And also, of course, hugely formative.

When painter Bushnell Keeler, the father of a high school friend and an important mentor in Lynch's life, gave the teenage Lynch a copy of Robert Henri's *The Art Spirit*, the aspiring fine artist adopted it as his personal credo, amending it along the way to "the art life." This would in turn go on to serve as the name of the aforementioned documentary about his early life and work. Still, that certainty of direction didn't insulate Lynch from the choppy waters of young adulthood. He may have had vision, but not yet visibility.

Lynch had left two art schools by the time he enrolled at the Pennsylvania

Academy of Fine Arts, where good friend Jack Fisk was already matriculating. Lynch registered in late 1965 and met fellow student Peggy Reavey (née Lentz). Their friendship eventually blossomed into romance. The pair would marry in January 1968 and welcome daughter Jennifer in April of that year.

This period of Lynch's life has been fairly well chronicled in both *The Art Life* and his 2018 memoir, *Room to Dream*, among other sources. Lynch of course has long cited the city of Philadelphia as his biggest influence because of the pervasive fear he felt while living there. But it's still worth touching upon this era if only to situate and better understand Lynch's interests and noninterests. There's also the fact that some sources credit Lynch as an actor in "Sailing with Bushnell Keeler" and "Early 16 mm Experiments," the latter released by Lynch himself in 2008 as part of his *Lime Green* box set. [Photo below]

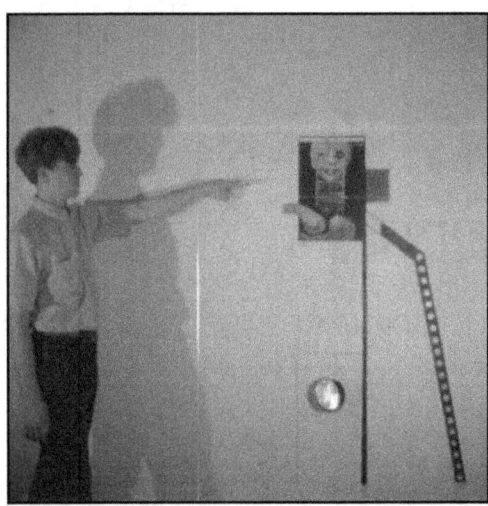

The former is a home movie Lynch shot on a Bolex 16 mm camera of him accompanying Bushnell and Dave Keeler (and a dog) on a daytime boat trip in the Chesapeake Bay; a life-jacket-clad Lynch appears in one three-second shot, seemingly mouthing a greeting. The short showcases a couple of hallmarks of later Lynch work—inventive framing and a heavy investment in mood, inclusive of a melancholic fade-out, plus a haunting, windswept soundtrack presumably added much later. Lynch seems incidentally captured. While he makes the choice to include himself in the footage, in my view this doesn't really clear the bar and count as a performance.

"Early 16 mm Experiments," meanwhile, consists of almost twenty-two minutes of material from Philadelphia strung together under music by Krzysztof Penderecki. Some footage is from the production of the trio of works that Lynch would self-recognize and canonize as his first three "official" short films on a 2001 DVD release, while other footage involves bits of animation tests and mirrored frames to create snowflake-like patterns—some abstract and some featuring Reavey.

Lynch's sole appearance is a clip running around two minutes and fifty seconds. In it, he acts out various measured movements with his hands while standing to the left of frame in front of an in-progress mixed media sculpture on the wall, never looking at the camera. While his actions (complete with, yes, characteristic finger flutters) could be adapted into a very fashionable modern dance routine, they would not strike most viewers as a performance. Lynch himself described the work as "a montage of those 16 mm experimental things, with a few pieces from 'The Alphabet' and 'The Grandmother.'"

In my discussion with Reavey, she joked that maybe what is regarded as Lynch's earliest short film offers a hidden indication of his future flirtation with on-screen performance. "That first movie he did ['Six Men Getting Sick'], which was on the sculpted screen, it was all his head and his arm, I believe, doing this," she said, gesturing to indicate their position. "And he was young and beautiful, so it was a good choice."

To hear Reavey tell it, she and Lynch were bound by similar creative sensibilities at the time. "I think we really were moving around in the same kind of territory," she said. "He was a much more advanced, sophisticated painter. He'd been studying painting for a long time before he even went to art school. But he barely went to high school, and I went to a really good school where I learned literature and all this stuff.

"In fact, he barely read," continued Reavey, more good-naturedly than chidingly. "I introduced him to [Kurt] Vonnegut pretty early on, that book *Cat's Cradle*, which he really liked. In fact, he mentioned it not that long ago. That's the book with ice-nine in it—I mean, you could see why he'd enjoy that. But I had this sense that you come out of studying all that literature, *Heart of Darkness* and *Man's Fate* and *Moby-Dick* and all the rest, and you have a dark view of mankind—a lot of that literature was about the darkness underneath. So I was definitely connected with him in that way. And I felt like I understood the territory he was moving around in—I mean, experimental film, *The Seventh Seal*, all that stuff."

Caught up in the push and pull between the beauty of youthful ignorance and the struggle of being young parents, the pair used money from their parents as a wedding gift to buy a house for $3,500. It was in a rough neighborhood, but its spaciousness afforded them plenty of room for their art. While Reavey described herself as "a painter, period," she was crucially active in helping Lynch hone his instincts and pursue his nascent visions in moving pictures.

"When he started to do film, both of us were equally ignorant, and that was a big, important thing," said Reavey. "We knew nothing, neither one of us. And he really—I mean, I think it's fair to say—did want my input much more than he would later, because later he was a lot more confident and had had training, and the women in his life were designed to do his laundry and take care of the set and all the rest of it."

The original idea for "The Alphabet" came from Reavey telling Lynch about her niece's dream, where she was vocalizing in her sleep. "With 'The Grandmother,'" said Reavey, "we were working together on trying to figure out this kid wetting the bed, which David never did. I did. My brother did. And so I understood the trauma of that, and we're trying to figure it out [because] if we just have a wet bed, you can't see it. So I said, 'Well, let's make it like a cartoon—let's paint that thing chrome yellow, just a big yellow dot.' That was one of the ideas that we [used], and it was never like, 'Oh, that was my idea, that was his idea.' It was his film, but I participated."

Outside of its footage from the discrete and fully actualized short film projects Lynch completed, "Early 16 mm Experiments" provides a snapshot of active spirits and minds at play. It contains a grab bag of creative exercises and perhaps, occasionally, even little objects of art in and of themselves. Mostly, though, it shows utilitarian work that served the primary function of helping Lynch and Reavey educate themselves on how to use cameras and other equipment and better achieve intended effect.

"I think he took a lot of stuff just for fun," Reavey said. "I remember in that *Lime Green* thing, there's a lot of footage of me running around pretending to water things and stuff. I think he was experimenting, just seeing what different light would do.

"I don't know if he would even say a lot of them were particularly films [or even projects]," she continued. "I guess he put it out, but it was more just stuff he did when we were sort of figuring things out."

While Reavey appeared in "The Alphabet" (as well as some of Lynch's other short-form work, like "Absurd Encounter with Fear"), she didn't ever consider herself an actress. "I thought of myself as paint, do you know what I mean? And I knew I had to do this," she said. "I didn't think of myself as a performer. I really didn't."

And if she wasn't a performer, Reavey said, Lynch was even less of one— apart from the usual rhythms of courtship and relationship patter. "He would sometimes do little performances, but they weren't on-camera things; they were just goofy," she said, recounting an in-joke the pair would indulge in when they would alternate imitations of a bird and the man who worked the cash register at the drugstore they visited around the corner from art school for lunch. "We thought it was hilarious. Nobody else did."

"Honestly, though," Reavey said, "he wasn't thinking about being in front of the camera. He was strictly thinking about what [things are] going to look like through the lens."

–CHAPTER 4–

"THE AMPUTEE" (1974)

"The Amputee" is Lynch's first completed short film after he and his young family moved west to Los Angeles following his acceptance into the American Film Institute. Shot in 1974, during one of the down-period breaks foisted upon the production of *Eraserhead* by a lack of funds, the project came to be when Lynch heard classmate Frederick Elmes needed to test two different black-and-white video stocks. Two versions of "The Amputee" exist—one running four minutes and fifty seconds, the other four minutes and four seconds.

As Lynch himself explained in the introduction contained on the DVD release of his short films, "When Fred told me that AFI was buying videotapes, it gave me a sadness, and I worried that they might have to change the name of the place. So I looked at Fred and I got an idea, and I said, 'Fred, does it matter what you shoot?' And he said, 'Well, what are you talking about?' And I said, 'Well, could you shoot anything you want twice, one with one stock, one with the other, and go like that, for the test?' And he said, 'Well, I don't see why not.' So I said, 'Could I write something, and make something for tomorrow?' And he said okay."

In a locked-down shot, a bespectacled woman (Catherine Coulson) whose legs are both amputated above the knee sits in a cushioned recliner, smoking a cigarette with her left hand and writing longhand on a pad with her other, as voice-over plays out over the scene. The full text of the script runs under three hundred words, referencing in first-person prose the shifting interpersonal dynamics and amorous feelings of various characters we never see (Jim, Helen, Harry, Joanne, and Paul) as well as the speaker herself and whomever she's addressing. In both form and style, it recalls any number of audition short scripts used in high school theater productions (more typically rendered in dialogue, but here as a monologue) where there's enough ambiguity in the words to invite multiple readings.

At around the thirty-five-second mark of the longer version, we hear a door open and then three seconds later slam shut. A nurse (Lynch) enters, clad in a white short-sleeve shirt and wearing an apron or smock. We hear the sound of water being drawn and some rustling of paper. Lynch begins treating the left stump, removing stained bandages, aerating the hole, snipping at sutures, and scraping the stump. Fluid starts to slowly leak out. At around 3:17, the wound spurts pus and blood, and Lynch dabs at it and

places a towel underneath. At around 4:22, Lynch exits, scampering out of frame. [Photo to side]

Lynch is of course notoriously a stickler for detail, so it's amusing that except for two words being transposed and a slightly more relaxed and matter-of-fact line reading on a single clause, Coulson's performance is remarkably emotionally consistent, while Lynch's silent actions account for most of the differences in the two versions. There's clearly an effort to maintain some continuity in movement and gesture (he touches his nose in both versions, though at different points and in different fashion—once rubbing it and once just with the back of his left hand), but it's nothing in comparison to Coulson's uniformity. Lynch is also dealing with the vagaries of practical effects throughout; the shorter version of "The Amputee" is the messier of the pair—the bloody mixture spurting out much more aggressively, up on to the woman's notepad—and because of that the more memorable. That moment gives the scene a jolt of unexpected dark humor, especially upon a repeat viewing.

While delivered by a single party here, the disjointed and open-ended narration, studded with non sequiturs, reflects a certain emotional kinship to the dialogue of *Rabbits* nearly thirty years later. Also, it's interesting to note that while one assumes the voice-over and the woman's scripting are presumably related, the pace of her writing—both languid and sporadic— doesn't really match what we hear on-screen. So is she recounting her own life preaccident? Crafting fiction? Daydreaming while penning something else? That's open to interpretation, let's say.

Again, knowing the background of "The Amputee" makes it difficult to truly judge Lynch's appearance (in which he's only ever glimpsed in one-quarter profile) as a full-fledged performance. It's certainly reflective, however, of his lifelong fascination with atypical physical forms, or deformity. While he's inarguably portraying a character here—and thus, if one discounts the previously mentioned snippets, this short film qualifies as his first bit of acting—it also seems clear that "The Amputee" isn't really about Lynch indulging an interest in performance per se. Instead, it more straightforwardly affirms his interest in DIY, hands-on (quite literally) filmmaking as well as working with dear friends.

That absorption and love with physicalizing the filmmaking process in very tangible ways would be a hallmark of his career, and last his entire life—as richly evidenced in behind-the-scenes material from the third season of *Twin Peaks*, where Lynch, his plate more than full with directing and acting, still spends time personally prepping everything from the pillow on the bed with Major Briggs's body to the hole in the floor in Sheriff Truman's office from which a bubbled Bob reemerges.

−CHAPTER 5−

HEART BEAT (1980)

Heart Beat, starring Nick Nolte, John Heard, and Sissy Spacek, opened in theaters on April 25, 1980, the eleventh film released in the second full year of operation for the fledgling Orion Pictures, an upstart film production company formed in the wake of the contentious exodus of five United Artists executives who then secured a significant line of credit and struck an exclusive distribution deal with Warner Bros.

Its first year's slate found some success. Jonathan Kaplan's influential *Over the Edge*, *Monty Python's Life of Brian*, Blake Edwards's box office smash *10*, and *The Great Santini* (which scored Oscar nominations for Robert Duvall and Michael O'Keefe) were among the company's notable 1979 releases.

The second film behind the camera for *Inserts* writer-director John Byrum, *Heart Beat* is crafted from a memoir by Carolyn Cassady ("suggested by" is the official credit), the widow of Neal Cassady, a major figure of the Beat Generation. Long before the term "throuple" existed, *Heart Beat*, spanning more than a decade, explored the complex and intertwined relationships among Neal (Nolte), Carolyn (Spacek), and novelist and poet Jack Kerouac (Heard), whose seminal *On the Road*, chronicled here from its embryonic form through its publication, would come to define the Beat Generation.

Lynch's first screen appearance on a project outside of his own creation comes in the form of a nonspeaking, blink-and-you-miss it cameo at the film's 19:21 mark, as a painter in the deep background. Lynch was married at the time to Mary Fisk, the sister of good friend Jack Fisk, who served as production designer on *Heart Beat*. According to Byrum, Fisk was his first hire when he received a green light on the movie. Since Byrum typically chose a painter whose work would define the look of each of his films, the pair met and decided on Edward Hopper as the inspiration for *Heart Beat*. Fisk then suggested Lynch for the project.

Running nearly two and a half minutes, the scene takes place at an art gallery. Unfolding in an uninterrupted shot, it focuses on Neal and Jack, who have fairly recently met and each obviously harbor feelings for Carolyn. She's studying to be a painter at the Art Institute in San Francisco but, as she tells the young men, also entertaining a marriage offer from an old friend of Neal's whom viewers have met in a previous scene. While Jack chooses a more subdued tack to convey his attraction, Neal, in rakish fashion, banters back and forth with Carolyn, teasing her about the idea of marrying "an asshole." After Carolyn walks off, out of frame, Jack and then Neal follow to continue their conversation, the latter heading over to a table and stuffing hors d'oeuvres into his jacket pocket. Before they can catch up with Carolyn, in the background we glimpse a figure of apparent success and coolness, his future so bright that he's wearing sunglasses indoors. Standing directly in front of a monochromatic painting, so close that his back could be touching it, is a painter surrounded by a small gaggle of admirers, possibly interviewing him about his work.

There isn't really a performance to speak of here, as Lynch is essentially an extra who is visible only if one is really looking (quite hard) for him. While online databases list Lynch in the project's cast, most properly note he was uncredited (meaning his name did not appear in the movie's closing credits). It's Byrum's recollection, though, that the artwork in front of which Lynch appears was his own.

The film itself, while not a masterpiece, is a quite engaging look at two highly notable historical figures, but also the destructively symbiotic and self-reinforcing nature of friendships that can form when people haven't yet arrived at the best versions of themselves. While effectively charting the death of innocence, it hangs its hat on rich, frequently playful performances (particularly from Nolte and Spacek) that belie one's expectation of a film about such revered, seemingly serious figures.

Leaning into romantic drama far more than any counterculture "scene," the movie is surprisingly candid and even irreverent about its characters' sexuality. In addition to partner swapping and a live-in love triangle, Neal is portrayed as bisexual. In one scene reminiscent of a circus clown car gag, Neal exits a small bathroom stall followed in slow procession by five other men—one of them carrying a saxophone.

For those looking for a few fun connections to Lynch and other collaborators, though, *Heart Beat* is produced by Edward R. Pressman, who would go on to produce *Wall Street* and a number of notable films in the 1990s, including Mark Frost's *Storyville*. The film's costume designer is

Patricia Norris, who served in the same role for Lynch's *The Elephant Man*, released later in 1980, and would go on to have a long and fruitful working relationship with him, serving as production designer and costume designer on various projects.

Additionally, one can't help but note that *Heart Beat* opens with footage of an atomic bomb test, which for many will summon to mind Gordon Cole in *The Return* whistling in front of the framed picture of the White Sands atomic explosion on the wall behind his desk.

To the strains of "Love Is a Many-Splendored Thing," by the Four Aces, this shot gives way to an aerial black-and-white view of an undeveloped parcel of land that in short order, by way of a time-lapse overlay, transforms into a look at tract homes—very much of a piece with the suburban cookie-cutter Las Vegas development in which Dougie Jones lives.

−CHAPTER 6−

THE ELEPHANT MAN (1980)

Given the years spent making *Eraserhead* and the frequency with which Lynch talked about movies creating a world to enter, one might think it surprising that he didn't slip into a featured role himself in his long-gestating feature debut. That he never seemed particularly tempted reflects Lynch's heavily partitioned mindset as described by Peggy Reavey, a holdover from the couple's Philadelphia years. He saw the art he wanted to create, but as of yet had no desire to step into it.

On *The Elephant Man*, though, Lynch was stepping forward in his career in just about every conceivable way. He was tackling complex subject matter rooted in historical biography—the story of Joseph (John in the film) Merrick (John Hurt), a severely deformed man who lived in nineteenth-century London. He was dealing with a much bigger budget than with *Eraserhead* and a fixed shooting schedule. He was also in charge of a full professional film crew instead of an intimate core group of collaborators filling multiple roles.

It would seem to chart, then, and fit a tidy narrative arc if Lynch had taken yet another step forward and slipped himself into his sophomore film—working in tandem with cinematographer Freddie Francis and his team to successfully conjure Victorian-era London, and then literally placing himself within it.

Lynch is widely credited online (though not in the movie's end credits) as Man in Bowler Hat in Mob Chasing Merrick, from a scene late in the movie. Merrick has enjoyed a brief respite from a life full of indignities only to be kidnapped from his hospital apartment by the alcoholic Bytes (Freddie Jones), his cruel showman "minder," and whisked away to a traveling freak show overseas. There, some of his fellow performers take pity on him and eventually book Merrick a ticket back home to England. When he arrives, clad in a hood and cloak that disguise his physical abnormalities, he's teased and followed by several children. After accidentally knocking over a little girl, Merrick is pursued by an angry crowd and cornered in a lavatory.

The latter part of this action is presented in a mad rush. Conveying with piercing clarity the surging panic of our titular protagonist, the sequence builds to the cathartic bellowing of the iconic lines, "I am not an elephant! I am not an animal! I am a human being! I am . . . a man!"

Earlier, near the beginning of the chase, at the 1:45:30 mark, the figure in a period-appropriate bowler hat crosses hurriedly in front of the camera left to right, mouth slightly open. It's a fleeting shot, not at all designed to showcase his visage. In fact, without the benefit of home viewing, most viewers probably wouldn't even spot this.

Though the man in the bowler hat is only one of many people chasing after Merrick, one could call this appearance as an extra a disproportionately crucial link in Lynch's on-screen filmography, notable for what it conveys about a small movement in his comfort level with appearing on camera in his own work.

There's only one problem with this narrative—those in a position to know say that's not Lynch in the shot.

"I don't remember that, and I was there," said *The Elephant Man* producer Jonathan Sanger, who went on to helm a second-season episode of *Twin Peaks*. "He was behind the camera the whole time, and behind the camera was the whole kiosk, in fact, because of all the modern elements."

The sequence was filmed at the London Underground's Liverpool Street station, which opened in 1874, and while it retains rich historical detail, it required a lot of careful planning. "We had an old train there, and John Hurt getting off the train, and shots up the stairs . . . we didn't do very much in terms of redressing the place because it was so big, so we had to really watch the angles," said Sanger. "It was a lot of work and [attention to detail], so that's where David's focus was, and I really don't remember [any cameo]. We shot everything in the scene there until you see [Merrick] going downstairs into the urinal, and that was in a different location . . . a urinal in a park in Shepherd's Bush."

Meanwhile, Jennifer Lynch, eleven at the time of filming, arrives at the same conclusion as Sanger, by way of a different recollection. "He did do something, but I believe that was cut out. That is my memory," she said. "I was not there that day, I'd gone back to school. But my memory is of him saying that he had done a little cameo to be in the background like Hitchcock did, for the fun of it, but then cut himself out."

Part of the lingering confusion perhaps stems from the fact that the man in the bowler hat is wearing a scarf similar to one Lynch is seen wearing in many production photos from the set. And while it's true that the most widely circulated screen grab of the purported cameo might resemble Lynch, the first frame of the man, which features a more direct shot, shows a seemingly much older face, with thicker eyebrows and slight bags under his eyes.

This contradiction of the incorrect credit notwithstanding, to say Lynch proved his talents on *The Elephant Man* is an understatement. A stirringly compassionate work that skirts easy sentimentality in favor of trawling the deeper waters of anguish, loneliness, and essential human connection, the film was both a critical hit and commercial smash. It secured eight Academy Award nominations, tying *Raging Bull* for the most that year. The professional opportunities its success presented—to step up to a big studio movie (*The Elephant Man* was released by Paramount, but actually independently financed by Brooksfilms), and the type of tentpole franchise entertainment becoming more in vogue in Hollywood—would set the table for Lynch's next film.

–CHAPTER 7–

DUNE (1984)

No recap of the troubled and compromised production of Lynch's third feature directorial effort is particularly necessary (though Max Evry's exhaustively researched *A Masterpiece in Disarray* exists for those interested in that story); the filmmaker's feelings about *Dune* are well-known.

"I brought up *Dune* once, and I said how much I liked it," said Louis C.K., who cast, directed, and acted opposite Lynch in *Louie*. "And he said,

'I died the death on that one, Louis. I died the death.'"

Jonathan Sanger recalled that while Lynch had smoked since he was quite young, during production on *The Elephant Man* he had stopped completely. "During that whole period, he never smoked at all while he was in London, where everybody was smoking. That was not part of his life," he said. "It only came back afterwards . . . probably around *Dune*, which I think may have done it."

"He said, 'Don't ever talk about *Dune*, ever. I don't even want to think about it, or hear the word *Dune* said,'" added Eric Bassett, who was integral to the creation of Lynch's eponymous website and went on to serve as the managing partner of his company Absurda.

And yet in an April 2022 interview I did with Lynch for A.V. Club regarding the restoration and rerelease of *Inland Empire*, when I asked if he considered a new cut of that film—because just as a viewer's relationship to a piece of art can change over time, so too can a creator's—Lynch pivoted, instead proactively mentioning *Dune*. For the first time, to my knowledge, he seemed if not outright desirous of a "director's cut" (something he had long denied was even possible with *Dune*), at least wistful about it and tempted in a vague, free-floating way by the cosmic possibility.

"I started selling out, and it's a sad, sad, pathetic, ridiculous story. But I would like to see what is there. I can't remember, that's the weird thing," Lynch said with a laugh. "I can't remember. And so it might be interesting—there could be something there." Here he paused. "But I don't think it's a silk purse. I know it's a sow's ear."

Intriguing words. While definitely not open, the door wasn't as tightly closed as it had been for most of the previous four decades.

This tidbit is, in my view, somewhat worth considering when revisiting Lynch's cameo in *Dune* (which isn't in question). It's purely speculative, but it feels as if Lynch's heartache over *Dune* hadn't been so deep, and his divorce from the movie so drastic, he might somehow have eventually found a way to pay homage in cheeky fashion to his act of self-inclusion. It is after all his first inarguably legitimate feature film performance.

This is Lynch planting a flag as a performer in a low-key but radical way—albeit in an uncredited cameo. Ergo, I like to imagine him incorporating "Spotter control, give me a report by the numbers" into a segment of the pandemic-era YouTube web series *Today's Number Is . . .* or dropping "Ordered by whom?" into a hardboiled interrogation of a monkey or perhaps making a short-form video for early-days DavidLynch.com in which he visits a grocery store cooking aisle, glances about forlornly, and intones, "We can't leave all this spice."

The above lines are all part of Lynch's *Dune* cameo, which comes in a forty-second portion of a scene charged with no small amount of energy, as Duke Leto Atreides (Jürgen Prochnow), Doctor Kynes (Max von Sydow), Gurney Halleck (Patrick Stewart), and Paul Atreides (Kyle MacLachlan) rescue a group of spice miners from a giant sandworm attack on the desert planet of Arrakis.

Arriving at just under fifty-one minutes into the film, the performance consists of a dozen short lines totaling a bit over fifty words in a radio transmission back-and-forth. Featuring four cutaways to Lynch's unnamed character, goggles pushed up to the top of his head and his handsome face smeared with dirt except for around his slightly glowing eyes, this sequence evinces a level of comfort with at least the *idea* of performance far greater than anything else Lynch had done up until this point.

Do we come to know this character? Maybe not deeply, but the brief sequence effectively communicates the preciousness of spice and the ingrained sense of duty and obligation its "worker bee" miners feel with regard to its harvesting. It's not a nonspeaking role, or dashing through the frame or appearing in the background of a shot as with Lynch's planned cameo in *The Elephant Man*. This is Lynch taking ownership of a small but important moment in a large-scale production with an extremely complex narrative. That in and of itself says something about how he was coming to view acting—despite the feelings about the overall finished product that would sit with him for most of his life.

—CHAPTER 8—

ZELLY AND ME (1988)

Tina Rathborne is probably best known as a *Twin Peaks* episodic director, having helmed season one's third episode, which includes Laura Palmer's funeral, and season two's tenth episode, which immediately follows Leland Palmer's death and finds Agent Cooper being suspended from the FBI and Major Briggs disappearing during a camping trip in the woods.

But Rathborne also wrote and directed 1988's *Zelly and Me*, an achingly tender, little-known drama of uncommon sensitivity. And if his few previous on-screen appearances represented incidental or flirtatious engagement, Lynch's first legitimate acting role in someone else's work marks *Zelly and Me* as the Trinity test of his performative career. Unpacking and understanding the circumstances that informed the film, ultimately paving the way for Lynch's participation, are valuable in understanding his decision to tackle acting and how and why it came in this form, at this moment, with this group of collaborators.

Born in Louisiana, Rathborne got her film education at The Brattle, a movie theater in Cambridge, Massachusetts, seeing foreign films as a child. She graduated from Harvard University and later attended Columbia Film School, studying under Frank Daniel and Miloš Forman.

Yet she also lived a life with no small amount of childhood tragedy, which would enormously inform her feature film debut. Rathborne's mother died in a plane crash when she was two years old. Only three years later, her father passed away. Separated from her siblings as different members of the family took care of different children, Rathborne was sent north to live with her paternal grandmother, who at that point was already in her midseventies. The emotional abuse through which she lived would form the spine of the heavily autobiographical *Zelly and Me*, which asks viewers to consider both the intensity of a young girl's feelings and the actions of those who would try to do right by her.

Set in 1958 Virginia, the movie centers on orphaned Phoebe (Alexandra Johnes), who lives with her wealthy but dictatorial and narcissistic grandmother Co-Co (Glynis Johns). Phoebe latches on to the love and kindness she receives from her live-in French babysitter Joan (Isabella Rossellini), whom she calls Zelly as an abbreviation of the title mademoiselle.

Co-Co clearly desperately needs love herself (watching the movie, one is reminded that hurt people hurt people) and is resentful of Phoebe's attachment to Zelly and indeed anyone other than herself. To that end, she attempts to break her granddaughter's spirit through emotional manipulation and outright cruelty, making Phoebe's life a series of tests she can never pass. When Co-Co's mistreatment of Phoebe becomes too much, Zelly confides in her sympathetic, seemingly well-to-do boyfriend, Willie (Lynch), that she wants to rescue Phoebe and take her away from Co-Co.

In addition to its highly affecting centering of a little girl's feelings—atypical of American studio fare during that era—the film depicts familial emotional cruelty and coercive language as a mechanism of control and abuse (drawing a child into a secret, for example) with a forthrightness far ahead of its time. These scenes land as not only perceptive (an unfortunate testament to Rathborne's lived experience, with many incidents and lines being lifted from real life) but also at times quite devastating.

There's a novelistic quality to the movie too. While evoking a very strong sense of primary identification with Phoebe, it also slowly manages to expand its canvas. At first blush, Lynch's character might seem extraneous. But by utilizing a bit more of a literary frame and showing viewers this separate part of Zelly's life, the film allows us to see Willie as one of several characters handcuffed to behaviors and mindsets from which they can't break free.

Rathborne's film is in some ways a spiritual forerunner to *Ponette*, Jacques Doillon's searing 1996 French drama about a four-year-old (Victoire Thivisol) who loses her mother in a car crash. Though *Zelly and Me* features an older protagonist (Johnes was ten at the time of filming) and focuses on the toxicity of Phoebe's relationship with Co-Co, both films are about little girls either abandoned by or largely lacking male figures in their lives and coping with the grief and trauma of losing a parent. In Phoebe's case, there's also the retraumatization of having her beloved primary caregiver ripped away from her.

That the "solution" to Phoebe's terrible dilemma, a half-sketched plan to abscond and craft a surrogate family, actually springs from adults and not Phoebe says something about maintaining moral certitude and radical innocence into adulthood—that there are utilitarian benefits, but maybe also limits.

• • •

After having directed a couple short films, Rathborne helmed *The Joy That Kills*, an hourlong adaptation of Kate Chopin's 1894 short story, which Rathborne characterizes as "essentially about my marriage, long before I knew that was the story of my marriage." The effort was broadcast on PBS in 1985 as part of the *American Playhouse* anthology series.

A year later, David Puttnam, the British producer of *Midnight Express* and *Chariots of Fire*, was appointed chairman and CEO of Columbia Pictures, a title he held for a little over a year, from June 1986 until September 1987. His brief tenure, however, was notable for his immediate and systematic plan to embrace young, unknown directors and low-budget features instead of bigger-budget, star-driven packages.

When Puttnam, by way of Rathborne's mentor Daniel, saw *The Joy That Kills*, he was floored, believing Rathborne to exactly fit the mold of his hard-charging vision of reshaping and revitalizing Columbia's film slate. He phoned and offered her a three-picture deal if she would fly to Los Angeles.

Rathborne, a quiet and composed figure who self-describes as "a lady with a very thin veneer of elegance, under which lies pure chaos," understandably jumped at that offer, and she took her recently completed screenplay for *Zelly and Me* with her. Having always been obsessed with Joan of Arc, Rathborne was watching Victor Fleming's 1948 film version, starring Ingrid Bergman, when she first heard that her beloved real-life live-in babysitter, the character upon whom Zelly is based, had died. "So I went straight to the dining room table and started writing, because I can only write out of pain," she said.

Upon landing in LA, Rathborne found that Puttnam didn't much spark to *Zelly and Me*. "They offered me some [other] scripts. One was about a woman who couldn't get pregnant," she recalled. "But really, the auteur filmmakers, Fellini and Bergman, who were visionary, wrote and directed their own material. That's what I thought filmmaking was about. I didn't think someone else wrote the script and someone else cast it. I thought it came from your gut, you had the vision, and your job was to execute your own vision."

When she took a risk by politely turning down the other scripts, Puttnam relented and gave Rathborne a green light for *Zelly and Me*—with a couple of catches. The budget could not exceed $1.5 million, and she would have to shoot nonunion.

"I was living at the time with Brian De Palma," said Rathborne, "and when it became clear that David was just going to shake up Hollywood, Brian pointed out this was going to last a very short amount of time. So there were a lot of compromises, but I at least had a choice." She chose to say yes and make her movie under those conditions.

• • •

When Rathborne returned home, she thought of Rossellini, whose mother, Bergman, had starred in the film she was watching when she first threw herself into writing *Zelly and Me*. Rossellini, as chance would have it, lived five blocks away. "I had always thought she was so beautiful. I had completely superficial interest in her," Rathborne said. "So I went and left the tape of *The Joy That Kills* and the script at her front concierge."

Rossellini received the package and, her curiosity aroused, dove into the material. "The first film she did, I was very impressed by it. There weren't too many women directors at the time, so I was intrigued to work with a woman," she said. "I was also working more as a model than as an actress, and I was wondering if there was [such a thing as] a woman's point of view—did they photograph women differently than men and all that? It's still a question that I have today."

The script for *Zelly and Me* also resonated with the actress. "My mom had a full career," said Rossellini. "She would always say, 'Of course I have to thank Hitchcock, Selznick, my father—whoever she worked with. But most of all, I have to thank Argenide.' That was the name of the housekeeper, the babysitter we had. Because Mama said if she didn't have Argenide and could leave us four children to her care, she wouldn't have had a career. So I did have a babysitter that I was very attached to, and I could relate to Tina."

Another point of connection was the script's early invocation (by way of a conversation between Zelly and Phoebe) of Joan of Arc, whom Bergman had played in two different stage productions in addition to Fleming's film. "I never understood why Mama was so fixated about Joan of Arc, but I think maybe it was the independence," said Rossellini. "She was a kind of a woman who was independent, a warrior. And Tina had the same kind of calling. Tina was very much a rebel in her aristocratic American family, even just wanting to work and wanting to be an artist. Mama didn't come from the same wealth as Tina but certainly had the same drive and love for work. And I think her passion for Joan of Arc was something that I identified with." Taken in sum, the elements felt like a sign. When the pair met in person and hit it off, their collaboration was sealed.

With Rossellini on board, attention turned to casting. "It was hard to get people to come in—men, males," said Rathborne. "Isabella didn't like the people who came in, and I didn't like them either. She said, 'Why don't you try David?' And I said, 'No, he's a director. He's not an actor.' But then she kept on."

"In the testing, a lot of them were manly," said Rossellini. "And I just thought that Zelly was never married [and was] somebody a little afraid of men. And so I thought [of] David, because David is very sweet. His nickname is Choir Boy. He's very charming and soft-spoken, and he comes across like a child a little, a bit naive, the way he speaks with the Montana expressions like, 'Oh, gee whiz,' all these things he says. I said [to Tina], 'He has a sweetness that I think he would justify more easily for Zelly to accept a man, because she's happy with the child and probably intimidated by men, and if you get a macho guy it's going to be hard.'"

At this point, Rathborne was already familiar with Lynch through her friendship with Rossellini. "He was her man. We used to hang out together. I knew him quite well by then. He's a great tease. We liked hacking around," she said. "And I called him Dave, to which he said, 'Nobody in the world would be allowed to call me that except you.'"

Still, Rathborne didn't see Lynch as a performer. Eventually, though, she relented. "He came, he read, and it was clear—he was perfect," she recalled. "I just was astounded. I don't think he got through the first page. I remember going, 'Oh my God.'"

"He was curious," said Rossellini "I mean, we were all at the beginning. So he wasn't that David Lynch of today, a superstar. And I was the girlfriend asking him a favor. He was experimenting and trying different things, and maybe acting—why not?"

"I remember he and Isabella being very close," said Jennifer Lynch.

"There was a lot of love there. And it makes perfect sense to me that Dad is a fine actor, because he's so good with actors. He so deeply understands what they're doing and how to support them. He really wanted to be better at both jobs, and *Zelly and Me* provided him an opportunity to work with people he was familiar with in a role that was gentle."

After the audition, even before filming, *Zelly and Me* delivered a revelation of sorts for Lynch. "He said, 'I didn't realize how difficult it is to go for a reading,'" Rossellini said. "'When I sat there with Tina and I was doing you, Isabella, a favor, I wanted so badly to have the role. I wanted so much to be accepted. And I realized how difficult it is to be an actor that is judged in five minutes, three minutes, and then dismissed.'

"So David said that since that experience, he has become a much kinder director when he does his own reading and casting. So that's good," added Rossellini with a laugh.

The rest of the film's casting involved plenty of drama, though. For the role of Co-Co, Rathborne originally wanted Linda Hunt, who turned her down. Irene Worth came in to audition and left an impression. "She threw the script at my face and said, 'This is disgusting. I just wanted to meet the person who wrote something so disgusting,'" recalled Rathborne with a slight shrug.

"My grandmother was feisty, diminutive, iconoclastic, and said what she thought—totally different than Glynis Johns," she continued. "But Glynis was a good actor, so I went with her. She could do it, but she did it in a more sentimental way than maybe I would've wanted. But I thought she was excellent, and she had been tortured as a child—so hence the connection to the material."

Naturally, making a movie with a child in a prominent starring role is a big risk. You need a sturdy peg upon which to hang your film. "I was there because it was important to cast a child with whom I had some chemistry, as they say," noted Rossellini. "So I was helping Tina, which is always hard, because a child doesn't have experience as an actor, and so it's not that you can look at their jobs they've done before."

For Rathborne, casting her surrogate was a challenging experience. "I wanted someone who looked like me as a child. My ears stuck out. I had my bangs. I was not looking for a beautiful child," she said.

The room out of which Rathborne and Rossellini were running the casting sessions was adjacent to a room where a casting team was looking for a young girl for a Saks Fifth Avenue ad. In what turned out to be a stroke of luck, the college student apprentice at the check-in desk for the latter sent Johnes into the room for *Zelly and Me* by mistake. "She came in and she read, and she had a presence," said Rathborne. "I was against her because of her beauty. You can see I'm perverse."

Rossellini was equally struck by Johnes, and Rathborne saw a tender, obvious connection between the two. Together, they felt they had their Phoebe. "She's a remarkable human being, unflappable. She had incredible equanimity," said Rathborne of Johnes. "The only drug I ever gave her was Coke. And a chocolate chip cookie when the days got really long."

• • •

Zelly and Me was shot in the summer of 1987 in Virginia, with one day of pickups on Long Island needed mostly for a close-up of Lynch's character when he comes out of his plantation home.

"We were shooting in a very beautiful estate, but we were staying in a very horrible motel on the freeway, as always happens," said Rossellini with a hearty laugh. "So we were looking so much forward to being on the set each day, because the set was beautiful and the motel was horrible and sad—you'd always hear the highway traffic, and the pool was the saddest thing I've ever seen."

Rathborne described a power struggle with producers Sue Jett and Tony Mark (who had also produced her previous work) in which they undercut her authority in ways both subtle and more pronounced in an attempt to inflate their own influence and prominence. "I think Sue and Tony did not like the fact that I had so much power [on *The Joy That Kills*]. So [for *Zelly and Me*] they gave me . . . I interviewed a cinematographer [Mikael Salomon] who I did not like at all," she said. "That would not have been the look of the film that I would've wanted."

With Salomon's selection—one of those little out-of-the-gate compromises that, in accumulation, loomed large—Rathborne embarked on a shoot that she felt was, if not fully at odds over the visual language of the film, still marked by a certain tension and difficulty in communication. "He was just very cold and unsupportive," reflected Rathborne. "And I think Sue and Tony had told him they were the producers. I don't think they said Tina's in charge. And in the end, that was all right. But it just was a very painful experience. I mean, I think he was competent, but I was very alone, whereas the cinematographer on *The Joy That Kills* [Misha Suslov] and Franny [star Frances Conroy] and I were very close—it was a very intimate, loving relationship."

Asked if that coldness was in any way gender related, Rathborne demurred. "I think it was his personality," she said. "I never once felt in all the time that I worked that my sex worked against me."

Despite such friction, *Zelly and Me* came in under budget and ahead of schedule. "I think it's because I drew everything, and we rehearsed so much," said Rathborne. "I write every single square, every single shot of the film."

Still, the battles and stress left their mark. "In the end, it was David and Isabella and Alexandra who kept me alive," said Rathborne. "They circled around me and gave me the love to get through."

"Listen, films are hard to make because you're always against deadlines," Rossellini said. "There's always everything that works against you. You imagine the scene on a beautiful sunny day, and it rains. You have an actor who may not remember the lines or doesn't exude what you thought they could exude and so there's no chemistry. I mean, technical problems. So you're constantly overwhelmed. It's difficult to make films, very difficult. There's so many elements and so many people that have to be coordinated.

"But I believed in Tina's talent and so did David, [so] I think we gave her encouragement. . . . We were all at the beginning of our careers, but we were appreciating each other's work. And sometimes you need that kind of trust from people saying, 'Yeah, you can do it. You have talent. You can make it.' So I think that's what Tina felt from David and I, and it was completely sincere. We really loved Tina."

• • •

Lynch's ten or so scenes in *Zelly and Me* total around fourteen minutes, or roughly one-sixth of the movie's running time. They compose their own arc—such that with just a bit more connective material, or perhaps a scene of Willie and Zelly first meeting, they could constitute their own short film.

We first glimpse Lynch early in the movie, when Phoebe's bus passes by and Willie walks out of a sprawling estate (the aforementioned pickup), while a voice-over ("If you get married, you have to promise to take me with you") establishes the depth of the bond between Phoebe and her nanny.

The scene that properly introduces Willie, running about two minutes and forty seconds, takes place, appropriately enough, at a diner. As Zelly drags in a suitcase behind her, a worried Willie rises from his table and asks her what happened. Zelly says she's leaving, and after she relates some of the particulars of Co-Co's abuse, Willie says "poor Phoebe," with great feeling. Their conversation continues, and Willie, reading Zelly's anxiousness and despair, performs a sleight of hand with his fork—a direct contribution from Lynch, Rathborne noted—causing her to smile. "I'm going to be missing our little meetings," she says, to which he replies, "Me too." The intimation here is that Zelly is considering leaving town anyway, but Willie has also had experience talking her down from similar emotional ledges.

A moment later, after she notices a monogram on his handkerchief, Willie says, "Joan [he calls her by her proper name throughout], I'm not who you think I am." Zelly replies, "I know. You don't have to explain to me anything. You're a very nice man, and I'm a very practical woman." As they talk a bit more, Willie asks Zelly about staying for Phoebe and then, haltingly, "What about... stay for me?" Throughout this scene there's an almost breathy quality to Willie's quietly spoken dialogue, firmly establishing the aching sincerity of Lynch's characterization.

After an interstitial sequence in which Willie takes Zelly home, there follows a second diner scene, running around seventy-five seconds. In it, Zelly slips into heels instead of sneakers outside, then enters, and the pair sit on the same side of their table. A totally besotted Willie gazes into Zelly's eyes as she talks about her lipstick ("Rapture red—I never wore red before") and how she feels the shade complements her cheekbones. At the end, Willie says, "Let me ask you a question: How in the world did you get so beautiful?"

Another interstitial drop-off follows, in which Willie blows a kiss and loudly says good night long after Zelly has exited his car.

Lynch's next scene is his longest, running over five minutes. In it, Zelly visits Willie at his home, tells him she's been fired ("Holy smokes" comes his reply), and informs him of her plan to take Phoebe with her back to Lyon, France. Willie pledges his help. After Zelly falls asleep while he makes her a cup of tea, Willie goes to his room, takes out a suitcase, packs up some bric-a-brac and an envelope of cash, and returns to wake Zelly.

"Joan, I've been thinking. I really wanna go with you and Phoebe," Willie says. "Now listen, tomorrow morning we'll go together and pick up Phoebe at her bus stop. You ask Phoebe if she wants to go with us, and if she does, we'll get a flight to Paris and get on that train to Lyon."

The next scene, running just under a minute, takes place in the morning light as the lovers lie in bed, Zelly wrapped in Willie's arms. When the phone rings, a shirtless Wille leaves the room to answer it. "The Alexander residence, good morning," he says. The rest of Willie's side of the conversation makes clear that the well-appointed home is his residence but not his house, and that he is in fact a live-in butler.

According to Lynch's daughter, this scene gave her father the most anxiety. "He was absolutely terrified," Jennifer Lynch recollected. "I've just always thought Dad had the most gentle, sweet chest. So I said, 'Dad, that's perfect for the character. You have the perfect chest.' And he just said, 'I have to get over the fact that I look the way I look. I have to learn to celebrate that. They're asking me to do this, and I don't want to disappoint anybody.' And he knew that the scene was important that we see him without a shirt on, we see him in both an emotional and physically vulnerable position. But that was a really big deal for him.

"It's so fragile a position to be in. [Willie] has done these incorrect things for all the sort of most loving, right reasons. So we understand him, but we also know he sort of fucked up [by hiding his true identity from Zelly]. Him being exposed I think was a really important part of that story."

The scene concludes with Willie (still shirtless) returning and informing Zelly of a change in plans and that he will meet her and Phoebe at an airline ticket counter.

"I know he gained great comfort from it being with Isabella. She was, as always, a great comfort to him and a great support," said Lynch. "She reminded him that making films, telling stories—all of that is playful. He knows that when he is directing. But I think when he got nervous or concerned about doing a good job for somebody he would forget, and she was very good at reminding him on a regular basis that this is the best job in the world and that he should be enjoying himself. I think that gave him a sense of . . . I don't know if it's bravery as much as just a gentle self-acceptance, like 'I'm playing this character and this is what this character's chest looks like.'"

Lynch's final scene comes when Zelly and Phoebe show up at Willie's residence and Zelly finally discovers his lie by omission and that it's actually also his place of employment. A heartsick Willie begs Zelly to take his money and says, "I love you, but don't you see? This is who I am." As Phoebe intervenes and helps Zelly get back into their waiting taxi, Zelly tells Willie, "It wouldn't have mattered to me."

• • •

Rathborne's own judgments about her film are rather harsh. "I'll tell you, I have many arguments with *Zelly and Me*," she said. "I've often done extremely self-destructive things." Earlier in her career, for example, she turned down an offer to play the lead in mentor Forman's *Ragtime*, something she still feels sad about. The weight of compromises on this movie and feelings of self-reproach regarding her professional life more broadly colored every nook and cranny of our lengthy conversation, frequently blinding Rathborne to her accomplishments and successes.

In addition to disappointment over *Zelly and Me*'s visual vocabulary, one of her biggest regrets has to do with the film's score.

"James Horner . . . said that this [was] the one film [that year] he would like to score," said Rathborne. "James came to New York, we met, and he did some examples. He was dead-on." Instead, Rathborne chose composer Pino Donaggio, a frequent collaborator of De Palma's, even though De Palma didn't influence her and in fact wanted her to use Horner, she said. "And when I heard the violins when they were recording the score, I thought, *Oh my God, this is not good.* It would've been a much better film, in my belief," with a score from Horner.

The crucible of production and these self-flagellations aside, nothing would fully prepare Rathborne for the experience of the film's path to release. She had already finished a first-pass assembly edit when Puttnam was ousted at Columbia, replaced by Dawn Steel. This left Rathborne in the position of having to ask a new regime to commit additional resources to a project it hadn't fostered or supported.

"I went to Dawn and said, 'May I have the money to, I don't know, remix it or to at least lower the volume?' And she said, 'Well, I'm not going to be a cunt about $40,000,'" said Rathborne. "Now, my reaction to that was, 'God, that is a brilliant line. If I used that line in a film, everyone would know exactly who that character was.' I wasn't the least bit put off by the language."

Once editing was done, Columbia set a test screening in New York. "I don't remember what theater it was, but it was big and it was crammed, and I was jammed up against the wall next to Brian," recalled Rathborne. As the movie unfolded and the rustling of popcorn bags subsided, De Palma leaned over and said reassuringly to her, "You have them."

Then, an unsettling disruption. "The lady next to me, a young woman, started sobbing so hard I thought she was going to get sick. So I leaned over to her and I said, 'Are you alright?' because I was concerned," said Rathborne. "When the lights went up and pieces of paper were handed down, I saw her write, 'This is the worst film I've ever seen.' Then someone—and you can imagine that I will never in my life forget this experience—a woman, who I know exactly what she looks like in my mind's eye, stood up and said, 'I'm going to kill the person who made this film.' Of course, I was dressed like everyone else, jeans and hiking boots or whatever. And you know the short story by Shirley Jackson, 'The Lottery?' I thought, *I've got to get out of here. I'm going to get killed.* As you can imagine, it was devastating."

Zelly and Me premiered at the Sundance Film Festival on January 23, 1988, and was released in theaters on April 15. While reviews of the movie weren't as unhinged as the test screening response, many weren't kind either. "Vincent Canby [chief film critic for the *New York Times*] was the making and breaking of the film," said Rathborne. "And so Isabella said, the night the paper was coming out, 'Okay, get in the cab. We're going to the loading docks.' So we went to the loading docks. She pulled out a [copy of the] *Times.* We got back into the car. She looked at it. She threw the paper out the window and said, 'We're going to have a glass of wine.' So I knew that it was not really necessary for me to read the article, and I didn't read any pretty much after that. I did read the *LA Times*, which said it was this sticky bun of a movie. And I have a lot of argument with the sentimentality of the film. I would do it very differently."

Rossellini didn't recall that specific anecdote but admitted to having the instinct even then to want to shield Rathborne, with whom she is still good friends today, from reading bad reviews herself. "I said, 'This is not the end of the story.' Yes, the review is bad or so-so or certainly doesn't make your direct producer want to make another film with you. Or there are some difficulties in gathering more money for your next project," she said. "But it's not the end. Because all my life I lived around independent filmmakers, and I heard how hard it is to find financing for their films. So basically I was telling her what I had seen, what I had experienced."

If Rathborne was at the time protected from the worst slings and arrows of film critics, there was one reaction which at least seemingly held the potential to sting a lot more: Lynch's negative response at a private LA screening.

"I remember it was a Columbia screening room, a small one," said Rathborne of Lynch's viewing of the movie. "I remember he was sitting at the end of a row, and as soon as the lights came up, I think he was wearing a leather jacket, he got up in a rage and swung his jacket against the chair and said, 'This is a chicks' film,' or something derogatory—maybe not chick, but like a girls' film, or something like that. And then [he] left. It was the only time [I ever saw him in] a rage. . . . But we never spoke about it again.

"And I understood his reaction completely on reflecting. I feel that because he showed his true feelings in the film with Isabella, that he was made too vulnerable. And also, I think he reacted the way that many reacted. I think there was a personal reaction, probably more personal in the sense [that] he [felt] too naked, or felt exposed.

"I can't remember my reaction. I was obviously saddened, but it didn't make me feel negatively towards him," she said. "[The comment] did nothing to our relationship."

Rossellini didn't recall when she first screened the movie, nor the forcefulness of Lynch's response. "Oh really?" she said when told of Rathborne's recollection. "I mean, this is what I liked about the film—that it was a woman's voice and sensitive and there weren't any guns or any explosions. And yet it was also very emotional. But I could see that also David would maybe say, 'Oh, is this enough to attract the public? Maybe it's not, because there's nothing sensational.' But I don't remember him [getting angry]. I remember him feeling like, 'Oh, I hope the film can find an audience.'"

Rathborne's characterization of Lynch's reaction would seem to be borne out by a contemporaneous interview with David Breskin in *Inner Views* (the same one in which he mentioned taking on the role in order to face his fear of acting) in which Lynch said, "I don't think Tina set out to make the movie as sweet as it was. It was her first feature film. One thing happened after another."

• • •

Regardless of response at the time, *Zelly and Me* stands as a moving, overlooked curio—not without flaws, but worth engaging with on its own terms. Like *Fire Walk With Me*, wildly misjudged by many critics upon its release, Rathborne's film is the victim of considerable bias and misinterpretation. While its tone or packaging may at times belie some of its heavier themes, its portrayal of psychological and emotional child abuse is evocatively rendered. Almost no reviews at the time substantively grappled with the darkness of this element of the film.

It's also fascinating that several high-profile critics talked about being unnerved particularly by Lynch's acting, but also sometimes Rossellini's turn. Even Jay Carr's largely positive *Boston Globe* review, in praising Lynch, said "there's always something scary about him."

Lynch's performance, to me, is incredibly sincere—the product of his personality, yes, but also a counterbalance to other characterizations in the film. Reactions like the one above are about something that's not on the screen, but rather something that seems to have existed at the time in people's minds as a vestigial reaction to *Blue Velvet*.

"I think a lot of the reaction to the film, in retrospect, was [viewers'] unresolved emotions towards their childhood major caregivers," reflected Rathborne. "I mean, I'm not saying it was flawless, because you've heard me speak about it. But I think the most violent reactions came probably from that.

"Isabella did say something very interesting," Rathborne continued. "She said, 'In Italy, I was always on the ramparts for feminist film, feminist art. And *this* is feminist art.'"

"It seems like maybe the film did come out a little early," Rossellini concurred, noting both *Zelly and Me*'s centering of topics typically more central to women's lives and the proliferation of modern-day spaces and platforms that allow for such works to more readily connect with audiences.

Did the more monstrous abuse eventually depicted in the Laura Palmer storyline of *Twin Peaks* flow in a small way, even if indirectly, from Lynch absorbing and pondering the themes of emotional manipulation and domestic trauma into which he had just dipped his toe as a performer a year earlier? One can't say for certain, but it's interesting to ponder.

Whatever else it is, *Zelly and Me* was also inarguably a leap of faith for

Lynch, an act of overcoming something of which he was afraid. In taking it on, alongside both a romantic partner and trusted friend, he established the basic template for so many of his forays into performance: that acting, for him, was less about radical transformation and more about indulging a sense of playfulness or leaning into a provocative space with collaborators with whom he felt confidence and kinship.

–CHAPTER 9–

TWIN PEAKS SEASON 1 (1990)

I f *Zelly and Me* helped Lynch conquer his fear of acting, then *Twin Peaks* would give him much greater confidence in the performative space. Another way of saying it might be, to embrace a popular idiom, that Willie walked so FBI Regional Bureau Chief Gordon Cole could run. Or maybe Willie talked so Cole could yell?

Perhaps it's stating the obvious, but this and other sections on *Twin Peaks* will assume a certain familiarity with the series and forgo plot descriptions with the same level of detail as some of the other projects explored herein. (If spoilers are a concern, it might be best to skip these chapters and return to them once you've completed the series.) Also, let's go ahead and dispatch with the notion that the reflection of Lynch in the glass in the sheriff's station during the *Twin Peaks* pilot registers as a performance because it's really him laying down a marker for the entire show's metatextuality or flagging that it's all really his dream. Or (and I'm looking at you, Galaxy Brain YouTube commenter) that it's somehow even him actually appearing *as*, or foreshadowing the appearance of, Gordon Cole. It's a production slipup (things happen), and just because a similar incident with Frank Silva reflected in a mirror was left intact and then integrated into the show's mythology doesn't mean Lynch was playing 4-D chess and calculatedly crafting a future performance.

• • •

The entirety of 1989 was a busy time for Lynch. The *Twin Peaks* pilot commenced its twenty-two-day shoot in Snoqualmie, Washington, on

Tuesday, February 21. Postproduction back in Los Angeles ran throughout April. On Monday, May 22, ABC picked up the pilot and ordered seven additional episodes. Then there was the scripting, shooting, and editing of a closed ending for the contractually obligated international version of the pilot, which included twenty-two minutes of additional footage.

In early summer, Lynch and Mark Frost sketched out the show's first season and cowrote the first two episodes—drafts and revisions are dated between July 12 and August 18. At the same time, Lynch was scripting and prepping *Wild at Heart*, which started shooting on Wednesday, August 9. "We were so busy we didn't have time to stop and think," said Duwayne Dunham, editor on *Wild at Heart* and editor and episodic director on *Twin Peaks*. "David finishes shooting *Wild at Heart* the same day I finished shooting episode one. We meet at the cutting room. He's prepping to shoot episode two, and we've got two cutting rooms set up, one for *Twin Peaks*, one for *Wild at Heart*. It's like musical chairs: where do you go? And then sometime in October David decided, even though *Wild at Heart* was nowhere near finished, it still was four hours and twenty-seven minutes long, he wanted to take it to Cannes. And so from that moment, from sometime in October to May, when we were in Cannes, it was full steam ahead."

In sketching out season one, Frost and Lynch might have had some loose sense of the potential fun in exploring the dynamics between Agent Dale Cooper and a FBI superior. Still, it would have been a difficult lift schedule-wise to fully integrate any character portrayed by Lynch. There was also not really a significant enough reason, in story, for such a character to make a physical appearance.

Ergo, Cole makes a voice cameo in season one—his name taken, as is fairly well known, from a character in 1950's *Sunset Boulevard*, one of Lynch's favorite films. In the one scene in which studio executive Cole (an uncredited Bert Moorhouse) appears in that movie, he's briefly glimpsed as director Cecil B. DeMille (playing himself) connects with him and discovers the real reason he's been phoning increasingly delusional silent film star Norma Desmond (Gloria Swanson). This is one of many examples of *Twin Peaks*'s dense cross-references to classic Hollywood movies, including *Laura*, *Vertigo*, *One-Eyed Jacks*, and more.

The character's name also has roots in two parallel streets in Hollywood, Gordon Street and Cole Avenue (their respective intersections with Sunset Boulevard roughly a half-mile apart), which Lynch and others have reasonably hypothesized was the original inspiration for the film's cowriter/director, Billy Wilder.

To hear Lynch tell it, as he did in *Room to Dream*, "Gordon Cole came when we were shooting a scene where Agent Cooper needs to call his unnamed boss in Philadelphia. I decided to do the voice just to make it more real, never thinking it would actually end up in the show. I was talking quite loud so Kyle could hear me, and that was when the character was born."

This recollection is charmingly illustrative of Lynch as either an occasionally incomplete or not always reliable narrator of his own creative life. To say that's when the character was born sort of ignores, you know, the script. Plus, Kimmy Robertson, who portrayed secretary Lucy Moran in all three seasons of the series, recalls Lynch sharing his dialogue with her beforehand, since her character connects Cole's call to Cooper. "If I remember right, which I'm pretty sure I do, he read it to me before, so I knew what it would sound like and what was going on," she said. "Which was rare, to know what was going on." Regardless, it seems fair to assume and say that Lynch slipping into the role of Cole came about from a feeling of "sandbox delight," of playing around within the world of *Twin Peaks*. Already established parallels, in both personality and interests, between Lynch and the character of Cooper created a fun lane where the former could engage with his on-screen alter ego.

Lynch's voice cameo comes in episode four, written by Robert (Bob) Engels and directed by Tim Hunter. The first draft of its script is dated September 26, 1989, with three revisions, on October 23, 27, and 31; revisions to the Cole scene came in the October 23 "blue" draft. The episode aired May 3, 1990.

Coming immediately after Cooper's conversation with Dr. Jacoby (Russ Tamblyn), which Sheriff Truman (Michael Ontkean) joins in progress, the call is mainly about providing evidentiary updates for Cooper (and by extension viewers), and Cole filling him in about the complaint filed by Albert Rosenfield (Miguel Ferrer) after Truman had slugged him. Cooper settles in in front of a small, corded Duofone intercom, creating a sense of

anticipation, and connects the call patched through by Lucy.

Cole's first words on the series: "Cooper, where do we start: the Palmer girl or Albert's new best friend, Harry Truman?" Cooper, naturally, focuses on Laura, and Cole says, "Albert has been very busy. The twine he found on her upper arms is a common household variety: Finley's Fine Twine."

Asked about the twine on her wrists, he replies, "Definitely not a match. No ID yet. And those marks on her shoulders? Bird bites." After a puzzled repetition of the last two words by Truman, Cole continues, "He'll also be faxing a reconstruction of the plastic fragment from her stomach."

After Cooper's reply, Cole continues, using acronyms for obstruction of justice and assault on a federal officer: "Now for the bad news, Coop. I've got an OOJ and an AFO here from Albert concerning his mano a mano with the local Sheriff Truman. Albert wants this guy's badge, Coop."

Cooper sticks up for Truman, releasing a wound-up, righteous passion that Gordon has clearly been on the receiving end of previously, as this portion of the scene ends with Cole squeezing in a couple interjections and "Don't get excited and hang up on me now," before exactly that happens.

This seventy-second exchange crisply and effectively establishes the basic relationship between Cole and Cooper—one of professionalism and mutual respect, but a bit of leeway granted Cooper in pushing back on decisions he deems unjust. The script also reflects some leeway afforded Lynch as cocreator, as one clause and one sentence are dropped from the broadcast version's dialogue:

The clause: "Despite the handsome shiner," after Cole notes that Albert has been busy.

The full sentence: "Albert thinks he'll have specifics this afternoon vis-à-vis genus and species," after Cole references the bird bites.

It's interesting to note that Lynch's 1988 short film "The Cowboy and the Frenchman" features a hard-of-hearing character played for laughs in the form of Harry Dean Stanton's ranch foreman, Slim. And Cori Glazer, who was script supervisor on both that short and many other projects with Lynch (and also had him saved as "Gordon" in her cell phone), finds it reasonable to assume there was at least the seed of inspiration there for Cole's partial deafness. "I'm sure it was," she said with a wide smile.

It's also amusing to flag that while Cole's loudness is clearly established, and Cooper raises his voice in pique defending Truman, we don't get the full stentorian effect of the character and there isn't yet any comic misunderstanding or back-and-forth in which Cooper has to repeat himself due to Cole being hard of hearing. "I think you could say, regrettably I suppose, that was a mistake the first time," said writer Harley Peyton, "but I think in series [later on] probably that would come from Mark or the director. I think it would've been very easy for either of them to say, 'Wait, [Cole] can't hear you. You need to raise your level to meet his level.' There's a comic element of it, and Mark always loved that kind of stuff. So because Mark would work with directors very much like he worked with writers . . .

they did a walk-through of every script, and I wouldn't be surprised if that's the part of the process that came up in."

For Engels, who scripted the episode (subject to Frost's final revisions), while Lynch's casting could have been spontaneous, it was nonetheless indelible. "I just thought, *This is a natural, to get him involved in this,*" said Engels. "So that was a fun one to get him to do. As I recall, we all could tell from the way that worked that this would be a great character to bring [back] in. David, he just played himself, do you know what I mean? He was a lot like Gordon Cole. We didn't change much. And it was just a fun idea."

For Hunter, the scene wasn't as remarkable—and certainly less memorable than other elements of his production week, like the llama he was able to corral for the scene at veterinarian Bob Lydecker's office. "I wouldn't have remembered [Lynch's voice work] if you hadn't pointed it out," said Hunter. "What I remember most about [the show], apart from the fact that the material was very good and very unusual and we did all think that this was something new, was the degree of freedom that they gave the directors to shape the episode the way they wanted. And also they would tolerate a certain amount of overtime if it was necessary, which I believe came out of David's and Mark's producer fees to some degree. They were very understanding, and of course I remember that especially, because later on in my career as a TV director nobody tolerated anything. It just became such a tough business in terms of making the hours and cramming impossible amounts of material into a single twelve-hour day."

While the secrecy surrounding *Twin Peaks* during production wouldn't fully take root until its second season, once it had become a bona fide cultural phenomenon, for a lot of the crew even Lynch's voice cameo came as a bit of a surprise. "I wouldn't get full scripts, but our department head would, and certainly we'd hear about new characters or people coming in or what was going on in other scenes," said a first-season crew member who wished to remain anonymous. "And I never heard anything about Lynch doing that voice. I don't think I knew or realized it until I saw it when it aired."

Still, even if they were caught unaware, folks working on the series weren't exactly shocked, and they felt it made sense. "That [casting] was talked about all outside of the crew," confirmed Ruurd Fenenga, who worked as first assistant camera on the first season of the show. "But the way David acts [in the scene], that's more or less how he is—as I knew him on the set."

"I don't remember, but I'm sure when I found out that David was going to play Gordon Cole, it was no big deal to me," said Dunham. "David had appeared in small movies before, and if he wanted to do that character then great—he'd do a good job."

The consensus regarding Lynch's season-one voice cameo seems to reflect the fact that whenever and however it was specifically decided, Lynch as Cole was either a casting decision made unilaterally by Lynch or in tandem with Frost. Either way, it more deeply personalized the project at a time before *Twin Peaks* had any guarantee of success. Lynch plays Cole with a crisp yet personable authority, lines delivered in the same timbre as his regular speaking voice, and there are trace elements of the delightful Cole-Cooper interplay viewers would come to witness more literally in season two.

It was a fun way, not unlike Frost's cameo as reporter Cyril Pons in the pilot, for Lynch to slip himself into the world the pair had created and the ever-expanding edges of its narrative parameters. The extent to which the idea of any further interactions or personal history between Cooper and Cole was formally fleshed out is largely irrelevant, as those questions would be addressed more organically once *Twin Peaks* was renewed for a second season.

—CHAPTER 10—

TWIN PEAKS SEASON 2 (1990-1991)

The first season of *Twin Peaks* was charged with ambition and an undeniable artistry. Eliciting a pleasantly woozy disorientation even as it challenged viewers, it became—against considerable odds and all expectation—a cultural juggernaut, racking up seven Emmy nominations and spawning three official tie-in books that would further stoke the fires of anticipation heading into its sophomore season. Making good on the possibility raised by season one's voice cameo, Lynch made his first on-screen appearance in season two as Gordon Cole, stepping, in literal fashion, into the world of Twin Peaks.

"I would talk to Mark pretty regularly," said Harley Peyton, a writer-producer on the second season. "We used to have lunch every day during production. But Gordon was something that [Frost and Lynch] hatched together, and I had nothing to do with. It sort of came out of nowhere. So then you would write for him. But David, I think, probably wrote a lot of his own stuff, although Mark really did so much of the writing. But that was a character that is sort of singular, in that it felt obviously a wonderful part of the context, but for me it felt a little out of context as well. And it's David Lynch—I mean, for God's sake, I'd never seen him do any acting before, so that whole thing was also a surprise and not something I expected. And of course it was wonderful on screen."

If Cole popping up was a surprise to some, it wasn't to others. "I will say this, David's very good at seeing the big picture," said Mike Malone, who worked for the duration of the series as its on-set dresser. "He can see an entire movie and say, 'Okay, I can insert this scene here. We can write this today and shoot it tomorrow, and I can insert it here.' He knows the whole thing, and all great directors do. [Steven] Soderbergh does [too]. So I'm sure he had it in his mind that 'Next season, if we get picked up, I'll be on camera.' He probably already had the big hearing aid thing in his mind, I'm sure. I can't imagine why he wouldn't have already thought that out."

"I completely understood it," said Michael Horse, who played Deputy Hawk, of Lynch's acting turn. "I mean, I found nothing odd about *Twin Peaks*. I found it a very organic experience. Being an artist and not really being an actor helped me navigate *Twin Peaks* far more easily than a lot of these other people."

"As long as I've known him, David has always been a bit of a provocateur—the kid who heard, at an early age, the Frankie Laine version of 'Don't Fence Me In,'" added Michael Ontkean, who portrayed Sheriff Truman. "One of David's mantras is clearly 'What can I get away with?'"

"I think . . . he loved the world of Twin Peaks so much that he could not help himself," said Kyle MacLachlan in a July 7, 2025, conversation with British Film Institute CEO Ben Roberts after the country's first-ever screening of a 35mm print of the pilot episode. "And he became part of the world of Twin Peaks when he put on the character of Gordon Cole."

To some, Lynch's love tipping over into the performative space may have even had an additional little nudge. "I do think Kyle had a lot to do with bringing him into it, because Kyle always thought David should act," said Jonathan Sanger, a second-season episodic director. "It seemed to me that he saw something in David he thought would be great for performance, which was not necessarily where David was coming from."

"Kyle and Dad are very similar people," said Jennifer Lynch. "Kyle is a version of my father that my father could interact with and appreciate in ways that he couldn't appreciate himself, just solo. So he and Kyle got to work together, and he got to yell at Kyle. . . . It brought him great joy, and it gave him permission to have a story go any way he wanted it to."

"You just thought, *Jeez, why not put him in here?*" added staff writer Bob Engels. "The great thing about *Twin Peaks* is we had such freedom to go any direction we wanted. It was so, in a weird way, free-form. Obviously we had to solve Laura Palmer and all that, but so much of it you could write in tangents, and some of it we gave up on and some we didn't. But the fun was trying to be more mysterious and at the same time have more fun with it, if that makes sense. It wasn't like we were trying to fool America. It was more, I always felt, that we wanted to make sure it stayed unique."

Lynch directed the first two episodes of the second season (Episodes 8 and 9 overall) and didn't appear on-screen as Cole until Episode 13. Unsurprisingly, the characterization was a hit with the cast and crew, in no small part because of its idiosyncratic spin on Lynch's disarming friendliness. "I just remember pure joy when David played Gordon Cole," said script supervisor Cori Glazer, assessing the character as a blend of familiar mannerisms and distinct acting choices, "maybe 50 percent David and 50 percent the character [just being] turned up to eleven."

"David had a joyful funniness about him," said production designer Richard Hoover, who saw in the character some satire of American cultural excess. "I don't remember how we found out. It was funny. We didn't realize he was going to do what he was going to do. He just kind of came in and did it. It was somewhat of his own little playground. But I think it was his fun moment, to tweak everyone's butt a little bit."

"I think he was certainly a natural at inhabiting certain characters, [and] in this case, he just walked into it and he just had it," said Peyton with a laugh. "The volume he spoke at, the hearing problems, the interesting, weird angles that he came at things, I mean, it made him a little bit of a cousin to Cooper, which would suggest the kind of bond between them already. I thought it was fascinating."

"Just seeing the character, it seemed over-the-top, but it was so funny," added Sabrina Sutherland, who served as second-season production coordinator. "And then, when you see it on screen, it was like, 'Whoa, this is perfect.' But I think when I saw it first being shot, I was thinking, *It's funny, but is it too much?* Because I couldn't really tell what it was."

"I always thought Gordon Cole was good, solid comic relief," said Malone. "Even in the scenes where he's more serious, it's still got that undercurrent of humor. David's got kind of a funny timbre and funny way of talking. And if he's going to raise his voice as part of the character, it's going to be funny. And *Twin Peaks* is so full of offbeat humor, so I think David knew that the character, the hearing aid and everything, was going to resonate."

At least one person close to Lynch, however, remains unswayed by his performance as Cole: Lynch's first wife, Peggy Reavey. "I talked to my daughter yesterday about this—she really loves the scenes of Gordon Cole, and I am like . . ." Here Reavey waved her hands, good-naturedly pantomiming aggravation. "They put my teeth on edge. To me, that's just too broad. But there are different ways of experiencing things, and Gordon Cole to me was . . . all one flat thing. But that's just me. I'm not saying that's objectively true."

"That is still one of the things I love about my mom, but that I really loved about my mom and dad's relationship and their friendship over the years—they stayed great friends all my life," Jennifer Lynch said. "And when we would Zoom on Sundays, that's the kind of thing she could say to him: 'Dave, it's one joke. The guy's deaf, I get it.' But he'd say, 'Okay, Peg. Okay, Peg, I get it.' She found him so much more interesting when he wasn't [just] one thing. She'll say, 'I totally disagree with you, Jen, but anyway, I love you madly.'"

• • •

If Lynch seemed to tap into a certain freedom in Cole, artistic leeway was likewise granted to the episodic directors of *Twin Peaks*, collaborators who abetted Lynch in bringing his character to life. Of the five season-two episodes in which he appeared, only one was directed by Lynch himself. One was helmed by Lesli Linka Glatter, who'd directed several episodes of *Amazing Stories*, an anthology show that ran on NBC from 1985 to 1987 and on which Johanna Ray, a longtime Lynch collaborator, worked as casting director. Glatter accompanied Ray to an early screening of the *Twin Peaks* pilot.

"Of course I flipped out when I saw it, and met David that night and said if this goes forward, which was hard to imagine that it would on network TV, I'd be honored and thrilled to direct," said Glatter, who spent twelve years as a modern dancer and choreographer before being nominated for an Academy Award for Best Live-Action Short Film altered the trajectory of her career. "And lo and behold, it did get picked up and I did get a call, and it was an extraordinary, life-changing experience."

Glatter directed one episode in the first season and four overall—second in the show's initial run only to Lynch's tally of six. "It felt like this ongoing repertory film company where everyone was around a lot, which was amazing," recalled Glatter. "And obviously David encouraged incredible creativity and to tell the story in the best possible way that you felt—there wasn't a codified method of what you were supposed to do, which made it intensely creative, collaborative, fun, and extraordinary." Glatter made it a point to be on set when Lynch was directing and found that illuminating. "I guess nowadays it's called shadowing," she said, "but I suppose that's exactly what I was doing. I couldn't wait to be around and watch him work, because it was so in the moment and intuitive. It was an education."

The other two directors who helmed episodes featuring Cole had even deeper connections to Lynch. Duwayne Dunham had edited *Blue Velvet* and directed the first episode of *Twin Peaks* after the pilot. Sanger had produced *The Elephant Man* and knew Lynch well. While the world of episodic television was generally rigid, these and other directors on *Twin Peaks* were accorded levels of flexibility and creative autonomy unprecedented for the time. "I just remember having fun because it was doing director stuff, not just following the bouncing ball and doing exactly what you were told to do," said Sanger. "I think most of the directors felt like that—that they could actually bring something to it. There was a style that existed, but you could play and have fun with the scenes and add stuff to them."

It's common now, but for those who didn't experience the show first run, it's difficult to describe how just about all abundance of mood on modern "prestige" television flows from *Twin Peaks*—that the saturation of atmosphere was integral to its hypnotic hold on viewers. It wasn't just a complementary seasoning, but in fact a vessel upon which all these characters had booked common passage. Lynch is largely credited with creating that tone with the pilot; other directors sought to follow his lead and find ways to put their stamp on material while honoring and enriching it. "I believe I speak for all the directors and David—we were making little movies," said Dunham. "I think we all shot it that way . . . and we shot them all like a movie because David had shot the pilot like a movie."

Sanger came to the series not only having "watched it very carefully, religiously," and having keen insights into Lynch's visual style and preferences, but with the added benefit of a comprehensive "cheat sheet" from his then college-age son (a huge fan) outlining the show's tangled relationship dynamics and hinted-at backstories. That came in handy because, dropped into a late-run slot heavy on Black Lodge lore after scheduling on an earlier episode didn't work out, Sanger often found concrete answers tough to come by. "Harley had adopted some of David's mannerisms," said Sanger with a smile. "I mean, if you ever asked David about the baby in *Eraserhead*, he shuts you down with a smile. He won't tell you anything. And that was something that Harley, in fact, had a little bit of—it was like he didn't want to explain too much. . . . I could never get a deep dive into the mythology any more than what I could ascertain from the stories I'd already seen. So you just had to go with it."

"Certainly one of the reasons why we got so many good directors to come there [was] because they had freedom that they normally don't get on television," said Engels. "There were a lot of feature directors that did it, and they had a great time." While the directors who helmed Lynch in his episodes as Cole weren't of that bunch (they had one feature directorial credit among them at the time), they were highly trusted collaborators, each able to bring to the table skill sets that helped put Lynch in a position to succeed in his biggest acting challenge to date. Lynch appeared as Gordon Cole in the following five second-season episodes.

• • •

Episode 13 (Airdate: November 3, 1990)

Our introduction to Cole arrives with a bang, scripted by Peyton and Engels. This was no soft-toss cameo: Lynch appears in three scenes totaling a bit under nine minutes. "I think that the introduction of Cole was something that was very carefully devised, but devised by Mark," said Peyton. "I mean, that whole scene break, the way he comes in to do those three scenes, and then the idea that he would be this character who was both comedic but also a really good way to get out exposition was something that was super valuable. And so just as a writer, you knew the points you had to get out, and you would try to get into the rhythm of the way he spoke. The two characters on the show who were the most challenging were Cooper and Cole, obviously, because they had very idiosyncratic dialogue rhythms. And for whatever reason, Cooper sort of came naturally. I never had a problem with that at all. Cole I found more challenging and maybe just because you never knew how David was going to approach it. It was just such a weird character."

"David did come to me [and] ask me if I would direct him, and I was so honored," said Glatter. "I couldn't believe it. I'm like, 'Are you kidding? Absolutely.' So I knew that [he would be acting] going in. It was a huge compliment. I was thrilled."

The first scene with Cole, interrupting the end of a conversation between Sheriff Truman and Donna Hayward (Lara Flynn Boyle) about Laura's secret diary, finds him walking past an open door in his zealous quest to locate the former. Sporting corded hearing aids and speaking quite loudly, Cole introduces himself with his full FBI title ("That's a real mouthful, but I can't hear myself anyway") and, when talking privately with Truman, delivers evidentiary updates on vicuña coat fibers found outside Cooper's hotel room (Truman's repetition of which Cole mishears as "tuna"), the One-Armed Man's syringe contents ("a combo, really weird stuff"), and papers found near Laura's murder site.

In writing for Cole, Engels drew inspiration from his hard-of-hearing mother. But much of the character flowed from Lynch. "A lot of Gordon Cole's beliefs or M.O. were David's; it was written for him," said Engels. "And David, as a writer, would have an input on that. David had approved the script, obviously, and then he would adjust how Gordon would fit in those things. He and Mark would do it initially, and then eventually it was all of us sitting with him. It was fun. You'd write one of his monologues, and then you knew he was going to adjust it. He did the rewrite on his dialogue, but it wasn't much. It was usually making it shorter: how about I do this, how about if I do that? And also, even if it isn't his episode that he's directing, he's directing that monologue, do you know what I mean?"

For Ontkean, a self-described "blind man when it comes to all the top-text mechanics and procedures" on set, the episode and scene were enjoyable but memorable chiefly for their lack of extraordinariness. They seemed familiar, in other words, despite the novelty of Lynch's appearance. "Nothing David ever said, or did, required any adjustment from me. Gordon Cole, or a character like him, was inevitable—fun from the get-go, a highly pleasurable dance partner," said Ontkean, who went on to describe Lynch as "being purely and absolutely attentive to whatever is humming in the immediate air" as a director but also an actor. Horse likewise noted that if Lynch was nervous, he didn't show it. "It seemed effortless to me," he said. "I don't know, maybe the guy studied, but I've never seen him seem to struggle at all."

It's striking how much informational output is required from Cole in a short period of time. Even as an acting neophyte, Lynch puts an appealing topspin on dialogue while powering through it in a believable way. "It's an incredible talent, because usually that's the dull part," said Glatter. "But I think for David, nothing was dull, everything was interesting." Part of the impact is in the writing, the verbal misunderstandings and call-and-response exchanges with Truman. But it's a smartly crafted performance as well, with Lynch making an immediate impression.

"There was never a time when you went, 'I have to make this shorter, because David won't be able to handle the dialogue,'" said Peyton. "You just didn't have to do that. I mean, happily you didn't have to do that with any of our actors, but not with David either. And again, it's funny because as a director, or producer, really, he wasn't always great at long-term planning. I feel like David was so instinctual and so in the moment. And that's a great thing on a movie set, but in television you're telling stories that have to make sense six episodes from now, and sometimes David wouldn't really worry about that. And so it became

my job and Mark's job to try to not clean it up but just kind of make sure that things were going to make sense. But I think as an actor, for whatever reason, he never failed to get the gist that you needed from him. He never failed to get the exposition that you might've thought, *Well, listen, he doesn't really think in that linear way. Maybe he just won't care.* But obviously he did. He came to the set every day. He was wildly prepared, and he was really great. If it was just some guy, you would've thought, *Wow, what a great addition to the cast and what a singular character,* because he was certainly that."

Cole's second scene, at the sheriff's office, was actually shot first. "It was David, and I wanted do a good job for him," recalled Glatter. "I remember being nervous, but then within a second I was totally comfortable because he made everyone feel comfortable. That was one of his many, many superpowers—being a genius, but the most down-to-earth genius."

The sequence opens with a close-up on the hearing aid in Cole's right ear, and as the camera pulls back, Cole's eyes scan back and forth ever so slightly. Cooper enters and, instinctively sensing his supervisor, snaps and points at him. "Agent Dale Cooper!" bellows Cole. With Truman and Hawk expertly placed in the deep background, reacting with bemusement, volumes are communicated about the warm acceptance between various parties—especially after a "private" moment between Cole and Cooper expands back to include Truman. The scene's comedy flows from Cole echoing questions ("You might ask the sheriff if we could use his office!") or flat-out repeating lines ("Looks like a chess deal!"), but the scene also establishes the depth of Cole's relationship with his agent, whose health he inquires about ("This worries me Coop. I feel a certain responsibility") before delivering a letter from Cooper's ex-partner, Windom Earle (Kenneth Welsh).

"Dad loves the absurdity of somebody who has to yell all the time and a man who was good at his job, but any interaction with him was innately absurd because he was constantly yelling and couldn't hear what you were saying," said Jennifer Lynch. "So there was an opportunity for misunderstanding but also this great authority. And he was a genuine down-to-earth American guy, Gordon Cole. When he got to play him, it just always felt like he had realized the celebration of it. And he trusted himself. He wanted Gordon to be great and loving and good, but he also wanted him to be deeply absurd."

"I have to say, being on the set, it was hilarious," Glatter said, miming stifled laughter and describing the crew struggling to stay quiet during filming. "We were all literally on the floor. He was so invested in it. I mean, it's hard to imagine anyone else doing that role."

"Yeah, we were just cracking up," agreed Malone. "David was injecting another fun element into it, and we were happy to be there and be the audience . . . there were probably people ruining takes from laughing out loud. It was great stuff."

For Horse, these first two scenes were funny but also made a statement, particularly when juxtaposed with the final Cole scene of the episode. "You know, all the tribal ceremonies that I've ever seen have sacred clowns, because humor is very important to the human condition, and I think David understood that," Horse said. "As we went into the darkness of the human condition, David would lighten that up. I mean, *Twin Peaks* spanned the whole spectrum of the human condition, but his understanding of humor—not just for the sake of humor, but the sake of how it helped with the lesson of the dark things that David was trying to explain to people—was so important."

If his introduction set the parameters of Cole, it's this scene with Cooper that demonstrates the character's most indelible qualities (that unique blend of earnest compassion and ridiculousness), affirms his place in this world, and establishes Lynch as a wholly credible performer. The off-screen rapport between Lynch and MacLachlan transitions on-screen naturally.

The provenance of Cole's utterance "You remind me today of a small Mexican Chihuahua," (much like the line's coded meaning) remains a mystery. "Engels was pretty funny—that sounds a little bit like an Engels line," said Peyton. "It was not mine. But to be perfectly honest with you, it also sounds very much like a David line. And David didn't write much on the show, but I remain convinced that when it came to Gordon he was an active participant. It wasn't like he was just improvising everything, but that's the kind of line that there may have been a line from Bob and then David just came up with his own."

Engels concurred. "It was probably an adjustment so that David could say it that way. He probably controlled the signal there."

Cole's final scene in Episode 13, coming at its end, is his most straightforwardly serious of the entire initial run. In the sheriff's station conference room with Cooper, Truman, Hawk, and an addled Phillip Gerard (Al Strobel), Cole has two lines as he draws a drug into a syringe. Letting Cooper lead the questioning of Gerard, the latter line ("If we give him the drug, Coop, you'll never see the other side") is a more than tacit endorsement of his agent's risky, withholding interrogation technique. The rest of the scene, a dialogue between Cooper and Gerard with riveting performances from MacLachlan and Strobel, fills in more of the story and relationship between inhabiting spirits Bob and Mike. Along with his scene partners, Lynch reacts nonverbally to these parceled-out, unsettling revelations. It's a different and intriguing side of Cole from the one glimpsed anywhere else in season two, one that would pop up again in *Fire Walk With Me*'s FBI office scene and be further explored years later with a more mature Cole in season three.

Episode 14 (Airdate: November 10, 1990)

It's here, ironically, in one of the most striking and rightly lauded hours of *Twin Peaks*'s original run, that Lynch's comparative lack of "ownership" or forward-leaning investment in his character, relative to where he ends up both this season and beyond, is most handily illustrated. In an opening-scene send-off in the episode, directed by Lynch, Cole stands in the sheriff's station lobby with Cooper, Hawk, Truman, Andy (Harry Goaz), and Gerard as the bulk of the group prepares to head to the Great Northern Hotel, where Gerard will attempt to help identify Bob. Perhaps further illustrating Horse's "sacred clown" point, Lynch and/or Mark Frost, to whom the script is credited, has Gerard repeat his last lines from the previous episode, but undercut their portentousness both through staging and by immediately moving on to other dialogue. At the scene's end, Cole, preparing to leave town, says his goodbyes to each character and theatrically clinks coffee mugs with Cooper.

It's quite easy to see—if Lynch had strongly desired—a larger role for Cole in the episode's narrative. The character wouldn't have had to be driving the action, but he could have been present, alongside Cooper and the Log Lady (Catherine Coulson), for the iconic concluding scene at the Roadhouse set to "The World Spins" (a song Lynch co-wrote), placing Cole even closer to the show's main mystery. His absence from the scene might suggest that Cole was not yet in Lynch's mind a significant filter through which to view the series. As a performer, Lynch was a *part* of the world but not quite so close to its center.

Interestingly, at a Hollywood Foreign Press Association press conference on September 8, 1990, three weeks before the show's second season premiere, Lynch responded to a couple of questions about his on-screen appearance—news of which had leaked in advance. He gave mostly anodyne answers, speaking glowingly about working with MacLachlan and Ontkean. But pressed with a follow-up, he eventually let slip a remark that with the benefit of hindsight lands more intriguingly. "I'm in one episode so far," said Lynch, "unless I can convince Mark if he'll write me in, you know, more."

Episode 18 (Airdate: December 15, 1990)

In this episode, directed by Dunham and credited to writer Barry Pullman, Lynch is again heard but not seen. The scene comes after a visit from Betty Briggs (Charlotte Stewart) to discuss her husband's disappearance and before Cooper's meeting with the FBI team sent to investigate his various north-of-the-border actions at the end of season one. With secretary Lucy Moran (Kimmy Robertson) out, a temp connects a call from Cole, who offers Cooper his full support before asking if any of the allegations are true. Otherwise, the call serves largely as a litany of positive-minded affirmations: "These are hard times, but we get through them," "Don't let 'em rattle you, Coop. These guys make a living looking through other people's drawers. We've all had our socks tossed around from time to time," and, finally, "Couple words of advice: Let a smile be your umbrella."

Even though it entirely makes sense in-universe that Cooper's boss is the one delivering the news, with the considered benefit of the bookend season three provides, it feels a bit notable that Cole is the one introducing the arrival of Agent Bryson (David Duchovny).

Episode 25 (Airdate: April 4, 1991)

Cole appears in two scenes in this episode directed by Dunham, the second, when it aired, after a five-week forced hiatus. Peyton and Engels wrote the script, the first draft arriving on January 9, 1991, with revisions coming through January 24; seven weekdays of shooting during the final week plus of the month ended with a production day on Wednesday, January 30, split with Episode 26. During the time leading up to filming, ratings had continued to slide, with four episodes having been broadcast since the arrest and death of Leland Palmer (Ray Wise)—two apiece in December and January, on either side of a lengthy holiday break. On Saturday, January 19, *Twin Peaks* won Best Television Series-Drama at the Golden Globes, while MacLachlan and Piper Laurie won acting trophies.

The first scene unfolds in Sheriff Truman's office, where Cooper, Truman, and Doc Hayward (Warren Frost) are wrapping up a conversation about a bonsai said to be sent by Truman's recently deceased girlfriend Josie Packard (Joan Chen).

Making a loud entrance (which does no favors for the brutal hangover Truman is nursing), Cole delivers to Cooper the classified portion of Earle's dossier. In a scene intercut with Earle absorbing their conversation via a planted listening device, Cole again delivers a blend of humorous non sequiturs ("Banzai!") and exposition. Before heading out to the Double R Diner ("The word linkage reminds me of sausage. Never cared much for the links, preferred the patties. But breakfast is a real good idea"), Cole asks Cooper to hang back. As the music swells, the audience prepares to take return of a version of Cooper who has been absent for a while. Cole reinstates his agent to the FBI, giving him back his badge and a brand-new-issue gun (described in detail) before he and Cooper exchange thumbs-ups.

"In television, generally speaking, the actors need to say the lines that are written," said Dunham. "In *Twin Peaks*, I think we had a little leeway there where we could play around a little bit, especially when you have David and Kyle together in a scene. I'm sure I gave him little notes here and there, but because David and Kyle are such good friends and then the three of us [had] the association with *Twin Peaks* and *Blue Velvet*, it was so easy. It was like each of us had the other's back, so to speak."

For cast and crew, it was another uplifting moment. "His hair was slicked back, which he never did," recalled Robertson. "I thought how handsome he looked in a Dale Cooper-type suit, and I felt a lot like I felt when I first walked into the conference room and saw all the donuts stacked up two seconds before we shot that [pilot scene], where they said, 'Lucy does this every night.' He surprised me totally, and it thrilled me because he was just somebody else. Then he did the scene and I have to tell you, everything was just perfect."

"There's a splendid formality to Gordon Cole, and that is entirely a creative character choice by David," added Ontkean, before landing on a two-word description that he felt best summarized Lynch's performance: impish solemnity.

Cole's second appearance is his longest overall scene and the most heavily circulated online, a beloved distillation of his (and by extension Lynch's) earnest wonderment. The scene begins with Cole, Cooper, and the still-queasy Truman entering the Double R, with Cole providing his hangover cure ("Raw meat and plenty of it, you break an egg on it, add in some salted anchovies, Tabasco, and Worcestershire sauce"), which sends Truman running to the bathroom.

After yet another thumbs-up exchange with Cooper, Cole spots waitress Shelly Johnson (Mädchen Amick), noting among other things, "That's the kind of girl to make you wish you spoke a little French."

Approaching the counter, where the Log Lady is eating, Cole earnestly and awkwardly pitches woo at Shelly ("I was wondering if I might trouble you for a cup of strong black coffee and in the process engage you in an anecdote of no small amusement") and is shocked to discover he can hear her perfectly. Asked if he wants pie, Cole excitedly exclaims, "Massive, massive quantities and a glass of water, sweetheart. My socks are on fire!"

In the scene's button, Cole, pie filling smeared on his lips, requests even more pie, plus a piece of paper and pencil to write "an epic poem."

The other side of this scene involves Cooper's flirtation with Annie Blackburn (Heather Graham), the innocent but troubled half sister of Double R owner Norma Jennings (Peggy Lipton), introduced in the previous episode. "I was a huge fan of the show," said Graham. "I was watching it, and I definitely loved it, and I also had a crush on Kyle MacLachlan." Graham had met Lynch after getting called in by Johanna Ray for a series of Calvin Klein Obsession commercials Lynch directed. She'd booked that job, opposite a young Benicio del Toro, and found herself in line for another in short order.

"He lived in the Hollywood Hills in a modern house, and I remember he had some kind of little project going on when I went over there," Graham continued. "He had a plate of meat he'd laid out and ants were crawling on it, and he was taking photos of that, and I just thought, *Wow, that is so bizarre.* After the commercial, I think he called me back. He used to do meetings at his house, and I think he said, 'There's a part in the show and her name's Annie, and she's kind of like a sports car—she's like a finely tuned machine, but it can go wrong easily because it's so complicated.'"

The notion of Cole hearing Shelly was struck upon early in the decision to revisit the character, according to Engels. Peyton, however, harbors thoughts of an alternate narrative path. "I kind of wish it'd been Norma, but I still understand the idea," he said. "I mean, it's such a nice metaphor for something. And in that sense, it's really, really smart." The scene was a blast to film. "Everybody was up for it. David was up for it, [Mädchen] was," said Dunham. "I mean, you couldn't wait: 'Let's shoot this.'"

Graham, not yet twenty-one at the time, remembered the experience as harmonious—but mainly funny, owing to her impressions of the persona she saw in both Lynch and the character of Cole. "David is such an interesting, unique person. I've never met a single other person who speaks in that kind of voice or tone, [it's] very distinctive. I find him really funny—I always feel like laughing when I listen to [him]. He's very quirky, and I probably am a little quirky too . . . so I can enjoy [that]."

For Jennifer Lynch, meanwhile, the scene most reflects Cole's abundance of joyfulness, which puts a smile on her face. "There was a tremendous amount of Dad and my grandfather and an old neighbor and just sort of things that made him giddy in Gordon Cole, so that it ended up being a celebration of people he knew and loved, but also an invention," she said.

Episode 26 (Airdate: April 11, 1991)
Directed by Sanger and cowritten by Frost and Peyton, this episode presents another send-off from Twin Peaks for Cole, much discussed and markedly different from the coffee klatch of Episode 14. "I remember him having to kiss Shelly. That was like, 'Oh, did he write that?' I think everybody was jokingly asking that," said Sutherland with a laugh.

"I don't think it's that controversial, but David likes the ladies," added Malone. "I can see why David would write that in or add that as a thing."

For Sanger, who was already working regularly as a director in TV and film, the opportunity to jump into *Twin Peaks* was fantastic, even if he didn't initially know that Lynch was going to be acting in his episode. "I was thrilled that he was going to be there, because he really wasn't around much in the preparation period," said Sanger. "He was there before I started prep, and he told me a little bit about [the episode], but he was not available during the prep period. I was hoping he would be, but he wasn't, so we just had to get along. But I like Mark very much, and Mark was great.

"The schedule at first seemed very ambitious, until I met the actors. Then I realized that we could actually accomplish what was scheduled in a day, because we didn't do tons of takes. I mean, they pretty much nailed it once you gave them what you wanted in terms of where the camera was going to be."

"I was thrilled to have him in the episode. I loved it," continued Sanger. "As an actor, David took it totally seriously. He was Gordon, you know, and that was it. When he was on set, he wasn't telling anybody how to do anything. He was Gordon. He was that character, and I could see his commitment to that role."

On the afternoon of Thursday, February 7, 1991, the penultimate day of Episode 26's shooting schedule, Lynch filmed his last scene as Cole for the regular run of the series. This was a little over a week before ABC announced, on February 16, an indefinite hiatus for *Twin Peaks* (ratings were in a free fall, the show having lost roughly one third of its audience since its return

in the new year). It was also exactly one week before the first draft of the series finale was filed, which Lynch significantly reworked when directing it. These facts lend some context to both the nature of Cole's final appearance and even, perhaps, specific lines (as when Cooper enjoins Cole to "hurry back" to Twin Peaks, and the latter says he will). The scene finds Cooper and Annie returning from a date and joining Cole and Shelly at the Double R, where the quartet share pie as Cole, preparing to leave town, speaks from the heart to Shelly.

While substantively the same as the television version, the revised (yellow) shooting script, dated January 31, does include differences in some of the dialogue, with handwritten notes that offer a window into the fine-tuning of Cole's characterization. The broadcast version, pulling back from a close-up of Cole's hearing aid as he and Shelly sit in a booth, opens with an unscripted line from Cole's tale of derring-do: "So he came slowly out of the shadows, leaving the dead girl behind." The scripted version also includes a line struck from the televised version, "Nothing like a colorful verb to strike fear in the heart of a common criminal."

A reference to the world being filled with beautiful women is slightly tweaked and made specific to Twin Peaks, while the number of pies ordered by Cole ("three each") is humorously upped. What might be a passing Jerry Lee Lewis lyric reference ("drives a man insane") gets dropped from the middle of the line "Coop, they say that love makes the world go 'round. Makes people who need people the luckiest people in the world." A couple of other changes are cosmetic or around the edges, a word added or dropped.

Until, that is, the aftermath of the scene's famous lip-lock, when Bobby Briggs (Dana Ashbrook) walks in to see his girlfriend in this unexpected clinch. A handwritten note for Bobby's dialogue ("I thought you were working") is *not* included in the televised version, in which he simply yells, "Hey, what the hell's going on?" The scripted lines "Two adults are sharing a tender moment, what does it look like? Poor kid acts like he never saw a kiss before. Watch closely, son. It goes like this" are significantly altered. The broadcast version, also annotated here, finds Cole saying, "You are witnessing a front three-quarter view of two adults sharing a tender moment. Acts like he's never seen a kiss before. Take another look, sonny—it's gonna happen again!" In both versions, Bobby stands slack-jawed and confused.

Revisions and adjustments are part of every television show. But the refinement here—in Sanger's recollection dictated by Lynch, though not in his handwriting on these pages—shows the scripting of Cole to be a living thing, open to molding with specificity and idiosyncrasy. There's a bit more edge and swagger to the version ultimately broadcast. In aggregate, these insertions and changes, while small, offer evidence of Lynch being

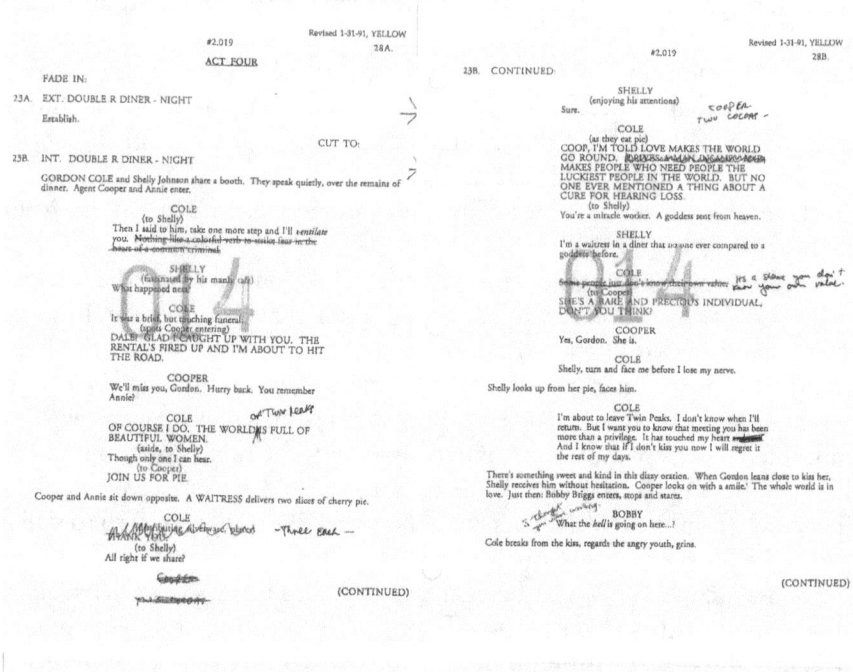

The changes for Cole's lines can be seen in this copy of a revised script from Episode 26, the final episode Cole appeared in on the original series. Script courtesy of Jonathan Sanger.

comfortable and in control of his character, applying a distinct vernacular filter.

Lynch and Amick reminisce about the kiss good-naturedly on the uncut version of the documentary featurette "A Slice of Lynch" on several home video releases, with the former calling it one of the highlights of his life and joking, "I remember thinking, *How sick is this, writing that into it so I could kiss Mädchen?*" ("But still the pen kept moving," jokes MacLachlan.) Both here and in *Room to Dream*, Amick talks about being honored. Clearly, their experience was rooted in a genuine warmth. Some younger fans who came to the series over the last fifteen years, however, seem to have . . . strong feelings about it. If you read the comments sections of videos posted on YouTube or message boards when the topic comes up, you'll see phrases like "weird and uncomfortable," "super creepy," "unnecessary," "always skip," and yes, many invocations of that Generation Z catchall, "cringe."

Asked about his thoughts on the scene, Horse said, "David doesn't have an arc," meaning that given Lynch's fine arts background, his more abstract approach to narrative and meaning renders largely irrelevant any need to dissect a plot strand too deeply. Interestingly, though, the segment sparked friction even at the time.

For Peyton, it felt unmotivated. "That's actually a thorny one for me," he said with a laugh. "I do remember being on the set that day—and this is my memory of it, and it's imperfect but definitely my memory—because I was angry. Somebody came up to me and said, 'David thinks Gordon should have a scene with Shelly, and that she kisses him.' And I thought, *Why? That doesn't make any sense to me. It doesn't make any sense to me based on who Shelly is, who her emotional relationships are, and (how they) have been developed.* I never saw Gordon Cole as that either. Rest in peace, David loved actresses a lot, and, I mean, if you want to know why Monica Bellucci was in *The Return*, it's just because David thought she was awesome, right? So that was part of him too. And I don't mean that in a creepy way at all. But the fact of the matter is that I found this idea creepy at the time, and so I resisted it and was not happy about it. And then it happened, and I remember writing a line for Bobby, but the fact of the matter is you're going to have to tell me if it made it into the cut because I don't remember. But I wrote a line for Bobby saying, 'What are you doing with that old guy?' That was my way of countering what I thought was sort of a weird, dysfunctional moment. David and I had a very complex relationship, and apparently David was not happy with that line of dialogue.

"I have many memories of the show, but I can absolutely remember being on set—and I had several of those moments with David—just thinking, *Oh man, we should not be doing this.* And I don't know if Mark was there or wasn't, but look, if David wanted to do something, it was going to happen.

"But I did oppose it at the time, and I still do . . . because I loved that character of Shelly so much, and I thought Mädchen was such a wonderful actress. As we were charting everyone's paths, I really felt that hers was one of the most consistent and best ones we did. I mean, there are other ones that were a little more inconsistent—James, for example."

Engels, though, had a different assessment. "Oh no, I liked the kiss," he said with a laugh. "That seemed like something that . . . it's like you want to keep twisting stuff. A lot of television episodic is just twisting the story as much and as long as you can get away with it. And that's what I thought about that, as I remember." Asked if he remembered it being a late addition or from where the idea was generated, Engels didn't recall.

• • •

From frame one, Gordon Cole felt like a force. Always seemingly coming from or going to Bend, Oregon ("Whole lotta shakin' going on in Bend"), he served a valuable function plotwise but also delivered no small amount of character-based comedic entertainment in a series full of colorful players. "It feels like David is so distinct and one of a kind that he's always going to be interesting on camera," mused Malone.

Looking back, it feels like Lynch's second-season work as Cole— consisting of just over twenty-one minutes of screen time spread out over eight scenes—helped his creative life evolve in useful fashion, perhaps tipping him even further into trusting his intuition. There's undeniable playfulness in Lynch's performance across these episodes, but one can't help but also notice it brims with confidence. Not far removed from *Zelly and Me* and a time when Lynch had described acting as phenomenally fearful, this was a jump into the deep end of a pool. But it was a familiar pool. He was surrounded by friends and trusted collaborators, and *Twin Peaks* was a project he knew completely.

His efforts were embraced by viewers and colleagues alike. Ontkean connected Lynch's performative sensibility to his supreme empathy for actors and ability to inhabit, in his mind's eye, multiple characters while directing. Other interviewees made similar points, comparing the joy that Lynch conveyed at helping guide an actor's performance to the gleefulness he radiated as Cole.

"I think if he was an on-screen character, it always feels to me like it's a certain aspect or extension of at least a part of who he is," said Jay Aaseng, who worked for Lynch for seven years as an assistant. "The Gordon Cole character feels very much like he's letting his inner child out a little more. He already speaks with a lot of intent in that way, so for him to just kind of amp that up a little more is such a perfect thing for him."

−CHAPTER 11−

TWIN PEAKS: FIRE WALK WITH ME (1992)

Following its cancellation by ABC, *Twin Peaks* faced an uncertain future. Streaming services didn't yet exist, and the cable television landscape was radically different; the market for "prestige" TV, shows that consistently employed high film production value and cinematic language, would be born and evolve very much on the back of *Twin Peaks*, as creatives like David Chase, Matthew Weiner, and Vince Gilligan would later attest. Aaron Spelling Productions explored jumping to another network, which was rare at the time, but the hurdles for that type of move were substantial—ranging from high production costs to the frayed partnership between Lynch and Mark Frost.

So it was that remaining hardcore fans waited on tenterhooks as difficult-to-source reporting ping-ponged back and forth over the fate of a potential *Twin Peaks* film. There was interest in a movie! Wait, funding snagged. It was greenlit! Wait, theatrical rights, involving multiple companies spanning two continents, were a tangled mess and under legal dispute. That's been resolved, and it's back on! Wait, Kyle MacLachlan was leery about being typecast and not keen to return, so the whole project was in jeopardy. The character of Chester Desmond was born, absorbing some of Cooper's actions; MacLachlan signed on for less than a week of shooting, and eventually *Twin Peaks: Fire Walk With Me* was born.

Reported in less detail at the time was the creative impasse: Frost wanted to push the story forward, while Lynch preferred a prequel examining the last seven days of Laura Palmer's life, and the previous murder tied to her case. In the end, Frost stepped aside. He retained an executive producer credit but had no creative input. If relations between Lynch and Frost were strained, they were even worse between Lynch and one of the other driving creative forces of *Twin Peaks*'s second season, Harley Peyton. During the time Frost was off shooting his feature directorial debut, *Storyville*, Peyton was given the impossible task of attempting to enforce creative decisions and production exigencies upon one of the show's cocreators and bore the brunt of Lynch's displeasure over these efforts. *Fire Walk With Me*, then, would stretch in a different direction.

"Well, David and I clearly were not getting along, so I didn't talk to him that much," admitted Peyton. "I would hear this kind of laughing and chuckling, and Bob Engels, who's a very funny guy, he and David would be sitting in Bob's office kind of just laughing it up and hanging out. I [went], 'Well, that's interesting.' It just seemed weird to me. David didn't do a lot of socializing like that."

In Engels, Lynch found a kindred spirit with whom he would forge both a friendship and working relationship that would extend across a couple other projects, the short-lived *On the Air* being the only other one to see a screen. "Clearly he and Bob got along, although I suspect . . . I mean, I don't want to insult Bob, but I suspect [on *Fire Walk With Me*] he was taking dictation most of the case," said Peyton. "And maybe that's what David needed—that he just wanted to write and direct it himself, and he wasn't going to be in a world where Mark could tell him that maybe something didn't work or something worked better or whatever."

Principal photography began on location on September 5, 1991, in the Snoqualmie and North Bend area of Washington state and moved to Southern California after about four weeks, with both location and soundstage filming continuing, the latter at City Studios, the same San Fernando site used during the TV show. Laura's death scene would end the official shoot on Halloween, with a day of insert shots being filmed on November 1.

In the prologue, set before the action shifts to Twin Peaks, Lynch appears as Cole in three scenes, filmed in Washington during the first and second weeks. The character was always set to be part of the mix, and the number and scope of his scenes were unaffected by script changes dictated by MacLachlan's reduced participation, said Engels.

In the first scene, coming just past the three-minute mark, after a shot of Teresa Banks's body floating down a river, Cole appears standing, in profile, in his Portland, Oregon, office, barking directions ("Get me Agent Chester Desmond out in Fargo, North Dakota!") to a brunette secretary who, pencil and pad in hand, does not bother taking dictation. Cut to Desmond (Chris Isaak) in the field making an arrest of two presumed prostitutes in front of a school bus full of crying children; he takes a phone call from a yelling Cole, who tells him about the murder of Banks. Still standing, Cole receives a mugful of coffee (holding it from the bottom) from a blonde secretary and finishes up his briefing, saying, "Chet, I've got a surprise for you— something interesting I would like to show you. Arrangements are being made, and I will meet you at the private Portland airport."

While *Fire Walk With Me* would go on to reveal both its narrative audaciousness and ambition—depicting Laura's hellish final week but also sprinkling in elements that pushed the story forward or at least hinted at new narrative connections—opening the movie with thirty-two minutes before ever getting to the town of Twin Peaks was a radical choice. "Part of it is trying to reward people that have seen the shows and now they're at the movie," said Engels. "And another part of it is 'Jeez, we're making a movie. Let's do other stuff. This is a movie now—and it's a Lynch movie.' And so a lot of things we hoped we could tie in to the *Twin Peaks* [mythology], but a lot of times it was just 'Let's try it this way.' Do you know what I mean? And that was the wonderful thing about David—improvisation is a bad word, but he had his own way of doing things, obviously, and sometimes it would go off a different way than anybody planned.

"I can remember when we were shooting and there were these two guys way off the set, either fans or something, two kind of odd-looking guys, and David turns to [cinematographer Ron Garcia] and says, 'Get a shot of those two guys.'" Here Engels laughed. "I don't think they're in the movie, but he had something occur to him about what he could use them for. And working with David was full of those incidents, full of them."

Cole's second scene is one of the most colorful and memorable of the film's prologue. It takes place at the aforementioned airstrip, where Cole, with FBI Agent Sam Stanley (Kiefer Sutherland) in tow, greets Desmond. Shot at the rural Fall City Airport in Washington, the sequence follows an in-cockpit shot showing Desmond's plane arriving. Cole introduces the pair ("Chet, give Sam Stanley the glad hand") outside, near a hangar, and then reveals his surprise: Lil (Kim Bendheim), a woman whom he deems his "mother's sister's girl," standing knock-kneed next to a yellow single-propeller airplane. Sporting an artificially bright red wig and dress to match,

Lil performs a contorted dance with a scrunched-up face—the decoded meanings of which Desmond will, in the scene that follows, explicate to Stanley. Cole emphatically advises Sam to stick with Chet ("He's got his own m.o., modus operandi") and announces he's off to the FBI's Philadelphia offices. Bendheim, an author and educator who lives in New York City, is credited on the film as Kimberly Ann Cole (a nod to her grandmother's maiden name), which she now regrets. "That was a mistake. I felt like nobody in LA could spell my last name," Bendheim said. "I was sad afterwards I just hadn't kept my

own name. I also write, so I had pieces in the *LA Times Book Review*, but they were under my name, not a pseudonym," she added, admitting to concern at the time about not wanting to connect those two worlds.

Lil is one of the more striking additions to *Fire Walk With Me*, a fan favorite who initiated the Blue Rose mythology. How Bendheim came to land the role is an interesting story. Intrigued by acting but not very actively auditioning, Bendheim had met Johanna Ray, Lynch's frequent casting director, through a friend from Harvard University, where Bendheim had majored in history and literature. "[Johanna] was very positive and interested in me, and I have friends who are actors, and they said, 'Well, you should just stop by when you have something new to tell her.' So I did," she shared. One early summer day in 1991, around three months before the movie began shooting, Bendheim dropped in on Ray to provide an update.

"I was wearing black-checked trousers and a black top, and she said that she wanted me to meet David Lynch," recalled Bendheim. "And I was like, 'Oh, okay.' I was thrilled. I went in, and he introduced himself and asked me what was on my mind. And I said at that point I was worried about an actor friend who was depressed because he hadn't worked. And David Lynch said, 'Well, what I remember hearing people say when they're depressed is they're supposed to remember a time when they were really happy, and that helps.' And then he called me a sweetheart, and that was about all we did in terms of talking."

Bendheim didn't hear anything for a while, but when she called Ray to check in, there was good news. "The next thing I knew I was being picked up in a white stretch limo and flying to Seattle," she said. "I went to the hotel, I think it was in Bellingham, and then when I woke up the next

morning and went to have breakfast, I met Chris Isaak. He started teasing me immediately, and I said, 'No, that's not fair—I haven't had enough sleep to be teased like that,' because he said, 'I think you have a strange face . . . It's just that it's very unusual.' And I said, 'Well, there are a lot of women who look like me in paintings.' Then I asked him if he knew what the script was about, and he said no. And I said, 'I can't tell what it's about either.' So we had established a rapport, and then on set I went to the makeup trailer and David Lynch was there, and he had told me by now that he wanted me to play Lil, his cousin."

Bendheim had watched *Twin Peaks* casually during its TV run and found it "fascinating and dark" but wasn't particularly familiar with Cole as a character. Told only of their characters' familial relationship and that she was supposed to communicate secret information in code by doing a strange dance, Bendheim began to wonder what music would be used. "While he was getting his makeup done, there was some samba music in the background, and he said, 'Do you like this?' and I said sure.

"So that's what he used for the take that I danced to, but he wanted me to do it more like a machine, like an automaton. So I made that up and did that, and that was how I worked. . . . I just thought, *Imagine you are his cousin and he wants you to do this and it's very important to him, so make it very important to you.* That was my non-Method acting way of doing it."

Bendheim felt Lynch was crystal clear about both the scene's tone and visual framing but still engaged in a dialogue about her character. "I had some give-and-take with him, and I said at one point, 'Could I have a line, because then I can join SAG?' And he said sure and he gave me a line, which was cut, when I said, also in code, 'I'm your mother's sister's girl.' And I was sorry it was cut, because then you could see that I was a normal person and not just this strange apparition," said Bendheim with a smile. "[Mary Sweeney] told me that what I did was kind of moony and ethereal, and I thought, *Oh, that's nice.* But that's not what ended up on the screen."

Bendheim did succeed, however, in retaining an element of Lil's unique look, even if it came at the cost of her comfort. "The red wig was crazy—the hair guy said it was like Marilyn [Monroe] gone to hell and I thought I looked like a clown, but I wasn't going to argue," she said. "It was my first movie. I remember that I had the red dress and also had a pair of red stilettos with wire net on them that I was supposed to wear. And I guess when we were rehearsing . . . someone gave me sneakers, blue high-tops, because those heels were not easy to walk in. And David said he kind of liked those high-tops. But I was like, 'Oh no, please, can I wear the other shoes? They're so elegant.' And he said, 'Oh, all right.'" Bendheim finished her portion of the scene in one or two takes and then watched the filming of Isaak and

Sutherland's exchange with Lynch that introduces Lil.

Cole's third and final scene, running four-plus minutes, is one of the most analyzed in the film—shot through with mystery and mounting dread. Back in the FBI's Philadelphia offices (actually a now-demolished building in downtown Seattle), Cooper enters a spacious room and says, "Gordon, it's 10:10 a.m. on February 16," a date he's worried about because of a dream he shared with Cole earlier. Cole checks his watch but gives no verbal reaction.

Cooper then walks into the hall, testing several times the recording results of a mounted video camera. Phillip Jeffries (David Bowie) exits an elevator down the hall and walks past a frozen-in-place Cooper on camera, staggering into Cole's office. As an alarmed Cooper runs in to join them, Cole and Albert Rosenfield rise to greet Jeffries, and Cole makes an introduction ("Cooper, meet the long-lost Phillip Jeffries—you may have heard of him from the academy"). Clearly unnerved by Cooper, Jeffries points at him and asks, "Who do you think this is there?" For the next 1:50, cross talk among the four FBI agents is intercut with subtitled scenes as a dazed Jeffries describes his meeting above a convenience store with otherworldly beings. Jeffries then suddenly disappears from the office, and Cole cries out, "He's gone!" Cooper and Cole check the video recording in the room adjacent to the hall, affirming Jeffries's presence was real. "But where did he go?" asks Cole. In an unscripted line seemingly added in ADR, he puts a button on the scene: "And where is Chester Desmond?"

This fascinating scene, which has been analyzed in detail countless times and interpreted many ways, places Cole closer to the center of an expanded mystery. In a film not short on experimentation, this is one of the headiest, most avant-garde sequences, and it's interesting to unpack Lynch's performance here due in large part to his rearranging of the scripted material, shuffling certain lines and placing others under an entrancing sound design marrying Angelo Badalamenti's score and dialogue from the convenience store denizens. Whether Lynch's reconceptualization was related to feelings about performance (his own, or others') or edit bay inspiration is an unresolved question.

The casting of Bowie and the creation and writing of the character of Jeffries went hand-in-hand, according to Engels, and additionally drove the direction of the scene. "Overall, [that scene] was really just a way to move the story along, find something that's different than what people are expecting," he said. "That was a great thing about David—he was never afraid to try stuff and to be different from what had gone before. I think it was his idea. And if he got an idea, then we did it. He just had such a unique way of making it seem like it was playing into something."

According to Engels, this intuitive-driven "modus operandi" was employed on *Fire Walk With Me* in general and this scene specifically. "Maybe another way to look at it is 'Let's stick to that world—but let's bend it, let's have some fun with this,'" described Engels. "I'm talking for David, but his was such a unique view it would just happen that way. It was really his view of things that would put these weird little twists in there that often paid off. And sometimes they didn't, but sometimes he wouldn't care."

For Bowie, the working experience on this scene was every bit as heady as the finished product was for viewers, according to on-set dresser Mike Malone. "That was one of my favorite days," he said. "Usually, when an actor's not working they go back to their trailer. Bowie hung around because David [could] establish that vibe on a set where it's just such a creative buzz going on that you want to be around. He said, 'I'm not going back to my trailer. I'm having fun watching David work.' So [when he wasn't acting] Bowie was sitting there with us, watching David performing and David directing."

The notability of Cole being the first (living) character viewers see can't be overstated. Taken in tandem with the smashing of a television after the movie's moody opening credits, it delivers a definitive statement: this *isn't* television anymore, and this is David Lynch's *Twin Peaks*. While keeping one foot grounded in Cole's unique blend of authoritative earnestness and folksy formality, Lynch's performance dials back some of the go-go energy present in Cole's second-season incarnation and leans into quietness or pauses in interesting, multi-interpretive ways—cutting, for example, his scripted lines in response to Cooper's mentioning the date and time, just letting Cole . . . be silent.

While there's additional material with Cole in the August 8, 1991, shooting script that was excised from the film's theatrical release, *Fire Walk With Me* as a whole underwent so many trims from first-draft screenplay to final cut that that hardly seems the most insightful means of appraisal of intent. A bit more Cole pops up in the longer version of the Philadelphia scene in *The Missing Pieces*, while other scripted scenes, like an extension of the sequence following Jeffries's disappearance, do not. One valuable way to evaluate Lynch's performance is simply through a comparative look at scripted dialogue and what appears on-screen in Cole's scenes.

Cori Glazer, who worked as a script supervisor for more than a quarter century with Lynch, spanning eight projects, including *Fire Walk With Me*, attests to the filmmaker's preference for extreme specificity in dialogue. "He did not like actors going off script," she said. "David really wanted people saying the lines." Not surprisingly, though, this exactitude would receive more flexibility when it came to Lynch as Cole.

Some of the dialogue reflects on-the-ground changes to match shooting realities (the word "private" being added before "Portland airport," for example, to better match the dirt runway on which the plane lands). But other bits show creative privilege that comes with proprietary rights. A couple of incidental words not in the shooting script are added in Cole's initial phone call to Desmond. In the airstrip scene, Lynch adds the opening, "Chet, good to see you"; transposes Chet's name in another line; throws in a "fellas"; and changes a scripted thumbs-up to a simple nod—perhaps reserving the former salutary affirmation for Cole's interactions with Cooper. Small changes in the grand scheme of things, yes, and not born of any actorly grandstanding—but showing a level of comfort and confidence that in Lynch's view he (and perhaps he alone) is tuned in to the movie's specific wavelength.

Despite all its darkness, the film still manages to establish Cole as, ahem, a man who appreciates women. While he doesn't ogle the secretaries in the opening scene, the fact that there are two of them in such close proximity and both exist in wordless servitude to a standing, authoritative Cole makes a statement about the character. While other objects of Cole's affection, both previous and future, exhibit far more personality, the secretaries here exude a representational quality that can't be missed.

Fire Walk With Me is Lynch's most sharply defined and wholly crafted performance in self-generated material at least until *Twin Peaks*'s third season. And while it's true that the film is darker than the series in its depictions of abuse, stemming largely from its chosen period of focus, I would assert that Cole's appearance, especially in his first two scenes, serves as a small but important reminder of the presence of lightness and its essentiality in confronting the world's bleakness. There's the stamp of idiosyncratic personality even as his character breaks the news of a murder and metes out information regarding its investigation. Yes, Lynch wasn't done with Laura Palmer, and he was gripped by the notion of exploring that massive contradiction of her character—radiant on the outside, dying on the inside, as he put it. But perhaps he also deeply wanted, or even *needed*, to step further inside *Twin Peaks* himself.

"Needless to say, I knew [my involvement] was not going to be happening," said Peyton with a laugh. "But for me, the shock was he wasn't calling Mark. I mean, I always saw that as a kind of betrayal. I'm not going to speak for Mark, but it was never a movie that I was willing to almost appreciate because I was so angry that Mark wasn't doing it. And look, again, we keep talking about how David is and how complicated he is . . . but David did embark on a sort of thirty-year tour where he was trying to acquire as much creative credit for the show as possible. And it wasn't like he was stealing anything from Mark, I think, in a weird way. But I think making *Fire Walk With Me* was like 'Okay, this is my thing now, and this is how I'm going to do it.' And at the time [after the film's release], there was a very good chance that would've been the end of it forever. So we're all very lucky that [David and Mark] managed to repair whatever feelings might've been the result of that and got back together to make the third season, which I thought was just masterful."

An actor who worked multiple times with Lynch (though never directly in a scene with him) and requested anonymity in exchange for their candor agreed that Lynch used the film to stamp his ownership on the material, but phrased it differently: "Everything about *Fire Walk With Me* seemed to me to represent a sort of through-the-looking-glass moment, or whatever," they said. "Whenever and wherever more of *Twin Peaks* came about, I think Gordon Cole was always going to be part of the equation in David's head from [the end of its original television run] onward. I saw that even then. The film was an act of repossession, in a way, and I think his character came along with that. He was in that world now, part of its mythology."

If Lynch himself didn't quite describe it that way in a lengthy 2002 interview with me for *Entertainment Today*, he at least conceded that he had strong feelings about Cole, describing him as "an interesting character, and a guy that believes so much in what he does, and the rightness and value of it." More *Twin Peaks* was definitively not on the table at that time, but when asked offhandedly about other potential stories that could involve Cole— stories that weren't part of *Twin Peaks*—Lynch seemed to draw a clear line of demarcation, associating his interest in the character only with that world. "Well, no, I haven't really thought about any of that," he said, "but I'm sure he's had an interesting career."

As I wrote in a 2022 piece for A.V. Club on the occasion of the film's thirtieth anniversary, sometimes society catches up to art. One of the more mesmerizing things about *Fire Walk With Me* is the manner in which Lynch, almost like a double helix, interweaves the tender and terrifying, the quiet and emotionally heightened. In investing so deeply in Laura Palmer's trauma and pain, Lynch is both embracing and foreshadowing an idea even more central to the 2017 return of *Twin Peaks*—that the tragedy of a single story can have larger, deeper reverberations we can barely comprehend.

Lynch's performance expanded the parameters of Cole and placed him closer to other characters and mysteries (Phillip Jeffries, the Blue Rose, et al.) that would feature more prominently in *The Return*. Cole is inarguably the on-screen character for which Lynch is best known as well as the closest to his heart, and *Fire Walk With Me* would plant the seeds that allowed for an even more robust fleshing out of the character twenty-five years later.

—*CHAPTER 12*—

NADJA (1995)

After the commercial and critical disappointment of *Fire Walk With Me*, Lynch was a bit at sea, an auteur without welcome harbor. He'd made a film of which he was proud (and one that would be substantially redeemed by way of reevaluation) but found himself, just two years removed from being on the cover of *Time* magazine, locked in movie jail, at least domestically. Foreign financing would arrive through a multipicture deal with French film company CIBY 2000, though that would bring its own complications (Lynch would eventually win a 1998 lawsuit for $6.5 million on breach-of-contract claims). In the interim, as Lynch worked on his own projects, he also turned an eye toward producing with his partner at the time, Mary Sweeney.

One of the films that entered their orbit was writer-director Michael Almereyda's *Nadja*, which served up an art house spin on a familiar horror character. The script's roots stretch back to an earlier Almereyda screenplay Lynch and Sweeney had offered to support—an Edgar Allan Poe project called *Walking the Black Cat* that kept locating red lights, deemed too unclassifiable. The pair then urged him to come up with an idea that could fit within a stronger genre framework, so at an October 31, 1993, meeting at Lynch's house, Almereyda pitched his unique take on a vampire movie with a ten-page outline. "*Nadja*, as people noticed only eventually, was grafted from *Dracula's Daughter*, a 1936 sequel to *Dracula*, with a few elements tossed in from André Breton's [surrealist novel] *Nadja*," said Almereyda. "David and Mary understood that the movie was intended as a kind of collage, shot [in black-and-white] on 35 mm and low-end Pixelvision video with patches of 16 mm, and we agreed that the idea was to follow a Roger Corman production model—to make it fast and cheap."

Still, even though budgeted in shoestring fashion, the production lost financing just a couple of weeks before its start date when Eric Stoltz, who was initially set to star, had to withdraw due to his mother's illness. "That's when David bravely decided to pay for the film out of his own pocket—an act of generosity that still startles me," said Almereyda, pointing out that it was also an indication of the trust and faith Lynch had invested in Sweeney, with *Nadja* serving as her first producing credit.

Lynch's cameo as a morgue security officer, running just over forty seconds, comes early in the movie. After an opening sequence in which the titular vampire (Elina Löwensohn) picks up an unsuspecting man at a bar and has a vision of the death of her father, Count Dracula, we cut to Jim (Martin Donovan) getting in some sparring work at a local gym. His wife, Lucy (Galaxy Craze), arrives and informs Jim that his uncle Van Helsing (Peter Fonda) is in jail for murder, saying, "It didn't make sense, but it didn't sound too surprising either—you know how he gets."

After Jim gathers himself and apparently prepares to bail out his uncle, Lynch's scene begins at the 7:28 mark, opening on his unnamed character sitting at a desk. To his left there's a rotary phone and a transistor radio, the latter's bent antenna hinting at altered airwaves; in front of his right arm sits an open lunch box and cup of coffee. A small, handmade Christmas tree sits at desk's edge above a sign reading "Undertakers and police officers print your names on arrivals."

Lynch's hairdo, which wouldn't fully manifest its distinctive upswept form until later, presents here as a gorgeously rumpled mop, with curls falling forward, covering his forehead. He's gazing downward, reading, as Nadja approaches with a scowling man by her side. Sensing their presence before they begin to speak, Lynch looks up slowly. There's a moment of pregnant silence among them all. After Nadja tells him they've come for the body of Count Dracula, Lynch blinks and slightly narrows his eyes, registering their words. "I believe there is a wooden stake in the heart," Nadja continues. Here the camera begins to push in on Lynch. "You will take us to him."

Lynch asks, "How'd you know about that?" The camera cuts back to Nadja, a low-angle shot also pushing in. "I'm a relative," she says. As the shot cuts back to Lynch, he asks, "Can you identify the body?" Nadja replies off-screen, telling him they will take the body as Lynch's eyes begin to slowly—almost imperceptibly at first—cross. Later in the movie, Van Helsing delivers dialogue that confirms Lynch's character blacked out but didn't meet a grisly end.

"The role of the morgue attendant was written for David, and he agreed to fly to New York to do it, his only visit to the set," recalled Almereyda of his film's five-and-a-half-week shoot in the spring of 1994. "Everyone was excited to have him present, and Mary, I remember, told me he'd been rehearsing on his own, really thinking about what it would be like, how it would feel, to be hypnotized. We did just a few takes, and I was pleased with all of them.

"When I suggested at one point that David might lift a cup of coffee to his mouth before speaking, he said, 'I can't.' When I asked why, he held out his hand, which was shaking. It was the only indication that this little acting job was causing him anxiety. I told him of course there was no need to touch the cup."

The sweetness of this memory seems to indicate that Lynch, despite those performances as Cole over the previous several years, still had an uneasy relationship with acting and—perhaps especially in material he didn't originate—one tinged with fear. His on-screen participation in *Nadja*, in a small, fun cameo without a heavy lift in dialogue, shows him willing to tackle that apprehensiveness head-on, however. Checking the performance boxes of experiential curiosity and personal connection, it would end up being the only feature film in which he acted and served as a producer without also directing.

"David didn't participate in the publicity for *Nadja*—that was never the plan—but there was enough buzz and fanfare following our debut screenings at the Toronto International Film Festival for Mary to receive an appealing offer from the Samuel Goldwyn Company, a deal that would have more than doubled David's investment," recalled Almereyda.

"I remember being a bit amazed that David and Mary agreed to a test screening of the film in Santa Monica, organized by the Goldwyn people, before the deal was signed," Almereyda continued. "I wasn't present for that but flew in from New York for a postscreening debriefing with the Goldwyn executives. Mary must have been with us, but in my memory it's just me and David riding up the Century City elevator and being greeted in the sleek, sun-struck office tower, getting the royal treatment, assistants hopping to bring coffee, people saying how honored they were to have David in the room, men in suits oozing a vibe of smiling deceitfulness. I remember David, unshaven, wearing a shirt buttoned to his neck, no jacket, looking unusually unpolished and uncertain while mutely paging through a sheaf of papers they presented to us, the execs talking brightly while the ash on David's cigarette got longer and longer, a thin stream of smoke twisting up into the air and dissolving in sunlight—just as the deal eventually twisted and dissolved."

While unfortunate, the setback of this unwound deal proved temporary. "David remained a cheerleader for *Nadja*, with Mary acting as intermediary and translator for all further business discussions. And as an assured editor, she guided the film through a fast revision, an attempt to appease our Santa Monica critics," said Almereyda, noting that a few shots were quickened and trimmed, with more Portishead layered in over composer Simon Fisher Turner's work.

Shorter by three or four minutes, this version screened at Sundance the following January and found the proper partner for a theatrical release. "Bingham Ray of October Films came to the rescue with a less lucrative but acceptable distribution deal," said Almereyda. "This turn of events allows me to assure myself, to this day, that in practical terms *Nadja* was not entirely a black spot or a lost cause for David."

Indeed, thirty-one years after its Toronto debut, in the fall of 2025, the film returned to the same festival with a 4K restoration director's cut in advance of a theatrical and streaming rerelease via Grasshopper Films— giving new, digital life to Lynch's unnamed morgue attendant.

−CHAPTER 13−

LOST HIGHWAY (1997)

There's a persistent rumor that Lynch appears in a deleted scene from *Lost Highway*. This credit has appeared on IMDb and Wikipedia for several decades now, listing Lynch as . . . a morgue attendant. Yes, his same character credit as from *Nadja*.

Again, though, this seems to be a Lynch performance that actually isn't. "I do not have any knowledge or recollection of that," said Jennifer Lynch. "I don't think it's in existence anywhere." No fewer than a half dozen sources in the know, including *Lost Highway* script supervisor Cori Glazer, either have no recollection of this ever being filmed or debunk it outright. And while Lynch's name appears in several online databases in the cast list, no actors are listed for the two other characters in the scene in question.

The 114-page June 21, 1995, script for *Lost Highway* contains a roughly one-page scene taking place after the murder of Renee Madison (Patricia Arquette), and in between the arrest and conviction of her husband, Fred (Bill Pullman). In it, a morgue attendant wheels Renee's corpse into a room in preparation for her autopsy. The medical examiner, dressed in a tuxedo for an evening date, enters the room with a woman identified as the mayor's daughter. The attendant shares two simple lines of greeting ("Hi doc—workin' late tonight, huh?" and "Howdy, Joyce") with each of them, then unloads and begins to unwrap labeled packages containing Renee's dismembered body parts. "Just like Christmas," says the medical examiner, tossing his cigarette to the floor. The camera tracks down to the ground, then holds there as the medical examiner eyes the body and he and his uneasy date, Joyce, converse.

However, this scene doesn't appear in the film.

"I don't have the greatest memory, but I don't recall David acting in that film at all," said first assistant camera Scott Ressler. "I do know that we delayed filming [one day] because David wanted to speak to someone attending an actual execution going on, so we stopped and waited as David spoke to someone at a real one on the phone before we started filming. And I don't remember if it was the actual execution scene that was delayed or some other scene. I just remember everyone sort of sat around as we listened to him on the phone going, 'Really?'" Here Ressler laughed. "We were hoping he would turn to us and say something, and I can't remember if he did or not. But the crucial part of the memory is that we actually stopped working [to accommodate this extra curiosity], and that's something that's not uncommon with David—in a good way, I mean."

"I don't remember him as a morgue attendant," added Sabrina Sutherland, who worked on *Lost Highway* as production supervisor and later helped oversee its restoration. "When we did do the deleted scenes [for the film's 2022 Criterion release], we didn't even go back to anything. We thought about what was there, and David said there really wasn't much there except for the prison [scene]. There was that whole walk-to-death-row thing that we did by the book. But other than that, he said there really wasn't much. So I don't remember the morgue scene at all. But maybe that was something he didn't want to see." Here Sutherland offered a short burst of laughter. "I don't know. I saw the cast contracts, and I don't remember David being part of that. It's possible, I suppose—but we never went back to that, for sure."

The pivot away from the scene reflects the complicated nature of Lynch's relationship with appearing in his own films, dating back to his earliest works: a deep-background cameo by Lynch for *The Elephant Man* was perhaps shot but not included in the final cut. Here, Lynch wrote a small, two-line role apparently with himself in mind but by all accounts ended up not filming it.

So what happened? Some folks likely saw a photo of Lynch from the little-seen *Nadja* (first published in *Cinefantastique*) and, knowing it wasn't present in *Lost Highway*'s theatrical cut but paying no mind to the fact it was in black-and-white, labeled it a deleted scene—a "match status" understandably bolstered by the existence of such a character in the latter's script. Especially since the film's home video treatment languished for years, the falsehood lingered unchallenged.

The mistake also tracks in an emotional sense, given Lynch's longstanding fascination with morgues, and the dark necessity of the work they do—an intrigue indulged in the pilot for *Twin Peaks* but dating all the way back to his time in Philadelphia, when he visited a morgue. There seems no strong reason to believe this performance exists, however, and there is abundant evidence it was not filmed. While *The Elephant Man* at least has a fleeting filmed image open to misinterpretation, this phantom credit seemingly exists only in an imaginary realm—perhaps appropriate for *Lost Highway*.

—CHAPTER 14—

"THE THIRD PLACE" (2000)

For an artist so strongly committed to his own idiosyncratic visions, Lynch had a healthy and not at all unrealistic relationship with commerce. The original incarnation of *Twin Peaks* was surprisingly commercialized for its time (perhaps contributing to the intensity with which a subset attached to it—I know I vacuumed up its print media tie-ins). Lynch was also always open about accepting advertising work, talking frequently about how it was a good way to keep up to date on the latest technology. The money certainly wasn't incidental, let's be honest. But whenever Lynch talked about the thrill of learning as a motivating factor in tackling commercials, it rang true because that's how he lived so much of his life—saying yes to things that sincerely interested him, exercising his creative instincts, and then figuring out what knowledge he could glean from the experience.

"The Third Place" is a prime example. Starring Lynch assistant Jason S—who also helmed *Lynch (One)* and "The Man with the Gray Elevated Hair," among other behind-the-scenes nonfiction portraits—this surreal one-minute PlayStation 2 commercial opens with a man walking down a hallway as a siren blares, followed by a burst of flames. The corridor shifts, seemingly contracting and then opening back up again. An assaultive sound mix disorients us as the camera tightens on the man's face. Looking to his right, he glimpses a woman floating upward who shushes him. Looking to his left at an angle, he sees a distant reflection of himself, with whom he exchanges a thumbs-up.

Hand fashioned out of Plasticine, the word "Where?" floats in the hall. "Not up, not down; not waking, not sleeping," says a narrator, through an echo. "Where are we?"

As the man continues walking down the hall, his head detaches and floats ahead of him, then reattaches and distorts as an object strikes him in the cheek. An arm comes out of his mouth and flies away. The man looks down to see smoke billowing from his jacket's armhole, his hand missing. Through this smoke, he makes out three figures sitting on a scalloped art deco-style couch—his own doppelgänger, a suited man with a duck's head, and a mummy wrapped head to toe in gauze, its mouth and one eye blackened.

Next to them is an arm, sprouting out of the ground, as big as each of them. Glances are exchanged, and at the fifty-one-second mark comes a close-up of the duck moving its neck to and fro and speaking. This serves as Lynch's first stab at animal voice-over ("Welcome to the third place," spoken as four discrete sentences), before the product logo appears and a female faintly yelling in the background reinforces its promotional pitch: "PlayStation 2—the third place!"

• • •

In the 1990s, Trevor Beattie [with Lynch in photo below] was creative director of the London office of global advertising agency TBWA, which spearheaded paradigm-shifting ad campaigns for huge brands like Apple, Absolut, and Nissan. In early 2000, Sony was looking to launch its highly anticipated PlayStation 2, a sixth-generation video game console that included a built-in DVD drive and was price competitive with stand-alone DVD players of the era and thus a potential two-for-one purchase for families looking to stretch their dollars and diversify their entertainment options. Sony came to TBWA, whose pitch landed on a creative idea based on the tagline "PlayStation 2 (to) the third place."

"It seems obvious now, but PlayStation were keen to occupy what used to be known as spare time," said Beattie. "I wrote a script as a kind of philosophy, or manifesto, describing a place that was neither work nor home, not waking or sleeping. I imagined it to be a road movie, and David was my clear dream choice to direct."

TBWA had the stature and connections to get Beattie a meeting, so he soon found

himself in Lynch's house, enjoying a damn fine cup of coffee with the man himself. "He'd just finished shooting *Mulholland Drive*," recalled Beattie. "He loved my script, was fascinated by the idea of condensing a movie notion into ninety seconds of action. He almost bought into my [original] thought of it being a road movie, but half jokingly explained it should be 'a road movie that's set in my house.'"

Lynch would ultimately have to leave home for the project but wouldn't need to go far for a two-day weekend shoot in downtown Los Angeles on October 7-8, 2000. For the commercial, Lynch pulled together a mostly old-hand crew of previous collaborators, including production designer Jack Fisk, special effects maestro Gary D'Amico, sound designer John Neff, and director of photography Scott Billups, who'd just completed a tour of duty as visual effects supervisor on *Mulholland Drive*.

The ambitious and disorienting spot wasn't conventionally storyboarded but instead was sketched out with what Billups called "graphical breadcrumbs." Utilizing a flamethrower and smoke machines, the ad also crams almost two dozen visual effects shots into sixty seconds. "As a shooter, working with David was never boring," said Billups. "Any time he said, 'yoo-hoo, yoo-hoo' [and pointed], it generally meant he saw something that tickled his fancy." In a behind-the-scenes video directed by Luke Forsythe and available online, Lynch can be heard exclaiming enraptured encouragement ("This is so fucking beautiful!" and "There ya go, buddy!") as well as good-naturedly chiding a crew member ("No more coffee for Dave Storm!") when he wanted an effect dialed back.

The ad was shot with a Sony DSR-PD150 DVCAM, the "prosumer" camcorder Lynch would come to favor for virtually all of his digitally shot forays over the next half decade, including *Inland Empire*. As such, production served in many ways as experiential proving ground for what the equipment could accomplish. Billups adjusted the camera's settings, fitted it with a wide-screen adapter to increase its field of view, and along with key grip Shawn Crowell designed and built custom-made camera plates and mounts that created extra mass, allowing smoother movement. Still, the PD150 had an autofocus feature that was difficult to disable for complex setups, so Billups kept a higher-end Sony HDW F900 HDCAM prepped just in case; they wouldn't end up needing it.

It was quite late in the process when Lynch introduced the notion that one of the final-scene characters should have the head of a duck. When he then suggested he voice the character himself, delivering the piece's signature line, no one batted an eye. "I was delighted," said Beattie. "You don't hire a duck and quack yourself, as they almost say."

At the end of the two-day shoot, full of complex problem-solving, the space was "left charred and smelling of MAPP gas and burnt Twizzlers," said Billups.

Postshoot, Lynch augmented the practical effects shot on set with desktop tools, including Adobe After Effects. And overseeing the edit with Lynch was none other than Bob Dylan . . . well, a *version* of Bob Dylan. One day, while talking about musical heroes, Lynch regaled Beattie with a portion of a story he would later tell in *Room to Dream* about how, many years earlier, he'd smoked some dope before a Dylan concert. From Lynch's seat in one of the back rows, Dylan was reduced to a distant dot. "David told me how he'd annoyed fellow concertgoers by complaining rather loudly in his hazy, high state about how *small* Dylan seemed: 'He's *tiny*! He's such a big star, but he's this little, tiny guy! Look how *small* he is!'" recalled Beattie.

Transfixed by this tale, Beattie hatched a plan after the ad's shoot, printing a tiny, one-inch photo of Dylan on stage, cutting it out and mounting it on cardboard, then adding a tiny bass stand. On his return to LA from London, Beattie presented Lynch with his very own "life-size" Tiny Bob Dylan. "He loved it and placed it atop his mixing desk for the whole edit," said Beattie.

Lynch was unfortunately less enthusiastic about the piece's eventual presentation. "During the editing, David showed us a version in black-and-white," said Beattie. "I bloody *loved* it. It was pure *Eraserhead*. Back in London, I convinced our wonderful PlayStation client (European Marketing Director) David Patton that this was the way to go. Back in LA, and at the time unknown to me, David was furious. He believed the ad should have run in color. I now love both versions, for different reasons." Both live on online, though the color version—which reveals the couch to be blue (velvet?)—does elicit a greater appreciation for the depth and interplay of its component parts.

The ad—which would play in movie theaters in dozens of countries and successfully kickstart Sony's well-regarded PlayStation 2 campaign—is driven by urgency and tension, counterbalanced by its dreamlike, off-kilter sensibility. Did Lynch wake up one morning gripped by the idea of lending his voice to a duck? Or even, upon taking a meeting on the project, have the thought, fully formed, that this would be a great vehicle in which to flex his vocal talents? No, I feel confident saying neither of those things happened.

And yet if one places an asterisk next to the first season voice cameo of Gordon Cole, given his later appearances in physicalized form, here we have Lynch's first stab at voice work—embracing its performative qualities as yet another avenue for creative expression, another way to live the art life.

It also seems to reflect, however consciously, Lynch's desire to step into a world he'd created—even if the world was far less expansive and defined than something like *Twin Peaks*.

—CHAPTER 15—

THE "NEW DEAL" OF DAVIDLYNCH.COM (2001-2011)

The winding road of *Mulholland Drive's* inception, production, narrative reconfiguration, and eventual release presented Lynch with at least two distinct creative paths. Rather unsurprisingly, he chose the road less traveled, and of more personal interest. While some then (and perhaps even now) looked askance at this choice, the rest of the 2000s was still a highly fertile period for him—just maybe not in the way others might have preferred.

Like many at the time, Lynch was intrigued by the creative possibilities and financial opportunities the internet provided. The difference was he was in a position to do something about it. The foundation for what would become his eponymous website had been laid a couple years earlier when Lynch brought *The Straight Story* in under budget and saw the return of a couple of hundred thousand dollars. (His company, Asymmetrical Productions, had cofinanced the independent production alongside Canal+ and several other companies.) Lynch directed that money back into a project that took the better part of three years before it launched to the public.

Thus, despite there being offers for him to direct scripts written by others, works that would have put his career on a different trajectory, the internet became the repository for almost all of his wide-eyed, optimistic creative output—a fact borne out by my in-person interview at Lynch's home in February 2002, just as his website was starting to get its legs underneath it. "It's a whole new deal," said Lynch of the internet, repeating the last four words for effect. "And the weird thing is that the internet is changing almost every day. So when do you jump in, how much do you put in for this kind of quality and this kind of speed and these kinds of restrictions? I'm learning, and we're going to have some fun doing it."

The person most responsible for practical back-end decisions that abetted and in some cases even inspired Lynch's creative visions was Eric Bassett, who met Lynch through Neal Edelstein. Edelstein had entered Lynch's orbit by producing his stunning segment of the *Lumière and Company* anthology film and was instrumental in turning the filmmaker's focus toward the emerging digital realm. Edelstein and Bassett, friends from their days at the University of Arizona, worked together on DavidLynch.com, and the latter drove its growth, going on to serve for thirteen years as the managing partner of Lynch's Absurda. While Lynch was extremely well-versed in cinematic technology, cutting-edge PC design programs and other elements of computer culture were new to him. One of the core priorities for the site when it was being built out was leaning into hardware and software that was intuitive, allowing Lynch as much flexibility as possible to implement his ideas.

Bassett cut deals with 4D and Macromedia Flash, and a last-minute Hail Mary with Apple proved hugely important, bringing into the fold QuickTime and Final Cut Pro. Bassett tackled tough problems and waded into deep waters, teaching himself how to build a file-sharing redundant system through Apple and constructing an infrastructure that wasn't beholden to others. "David didn't trust anybody, and he wanted everything to be under my roof," said Bassett. "I owned these buildings in Laguna Canyon, two buildings, and he wanted me to build my own server structure, which is not what anybody does anymore."

All of this technical heavy-lifting, and many late nights, endeared Bassett to Lynch. "David loved it because he loves when people work hard," said Bassett with a slight laugh. "So we really got along very, very well. I'd always say he was like another father, but he would say, 'No, we're too close in age. We're like brothers.' And I would say okay."

This laid the groundwork for an idiosyncratic website that could serve as a creative laboratory for Lynch, allowing him to experiment with new formats and technologies. When I talked to him in 2002, it was clear Lynch was enthralled by the digital frontier, seeing it as a source of inspiration as well as a way to create a self-sufficient ecosystem for his art.

A highly interactive pay site ($9.97 per month) with some complimentary features, DavidLynch.com launched as a Flash-laden site with two chat rooms, photos, clips from Lynch's short films, a store selling unique merchandise, short-form video experiments, music, and all sorts of other oddities, like solvable puzzles of, say, Frank Booth's iconic *Blue Velvet* mask. And speaking of booths, codes occasionally scattered throughout the site could be entered in virtual phone booths to reveal special content. When Lynch traveled to France in May 2002, where he served as the Cannes Film Festival jury president, he shared an ongoing travelogue in the form of the multipart *Cannes Diaries*.

"During *Twin Peaks*, I never went on the internet, but that was the beginning and people were talking, because that's all you could do, just talk and type," Lynch said to me. "But there was so much talk on the internet about *Twin Peaks*. People would bring in reams and reams of paper and say, 'You've gotta see what's happening.' Back then the internet was kind of a sorry place for visuals, but I started thinking about it.

"And so, anyway, somewhere in there I met the correct people," Lynch continued. "That was about two and a half years ago, and I started paying more attention to it and started building this site. Along the way I learned so much and got so excited, and I realized too how complicated it is to set up a site like this. This is an extremely complicated site. It may look relatively simple because, I think, it's pretty user-friendly, but it's misleading in terms of its simplicity because there's a lot of stuff that has to work. The technical side to it is huge. And now it's running better and better, but a lot of times you don't know really if it's going to run until you just pop the thing up. I think the first day we got three million hits, and it just fried the servers."

Indeed, an all-caps email blast had gone out for the site's specifically timed launch: 9:45 a.m. Pacific time on Monday, December 10, 2001. It wouldn't be the last time, but on that day, yes, David Lynch broke the internet.

"It instantly crashed. It was horrible," recalled Bassett with a rueful smile that still hints at memories of the stress. "It took us a few days, even a couple weeks, to get everything to where it was smooth. And it was mostly on 4D's end. They didn't really have the capacity for what we had built, so it would've been better to stage it differently rather than have everybody rush to the door at once. It was a tough lesson learned."

Once things were up and running, DavidLynch.com became home to a passionately engaged community, and Lynch was fairly active in the chat rooms. Almost all of the video content was produced on the property of his adjoining Hollywood Hills homes, one of which was made famous in *Lost Highway*. "Every medium talks to you, and once you get this kind of action and reaction thing going, the ideas start flowing," Lynch said in 2002. "It's been really great to get into those worlds and build stuff and shoot stuff— just fantastic."

"With the website, he was able to really celebrate one of his favorite things to do, which was experiment," added Jennifer Lynch. "The medium of digital was a perfect home for that. I think above and beyond anything else, he was curious enough that he was willing to try things and risk failing at them to understand how to do them and to learn how to make things."

Work debuted on DavidLynch.com would inform and flow into his next and ultimately final theatrically released feature film, *Inland Empire*, at that point probably his grandest swing for the fences in a career full of them—a spiritual successor to *Eraserhead* in its sprawling, immersive production. Some material, like *Rabbits*, was inserted or more fully absorbed; others, like "Axxon N.," were touched upon in ways distinct from what might have been their original vision for the website.

Some content inarguably indulges Lynch's performative instincts, which, if not fully burgeoning at this point, were at least finding interesting new avenues of expression. Other content falls into more of a gray zone.

What about, for example, Lynch's famous weather reports? Do habitual acts publicly presented not contain an element of performance even if one is not always portraying a character distinguishable from themselves? Many people would say yes. What then about a single, longer-form act of captured work? Opportunities for judgment calls abound.

Member questions, a regular website feature that Lynch loved, usually were simply ten to twelve aggregated queries from the message board. Lynch, sitting in front of a microphone, would typically respond with stories about his work or thoughts on other random topics. Sometimes, however, the back-and-forth took on a life of its own, spawning ideas that became . . . well, performative in a way. One of the best examples is a much-circulated clip of Lynch attempting to pronounce the consonant-laden username of one site member after ceremoniously stuffing the panties of another into his mouth.

It's hard for younger generations to grasp the notion, but everyone navigating the internet at that time lived in this same space, knowingly or not—forging and figuring out their online identity, before social media as we now know it existed. So, were random though striking pieces of ephemera like these performances, in a sense? These are some of the fun questions that an examination of DavidLynch.com invites.

This first incarnation of Lynch's website represented a pioneering approach to artist-controlled digital distribution, predating platforms like YouTube and modern subscription models. While it had benefits and even some successes, it also, by Lynch's own admission, became a drain on his time. At some point the creative value proposition went pear-shaped, and financials trended in the same direction. "I remember I got a call from him when I was at AFM in [early November] 2010, and he just said . . . it was cutting it too close," said Bassett. "It got to the point where he might've had to put money in, and I was like, 'Let's just shut it down.'" The site continued for a couple months after that, but certain elements were disabled and others not updated.

Lynch's digital presence would not end, however, merely evolve. On March 10, 2011—"sometime between 1:23 and 1:38pm Pacific time," he announced in an email to *The New York Times*—DavidLynch.com would relaunch as a website dedicated to Lynch's musical endeavors, hosting the "open-album" *Twin Peaks Archive* as well as videos and other collaborations.

After judging a short film contest for Vimeo in 2010, Lynch also posted a few videos on that platform. On November 16, 2018, his YouTube channel, David Lynch Theater, launched. This would become home to various short-form works and set the stage for what would become for many a virtual lifeline during the COVID-19 pandemic.

–CHAPTER 16–

BLUEBOB (2001-2002)

Right around the time 1997's *Lost Highway* was meeting a disappointing commercial reception, Lynch met John Neff, a veteran session musician and audio engineer whom he hired to design Asymmetrical Studios, his state-of-the-art home recording workspace. Roughly one year later, the duo would begin collaborating on a series of audio experiments to test equipment and help give Lynch a better sense of their capabilities. Out of this noodling, which included sequenced drum machine patterns, distortion effects pedals, and tuners, the instrumental backbones of several songs were created.

This process began long before physical production on *The Straight Story* (which Lynch shot on location in the fall of 1998) and continued past the film's Cannes debut and later theatrical release in 1999, into March 2000. During this time, the music was married to lyrics, some of which Lynch had written years earlier and some of which were new; Neff performed all of these mostly in a spoken-word style. The final product of these sessions was *BlueBOB*, a twelve-track studio album collaboration (three of which are instrumentals) released through Lynch's website on December 10, 2001.

An atmospheric industrial blues effort with pockets of paranoia, *BlueBOB* was described at the time by Lynch as "a music idea based on the pounding machinery of the smokestack industry and the raw, amplified birth of rock 'n' roll." The third track on the album is the thumping, catchy "Thank You, Judge." Lyrically the tune is a kind of alimony-driven riff on the Beastie Boys' "She's Crafty," in which Neff sardonically growls a list of all the items his ex-wife has taken in their divorce—everything from his swimming pool, motorcycle, and records to his leaf blower, fishing gear, and DVD player.

A music video for "Thank You, Judge," running just under six minutes, was shot in the San Fernando Valley region of Los Angeles. It's funny if incredibly literal minded for a Lynch-helmed work; the lyrical inventorying of the objects taken is shown mainly through shots of said items (plus a few winks and nods, like a brief glimpse of a Pabst Blue Ribbon can), mixed with some performance footage from Asymmetrical Studios. What gives the entire effort its bite, though, is a series of dialogue interludes that provide a through-line narrative. Throughout these segments—which show Neff in court getting screamed at by his ex-wife (Naomi Watts) and then standing outside a house while she throws his socks and underwear all over the front yard—Lynch appears as Billy the Groper, a sort of muttering, Beavis-like, masked figure of indeterminate origin whose own branded cans of "pork the beans" are also glimpsed briefly. The character queries Neff as to the particulars of his predicament and at one point morphs into a landlord sporting a bandaged arm and filthy white T-shirt with 911 (also the name of another track) written on the front, attempting to rent Neff a rundown apartment. Then, at the video's end, he becomes a cop who dresses down Neff while his ex-wife dances with delight, watching with her new boyfriend (Eli Roth). "Under arrest? I just came over to see the dog," protests Neff. "That's no way to talk about your wife, man!" retorts Groper, advising him to bend over for a strip search.

One of the shoot's locations, a residential neighborhood in Northridge, is extraordinarily easy to find given that a street sign appears prominently in the video. The other setup, located a little over four miles away in Van Nuys, I deduced by way of record searching commercial signage in the background. Nearly twenty-five years later, these locations still exude a certain Lynchian vibe—pedestrian but uneasy—if one takes a moment to luxuriate in their surroundings. While a large tree provides street shade, much of the residential neighborhood, at least around its intersection, is dotted with younger and thinner foliage, offering a spacious view of the summer sky (one can easily imagine Lynch holding forth on the quality of the light). Mockingbirds and Bullock's orioles dart around, feeding off palm tree seeds and the buffet of a nearby feeder. A thick, squat palm tree seen in the video in the corner of the lawn, nearest the sidewalk and street, is gone; a sapling now sits in its place. Across the street, a malodorous couch sits on the curb, cushions ripped open and white stuffing bursting forth, awaiting a bulk-item pickup that seems destined never to come.

The business location from the video sits less than half-a-mile from a high school, but along a stretch of road loaded with such an abundance of auto body repair and parts shops that it defies reasonable statistical per capita distribution. The smell of stale fried chicken hangs heavy in the air, the product of a nearby fast-food restaurant. On the ground is a pair of bird wings, with no sign of the rest of a carcass. The area is populated with the type of marginalized characters who often fascinated Lynch, and the building used in the shoot itself is (and was at the time, one presumes) a rundown, flaked-stucco-wall motel of the sort that offers weekly rates.

The character of Groper also pops up in a one-minute easter egg featured on the 2006 Absurda DVD release *Dynamic:01: The Best of DavidLynch.com*, protesting in profane terms his arrest. The demented glee of Lynch's masked portrayal comes across as wild as anything else in which he has appeared, untethered to any outside judgments. "Thank You, Judge" augured the arrival of a couple more out-there characters from Lynch, especially in the voice-over realm. "I feel like he only fully departed [in performances] from who he was when he could kind of put on the mask and be Billy the Groper or do the voices for *DumbLand* or things like that," said Jay Aaseng, who would come on board as an assistant with Lynch in January 2001.

In the wake of *BlueBOB*'s release, and in advance of the tandem's one and only live performance—November 11, 2002, at Olympia Music Hall in Paris, sharing a bill with Portishead's Beth Gibbons—Lynch concocted a special piece of performance art for French television in order to publicize both the album and show. As part of a four-minute interview for Canal+ with a French journalist with whom he was friendly, Didier Allouch, Lynch came up with the idea to create a small fake cave on a dirt berm on his property and stage a bizarre scene.

Allouch was kept waiting until dark and then given the green light for a conversation—the only caveat being not to ask about anything unfolding around him. What follows is a hilarious and surreal interview, appropriately hued in blue, in which a dirt-smeared, shirtless Lynch holds forth with soundbites about *BlueBOB* ("We're mainly a garage band, a studio band—it was an experiment, and it ended up being an album" and "There's something about factories and electricity and early rock 'n' roll that blended for us, and that's what we're thinking about as we're doing the music") against the backdrop of a flashing red siren, droning sound effects, and more.

Not counting his *Dune* set photo thirst trap, this clip is one of only three known filmed pieces in which Lynch bares his chest, for those keeping score (the others being *Zelly and Me* and 2016's *Shadows of Paradise*). He's not the only topless person, either, as a young woman, nude except for go-go boots, comes out to deliver two eggs, which Neff then adds to a pile of six. Pascal Nabet-Meyer, whose Soulitude Records would release *BlueBOB* across Europe plus in a US reissue in 2003, gets summoned out for an unusual cameo before departing. When the woman returns for a second time, she and Lynch sidle up to one another, and he whispers something in her ear.

While *BlueBOB* wouldn't find Lynch taking the lead vocally, the very extroverted presentations in these two affiliated works—one masked and one intended for a smaller audience, with the participation of a journalist with whom he was well acquainted—suggest a surging sense of performative interest and even confidence.

−CHAPTER 17−

DUMBLAND (2002)

It's difficult if not impossible to fully explain the mania of the early dot-com era, when the internet was wild and free, yes, but also fueled by a genuine playfulness and optimism that social media and its attendant biliousness and doom have now all but drowned out. Before SEO (and, later, algorithmic steering) seized the reins of web traffic, there were companies flush with venture capitalist funding looking around to throw wads of cash at familiar names, all in an attempt to grab enough eyeballs to justify their market caps.

It was against this backdrop, in 2000, that Lynch was commissioned by Shockwave.com, a young gaming and entertainment website launched by Macromedia chiefly as a way to promote its Adobe Flash and Shockwave media players, to develop an exclusive series of adult-oriented animated shorts. The announcement was made on Wednesday, March 22, at an event called (seriously) the Yahoo! Internet Life Online Film Festival in Los Angeles and reported on breathlessly as a stampede of big-name creatives (Stan Lee, Tim Burton, and James L. Brooks) inked deals with the company. The name of Lynch's show: *DumbLand*.

"It's going to be very crude, but sophisticatedly crude," Lynch said to *Variety* at the time. "It's very dumb and it's very bad quality." Crucially (and shrewdly), Lynch retained ownership of the characters he created. Two episodes ended up premiering on Shockwave in June of that year; eight (out of an originally planned fifteen-plus) debuted on DavidLynch.com in February 2002, following the dot-com bubble collapse. Later, in 2006, they were released on DVD, in the type of striking, bespoke, large-format packaging that Lynch favored for media releases via his website.

The series, with each episode running three to five minutes, centers on Randy, a coarse, scowling lout with a total of three teeth—two wide gapped on top and one on the bottom. Randy lives with his son (credited as Sparky, though his name isn't used) and his nameless wife. The former is half sketched, with round eyes, nose, and mouth on a bulbous head attached to a skinny body and spindly limbs—think otherworldly alien meets emaciated Casper the Ghost. The wife, meanwhile, is a shrieking ball of bundled anxieties who summons to mind Edvard Munch's *The Scream*—understandable, given her husband's steady stream of verbal and physical abuse.

The animation utilizes "line boil" technique, which is time intensive but creates both comedy and tension in the form of live-wire eyebrows and other wobbling effects. The end result lends the entire proceedings a jittery kineticism, an edgy and caffeinated vibe that abets the decidedly low-fi presentation and counterpoints the dialogue's frequent pregnant pauses. Visually, the animation becomes progressively sophisticated as the episodes advance. "To David's credit, he just got a few lessons from me, and from them he did those whole things himself in Flash—literally learned how to animate in Flash, which was pretty amazing," said Eric Bassett.

The series lives or dies entirely on one's embrace or rejection of the basic concept that there's humor in so-called low culture (hence lots of loud farting) and in the mixture of farce, idiocy, and preposterous violence—the last mentioned of which occasionally redounds upon those who inflict it. To some, its form obscures its social commentary or renders it irrelevant as a vehicle for such. To others, its quick-riff, heightened-reality jokes at the expense of modern life's cacophonous and overwhelming nature, its juxtaposition of the savage and the mundane, is hilarious. With an aggregate running time of just over thirty-three minutes, *DumbLand* is not a heavy lift.

• • •

The following is a summary of all eight episodes, each of which included the same preface text ("*DumbLand* is a crude, stupid, violent, absurd series. If it is funny, it is funny because we see the absurdity of it all") and a short credits bumper set to driving theme music that recalls the sound of a cheaply made lawn mower.

Episode 1: "The Neighbor" (2:52)
The first episode is also the shortest. Right out of the gate it establishes the crudity (in form and tone) that defines *DumbLand*, delivering profanity, flatulence, outbursts of anger, and a shocking act of physical violation, in

this case by a one-armed man (though no, not an Al Strobel cameo).

"I was just looking at that wooden shed over there," Randy says to his neighbor. "Oh, yes?" he replies. "I like that shed," Randy says. "That's my shed," the neighbor notes. "I know it's your fucking shed!" Randy screams and then lets out a loud fart before repeating his feelings about said wooden shed.

"I have a false arm," the neighbor says, pulling off one of his limbs and tossing it to the ground. A helicopter overhead sets off Randy, who unleashes a torrent of obscenities. Randy then turns back to his neighbor: "I heard once someone said you fuck ducks." After a beat, a duck comes waddling out of the shed. Another beat, and then the episode's stinger: "I am a one-armed duck-fucker," the neighbor intones.

Episode 2: "The Treadmill" (3:40)

DumbLand's second episode establishes Randy as both an abuser and, in the grand tradition of so many American sitcom fathers, a complete idiot. It opens with him frantically slurping a beer, watching football on TV. His wife is running on a treadmill in the next room, faster and faster, which eventually distracts him. Randy goes and slaps her off it, yelling, "Stop your fucking exercise!"

Sparky appears, pogoing up and down enthusiastically, saying, "Hey Dad, let me try!" When he steps on the treadmill, Sparky flies through the wall, leaving a small hole. "Fucking twit," Randy mutters dismissively. As Randy stares at the treadmill, though, his curiosity slowly gets the best of him. He repeats his son's action and suffers the same fate, leaving a much bigger hole. Outside, Randy lets loose a steadying fart and returns inside with a hammer for another go at the treadmill. This time, the hammer ends up lodged in his rectum.

A chipper salesman comes by touting "a household product that makes things smell good," and Randy responds by (literally) punching his face off, after which the head-dangling salesman begins to recite the Gettysburg address.

Episode 3: "The Doctor" (4:33)

This episode showcases Lynch's delight in commingling absurdity and depravity, as well as his strong but highly idiosyncratic comic timing, which stretches the boundaries of comedy's traditional "rule of three."

After a brief confrontation with the mailman ("Well, I got two letters for you: FU, stamp licker!"), Randy angrily spies a broken lamp. His wife takes responsibility for its state but runs out of the room. What follows is a slow build of tension as Randy eyes the fixture's filament, the lamp still plugged in. It's two dim bulbs, one figurative, one literal. Naturally, this doesn't end so well for Randy.

A doctor shows up and tends to Randy, whose eyes are spinning wildly (the sound effect here evokes a shaken aerosol can, which features prominently in another episode), applying a series of increasingly ludicrous pain tests, asking, "Does that hurt you?" after each one. After the last violent test, Randy beats up the doctor in a manner that would make Tex Avery proud before the doctor responds, "Just what I thought: you're completely normal."

Episode 4: "A Friend Visits" (3:49)

The fourth episode may, for some, trigger memories of Nadine Hurley's drape runners. Outside, Randy runs up to his screaming wife, her hands raised in manic defense of her "new clothesline," exhibiting a protective care for it that makes it seem the most important thing in her life.

"Not for long," Randy yells, wrenching the clothesline to and fro. "What if I had to come out in the yard at night to take a shit? I could slice my fucking head off!" Randy squishes his wife's head into silence, only to have it regenerate as a different face. Randy then tosses the clothesline into the street, where it hits a passing car.

After this, Randy sits with a cowboy-hatted friend drinking a beer. The pair discuss various animals they like to kill and behead, with the conversation heading down an increasingly dark path.

Episode 5: "Get the Stick" (4:06)

This episode is a simple and straightforward piece of physical comedy in which brutality and grotesquerie are cranked to the max—and also something one can envision being cited in handwringing fashion by the head of some culturally conservative group expressing concern for "the children."

Sparky, who repeats most of his dialogue multiple times, calls out, "Hey, Dad, there's a man with a stick caught in his mouth!" The action cuts to a wide shot, and there is indeed a man struggling as described, asking for help. As Sparky exhorts him to "Get the stick!" Randy violently shakes the man back and forth. In the process he breaks his neck, leaving the man writhing on the ground. More effort results in his eyes being gouged out before Randy is finally successful in dislodging the stick. The man's mangled body rolls away through the backyard's fence and out onto the road, where a truck runs over it. Randy profanely notes that the man never expressed any gratitude.

Episode 6: "My Teeth Are Bleeding" (3:55)

Set amidst a cacophony of noise, the sixth episode presents as an aural domestic hell, with the joke lying in the differences between what we each find most grating or are able to tune out.

In one of the series' more complex frames, a reverse-angle composition, Randy sits in the bottom righthand corner, his screaming wife in a chair to the left, Sparky jumping on a trampoline in front of him, and a TV to the right with the energy from repetitive blows of violence from a wrestling match emanating off the screen and into the room. In the background, through a window, cars and trucks drive by on a two-lane highway.

As Randy looks back and forth at all these elements, cars skid and gunfire erupts outside. Then there's a police car and people running. Sparky, meanwhile, falls off the trampoline, and Randy's wife begins to choke in exaggerated fashion. It's a fly buzzing around Randy's head that he finds most bothersome, however.

Episode 7: "Uncle Bob" (5:09)

The seventh episode expands our view of this most unusual family, as Randy visits his mother-in-law with his wife and Sparky in tow. This broad-shouldered woman with tiny hands communicates in no uncertain terms to her daughter that she's "not afraid of this dickhead husband of yours." Lest one think the character represents a strong condemnation of domestic violence, the woman hits her daughter too.

Noting that Uncle Bob is not feeling good but that she and her daughter are going shopping, Randy's mother-in-law charges him with looking after Bob. "You lay one hand on him and I'll cut your nuts off," she threatens, adding on the way out, "Remember what I told you about your nuts."

Uncle Bob is a curiously hunchbacked figure (shades of the Elephant Man, perhaps?) who doesn't speak, and we (like Randy and Sparky) don't quite know what's wrong with him. In sequential fashion, Bob pants, hits himself, stomps, burps, farts, and vomits. Finally, Bob lunges over and hits Randy. Sparky's eyes slowly track his father, waiting for a reaction. Randy hits Bob, but his mother-in-law suddenly appears and smashes Randy, sending him straight through a wall. Later that night, Sparky approaches Randy, who sits outside in a tree: "They're gone. You're safe. She took Uncle Bob to the hospital. Uncle Bob bit his foot off."

Episode 8: "Ants" (5:18)

The last and longest episode of *DumbLand*, "Ants" spotlights a longstanding fascination (and nemesis) of Lynch, ultimately elevating them to probably the closest thing to a winner in the whole series. Watching more and more ants crawl along his floor, Randy becomes irate and grabs a spray can simply labeled "Kill" from the cabinet. Lynch then indulges a classic, elongated comedic setup, showing us the can's nozzle pointed in the wrong direction. After Randy predictably sprays himself in the eyes and falls down screaming, his face rearranges.

In this semihallucinatory state, Randy watches a chorus line of dancing ants, à la the Rockettes, serenade him profanely, telling him what they see when they look at him. (Hint: it's not complimentary.) More misfortune befalls Randy after he comes to and tries to attack the ants again, this time with his hands. Later, when he's in a full body cast, he looks down at his exposed toes. One ant climbs down his cast, then two, and then it's a swarm. Randy bellows in anguished defeat.

• • •

It's not difficult to draw a line from *DumbLand* back to The Angriest Dog in the World, Lynch's four-panel comic strip that ran from 1983 to 1992 in the *Los Angeles Reader*. In the latter work, each strip is introduced with the same caption: "The dog who is so angry he cannot move, he cannot eat, he cannot sleep. He can just barely growl. Bound so tightly with tension and anger, he approaches the state of rigor mortis."

The four panels maintain a visual consistency. In each, a highly stylized black dog—with a pointy tail that makes him look almost like a bomb set to go off—strains against his chain, tied to a small post in a yard underneath the window of a house. The first three panels are in daylight, while the last shows nighttime, a light from indoors spilling out onto a darkened yard.

The content changes only by way of dialogue from the family inside the home, presented in word bubbles in one or more of the panels. Sometimes these interjections center on wordplay, but just as often they are non sequiturs or absurd exclamations, leaving a viewer to divine their meaning from their juxtaposition against this static, perpetually furious dog. (While Lynch said he had the idea for the comic strip a decade earlier, the fact it debuted during the period when he was editing *Dune* is perhaps not a complete coincidence.)

DumbLand is an animated work but similarly rendered in black-

and-white and confined almost entirely to a single dwelling—though both outside and indoors. While it's shot through with more overt violence, its indulgence of non sequiturs and absurdity is similar to its canine forerunner's, as is its overarching preoccupation with anger. The shared simplicity of the projects' visual styling and the absence of substantive information about family dynamics or the broader community in which the action takes place encourages viewers to fill in details with their own imaginations.

Here, though, Lynch lends his voice as well as his pen to the characters. And despite the show's physical outlandishness, it's the vocal performances that are probably the most interesting thing about *DumbLand*, checking three boxes of performative participation: indulging his experiential curiosity, expressing his sense of humor, and connecting with the art life.

In later years, Lynch enjoyed a good bit of voice work—especially in projects generated by other people. His voice was a known commodity and almost always built into the character. Sure, it could be dialed up and down, but Lynch wasn't going to be hired to do accents. He may have at one time had some reservations about the timbre of his voice, but it became a much-loved feature of his personality.

On *DumbLand*, it's easy to forget it's Lynch saying all these crazy things and providing assorted squawks and bellows. It would have been simple to rope in an assistant—or even John Neff, his in-house manager at Asymmetrical Studios, with whom he was working heavily on music at the time—to provide the voice of other characters. Lynch voicing them all himself shows not only an immersion in the technology, which by all accounts was fascinating to him before it became tedious, but also an absorption in the world itself, small scaled as it was.

Lynch altered his voice using a BOSS VT-1 Voice Transformer, which allowed real-time manipulation, granting Lynch the immediacy and ease of use he craved. "It's been completely invaluable. I need all these pieces because I love experimenting, and they open up a whole other world of experimentation," Lynch told *BOSS Users Group Magazine* in 2001. Working with Neff, he could save presets for his main characters and crank up the distortion for Randy's screaming fits but easily and quickly introduce completely new voices, implementing vocal gender changes plus all other manner of off-the-wall effects, all in a single recording session.

For a while, this volume of work was probably part of the appeal for Lynch. "He loves to work more than anybody," said Bassett. "He gets up in the morning. He wears the exact same outfit, comes to work day after day from early in the morning until late at night. And if he can't work, it puts him in a horrible mood. He just wants to work all the time."

Lynch refused to outsource and serve as more of a conductor overseeing the series. His joyful attachment to it was inextricably tied to both the physical acts of *doing* (learning a new technology, drawing, performing) and the experimentation and fine-tuning inherent to this type of creation. "He had a great time with that," said daughter Jennifer Lynch. "It was just all out in the open, balls to the wall, 'I think this is funny.'"

Eventually, however, the show's production ran into the buzzsaw realities of cost-benefit analysis—and the fact that there wasn't a business model to sustain it. In *Room to Dream*, Lynch tells a straightforward story about how *DumbLand* came to be. This account aligns with the view from one collaborator at the time (who asked to remain anonymous) that Lynch viewed the internet as potentially a way "to make silly money. He was into it for the art, for sure—that was genuine. But he also had dollar signs in his head, as did a lot of people at the time."

In his memoir, Lynch relates how a man from Shockwave arrived at his home in a limousine and pitched an offer for an animated series in exchange for shares of the company that, when vested, would be worth seven million dollars. As Lynch noted, "I said okay and started working." When the dot-com bubble burst, Lynch said, "all those 'new-sneaker people,' including the Shockwave guy, went up in smoke and those shares were absolutely worthless. I have the worst money luck."

Each *DumbLand* episode reportedly took Lynch around sixty hours to create. And without the windfall of that Shockwave payout (or anything close to it), Lynch's website subscription model wasn't a workable long-term economic replacement for a series that someone could binge in far under one hour and then simply cancel their membership. Ergo, any grander plans withered on the vine, and the series ended after eight episodes.

"From what I understood, David loved being able to do everything himself, but I think that might've butted up against the limits of the reality of exactly what that means when you're doing animation, because it was painstaking—as animation would be, especially if you're doing it all yourself," said Jay Aaseng, who came on board as an assistant with Lynch after the bulk of the work on *DumbLand* was complete.

"It was pretty labor-intensive," agreed fellow Lynch assistant Erik Crary. "I think he enjoyed it, and it was a great outlet for low humor, which obviously he had a place [in his heart] for that. But when you get into the volume of animating all of that, yes, by the end I think he was ready to wrap up."

Overall, the reaction to *DumbLand* stands as varied. Even among Lynch aficionados it's divisive. To those who worked most closely with him, however, the series reflected both Lynch's sense of humor and his curiosity about human impulse and behavior.

"I was a big fan, because it was so crass and stupid. I loved it," said Crary. "I have a big soft spot for a certain level of stupid. If it's kind of crass and it knows it and it's just trying to do a thing quickly, I'm usually a fan. And I think there's a lot of satire to it—the kid's very annoying and the dad's very aggressive and the mom's completely locked up in fear. He's playing on certain character types that you can see in some of his other stuff. But this is just the most unfiltered, raw, rough version of those [characters], which I thought was fun."

"The main character, now that I look back on it, seems to have a lot in common with that Billy the Groper character," added Aaseng. "Maybe that was just all part of a thing that he was exploring at that time."

DumbLand exhibits, as much as anything Lynch produced in long form, his anthropologist-like appreciation of the imbecilic. It also affirms his belief that a great deal of human boorishness, and the considerable ill and suffering that flows from it, is hardwired to unthinkingness—and thus worth examining or at least acknowledging with a laugh.

When I spoke to Lynch in February 2002, at which point *DumbLand* was halfway through its run on his website, he was still in a positive headspace with regard to the series and optimistic about its reception, despite the fact that it was likely entirely in his rearview mirror creatively speaking. A large part of those feelings seemed to exist as perverse affection for Randy, surely the most repellant character ever personally embodied by Lynch. That a less frightening approximation of Randy's visage would pop up years later in *The Return* as the head on Johnny Horne's therapy bear maybe ratifies Lynch's view of the character's peculiar sanative powers, acting as a sort of pressure-relief valve.

"The internet is really getting to be the place for a continuing story," said Lynch then. "When we first started working on the site, it wasn't a place for five-minute moving things. There were too many obstacles. And then it just keeps getting better and better. So I like that development and growth and the way that it is its own world that then itself offers up the opportunity to create and explore whole *other* worlds—just worlds within worlds, but finding other people along the way, too, who enjoy those worlds.

"And Randy seems like a guy that belongs on the internet, you know? He was just made for it, in a way," Lynch continued. "*DumbLand* is, as the name says, quite dumb, and so five minutes of Randy at a time is a good amount probably. Any more might cause people some distress."

−CHAPTER 18−

OUT YONDER (2002, 2003, 2007)

During Lynch's steady experimentation on his nascent website, one of the projects Lynch conceived was *Out Yonder*, consisting of three purposefully preposterous shorts released over a half dozen years, in which he starred with his oldest son. "It was whenever Austin was in town—that kind of drove that," said Eric Bassett. "He loved doing *Out Yonder* with his son, and Austin's the nicest guy I've ever met."

Characterized by extended squinty pauses and the copious use of a self-created discourse marker that renders verb tenses alliterative and largely irrelevant, these black-and-white efforts center on a pair of unnamed gentleman who sit outdoors and in elliptical fashion discuss various problems, from an empty fridge and milk-demanding neighbor to dental pain. As Lynch himself explained in an introduction on the 2006 DVD *Dynamic:01*, the idea for *Out Yonder* was born in large part simply from the phrase "be's bein'," which popped into his head, amused him, and somehow became a unifying narrative element in some longhand writing he was doing.

All the characters in the shorts speak in distorted, slightly tinny voices with an elevated pitch, and their dialogue is liberally sprinkled with slight variations on the aforementioned word cluster. (As an aside, some dialogue quoted here directly may include such filler words, but for exchanges paraphrased you can add your own "be's bein's.") In ways sometimes obvious and sometimes less so, *Out Yonder* can be seen as a live-action cousin of *DumbLand*, though each entry in the series features the same button for its ending.

• • •

"Out Yonder: Neighbor Boy" (9:38)

Released as merely "Out Yonder" on February 11, 2002, and then retroactively given its fuller appellation upon extension of the series, this short establishes the basic visual vocabulary of the productions: a locked-off exterior two shot with complementary close-ups and occasional handheld work. On the left side of the frame, Lynch sits in his familiar work outfit (khakis, white shirt buttoned to the collar), this time with a dark blazer and oversize and up-teased knit cap that makes him look, in a way, like a demented Shriner. To his left is an empty chair and in between a well-worn radio with a cassette deck, which he smacks. For a while Lynch tracks the sound of a bird fluttering back and forth, then those of several other animals.

Austin, sporting a tighter, darker knit cap, enters and sits, holding a book bag in his lap. "It bein' hot," he says, followed by, "It be's like this some days. It be's bein' hard to figure. That bein' the doorbell?" Each of these statements is followed by significant lulls in which Austin gazes downward, intercut with Lynch glaring at him. That ringing doorbell heralds the (off-screen) arrival of a large, stomping figure whose presence casts an affected shadow over the pair. "Damn son! He be's bein' one big neighbor boy!" exclaims Lynch. As the figure speaks in garbled, unintelligible fashion, Lynch says, "Damn, I be's feelin' we's be's not at this time having the quality of milk he may be's bein' requiring!" As the unseen, agitated neighbor scales their house, Austin leaves to fetch some milk in an effort to placate him.

A little past the eight-minute mark, as the sound of distant off-screen fighting rises, Lynch gazes out and asks, "What we be's seeing out yonder?" Told it's the Ninth Cavalry as well as some Native Americans, Lynch says, "Looks to be a ruckus," and then, after a pause, "Them be shedding blood." After a close-up and long pause, he swats at a winged-bug effect that appears on-screen, and the piece ends with the pair sitting in silence.

"Out Yonder: Teeth" (13:27)

Released on April 16, 2003, "Teeth" opens on the same tableau, this time with Lynch and an already seated Austin angled slightly inward, each facing the other. A wheelbarrow sits to Lynch's right, and a pair of binoculars are on the ground. The antenna of the radio between them is evocatively bent.

Lynch lifts up his leg as if to pass gas and holds it for twenty seconds. He then expels sporadic flatulence (a great junior high metal band name, I'm thinking) in a pained clench for roughly half a minute—undoubtedly the most robust live-action example of Lynch's "farthouse" appreciation, blending unconventional storytelling with everyman toilet humor.

An extended conversation ensues, Lynch's brow furrowed throughout, in which Austin complains of pain, "something like a functional incapacitation."

"What it is? An unknown etiology?" asks Lynch. "Evidence of inflammation and degeneration," says Austin. "It may be a neuralgia. It may be of psychogenic origin. But I've been thinking it may not be so." Lynch determines Austin needs a tooth extraction, saying, "You be's bein' shirking that which be's bein' needing facing."

As the camerawork shifts to tight handheld, Lynch's other son, Riley, about ten at the time, enters. Shot from behind so that we never see his face, Riley assists Lynch in examining the impacted area before the latter uses a pair of pliers to yank out one tooth, then another. Riley announces his hunger and leaves, while Austin, his shirt bloodied from this action, makes a request for brown salted nuts. As the sounds of the cavalry and battle arise once more, Lynch again notes, "Them be shedding blood."

"I'm going to say that one's directly related to some family stuff that was going on," said Lynch's assistant Erik Crary. "I can't tell you with 100 percent accuracy, but I do feel like that might've been . . . something David could see happening: 'We're going to shoot *Out Yonder*, let's weave this in.' I could definitely see that happening."

"Out Yonder: Chicken" (17:09)

Released on April 16, 2007, the last and longest *Out Yonder* episode extends the family affair, with Lynch's partner and later wife, Emily Stofle, appearing. "Chicken" opens with Lynch sitting alone staring at a white bucket at his feet filled with black goo. The mise-en-scène is mostly the same, but gone is the radio antenna. As the sounds of nature mingle in the background with a low rustling, Lynch's eyes move slowly back and forth, then up to meet an approaching figure—a woman in a bathrobe, her head bandaged and a Band-Aid on her face.

The woman introduces herself as a neighbor and then says, apropos of nothing, "This gonorrhea be gettin' me." This triggers the first of numerous expressionless reaction shots of Lynch, free for a viewer to interpret as they choose; this one lasts seven seconds. After she sits down, the woman notes that her breast is hurting and exposes herself to illustrate. Another pause from Lynch before a deadpan response that feels like it should be a very popular GIF: "That be's bein' one large area of hurt."

A discussion about her missing chickens ensues, and after the woman leaves, Lynch calls out to wish her good luck. Austin enters, and the pair sit chewing for a while, talking about what Austin is eating. In a flash of sudden violence, Lynch punches Austin in the face, prompting Austin to spit out a carcass of indeterminate nature. Lynch admonishes him for eating that which isn't his. Austin pulls out a chicken by its feet from underneath his shirt and explains he found it behind the refrigerator. He plops it on the radio, where a few flies buzz around it.

Talk centers on the chicken ("It's one for eating, once gutted") and what's in the bucket ("It's unknown to me"), which Lynch advises carefulness on exploring. When Austin reaches in, he pulls out a human leg—which, as a flash renders him one-legged, turns out to be his own. His exposed stump provides the only appearance of color in the entire *Out Yonder* catalogue. A repetition of the cavalry dialogue follows, and as Austin gazes into the distance and then looks down, Lynch bends over and sticks his head in the bucket and his rear end high in the air, farting out an animated series of a dozen winged creatures.

"That must've been one of the last things we did for the website probably, at least in that very produced kind of way," said assistant Jay Aaseng. The chicken that appears in the short was real, found by Crary during a trip to Chinatown in downtown Los Angeles. "One of the great, amazing things about working for David is just having to source things you never would've thought you'd have to figure out how to source, especially in the budding days of the internet, when it wasn't quite as easy to do this stuff," continued Aaseng. "So one of them was trying to find an actual chicken we could use that was dead."

• • •

Production on every episode of *Out Yonder* involved both Crary and Aaseng. "I was [Lynch's] writer's assistant at the time, so he would often either dictate to me or sometimes he'd just write on legal pads, and I'd have to try to make sense of it and type it up," said Aaseng. "But that was something where . . . he'd done a lot in *Twin Peaks*, obviously, and *Fire Walk With Me*, but other than very small stuff, he had not done acting for a little while. I even remember him talking about it a bit: 'Oh, I haven't put the acting hat on for a while.'

"He definitely got an idea that really took hold, though, and then when he thought about doing it with Austin, he got into it and said, 'I think this could be a fun thing to do.'"

Typically, Crary would break down the script and talk with Lynch about any items needed. Then he and Aaseng would shoot. "That was us setting up cameras right behind his gray house, which you probably remember, and setting up chairs," continued Aaseng. "Most of the set for that was honestly already there. We probably adjusted a few things, obviously, but those chairs, I think, were actually the chairs that were out there."

"I had no business [filming]," added Crary. "I'm not a trained cameraperson. There's a lot of things I had no business doing, but in the spirit of being around him, you're doing it. It was amazing. I couldn't afford proper film school. I really wanted to go, and I think I got away with a lotto ticket on just doing common-sense production with him."

It's Aaseng's recollection the *Out Yonder* shorts were written as discrete stand-alones, which would track with the long gap in production between the second and third entries. It's interesting, though, to think about why Lynch found these characters worth returning to (it was the only live-action character he ever reprised other than Gordon Cole).

"I mean, David was into all kinds of different things," noted Aaseng. "I think at one point he kind of went down a little bit of a rabbit hole with quantum physics and string theory and all this, and he kind of brought that into *Out Yonder,* which is the most absurd thing for characters like that to be talking about."

While *Out Yonder* doesn't explicitly reference those elements, Aaseng is right that Lynch made that connection. As he explained in a snippet from a recorded introduction on the mystery disc of his *Lime Green* box set, released via Absurda in 2008, "These people have an interest in oral pathology, quantum cosmology, general medicine, fertilization processes, and properties of soil." In his memoir, *Room to Dream,* Lynch went even further: "The idea is that this family is heavy into quantum physics, and they talk in abstract ways about things. They're interested in medicine and science, and they're quantum physicists."

Even if *Out Yonder* is not immediately readable as described above, is it emblematic of Lynch taking complex theories or ideas that caught his attention in the real world and transmuting them into a creative endeavor? "Possibly," said Aaseng. "I think just me having been around him, I would notice every now and then that stuff like that would happen.

"But I couldn't necessarily say with any certainty that the things he was doing in *Out Yonder* were also just related to things that were top of mind or just particular ideas he was fascinated with. I know that he, like everybody else, was very affected by 9/11 and how the world changed after that. I know he was thinking perhaps more, or at least more outwardly with me, about the world and where we were heading and just a little more concerned about politics and stuff like this. So sometimes I wonder if some of that might've influenced some of the things he's talking about, especially with that little speech they do at the end and just watching people fight off in the distance. But it's hard to say. I mean, the question of where David's ideas come from is going to be an eternal mystery for all of us."

• • •

An unforgiving cynic might view these shorts as a savvy way to commodify and monetize family time; they did, after all, help feed the content machine of DavidLynch.com. The best way to view *Out Yonder,* however, seems to be as loosely themed sketches that check the performative boxes of personal connection and sense of humor, as well as more generally through a lens that combines two of Lynch's favorite words: "absurd" and "experiment."

Readings on string theory may have served as a certain leaping-off point, but it's likely Lynch found an everyman's attempt to grasp or apply such postulations humorous and worked his way back to these characters. His framing of the idea as inspired by the vocal disfluencies of "be's bein'" is apparently sincere, given *Out Yonder'*s steadfast adherence to the bit. The expanding length of the series, meanwhile, especially with the last episode coming after the production experience of the three-hour *Inland Empire*, also reflects a comfort level with methodical pacing that would foreshadow some scene stagings in *The Return*.

Out Yonder is most interesting to ponder through a performative lens, however. While Cole wasn't necessarily a physically dynamic figure, he was certainly highly verbally expressive. By contrast, the characters Lynch sketches here are rooted in stillness. They read in part as an exercise in the effectiveness of controlled reaction—in terms of both the performances themselves and an audience's response. This is quite different than Lynch's previous acting work and much else of what he was exploring on his website.

"That was the first time to see him get into doing a character and seeing how much he would commit to it," said Aaseng. "That's what I think separates him. It's really all about commitment—how hard do you commit to what you're doing? And whatever he's doing, he's just absolutely, 110 percent, all there.

"I think a lot of times when he's on camera, he's playing sort of a comedic character. Not always, but a lot of the time. And it always made me wonder, [because] I think he did have self-awareness [that] what he brings to the table [as a performer] is just a very particular type of thing that is so singularly him but also can come off as surreal and fascinating and absurdly funny."

–CHAPTER 19–

"STRANGE AND UNPRODUCTIVE THINKING" (2002)

Strange thinking, sure. But strange and *unproductive* thinking, from David Lynch? Well, that seems unlikely.

With roots that stretch back nearly ten years and forward almost another decade, this hidden little curio from Lynch's website shows him at both his most playful and, quite possibly, philosophical. It also showcases his propensity for returning to themes, and even cleverly repurposing material that especially intrigued him.

Basically a mischievous indulgence of his long-discussed belief that "we're all like detectives in life," this one-minute-50-second video was only ever available on DavidLynch.com. One of the site's mysterious features involved various phone booths, for which codes—sometimes revealed  in a chat room, sometimes buried elsewhere within content—would unlock additional material. On the DVD release for Lynch's short films, if one cycles through the TV calibration settings, a colored test pattern appears. By pressing select on your remote control, a special code, X7507, is revealed along with the number 1 inside of a red circle, next to a vomiting figure. When entered in Phone Booth 1 on Lynch's website, a special clip appeared: "Strange and Unproductive Thinking."

Featuring Lynch's squinting, scrunched-up-face under a looped, massively sped-up video of him looking downward and ostensibly reading aloud, this work consists of around two-thirds of a 950-word chunk of text from his book *Images*. The monologue is a free-flowing, philosophically tinged verbal barrage touching on various energies and aphorisms (sample: "It is with this also on our minds that we see that the initial thinking on a subject is critical to all that follows"), plus ruminations on vital links between the subconscious and super-conscious minds and the idea of a world free of tooth decay.

Published in 1994, *Images* consists of many stills from Lynch's films, but also photos of his animal kits, abandoned factories, spark plugs, nudes, and other artwork. There's a bit of text here and there, ranging from non sequitur dialogue exchanges to a captioned photo essay on dental hygiene. The spoken-word monologue from "Strange and Unproductive Thinking" comes from a section titled "Meaningless Conversations" (itself a title that would be repurposed in singularized form for a song from Lynch and Angelo Badalamenti's 2018 album, *Thought Gang*, comprising material recorded in the early 1990s).

The full version of the above-mentioned text from *Images*, meanwhile, would go on to form a song titled "Strange and Unproductive Thinking" on Lynch's 2011 debut solo album, *Crazy Clown Time*—a seven-and-a-half-minute, groovily hypnotic spoken-word treatise, heavily processed via a vocoder and set underneath a gently percussive, driving beat.

This "Strange and Unproductive Thinking" (check the Internet Archive to give it a spin) seems to date from mid- to late February 2002, though the exact day of its flipped-switch availability is perhaps lost to the sands of time. The additional wrinkle is that the audio, which includes a bit of music in the background, is also sped up (the video and audio aren't synced), in a fashion that would make the Micro Machines pitchman jealous.

Again, stacked up, that's a two-decade span over which Lynch returned to this text, using it across three different mediums. Do the different presentations—one plain, one playful, one set to music that gives it a pleasantly woozy uplift—contain a special message or attitudinal shift? Maybe only that life holds multitudes, a theme Lynch always seemed inclined to underscore in his work.

−CHAPTER 20−

"THE DISC OF SORROW

IS INSTALLED" (2002)

As with ants, another interloper of nature, Lynch's battles with squirrels spanned decades, and his efforts to prevent their thievery of seed meant for birds took many forms over the years. "That was a lifelong struggle," said Jennifer Lynch with a laugh. "He didn't mind causing them sorrow, but he didn't want to hurt them. If I'm remembering correctly, he had killed a squirrel in his youth with a slingshot and never got over it. So it was a battle that he fought internally as well, because they frustrated him so much, but he did not want to hurt them." That Lynch's personal campaign would eventually be chronicled in an idiosyncratic performance-art piece on his website is perhaps not surprising.

"I remember that was always one of the best stories that David had, where he would talk about this disc of sorrow," said Jay Aaseng, who served as one of Lynch's assistants for many years. "It's always interesting when David tells stories, because he's so passionate and I feel like he's got the color sort of turned up in his world more than the rest of us. It's the way he'll talk about things, where you're like, 'How could that be?' But also, you kind of believe it when David says it. So he is saying squirrels were literally weeping on the ground. They were so upset that they couldn't get to this food that they'd had an unlimited supply of up until now. I remember we were just dying laughing at this story when he told it, and so I'm guessing that was maybe part of him realizing we could actually do something like that for the site."

The four-minute short "The Disc of Sorrow Is Installed" debuted in mid-2002, after an intriguing sign labeled "Future Home of Disc of Sorrow" had been glimpsed in the background of other website works. Shot by Aaseng and fellow assistant Erik Crary, the video (in color, but trading heavily in shades of black, white, and gray) opens with that placard still present and then pans up a long pole to a bird feeder, where several small birds are enjoying a meal. A quick cut to a single bird perched on the aforementioned sign then gives way to another shot of the birds scattering.

In the background there exists a droning soundscape, credited to Angelo Badalamenti—likely part of a cord of the sonic "firewood" which he frequently provided Lynch, to serve as the foundation for later compositions. Additionally, the entire scene is set up in front of a massive, matted industrial backdrop consisting of one of Lynch's photos dating back to *Eraserhead*'s production, from the construction site of what is now the Beverly Center. "He'd gotten a large-format Epson printer and had printed that photo in panels," recalled Crary. "From there we'd trim things up and help him glue or seal it to a large painting canvas, which was gessoed wood usually. He used that method as the base of a few of his paintings at that time—he really dug that huge printer."

In a wide shot, with the bird feeder flush left, Lynch stands close to the center of the frame, holding a large, blue, thin-cut metal circle—the diameter of which covers his entire chest—with a small hole cut in the middle. Lynch offers an emphatic pronouncement: "Squirrels above, birds below. These days life is backwards, don't you know? With the disc of sorrow it's a different show: birds above, and squirrels below."

Cut to a medium shot: "We will now install the disc of sorrow," Lynch says, turning his head to his left and nodding. Back to a wide shot: two men enter wearing black coats. One, Alfredo Ponce, sports a black toboggan and novelty googly eyes, the other, Ruben Nuñez, sunglasses and a dark blue baseball cap. Shots alternate between wide and medium as Alfredo unscrews the sign and Ruben removes it.

Together they lift the bird feeder out of the ground, hoisting it high up by its thin metal pole. Lynch lines up the circle's hole with the pole, threads it, and lifts the disc higher as the duo reinserts the bird feeder's pole into the ground. At the 3:10 mark, they reposition themselves in a line, Lynch in the middle. They flub a benediction, comically mistiming both an in-unison salute and their group exit stage left, sandwiched around Lynch intoning, "The disc of sorrow is [sic] been installed."

For many years, Ponce was Lynch's groundskeeper, though his jack-of-all-trades utility belied that tidy description. Nuñez, meanwhile, also worked around the property for several years, helping with upkeep. "David just surrounds himself with magical people, and Alfredo was just such a diamond in the rough," said Aaseng. "Now he's retired, but he had an unparalleled work ethic. He had the strength and endurance of five guys put together. And not only that, he could just figure out anything. David realized at a certain point that he could do groundskeeping—he was a master at that—but he could also build anything that he wanted him to build too."

Over the years, as necessitated by both the effects of weather and the problem-solving ingenuity of his rodent nemeses, Lynch had worked his way through several different versions of his homemade solution, involving LP records and plexiglass. As for this particular iteration of the disc of sorrow, there's every reason to believe it was made to be camera ready. "David definitely designed all of that stuff [but] Alfredo and David were very, very synced up," said Crary. "Alfredo sort of knew what to do to fabricate it and David would coach him, and then eventually they'd be working together or David would take it over. But there was a lot of history and a lot of craftsmanship—and collaboration—between those two. So I'm confident saying David would've designed it. Alfredo probably did the initial fabrication, and then at some point David probably did the painting or some refinement of it."

The particulars of Ponce's and Nuñez's costumes, on the other hand, are perhaps lost to the ether. "With the googly eyes, [Alfredo] could see directly in front, and that was it—he had no peripheral vision," said Aaseng. "So when they salute, and Alfredo is still saluting, he doesn't realize they're not doing that anymore. He's just looking to see what's going on, and it just adds to the incredibly absurdity of it all. I remember very distinctly we were shooting from a little ways away, so we wouldn't ruin anything. But even still, Erik and I—well, definitely me—was having to try to keep from laughing.

"And also, honestly, we were a little bit worried for Alfredo," Aaseng continued. "It was a little bit of a narrow path to walk there, and . . . the last thing you want to see is someone take a tumble down the hill."

More than one YouTube commenter has referred to this as a "classic David Lynch shitpost." But such pronouncements ignore the care with which the background is chosen, the mood imposed by the sound design, and of course the solemnity with which the entire event is staged, as if it represents a step forward in human achievement that must be recorded for posterity. "It just goes to show how sharp his sense of humor is, because it's almost not even offered as something that could be entertaining, just that he's documenting this critical function," said Seth Green, a fan of Lynch who would later cross professional paths with him.

It also ignores Lynch's decision to spotlight (albeit in anonymized fashion) two trusted deputies, to share the screen with employees he'd roped into his playful scheme. This again reflects commingled reasons for acting— expressing his sense of humor while also taking part in a creative endeavor with friends. Lynch's performance, meanwhile, amusingly leans into rhymed declarative authority—sort of like a circus ringmaster pretending to be a newsman delivering a scientific finding, if that makes sense.

So, given all the thought put into the production and installation, from both an artistic and utilitarian perspective, was its functionality ultimately successful? "I think that [particular] disc of sorrow, just by where it was, was a tricky one to be as successful as the one before, because it was on a hill and so squirrels could jump out of trees and still get there sometimes," said Aaseng.

"And so I think we had to keep tweaking things to try to make sure they couldn't reach the feeder and that they would just get foiled. But that said, I think it was, for the most part, pretty successful. Maybe it didn't quite get the same reaction as the days of yore from the crying squirrels," he continued with a laugh, "but it was pretty fun to see the whole thing come together."

–CHAPTER 21–

"BOAT" (2003)

Running just over seven minutes, "Boat" debuted on DavidLynch.com, and saw later commercial release as part of the 2006 *Dynamic:01* DVD. In the introduction for the video, Lynch says, "It kind of, like, started as one of those family videos, and I somehow got the idea that this would be a trip into night." He then notes that a voice-over he wrote "sort of put it in another place."

The video opens with shots of a tree canopy against a sunny sky. Other shots present a small, well-maintained watercraft, then its tank being filled with gasoline, a close-up of the boat's engine, some knots, and a small American flag at its stern. We push in on a coiled rope, then witness a finger turn on the engine and adjust other switches. We see the craft bobbing in a boat slip, empty.

The 175-word voice-over from Emily Stofle unfolds in fragmented fashion—emotionally impressionistic shards that give the piece a woozy, confused vibe: "It was so bright. I couldn't sleep. Trees . . . the dogs were barking. When things go wrong, it gets like this. . . . Essential beauty, I thought. I was so tired. I thought nature contains many mysteries."

At the 3:20 mark, as indicated by the voice-over, the boat begins to move and we see Lynch inside, backing it out alone, then another shot of him, from behind, out on the water. At 3:55, the camera now in the boat, Lynch looks directly into the lens and says, "We're gonna try to go fast enough to go into the night."

Shots intercut between Lynch; over the boat's edge, water speeding by; the flag whipping in the wind; and water trailing in the craft's wake. Throughout all this, no one else is shown. The rest of the voice-over is largely experiential ("I saw drops of water, and it was very bright . . . I was moving very fast"), and at around the 5:20 mark the shots transition to nighttime.

The ending juxtaposes the only other line of dialogue spoken by Lynch with a pause in the final line of voice-over: "I think I went to sleep, and I want to tell you . . . ["It worked"] . . . that I dreamed of you."

"Boat"'s roots may stretch back to "one of those family videos," but they also extend far outside of Los Angeles. "My hometown is Lodi, Wisconsin, and it's about twenty-five miles away from Madison, where David and Mary [Sweeney] had a house," said Erik Crary. "And just to be blunt, it was easiest for me to plan my vacation home to see my family when David and Mary weren't going to be at the house, which usually meant they were in Madison at the same time. So strangely, my vacation was very close to my boss, but it was a lot of fun because a couple of those summers—one summer, I think it was the summer that 'Boat' was shot—I went and played golf with them, and we went and got lunch at some tavern and then went for a ride on that boat.

"I sort of recall shooting stuff then. I don't think I was a part of shooting 'Boat' necessarily. I don't know if he and [son] Riley and Mary went out with [son] Austin and shot, but they just had this beautiful wooden boat. But the idea that they would go out as a family and shoot—that makes perfect sense to me. It was a very special couple of weeks in that sort of woodsy lake (area), but still in a beautiful city setup that they had."

In *Room to Dream*, Lynch tells an anecdote about first acquiring the vessel from "Boat," a 1942 Fitzgerald & Lee runabout named *Little Indian*. Lynch then recounts a story of staying with Isabella Rossellini and going out to meet her and some friends in Bellport, Long Island, for an afternoon of crab fishing. Afterward, heading back alone, Lynch encountered a rapidly developing storm that in an instant plunged a sunny day into darkest night, "like *The Twilight Zone*." Losing his way in fog and choppy water getting back, and possibly running low on gas, he was saved at the last moment by the sight of distant shore lights.

While shot on Lake Mendota in Wisconsin and married to a characteristically elliptical narrative, "Boat" seems at its core at least a partial reflection upon that incident and an attempt to reframe it as something more controllable, part of an active undertaking. Some might quibble around the edges with the notion of this ranking as a performance, but I would argue it absolutely reflects Lynch's ability to see both story worlds and an external reality the world foists upon us as equally valid, and sometimes blend and merge the two.

Clearly there exists both a narrative conceit (going fast enough to transcend the speed of light, and move into darkness), and an artistic, constructed rendering of it. It would be easy enough to explore the same idea merely through voice-over (whether Stofle's or via a separate track), but the fact that Lynch places himself (literally) in the driver's seat is rather notable—as seems the fact that it bridges elements among relationships with three of his longtime partners: Rossellini, Sweeney, and Stofle.

–CHAPTER 22–

"LAMP" (2003)

"Lamp," like "Boat," made its debut on Lynch's website, and was eventually released to DVD as part of *Dynamic:01*. Quite unlike that short, however, which bears traditional hallmarks of filmic construction, the thirty-minute "Lamp" exists more as a snapshot of nonfiction utilitarian content, with Lynch enthusiastically laboring on a titular fixture, his third such handcrafted piece. As narrated in running fashion by Lynch, however, it manages to transcend its workaday roots.

For Erik Crary, who shot much of it and is glimpsed briefly in the video's

end, "Lamp" might function chiefly as a valentine to Lynch's beloved Fix-It-All, a patching compound which Lynch refers to throughout as simply Fix-All, and explains is like plaster but much stronger. "He *loved* [that stuff], and if he's going to be making this lamp anyway, let's shoot it, let's see what it becomes," said Crary. "That's a good example of [something being] inherently interesting when he's doing it because he's so focused, and doing the thing."

For Eric Bassett, Lynch's partner at Absurda, the piece cleared the bar of workability simply by being something that Lynch was sincerely invested in. "He was the driver behind all of those ideas. I just told him if it was viable or not," recalled Bassett. "And I said, 'Look, most anything that you do people will watch, at a certain level.'"

"He was probably perpetually thinking about content," added Crary. "Some of it's very high value. *Rabbits*, huge effort. *DumbLand*, huge effort. Some of these things took a lot. And then some of these things, like 'Quinoa' and 'Lamp' are like, 'This could be interesting—let's shoot it.' There's one called 'Ball of Bees' [where] there was just a phenomenon that was happening in the backyard, so we shot it. There were targets of mutual opportunity that happened once in a while too."

For some viewers, "Lamp" might test the outer limits of patience. But those folks are likely not reading this book. Again, many (probably most) of Lynch's fans found reward in not only his films, but also the variedness and imagination of his other interests. They took enjoyment in the idea of Lynch the happy worker, pursuing his creative instincts wherever they took him. This work definitely checks that box.

Set under a simple, low percussive beat, with birds chirping in the background, "Lamp" takes place in and around the aerie of Lynch's compound, an open-air-accessible workspace situated on sloping grounds. Sporting his trademark white, long-sleeve shirt, with sleeves rolled up and hair game incredibly strong throughout, Lynch amiably sets the scene before one of the laughs occasionally found in the piece's edits. After a forty-five-second intro in which Lynch references his trusted handyman Alfredo Ponce creating the cold-rolled steel frame for his work, and four buckets of Fix-It-All and gauze having already been applied, thus setting up the day's work, there's a cut: "Before we do that, we have to have some coffee," Lynch says cheerily.

The rest of the video finds him mixing and then applying Fix-It-All, molding it while armed with a spray bottle and DuraSkin blue rubber gloves. Along the way there are breaks for American Spirit cigarettes ("This is a time to reflect on the next step") and beverages ("This is a petite noisette . . . it takes the edge off espresso") as different elements dry or set.

There's a fair bit of rhapsodizing about the depth of color in the summertime afternoon light as Lynch mixes and tests shades to match with the universal yellow he applies to the fixture's base. He dismissively deems one finalist, a slate-blue hue, "too weak," with what registers almost as sour parental disappointment. As he frequently did with guests, Lynch also shows off the special pullout, drain-friendly drawer built into his thin-ply wooden artist's sink, which was his preferred work urinal. The video ends, predictably, with a smile and proclamation: "Alrighty, coffee time."

Lynch would typically never call works like these short films—he deemed them experiments—though I will note that, interestingly, its *Dynamic:01* DVD presentation deems "Lamp" a movie and Lynch even refers to it as such in his short introduction to the piece. And if it's a movie, he's certainly its star. Does the artist's mask inadvertently slip here?

Reasonable minds can engage and differ on whether this constitutes a performance, and in all honesty "Lamp" exists on the edges. In terms of the representational buckets of performance, Lynch is working alone, doing something he enjoys but isn't necessarily engaging new learning centers, and not really actively expressing his sense of humor throughout—though there are moments of curious, oblique jocularity, as when he says in a down moment, apropos of nothing, "This is where it's very nice to have a female assistant, to share in the joys of work."

Is there a deeply "in-character" performance here? Of course not. But if a trained camera captures truth and presentation confers meaning, then the editorial self-selection of this work perhaps delivers one of the more direct, cogent, stand-alone portraits of Lynch as the enthusiastic art life devotee— not *talking* about his love of the art life, but actually just doing it. Maybe that makes his appearance a performance—an audiovisual statement of being, and purpose. And that makes "Lamp" (whose finished product now resides with a private collector in New York but could be loaned out for future museum exhibitions) special.

Brick Tamland would certainly agree.

—CHAPTER 23—
WEATHER REPORTS, PART 1 (2005-2010)

Probably no piece of DavidLynch.com content has achieved more renown than Lynch's weather reports. The bulletins were regularly uploaded between 2005 and 2010, added to the website's switchboard listing, and in their early days frequently featured Lynch recognizing site members by their usernames. No doubt this individual attention was a heady experience, but the cultural connection and staying power of the weather reports far surpassed the audience who initially saw them.

This is partly owing to YouTube cross postings and then their reincarnation during the COVID pandemic, which introduced them to an entirely different generation. But it's also an interesting example of the Mandela Effect: in my discussions with dozens of people, individuals expressed a wide variety of highly personal memories of when they first saw the weather reports, citing a dozen different years, some (incorrectly) dating all the way back to the 1990s. This reflects, I believe, the uniquely casual intimacy baked into the concept—the commingling of ordinariness and an always-lurking capacity for the unexpected or bizarre.

In reality, the first weather report was posted on Thursday, January 6, 2005. In the one-minute clip, cigarette smoke wafting into frame, Lynch sits in his familiar workspace and lays out the premise, beginning with an amusing digression about what day he believes it to be versus what he's being told. "If you can kind of feel the light, it's incredibly beautiful this morning here in LA, very beautiful sunlight," he says. "But big storms are coming in, so stay tuned!" Precipitation does follow over the next several days ("This place is completely socked in—the only news I have is rain"), with some handheld camerawork giving viewers a rare outdoor glimpse. On Friday, January 7, Lynch dryly says, "I'm gonna try to do this over the weekend, even though a lot of so-called trusty assistants will be missing."

Lynch does indeed stick with it, and the first month or so of the reports features a couple of guests (Chrystabell dancing, Laura Dern sitting silently with a backward sign showing the date), but also indulges various performative elements from Lynch, from crawling underneath his desk to investigate a sound to clapping himself out of frame through a jump cut. One of the more widely disseminated early entries, from January 21, features Lynch silently perusing a copy of *Maxim* with actress/model Brooke Burns on the cover while wearing thick gardening gloves.

Props are introduced in the form of a small painting of a sun against a blue backdrop (a literal antecedent to "blue skies and golden sunshine"), plus a fan sometimes used to indicate windiness. Occasionally Lynch spotlights newly acquired information ("Maybe you already know this, but today I learned that fleas can jump"), and on February 4, after several days of teasing viewers by displaying receptacles with question marks on them, he reveals another booth and a secret code to unlock additional website content. Within the established parameters of run time (around one minute for the first month, later trending down to thirty seconds or so) and previously mentioned setting, these entries were highly variable and performance oriented and interchangeably referred to as "weather reports" and "daily reports."

From 2006 to 2008, the weather reports also aired on Los Angeles radio station Indie 103.1 FM, where founding Vandals member and polymath Joe Escalante hosted a morning show and Lynch would call in live with the weather before eventually switching over to an answering machine that allowed him to leave a message the evening before to be broadcast the next day. "When I would have an important guest on and they would find out the real David Lynch was doing weather, they would look at me with a changed level of respect, like they were doing the right morning show," said Escalante in a 2009 interview with LAist.

While meteorological overview remained the unifying element, these early years of the online weather reports in particular were loose limbed and experimental, with certain bits dipping into either personalized sharing, commercialized pitches (Lynch's soft stumping for Fix-It-All, or more direct announcements of website offerings), visual gag components, or a combination of all three. Sometimes Lynch would also make a musical recommendation. On several occasions he expressed his considerable irritation at helicopters outside.

In March 2006, Lynch silently dons what looks like a white monkey mask with a towel wrapped around its head, muttering only an indecipherable phrase (perhaps "Hey kids, thank you for my eggs"?) in singsong. On June 13, 2006, Lynch cues a recorded drumroll to herald the availability of ringtones and wallpaper for purchase. Much later, on January 28, 2009, Lynch confirms his social media presence, saying, "That is me on the Twitter page."

"This is one of my favorite things," said assistant Erik Crary of the weather reports. "So shooting it, it was a whole thing at first—we had to shoot it and then we had to encode it and then we had to upload it, because this is early, early, early website days. But once we settled on a pattern, David wanted to make it sort of clockwork. So he designed an arm, like a wooden arm—then I don't remember if he built it, or [groundskeeper] Alfredo [Ponce] built it—that went up [and] had the camera already on it.

"So in the morning, whoever was going up to get him his coffee and shoot it, we would just crank this arm down, fire everything up, turn on the computer, and he'd shoot it. But it was almost like a Wallace and Gromit thing—it would come down, we'd shoot it, it'd go back up, we'd encode it, and then everyone's off on their day. I think he loved doing it, but it was not going to be a production every single day. We were going to [make it] routine, and he could even do it by himself if he wanted to. I loved that whole setup. I thought it was hilarious."

"Every morning, the first thing we'd do is meet in the painting studio," added Mindy Ramaker, who worked for Lynch for eight years starting in the summer of 2007 before transitioning to creative director with the David Lynch Foundation. "David would have a coffee, and we'd film the weather report. I'd tell him the date, temp, and we'd usually do it in one take. These are really fond memories of mine. David was always so present for them, the way he'd look out the window to see what the sky looked like."

With Lynch's other commitments during this first year-plus (he was editing *Inland Empire* at the time, which would premiere at the 2006 Venice Film Festival), the daily postings missed dates here and there. Naturally, they also accommodated his out-of-town travel schedule, so the weather reports eventually became less regular. At a certain point they ground to a halt.

"I think it was around 2009 or 2010, the weather report stopped," said Ramaker. "David had gone on a long international trip, likely to Paris, where he would make lithographs at Idem Studio. When he returned weeks later, a bird had built a nest on top of the weather report camera. There was a canvas bag that covered the camera from dust, and David told me he'd seen the bird flying in and out of it. When he described it, it was with a kind of shocked delight. He didn't want to disturb the bird and its nest, so we paused filming of the weather report. Once they moved out, he said, we could pick it back up again.

"During this time David got out of the habit of filming the report, and his routine changed as well. I think he was working on music, maybe for *Crazy Clown Time*, so he was starting his mornings in the recording studio instead of the painting studio. It was sad that the weather report ended, but it was for a really sweet and very David reason."

However and whenever people found them, Lynch's weather reports struck a chord with an enormous cross section of individuals, from strangers to even past collaborators.

"To me, to turn on the morning radio and hear him do the weather report completely blew my mind," said Aaron Lee, a writer whose career would later intersect with Lynch's. "If anything screamed to me 'I live in Hollywood now,' it was the local weather report being by David Lynch. That made me feel like I lived in the right city, I lived in the place that I always dreamed of being."

"I loved the YouTube weather reports a lot, both incarnations—a little garnish and a little seasoning to his profound catalogue," added Michael Ontkean. "He often went with suggestions of mine for the song or record of the day."

The flexibility of the concept—allowing for both simple repetition and the indulgence of asides and flights of fancy—is part of its genius. If Gordon Cole would represent his defining on-screen character, and voice work more consistently provided a vessel through which to showcase his sense of humor, the weather reports probably gave Lynch the most sustained and direct avenue through which to express different elements of his own personality as well as playacted shenanigans.

"That's acting, completely—oh, yeah. It wasn't like people were watching to find out the weather," said Bob Engels with a laugh. "And I don't know how that came to be, but I could see someone coming up with that idea or David coming up with the idea and saying, 'God, I wonder if someone would let me do weather?' It probably just amused him to do it."

"My memory and feeling is that it was in the generation-of-content spirit," added Crary. "It gave something for people to tune into that he would be doing regularly, and he wanted to do it. If he wants to check in about something, if he wants to pose a question, if he wants to do something, he's got an automatic schedule for that."

To Lynch's eldest daughter, the weather reports were connected to things he enjoyed himself and a way to orient and ground his mental state, but with a recognition of the palliative benefits it offered others. "He was able to joyfully start each day talking about the weather and wishing everyone a good day, and I think that was helpful to him in motivating himself to have a good day," said Jennifer Lynch. "In *Blue Velvet*, the radio song for Lumberton was 'Logs, logs, logs, Lumberton, USA,' right? And things like that were the birth of the weather reports—great big, white, puffy clouds and blue skies and sunshine all along the way.

"Those very simple, pure, Boise, Idaho, Americana-type things brought him great joy, and I think he knew that was a way to comfort people. We all share the weather, [so] he could reach people with something that was common for all of us and at the same time wish everybody a great day and set things off in a positive way."

—CHAPTER 24—

INLAND EMPIRE (2006)

Unpacking the totality of *Inland Empire*—its ambitions, its alleyways, its . . . let's say interpretations rather than meaning—would require its own book. But unpacking the era, circumstances, and mood that helped birth Lynch's acting cameo in the film are, thankfully, much easier.

By the time *Inland Empire* saw release in 2006, Lynch was five years removed from the triumph of *Mulholland Drive*, which had earned him some of the most rapturous reviews of his career as well as his third best director Oscar nod. Five years, for most top Hollywood filmmakers, would represent a hiatus too far extended, some type of problem.

But in that time Lynch had been busy working—quite busy. As some of the grandest predictions of the internet's great economic democratization receded, and corporate America began to wrap its rapacious tentacles around the more exploitable elements of this omnipresent new platform (a cycle that would repeat itself over the next two decades), Lynch kept making things for an online audience. While his website wouldn't be able to catapult him to untold riches, it still provided copious amounts of the thing he craved most: creative freedom. Then, slowly, some of these disparate ideas began to coalesce in his mind.

As is widely known, and chronicled in *Room to Dream*, Lynch ran into Laura Dern, whom he hadn't seen in a while, during a neighborhood walk. They expressed a joint desire to again work together, so Lynch spent two weeks writing something and then phoned Dern's agent to officialize the project, offering $100. They shot a scene. Then another. And another.

In a 2022 interview with me for A.V. Club, tied to the movie's remastering and theatrical rerelease, Lynch characterized the writing on *Inland Empire* as familiar to his normal process with one notable exception. "You get an idea, and you write that one out, then you're going along, you don't have any script, you had an idea and you wrote it out," said Lynch. "Then you go along, you get another idea and you write it out. Now you have two ideas, but you don't have a script. You go along a little bit more and you get a third idea, you write it out. And you look and you say, 'Wait a minute, I have three ideas and none of them relate to one another.' Fine! No problem. There's no script, just three ideas that don't relate. You go along and you get a fourth idea, and this fourth idea relates to the first three, and you say, 'Oh, something's happening.' And then, when something starts happening, more ideas flood in, *quicker*! Quicker they come, like schools of fish, schools of fish! And the thing starts to emerge, and a script appears. That's *exactly* the way it happens, and that's exactly the way it happened on *Inland Empire*. The *only* difference was that I happened to shoot each of those first three ideas. Not only did I write them down, but I shot them. I built a set, or I went to a location and I shot them, and they didn't relate. And then I got the fourth idea, which related to them, and now I'm stuck with the [technical format], because I've already shot these three."

What's obvious is that Lynch was captivated by the fact that digital video offered a return to the beloved but impractical creative model of *Eraserhead*, in which the potential for psychological "sink in" was valued far more than a larger budget from someone else saying yes to his vision.

Lynch will never get the full credit he deserves for *Inland Empire* because, outside of his website, he poured all his efforts into one dense, challenging masterwork rather than a series of discrete narrative experiments, as Steven Soderbergh did with *Full Frontal, Bubble*, and *The Girlfriend Experience*. But Lynch was pioneering digital film techniques before the technology had fully matured, embracing and rolling with its limitations rather than simply waiting around for better quality.

His radical commitment reminds me of an interview with Ang Lee, a gifted storyteller who for years (and with varying degrees of success) has leaned into cutting-edge special effects, high frame rate, and digital de-aging technology on diverse projects like *Hulk, Life of Pi, Billy Lynn's Long Halftime Walk*, and *Gemini Man*. During an April 5, 2018, set visit to Savannah, Georgia, for *Gemini Man*, Lee talked with me in somewhat wistful tones about the risks that living on the early curve of adoption entailed. "Sometimes [new technologies] work and sometimes they aren't there yet and maybe come up short. I wish more people would join me," he said with a shrug. "I may be using them wrong, but the only way we'll know and learn is to try, to experiment."

That was Lynch on *Inland Empire*, throwing caution to the wind and diving headlong into experimentation, backed by a small team of dedicated assistants. "From the production side of things, it was really helter-skelter.

And I think that because Erik [Crary] and I were so young and kind of didn't know what we didn't know, it kind of all worked in a crazy type of way. I would see other people on set seeming a lot more stressed, and I wouldn't really understand it," said Jay Aaseng, Lynch's assistant, with a laugh.

While he hadn't stepped into *Eraserhead*, his most analogous previous production experience, Lynch gave himself a small role in *Inland Empire*. His vocal cameo as an off-screen character, Bucky J, came during one of the production's rare studio days—part of a two-day weekend shoot on the Paramount lot in Los Angeles. For our purposes, a deep contextualization of the film seems not necessarily relevant, but the scene in question is itself built around a movie shoot.

At the 44:30 mark, in a sequence lasting roughly one and a half minutes, the director of that production, Kingsley Stewart (Jeremy Irons), calls out to an unseen gaffer, Bucky J, to adjust a lighting rig: "I think we haven't still got the 2K quite in the right place. I'd say up two feet. You'd know better than me."

Replies Bucky: "Boss, you want that 2K down? You want it down?"

As the camera holds on Stewart, using a megaphone to communicate in gently solicitous tones to his crew member up high above the set, Bucky struggles to respond sensibly. Gently corrected yet again when he moves the light in the wrong direction, Bucky irritatedly exclaims, "First goddamned time . . . I, I had to crap! Just a minute, I'm gettin' on it!"

"I'm curious if he planned to always voice Bucky J," said fellow assistant Crary. "I mean, he just did it so well. It might've been one of those things where he was like, 'No one else can play it. I know exactly the joke. I know exactly what I want to say,' so he just did it. That one felt a little more planned than some of the stuff. . . . I was trying my hardest not to laugh, as was everybody. And Jeremy Irons was failing, as he was laughing in the scene."

"That was in the script, I do remember that," confirmed Aaseng. "But I also think that David did a little bit of [improvising] on the day too, and that made it even better. I think he basically had written out that there was going to be a bit of back-and-forth between Jeremy Irons's character and this Bucky J. I don't think I actually realized it was going to be David playing that part, though, until we got to the set. I just didn't connect the dots until he started doing it.

"Certainly while we were writing it he didn't say, 'That's going to be me.' And even the way it was written, it wasn't entirely clear to me if we were going to see that character or not . . . David isn't always that concerned with writing properly in a script 'dialogue off-screen' or whatever."

However planned, Lynch's performance indulges his sense of humor and enjoyment of the absurd—as viewers we identify with the mask of Stewart's exasperation, and delight when it finally drops. Additionally, as with a chunk of the content (*Out Yonder, DumbLand*) from his website, this bit gives viewers a nudge to the ribs with a lowbrow laugh centered on excretory system bodily function.

As part of a lengthy interview for the film's 2007 Absurda DVD release, Lynch would seem to confirm some real-life roots for the character's inspiration—albeit in characteristically roundabout fashion.

Responding to an off-screen question, Lynch begins by praising John Churchill, who began as his driver and worked in various capacities on three Lynch films before going on to portray an assistant director in *Inland Empire* and appearing in the aforementioned scene next to Irons.

Describing a game he would play with Churchill, who in 2016 passed away from cancer, Lynch talks about how he would concoct stories for various people Churchill pointed out during their time in transit. "Churchill would bring out all these things . . . sometimes he'll prompt something," Lynch says. "And that's how Bucky J was born."

By way of ostensible further explanation, Lynch adds, "Bucky J was born during the shooting of . . . I don't even know what we were doing . . . I was on the floor shooting up at Justin [Theroux], and it was some kind of lighting test. And then Bucky J, the night before, had what anyone would say would be maybe one of the world's worst nights. And so he was like totally toast on this day. It's like one of those things that happens that's a life-changing event—and insurance companies are involved, police are involved, hospitals, doctors, nurses, drugs, rehabilitation, church and state, and national government." Here Lynch laughs, through a wide smile. "All these things. So things are not the same after that."

This embrace of slipstream reasoning, blending a personal recollection from production with a richly imagined backstory, is pure Lynch. Is Bucky J then based explicitly on a character biography Lynch created one day long ago, married to the scene through memories of a lighting delay on another sequence from the movie? Inspired by some specific interaction during the lighting test? A composite of the two, and therefore a good-natured tweak or maybe even metatextual commentary on the time drain of old production methods versus this surge of freedom felt with digital video?

"Oh, interesting, now that you're saying that, I can see that link," said Crary. "I don't know if that was intended, but that's the beauty of David's work—you bring a lot of intention to it, or can read into it. But I can definitely see the argument."

"I wouldn't be surprised if some of that could have perhaps been a commentary on how much longer these things take," mused Aaseng. "Not that I think he would ever disparage anybody in the lighting department for doing what they do, but just sometimes those things do take longer. But it is kind of funny . . . kind of a meta thing poking fun—here's how *we're* making this movie, and here's how it might ordinarily be done. And to hell with that!"

—CHAPTER 25—

"DAVID LYNCH COOKS QUINOA" (2007)

There is perhaps no other single piece of self-generated on-screen performative content that induces as much perplexed delight as the forthrightly titled "David Lynch Cooks Quinoa," both for those who embrace the singularity of Lynch's personality as much as his films and newbies alike—fans who perhaps came to *Twin Peaks* in the last decade and only discovered in piecemeal fashion that he also pumped out all sorts of short-form curios.

Alternately known as just "Quinoa" on the *Inland Empire* DVD release, where it first appeared, this singularly Lynchian enterprise takes the mundane and the slightly offbeat and fuses them with overwhelming sincerity, producing a highly evocative performance-art piece anchored by moody presentation and inventive narrative misdirection. A twenty-minute video shot in black-and-white, it chronicles exactly what it promises—a narrated mealtime, but wrapped around a story recollected from forty years earlier.

There are other film directors who, one supposes, could render making themselves dinner entertaining, but whereas they might dip into stories about movies during cooking time, Lynch does not. One could count on a single hand the number of contemporaries who, through the sheer gravitational pull of their personality, could execute this same concept with similar success.

From the yearslong stretch at Bob's Big Boy to lunches of tuna, tomatoes, and feta cheese, Lynch's food phases—embraced to limit the distraction of quotidian decision-making—are the stuff of legend. "Quinoa" was born from a routine that lasted an estimated six months, maybe a bit longer. There never seemed to be any particular trend or trigger attached to the end of one of his phases, according to those close to him.

"It seemed like it was just kind of a pattern," said Erik Crary, one of Lynch's assistants. "I think if you do that for six or eight or ten months, a chicken sandwich suddenly sounds better than a salad. It seemed like there would just be pivots, and then we'd be onto something else. There was also a big presence of Ayurvedic food that started coming in, [which is] related to the TM movement. It's an Indian style of cooking that's all based on your health, and an Ayurvedic doctor will come and meet you and take your pulse and create a spice recipe and stuff for you. So there were some periods where Ayurvedic food was making its way into the diet as well, which probably spurred some of those pivots on, here and there."

Lynch's mealtime habits aside, there's no clear reason for this wonderful oddity to exist. And yet once you've seen David Lynch cook quinoa—as over a million aggregate viewers on YouTube will attest—it's not something likely to leave your memory.

"Quinoa" doesn't dally, jumping straight into its premise. Lynch introduces his copper-lined cookware as if praising a pet's behavior ("Such a good pan . . . ") and emphasizes the need for fresh water, which he gets from the sink. The recipe includes sea salt, organic broccoli, and a vegetable bouillon cube, and while the quinoa itself ("They say it's the only grain that's a perfect, complete protein") is nominally measured to a little less than half a cup, other measurements are merely eyeballed.

At around the six-minute mark, with the quinoa needing more time before he adds the broccoli, Lynch heads to the patio for a cigarette, glass of red wine in hand. There, Lynch sits in deep, deep darkness, telling the story of a European train trip in August 1965 with good friend Jack Fisk.

During a brief stop late at night, he disembarked and visited a stand where "for the smallest amount of money, you could get a bottle of this sugar water." Of special interest to *Twin Peaks* fans is a seemingly random detail, tossed off in the middle of the story, that would surface a decade later in season three: "Moths were flipping and flying, like frogs— frog moths were pulling themselves out of the earth, and flying up in front of the stand," Lynch says. "Dust was blowing. It was like a

mysterious, strange wind sound, and out came the tiniest little copper coin that I'd gotten somewhere, and I gave it to this man."

Marveling at the paper money returned to him as change, Lynch relates Fisk befriending a Yugoslavian girl on the train who had never tasted Coca-Cola. He promises to buy her one upon their arrival in Venice, delighted at the prospect of witnessing her first sip of the beverage—a story whose culmination connects back to his sugar water purchase. Returning inside, Lynch finishes preparing his quinoa and, after adding a couple of squirts of liquid amino acids and olive oil, digs in, exclaiming, "Man! That is so good!"

"I think Jason [S, a fellow assistant] was definitely shooting some of that," said Crary. "I might've been shooting another camera. I was around for it; I just don't remember how much coverage we had. I want to say it might've been another one of those mutual targets of opportunity. He was in a storytelling mood. Dinner had to be made. He was getting really into his process with quinoa. Jason was there, and he was always very loose and sort of in ready-to-talk mode with Jason. So I don't recall it being set up other than someone saying, 'Hey, he's going to make dinner. We're going to shoot it.' But I love it. And to the point, David's performances, he's got something in mind. The opportunity's presenting itself. It's going to happen on camera, and that's the only time that was probably ever going to formulate. If he had just thought of it and said, 'We're going to shoot this next week,' I don't think 'Quinoa' exists."

"I think actually that was my idea," said Absurda managing partner Eric Bassett, noting that even though Lynch drove everything creatively, he was always trying to brainstorm for website content ideas that were light lifts, and this slotted within the context of a Lynch-fronted cooking show that was also discussed. "But if somebody else says it was theirs, that's fine too. I'm pretty sure that, good or bad, that was my idea."

Regardless of the piece's exact origins, the backdrop was not wildly different from that on many other evenings. "We would sit there all night long listening to David tell stories. He would tell the most amazing stories, and I was just like, 'Man, I wish we could get that on film,'" Bassett said.

"Some of the things . . . you know how he is," he added with a laugh, reliving some of "Quinoa"'s monologue. "He was just so descriptive, and so funny. And he would say to look into the pot [while the quinoa cooked], and then nobody could see into the pot because it was so dark. It was just a really fun thing to do."

"That was a fun thing that, in retrospect, feels like a little bit of a send-off," agreed assistant Jay Aaseng, who left his position with Lynch in 2008. "'Okay, we're going to stay late after work and we're going to shoot this thing, him making the quinoa.' He was super into quinoa at that time.

He was super into cooking—he wasn't always, but he would go through phases—and at this point he was just very much into cooking for himself. And he loved quinoa, so he did this video, but what we didn't know is he was going to do that whole story in the middle. We thought we'd just be killing time.

"I always wondered [about] the magic about that. There's a good chance he would've just been telling that story even if we hadn't had the cameras on him. I'm not really even sure how much of a performative thing that was. I mean, maybe it was. I just didn't see it. But that very much felt like David being David. That's classic. That's how he would tell stories, just like that.

"Checking with him every day, whenever he'd be telling stories, it'd be just that kind of thing. He'd be sitting down and [say], 'I remember a time . . . ' and then just go into it. And that story, because of the fact that it was night and we were out there—it was dark and you can't even hardly see him, and he's telling a story that happened at night—it just felt so natural in the moment. But looking back on it, it does kind of have a very cool performative thing to it, where afterwards I was like, 'Oh, is that all planned as part of this, or did that just happen organically?' It's impossible for me to tell, really."

Indeed, one can split hairs as to whether this is a true performance or merely Lynch being himself. It seems inarguable, though, that he possessed a self-awareness of his reputation and idiosyncrasies as well as the adroitness to leverage that sometimes—especially in short-form material. Ergo, "Quinoa" again speaks to the idea of public faces. Doing something you do frequently but knowing it's going to be consumed by a wider audience (albeit a friendly one) would, it's reasonable to assume, impact your behavior.

The notion that Lynch's appearance here isn't performative is clearly refuted at just under the fifteen-minute mark, when a series of intentional actions are married to added sound effects. Here, Lynch the director is making an unequivocal declaration, using Lynch the actor as his vessel.

"It definitely turned it into a whole different thing, for sure," said Aaseng. "What's also interesting is he got so interested in very unconventional storytelling later on in his career, but knowing him the years I did, he was very much just a conventional storyteller, where he would sit down and tell you a story. He loved doing that, and he was really good at it.

"That was just sort of the way he was. He has that natural [desire] to tell a good story, which is a certain performative thing that's just [part of] him, whether he's trying to or not."

"David Lynch Cooks Quinoa," with its amusingly straightforward and guileless culinary tutorial bracketing a complementary performance that edges into deeper waters, affirms that informed observation.

—CHAPTER 26—

TWIN PEAKS FESTIVAL GREETING (2008)

In August 1992, *Twin Peaks: Fire Walk With Me* held its US premiere in North Bend, Washington, and people flocked to the area to bask in the glow of the event and catch a glimpse of the attending cast and crew. For many fans of the still freshly canceled show, it felt like a reunion with family they didn't know they had. Several remarked how nice it would be to get together again, and a pair of fans, Pat and Don Shook, took on that challenge. The next year the Twin Peaks Festival, which would run annually through 2019, was born.

For the 2008 iteration, held July 25-27, organizers scored a coup. While the gathering featured *Twin Peaks* actors like Piper Laurie, Charlotte Stewart, and Kimmy Robertson and hosted the US premiere of Jennifer Lynch's *Surveillance*, a crown jewel came in the form of a handcrafted short-form benediction from, and starring, Lynch himself.

While released on DVD later that year as part of Lynch's *Lime Green* box set, the striking black-and-white piece made its world premiere at the festival. Running four minutes and twenty seconds and shot in reverse fashion, à la the Red Room sequences, the short opens on a doll face down in front of two folding chairs on a chevron floor. As the camera pans up, Lynch shuffles into frame crossing right to left, gazes upward and to the left off-screen as a spotlight hits his face, and grins in slightly unsettling fashion. He crouches in front of the left chair, striking it four times with his right hand. Both Lynch and the doll then reorient and end up seated in the chairs, the former with his tie askew and the latter revealed to be a half amputee with the iconic face of a deceased Laura Palmer pasted over whatever visage she previously possessed.

After a moment, in reverse speak, Lynch says, "There are three things I want you to remember. Three things." He holds out three fingers, and his hands shake violently. Lynch rocks to and fro, his body contorting into an almost horizontal position. He collapses onto the floor face down, struggles back into his chair, and speaks once more. "Give it over strong," he says in subtitled reverse speak again, making an arm gesture. "Make a purchase of a raincoat. Enjoy Twin Peaks Festival."

Lynch then stands, walks over and gently kisses Laura's closed eye, and looks at the camera as "Laura Palmer's Theme" starts to play and the spotlight traces up from the floor to his head, washing out his face.

"This was one of the first filmed productions I was part of," said Mindy Ramaker, Lynch's assistant at the time. The Twin Peaks Festival had invited Lynch to attend, but when he politely declined the organizers asked if he could record a short video greeting. Lynch agreed—but that didn't mean he sprang into action.

"I remember the deadline was looming, and it felt a bit like David was putting it off," Ramaker said. "We'd all assumed he was going to record a straightforward message, an 'I'm sorry I can't be there' sort of thing. But that wasn't what he had in mind.

"David could be secretive about things, I think to keep the ideas pure and leave room to experiment in the moment. So he would ask for things piece by piece—some black curtains, for example, a certain type of lighting, a doll, a printout of something, etcetera."

The unifying concept behind all those individual requests would eventually come into focus. Production involved a very small crew, consisting of Ramaker; Anna Skarbek, Lynch's other assistant at the time; Michael Barile, who was still only interning at Lynch's office at the time; and Scott Ressler, a cameraman who'd worked with Lynch many times before.

"It was very hands-on, because there were three of us who were setting this thing up," said Barile. "So I got to help design this whole set for specs, set up the lighting, get all the props together, and stay late after work and shoot this thing with them for a couple hours. It was a lot of fun."

"We filmed it at the office in the middle gray house living room," Ramaker shared. "I remember David coming into the room, bringing a lot of energy, mystery, and also some nerves. He would understandably get nervous before going in front of a camera—especially giving speeches at events. I don't think he enjoyed that at all. But he did enjoy a good interview and acting."

Ressler didn't learn about the reverse-speak element until showing up but recalled his biggest challenge from the shoot. "Almost every time I jumped up to [make a technical adjustment], I somehow got tangled or hit one of the fishing lines [used to manipulate the doll]. My brain was elsewhere," he said.

While the third season of *Twin Peaks* was not even a whispered possibility at this point in time, and this short curio is a tip-of-the-hat sign of appreciation rather than some canonically stamped decoder ring, it's still quite interesting to see Lynch physically inhabit a *Peaks*-ian space at this particular moment in his life and career. There's a rich symbolism in his kissing Laura Palmer, and while I wouldn't suggest he's actually *playing* Gordon Cole here, there's probably someone somewhere fervently advancing that argument. Certainly it's notable that he's wearing the type of skinny black tie Cole favored, which was definitely not part of Lynch's day-to-day wardrobe.

"This performance sticks out to me because it was very physical and he was totally committed to it," said Ramaker. "None of us had seen a script or been told what was going to happen. He gave each of us just as much information as we needed to do our parts. I think I was working the lighting, and Anna the doll. I remember how incredible it was to see it unfold live in front of my eyes, even if it didn't make a ton of sense because everything was happening backwards. I think this was done in just one take. David always knew when he got it."

Of the different boxes that Lynch's performative work could check, this greeting video seems hardwired to his desire to stay connected with the art life spirit. It's also clearly grounded in gratitude for fans of his work, who would keep the flame burning for *Twin Peaks* so many years after its cancellation. That Lynch expressed that appreciation in the form of yet another creative work forms a perfect circle.

"The other thing I'll say is that David really took these things seriously," said Ramaker. "He didn't have to create such special short-film-like videos. No one expected or asked for this at the time. But David really cared about his fans, and he took any kind of award or honor to heart. I don't think he ever took it for granted."

−CHAPTER 27−

HOLLYSHORTS VISIONARY AWARD (2008)

Short films, both an artistic proving ground and professional lifeline for many young directors seeking to jump to features, are notoriously difficult to publicly showcase. Some major festivals do a solid job spotlighting them, but for entertainment journalists typically caught up in the grind of turning around coverage on several high-profile films per day, they can unfortunately become an afterthought.

The HollyShorts Film Festival, held annually in Hollywood, California, has carved out a nice space for itself. An Oscar-qualifying independent-short-film festival that has undeniably benefited from its industry-friendly location, it programs an eclectic mix of short-form work from all over the world, savvily blending works from big-name talent alongside that of newcomers and unknowns.

The 2008 version of the festival was held August 7-10, with the historic Egyptian Theatre playing host to its gala opening night event and the rest of the festival taking place at the Laemmle Sunset 5, at the time one of the preeminent arthouse theaters in the United States. For their inaugural Visionary Award, organizers chose to honor Lynch and crossed their fingers for his attendance—it was, after all, local for him. Lynch, though, opted instead to produce another short-form video work in lieu of an in-person acceptance speech.

"This shoot was a slightly bigger production than the Twin Peaks Fest greeting but still filmed in a 'down and dirty' way in the backyard/patio of the office house," said assistant Mindy Ramaker. "I think this one was really impressive because David was juggling so much. Everything is done backwards, including his lines, and it's [a single] take. I always enjoyed these because I got to see another side of David than what I saw on the day-to-day. Like, it's him, but it isn't. I don't think I'd ever seen David dance, for example."

The four-minute black-and-white piece opens with Lynch rising from the bottom righthand corner of the frame and again employing subtitled backward speech, saying, "HollyShorts, thank you very much for Visionary Award." The camera pulls back to center Lynch a bit more and reveal one of his tall, thin lamp works of fine art behind him. "New filmmakers," Lynch then says, raising his arms and tousling his own hair, "find own voice."

Some music starts, and Lynch says, "Hey, hey, hey," and dances for fifteen seconds—if not quite a Little Man from Another Place shuffle, then at least an approximation. Pantomiming various actions, he says, "Catch idea you love. Practice juggle many things," also touching a paper heart to the lamp and then putting it up his jacket. Catching a tossed pastry, he says, "Keep eye on doughnut, not on hole," fingering its middle. "Be happy in work," he adds, walking in place, before intoning, "Peace and happiness."

As Lynch gestures to his left and then exits right, big band music starts, and three leggy dancers (Emily Stofle, Jenna Green and Ariana Delawari, from left to right) in high heels and costumes, holding paper doves, perform a short choreographed routine. Upon their exit, Lynch reenters, returns to the lamp, says "Goodnight," and adjusts a sketched dimmer that fades the lights.

Scott Ressler operated camera once again, but this time it took more than one take. "There were a lot of moving pieces, and I remember [me] being the reason we had to do more takes," said Ramaker. "I was in charge of throwing the doughnut, and my aim and timing wasn't always right!"

This performance by Lynch is very much a vibes-based thing—sincere in its appreciation but also reflecting a wisdom that comes with age, making a canny stab at dressing up profundity in short aphorisms and somewhat silly packaging. It's certainly of a piece with the Twin Peaks Festival greeting. While it's stripped of much of that work's iconography, they're linked roughly in staging and length, and of course the central reverse-speaking element remains.

While the festival greeting was first, it was perhaps the close proximity of the two works that opened the floodgates. "After this, people started requesting special video greetings all the time," said Ramaker. "It put a lot of pressure on him because the videos took a lot of work and creative energy."

"If he did all the videos people asked—first of all, he wouldn't be able to get through them—then he wouldn't be able to do anything else," agreed Sabrina Sutherland. "So if it got accepted, it was kind of a big thing.

"He had to get an idea for it, figure out what it was, and it took up all of his time thinking. He never did anything off the cuff or without any thought or just kind of haphazardly. Every single thing that he did he put time and effort into and made sure that it was something he was happy with and it was his vision of something important. Some people don't really take time with [such things]. He took time."

–CHAPTER 28–

DAVID LYNCH WORLD TOUR (2009)

Lynch's undeniable stature as a global cinematic icon stands in curious contrast to the fact that his films were often—and usually not incorrectly—described as distinctly American. The reasons for this embrace by international cinephiles are numerous, yet with a couple exceptions (*The Elephant Man* was shot and is set in England, while *Dune* filmed in Mexico), Lynch didn't stray far from his American roots. There's no European phase to his filmography, à la Woody Allen or Wes Anderson. Still, Lynch managed to leave his mark—and even, perhaps most surprising of all, pop up in several international productions as a performer.

In August 2008, Lynch made an eight-day trip throughout Brazil for the release of the translated version of his book *Catching the Big Fish: Meditation, Consciousness and Creativity*. Accompanied by David Lynch Foundation CEO Bob Roth, among others, Lynch traveled to Rio de Janeiro, São Paulo, Belo Horizonte, and Porto Alegre. He spoke on college campuses, held several news conferences, met with government leaders, and visited schools where students meditate. "You have a diamond; keep it for the rest of your life," he said at one such school.

In 2009, from April 6-12, Lynch traveled to Moscow in support of *The Air Is on Fire*, an exhibition celebrating his work as a visual artist, with paintings, drawings, photographs, lithographs, experimental films, and other artwork dating back to his teenage years. There, in addition to celebrating the showcase and signing copies of *Catching the Big Fish* (newly translated to Russian), Lynch again spoke to large numbers of mostly young people, this time a packed auditorium of university students.

Each of these trips yielded unusual and rarely discussed entries in the canon of Lynch as a performer. The recollections of the core creatives involved reflect the power of Lynch's career-long advocacy for cinema that embraced abstractions as well as the enduring impact of even his fleeting interactions with them.

"Peixe Vermelho" ("Red Fish")

As a cultural curator/manager, producer, and director, Andreia Vigo has always been inspired by Lynch's work, citing him as her greatest inspiration. In 2004, while organizing a film program in Porto Alegre, she dreamed of showing *Eraserhead*.

"Back then, getting access to the film wasn't easy," she said. "I had a friend who worked at Panavision Brazil and knew many people at Panavision Los Angeles. He helped me get the contact information for Asymmetrical Productions and David's assistant. I asked for permission to screen the film twice. The screening was authorized, but it had to be a single showing. I received a beautiful box containing the DVD and some rare materials related to the film—a truly kind and delicate gesture from [Lynch]."

Years later, Vigo put that contact information to further use. "In 2008, I was invited to create an audiovisual piece for a lecture series called Fronteiras do Pensamento (which translates as 'Frontiers or Borders of Thought'), which that year featured prominent artists such as Wim Wenders, Philip Glass, Bob Wilson and Fernando Arrabal, among others," she said.

Knowing *Catching the Big Fish* was soon to be released in Brazil, Vigo saw an opportunity—believing Lynch to be a perfect fit for this popular Brazilian

cultural project that, by way of both special annual gatherings and ongoing events, brings in highly regarded international talent in a variety of fields to highlight different mindsets, forge creative thinking, and advance problem-solving.

"I had the idea to suggest to the Fronteiras do Pensamento organizers that they invite [Lynch] to Porto Alegre to take part in the project, so I found the contact for the book's Brazilian publisher and connected them," she said. [Andreia Vigo and Lynch pictured above.] "A few days later, Lynch was confirmed for the Fronteiras program! Naturally, my audiovisual piece had to feature him—and it ended up becoming a short film. And due to the extremely tight deadline, the negotiations for his participation in the short had to be conducted directly by me." After reaching out, Vigo eventually received word that Lynch had agreed to participate, though he would have just fifteen minutes available for the shoot.

Simultaneously, Vigo got in touch with Matt Palasz, a friend and fellow Lynch fan who was a neighbor in New York City when she lived there briefly in 2007. The pair had seen *Inland Empire* together at that time, and Palasz came on board as writer, with the duo sharing a story credit. "Matt is an excellent writer, a master of narrative and suspense," Vigo said, "and he brought the central idea: a young couple is traveling when the man mysteriously disappears. From there, I started thinking about possible locations, characters, imagery, and atmospheres while Matt worked on structuring the narrative. The only scene fully developed was the one involving Lynch—all the others were written as extended synopses."

The result of their collaboration was the fourteen-minute "Peixe Vermelho," which translates as "red fish" but is also a colloquialism for "red herring." Shot in Portuguese and English and told in nonlinear fashion, the film centers on a woman (Carina Dias) whose boyfriend (Rafael Sieg) goes missing.

Interrogated by police and believing his disappearance to be related to their last meal, which was red herring, the woman connects with an older shaman (Sandra Dani) who tells her, "It is a false food. There is someone you should talk to." Cut to: Lynch's scene, at around the 8:40 mark and lasting roughly forty-five seconds. Sitting with Lynch at a lamp-lit table with a small, illuminated replica of Stonehenge in its center, the young woman hands Lynch (credited as the Knowledgeable One), a photograph of her missing boyfriend taken the previous evening. "What do you mean disappeared?" asks Lynch, responding to her statement. "You mean up in flames, like poof? Or was he abducted?" Told by the shaman that the boyfriend had red herring for dinner, Lynch replies, "There's no such thing as a red herring," a faint smile passing his lips. He then takes a drag from a cigarette.

Characterized by an enveloping sound design and unmoored sense of foreboding, "Peixe Vermelho" contains a couple of other totems familiar to fans of Lynch's work. Dani somewhat resembles Grace Zabriskie, and the shaman's meeting with Dias's character is shot in close-up from a slightly high angle that renders it reminiscent visually of Zabriskie and Laura Dern's *Inland Empire* scene. Vigo's short could also be described as being about "a woman in trouble," *Inland Empire*'s tagline.

Vigo describes her day shooting with Lynch—Sunday, August 10, 2008, the sun blazing overhead—as akin to entering another dimension. As soon as the possibility of filming with him arose, she was gripped by the image of a trailer as a potential setting. Vigo secured a motor home, and "with such a tight schedule, the most practical solution was to park the trailer near [his] hotel," she said. "In front of it, there was a vast and beautiful green park. And nestled inside that park was a small, retro, charming amusement park—absolutely cinematic."

Each of these locations ended up being used in the film. Even the facade of Lynch's hotel—which in the movie serves as the site of the boyfriend's disappearance—pops up. There's also a daytime scene of the woman walking through the park with the camera circling around her—conceived as a tribute to influential Brazilian filmmaker Glauber Rocha, best known for *Entranced Earth*.

"On the day of the shoot, scheduled for around 1:00 p.m., we arrived early and parked the motor home in a vacant lot next to the hotel—a space often used by circuses that spent seasons in the city," said Vigo. "We began setting up the film set, and one of the main tasks was to block all the windows of the motor home to simulate nighttime."

Lynch was scheduled to attend a press conference on the hotel rooftop before the shoot. "I was supposed to go up and meet him," recalled Vigo. "Around 10:00 a.m., I received a message from his assistant: 'David asked me to let you know he's already memorized the lines.' It was surreal.

"At the agreed time, I went to get him. In the elevator, he was incredibly kind [even though he probably] noticed I was a bit tense. As we reached the ground floor, he asked, 'Can I have a cigarette?' I replied, 'Of course. Can I have one with you?'" Even though she didn't smoke, Vigo felt moved to share a cigarette with Lynch.

Once finished, the pair dove right in, entering the blacked-out motor home. Inside were two cameras, a lot of lights, and about fifteen people—cast, crew, a photographer, and a videographer from Fronteiras do Pensamento. "The fifteen minutes we had with him seemed to stretch into an eternity," Vigo said. "The first take was absolutely perfect, but I asked to do two more, and he, with his boundless generosity, agreed. He said, 'Of course, as you wish.' Then I asked for one final take of him just smoking and he did that too.

"When we opened the trailer door, several journalists were waiting outside. We stepped out, and I asked if we could take a photo with the entire crew. He said yes. He was clearly having fun with the whole experience."

As a condition of Lynch's participation, Vigo agreed to send along the finalized version of "Peixe Vermelho" for his formal approval. "A year later, we finished the film and I sent him the cut," she said. "The link was private and accessible only to him. It was a Friday. When I checked, the link had thirteen views. His response came on Monday: 'Use the shoot with my blessing.' I couldn't have received a more beautiful and meaningful message than this."

Clearly, Vigo's admiration for Lynch and love of his work were driving factors in shaping "Peixe Vermelho." But she also viewed his involvement as an important way to anchor a mysterious story about loss. "I see Lynch as an extraordinary actor," Vigo said. "I believe his skill as a director of actors enhances his own performance on-screen."

Indeed, it's surprising just how well-calculated Lynch's performance is—totally relaxed but with a hint of awakened curiosity, fitting the tone of the overall piece hand in glove. The delivery of his last line of dialogue in particular leaves viewers free to extrapolate everything from his character's basic identity and motivations to the actual nature of his advice. The ambiguity was something Lynch clearly thrived in.

Traveling in a foreign land, pulled in other directions, and having no personal connection to those involved, Lynch had no particular reason, and certainly no obligation, to take part in "Peixe Vermelho." But he opted in as an assistive act of art-life amplification for a younger generation of filmmakers he perhaps saw as kindred spirits.

"The Soul Detective"
The second short film project from Brazil involving Lynch also comes from

his time in Porto Alegre during the same trip and provides an interesting comparative study in creative construction with "Peixe Vermelho."

The nine-minute "The Soul Detective," known occasionally as "O Passageiro Obscuro" ("The Dark Passenger"), unfolds in English and Portuguese. The movie's logline is fairly straightforward, even if the premise is inventive: a detective (Leandro Lefa) enters a rundown train car and, using his telepathic powers, attempts to access the mind of a recent murder victim before his memories vanish. During his work, the detective is visited by a woman in a red dress (Carolina Silvestre) who tells him that it's someone else's mind he's been inside for the previous twelve hours and that like him, she is "waiting for something to happen."

Lynch's participation is unusually situated. In some online databases he's erroneously credited as portraying a detective, and in others he's credited as himself—which is notionally correct, but complicated. What makes "The Soul Detective" unusual is that its narrative was both crafted after and substantively informed by a separate, fifteen-minute interview with Lynch, portions of which are intercut with the aforementioned narrative.

At the 1:13 mark, Lynch appears for about a dozen seconds, in and out of focus, adjusting a translation headset at a press conference—the same one that took place immediately prior to his participation in "Peixe Vermelho." All other snippets of him come from the one-on-one interview, conducted by director Davi de Oliveira Pinheiro [photo below], who is never seen. Lynch's first spoken words unfold over an on-screen image of a record player, layered and looped in repetition, while other ensuing bits ("It's very true we live in a dark world. We find happiness together" and "An understanding comes with the idea, and an even greater understanding comes from diving within and unfolding that") are played under the echoing word "together." In total,

Lynch speaks for about sixty-five seconds and is on camera for about twenty seconds. At no point is he introduced or identified; if one had no prior visual frame of reference, he could be any amiable proselytizer of ideas.

The reasons behind this presentation, and Lynch's place within it, are complex. Fronteiras do Pensamento, like many Brazilian cultural projects, can be susceptible to politicized funding and favoritism, according to Pinheiro and two local sources who preferred not to be named. This contributes to certain hierarchies within the arts and also self-reinforcing feedback loops in which mixed ownership companies, entities combining government funding and private capital, put an outsized stamp on cultural matters.

The 2008 sessions of Fronteiras do Pensamento, for example, were presented in part by petrochemical giant Braskem—a big cultural donor that, like other companies approved by the government through what's called Rouanet law, receives significant tax breaks on such sponsorships—and produced by a company called Fellows. The latter then subcontracted and partnered with V2 Cinema on short film content for Fronteiras do Pensamento; producing duties on V2's work fell to Pinheiro.

Upon learning and discussing which creative parties were coming to Porto Alegre, V2 selected filmmakers from a pool of candidates and paired them with participating talent based on their project pitches. "Peixe Vermelho" began its life as one of those selections.

"I'm going to be very candid about everything," said Pinheiro. "What happened is that Andreia was not a selection of directors that came from our company. It came from over us. But it was, at least for me as a producer with her, a very healthy relationship at the beginning, because of course even if it comes from above, we are going to try to make the best film possible. So she proposed 'Red Fish,' and we tried to create the best situation for her to make the film. We spent a lot on her production to guarantee that we had the best crew. I brought from my feature film my assistant director [Davi Pretto], who I thought was very technical and could give support to her.

"And the relationship was really good until she tried to take the film away from us, and she succeeded [in separating] the film from the project. But the thing is . . . we didn't get our budget back, our expenses. I think when she got out, we had only 40 percent of the budget still. So that's what happened. And I'm telling you because it kind of bleeds into how 'The Soul Detective' was made."

With no way to replenish the budget gap, and charged with the responsibility of delivering a short film with reduced resources, Pinheiro made a choice. "In deciding who was going to direct the next film I said, as a producer, 'Okay, I'm not going to impose 40 percent on any other person other than me.' So the situation was that we had to deliver a film, by contract, and at the same time they were kind of cutting off our time with David Lynch," Pinheiro said. "So we negotiated fifteen minutes of an interview with him, without knowing what film we were going to make."

The interview was conducted in a cramped dressing room—a setting that immediately dictated a certain look and feel for the footage. "I started to interview him, and he was in the Transcendental Meditation phase," said Pinheiro. "So every question I [asked] about creativity, about his films, he came back with Transcendental Meditation."

Pinheiro quickly surrendered any notion of control. "It was very special to have an interaction with someone who had been influential in my life since I was eight years old," he said. "And at the same time, I [got] a basic idea of what I'm going to make, but I know it's going to be very experimental. I know it's not going to be anything where I have any control over the form."

For further inspiration, Pinheiro reached back to a distant memory. "When I was a kid . . . I don't know if this was a misreading of mine or a misspelling in the newspaper, but it said that David Lynch had died. This was 1991, and it was David Lean who died at the time," he said with a laugh. "I always remembered that. Afterwards, of course, no, he didn't die, he was making another film, but that for me was [on my mind] when I got out of the [interview], and it was the basis of the idea I had for the short film—this misreading of a newspaper and that I was interviewing the ghost of David Lynch or something like that.

"And that was a good idea. But when I started to watch the material, I thought it was a betrayal of what he was trying to say, so it wouldn't be a good execution of the idea. I couldn't betray his thoughts. What he was saying was something he wanted to say at the time. It was something genuine. And if you listen to it enough, it's not about only the meditation. The meditation leads into his films. So I [decided on] a conceptual adaptation of what he had said."

That decision informed not only which of Lynch's answers were used, but also how they were presented, as Pinheiro attempted to create visual, thematic, and aesthetic associations with Lynch's responses. While the lawman's costuming—black suit and tie—and the evocative train car setting, with its graffitied and rusted exterior housing a homicide scene, may summon evocations of *Twin Peaks*, Pinheiro claimed he had no such association in mind. Rather, he was taken by its striking moodiness, and while he would later be turned away in his effort to secure the same location for his 2010 horror film, *Beyond the Grave*, the institutional power of Fronteiras do Pensamento in this case proved beneficial. "I said, 'We are going to get this location for this short film. I don't know *what* we're going to shoot there, but we're going to shoot there,'" said Pinheiro with a smile. That choice in turn provided more inspiration, further molding his idea.

The end result, pieced together from two nonconsecutive shooting days (the fifteen-minute Lynch interview on August 10, 2008, everything else on October 10), is distinctly its own—paying homage to Lynch while also indulging other stylistic influences. The "performance" here, then, is among the most associative and open to interpretation in Lynch's on-screen canon—no small feat. It's highly curated, yes, but put together with maximum intentionality; how one reads it depends on how they respond to the film.

To Pinheiro, Lynch's artistic authenticity and perseverance are universal lessons he's absorbed and applied to his own career. And, in fact, the short film still influences his thinking. "I'm working [on] a feature version of *The Soul Detective*," said Pinheiro, who has both a script and some storyboards complete. "It's a very different film nowadays. I'm changing a lot. It's very different because I'm a very different person. But I have been working on the project for nearly ten years, fifteen years, my God."

Lynch's connection to "The Soul Detective" is its own thing, but the fact that he was involved in a project that might be reincarnated decades later and have a complete other life feels desperately appropriate.

The additional coincidence? Centered on a morally dubious telepath, the first version of Pinheiro's feature script—since changed, but written well before *Twin Peaks*'s third season—actually began with one of the characters getting a cigarette and asking, "Got a light?" Said Pinheiro with a laugh: "That scared me a lot, to see how things are connected."

The Way of Samodelkin

If nothing else, this tome provides the answer to the trivia question of what Russian feature film Lynch appears in—arguably the most unexpected and perplexing, and inarguably the least well-known, entry in his entire performative canon.

In early April 2009, Lynch made a visit to Moscow with Emily Stofle, his recent bride, in support of *The Air Is on Fire*, an expansive exhibition of his work that had premiered two years earlier at the Fondation Cartier contemporary art museum in Paris and was now set to appear at the Ekaterina Foundation, from April 10 to July 12. As on other trips abroad, he held a minimaster class/Q&A session with young people. Lynch signed copies of *Catching the Big Fish* at a well-attended public appearance and then squeezed in a feature film cameo too.

Steeped heavily in experimental technique, *The Way of Samodelkin* is set against the backdrop of the Moscow art scene. Described in the broadest strokes as a mystical detective story, the film might more appropriately be called a sociocultural cinematic essay. Its main character, Felix (Ilia Korobkov), is tasked with finding the author of various works located in the basement of a deceased artist, sending him on a through-the-looking-glass journey as he sifts through clues and meets characters representing various figures from the Russian art scene over the previous three decades.

Credited as Stranger in a Dream, Lynch can be briefly heard on a car radio interview and then appears in two of Felix's dreams. It's not entirely clear, however, if he is supposed to represent the same individual in his physical appearances as in the radio interview.

Lynch's first scene comes at the fifty-minute mark. A freight elevator door opens slowly before we cut to a comfy, empty, deep-set armchair in front of a wall and curtain (less red than dark orange and yellow, with some stripes). Felix enters and sits down opposite in a matching love seat, gazing to his right out a window. We then cut to Lynch—clad in suit pants and an overcoat—tracking Felix with his eyes and looking up slightly, even though Felix has already sat down. Back in a wide shot, Lynch says, "Hey, Mr. Falix [sic], you've lost something," and reaches out with his right hand, eventually passing him a 35 mm film roll (the shots purposefully don't quite match). Felix looks at the object, turning it in his hand before the camera cuts to an empty chair where Lynch had been sitting.

Just under thirty minutes of screen time later, after Felix has been told that one of the people he's seeking moved to America following perestroika, comes an eighteen-second interstitial sequence in which Felix is listening to an interview on the radio while driving. Asked the main difference between life and death, Lynch responds with the beginning of a version of an answer he had given numerous times in previous interviews about the human consciousness living on: "When you're driving a car and the car gets very old and it gets rusted and it stops running, then the driver gets out of the car." Here the scene ends.

Finally, at the 1:27:10 mark, after Felix falls asleep while taking Polaroids of himself on a bed, comes a fifteen-second sequence, shot at a slightly low angle, in which Lynch, back in the chair, looks straight ahead for six or seven seconds before gazing downward. In a slightly slowed-down voice, he intones, "Remember the film," as those words also appear on the screen in English.

In aggregate, Lynch's scenes run just over a minute and a half, with his screen (or audio) time accounting for roughly half of that. Overall, the film is a dense work so steeped in cultural specificity and metaphor as to come off as largely impenetrable to most Western audiences, but there are moments of striking imagination and composition scattered throughout. The story of its production, though—and how Lynch came to land in the movie—is fascinating.

The Way of Samodelkin was produced in 2008-2009 as a group project by students of the video and media art department at Rodchenko Moscow School of Photography and Multimedia, also known as the Moscow School of Visual Arts. "At that moment we experimented a lot with possibilities of narrative video art and its intersection with film space—those were pioneering practices for the Moscow art scene of that time," said Petr Laden, the credited director on the project. "The collective was all our class, plus some extra students from other years—about twelve persons including our professor, Kirill Preobrazhenskiy, with whom we also started a video art group and magazine, *Vidiot*."

"It was essentially a full DIY project," said actor Korobkov, "made in the spirit of what David Graeber, in his book *Debt: The First 5000 Years*, called 'communism'—not in the state-political sense, but as any human relationship based on the principle, 'From each according to their abilities, to each according to their needs.' From the outset, it was conceived as total collaboration with anonymity in creation and production. The script existed only in the participants' minds.

"Dialogue was written on the day of shooting, or more often simply outlined and improvised," Korobkov continued. "Over time, however, as the footage came together, some participants gradually took over control of the editing and meaning-making—notably, Petr Laden began to call himself the director.

"At that point, I and other participants, who had been working under the initial principles of collective production, lost the ability to participate in the final cut of the film. So yes, I appear in the film as Felix, but in a sense as a disappointed Felix."

The structure and name of the movie come from a short text by authors Pavel Pepperstein and Sergei Anufriev, and its core idea, in a narrative sense, was to research and try to bring to light the creative practices of the unofficial Moscow art scene of the 1980s and how those in turn affected the work of artists in the 1990s and early 2000s. The result was intended to be a sort of lived-in contemporary art history piece, with the means of expression as well as figures of the past thirty years all given equal spotlight. The filmmakers chose to make not a documentary but a fictional film (hence the detective story) in which the actual could exist alongside both the fantastical and the representative.

"We incorporated into the film a lot of important background of the time—locations, art pieces, and more—and David Lynch was a big and important part of culture of the 1990s too, not only as a great director we all loved, but because *Twin Peaks* was one of first foreign TV series shown on new Russia TV, in 1993, and had a [massive] cultural impact," said Laden. "Thus, when he came to Moscow for his big exhibition in 2009, we had an obvious [desire] to include him in our movie."

Securing Lynch's involvement was a surprising stroke of luck, all involved agree. "I was searching to contact him," said Laden, "and as a result I was invited by Olga Sviblova [a Russian arts administrator who founded the Multimedia Art Museum, Moscow] for a dinner with him at Turandot restaurant—not a personal dinner, but for his team, sponsors, and several artists, [including Armenian-Soviet director] Artavazd Peleshyan, who was invited by Lynch, as I understood. At the end of the dinner, I had a chance for a short word with Lynch, and he agreed to give us five minutes of his time the next morning at 8:14 in his hotel."

And no, that's not a typo or misstatement. "He definitely said some nongeneric time," confirmed Laden. "I remember that was cute and in his style—so definitely not 8:15, and I am almost sure it was 8:14."

The group sprung to action and made plans on short notice. "I had all night to write the scene and organize people to come for shooting," said Laden, placing the date after the exhibition opening, which would've been either April 11 or the following day, the morning of Lynch's departure.

"We arrived early at his hotel and waited for him to come down before heading off to his next engagements. I remember him as an incredibly gentle person who, without unnecessary questions, simply did what we asked," recalled Korobkov. "I honestly don't even know if he ever saw his image in the film. Altogether, from memory, the whole encounter lasted five or maybe ten minutes. Possibly two takes—but I'm not sure."

The audio for the movie's car radio scene, meanwhile, was recorded during Lynch's press conference at the opening of his exhibition.

As with "Peixe Vermelho," any assessment of Lynch's performance in *The Way of Samodelkin* rests mostly in an evaluation of its fit in terms of mood.

Did he have a firm (or even *any*) knowledge of the film's plot? Of course not. Its collectivist production model? Perhaps, but likely not. Its tone or rhythms? None more than he could intuit from a quick conversation with Laden the night prior and from soaking up his surroundings when stepping out of his hotel's elevator. And you know what? That proved enough. There's a level of comfort that translates to his line readings.

Out of a desire to endorse the art life—and maybe some personal curiosity as well—Lynch accepted what by all accounts was a blind ask and leaned into a strange cameo in an unfamiliar land.

Watching the entire film now, in the shadow of the Russo-Ukrainian War and all the blood senselessly spilled by that invasion, it's difficult not to ponder the fact that so many idealistic artists and young Russians have had to make the choice to leave their native land. While in no way equal to the Ukrainian civilian loss of life, this represents its own tragedy—being driven out by an autocratic regime inhospitable to the freedom of political expression, certainly, but also the sort of creativity that is an essential part of the human soul. It

casts the optimism and experimentation of the film [Lynch on set to left] into stark relief—a relic of a moment in time that seems unlikely to soon return.

If that realization lands as depressing, the human benefit at least lives on. *The Way of Samodelkin* is an absorbing example of Lynch's unique ability to strikingly impact the lives of folks with whom he crossed paths only briefly—not merely through the depth of feeling present in his art, but because of who he was as a person.

"I love David Lynch very much, and he has highly influenced me in many ways," said Laden, who recently moved to Germany and is restarting his career there, working primarily as an editor while also as a multimedia artist and director.

Korobkov is even more philosophical. "My perception of Lynch now and fifteen years ago is very different. It's hard to unsee or disentangle my current understanding of him from my memories back then," he said. "At the time of the shoot, I probably respected Lynch primarily as the brilliant director of *Mulholland Drive*—one of my favorite films back then. But I didn't yet fully grasp his other work. You could say I saw him as a legend of independent cinema but without the nuance and layered meanings I perceive now.

"If I were to meet him today, my attitude would be entirely different. Since then, all of his work—his music albums, the third season of *Twin Peaks*, *Inland Empire*, *Lost Highway*, even his version of *Dune*—has become foundational to how I perceive the world. I see Lynch as a major artist, creating phenomenal statements with multifaceted meanings. I consider him an authentic feminist, someone who problematizes the systemic and thus invisible violence toward women. He is, like the Mystery Man in *Lost Highway*, pointing at problems everyone refuses to see, misperceived as a freak or oddity. The world would undoubtedly be a better place if more people understood his art."

-CHAPTER 29-

THE CLEVELAND SHOW (2010-2013)

Of all of David Lynch's acting endeavors, none may have elicited as much sheer, delighted confusion as his voice work as a recurring character on *The Cleveland Show*. And yet Lynch's participation is a simple illustration of the biblical aphorism "Ask and ye shall receive." Sometimes it really is that simple.

The series, cocreated by Seth MacFarlane, Mike Henry, and Richard Appel, was conceived of as a spinoff from *Family Guy*, the long-running animated sitcom that at that point was entering its eighth season on Fox. The idea was to take a supporting character, give him a new family in his old hometown, and mine that tension for laughs against a similar backdrop of unapologetically bawdy humor. Henry, who voiced the amiable Cleveland Brown and was an enormous Lynch fan, was the driving force behind the outreach to him.

The show premiered in September 2009, but Lynch didn't appear until the fourteenth episode of its debut season, which aired on February 21, 2010. Over the course of its four-season run, Lynch appeared in twenty-three of the show's eighty-eight episodes—three in the first year and no fewer than a half-dozen each subsequent season—becoming a valuable member of the background comedic ensemble.

The pilot sets the scene in effectively streamlined fashion, as Cleveland, financially crippled by the fallout from a divorce, leaves Quahog, Rhode Island, with his portly son, Cleveland Jr. (voiced by Kevin Michael Richardson), planning to head west. On the way they stop over in Cleveland's hometown of Stoolbend, Virginia, where he unexpectedly reconnects with high school crush Donna Tubbs (voiced by Sanaa Lathan), now a single mother to teenage Roberta (voiced for most of the show by Reagan Gomez-Preston) and the rambunctious young Rallo (also voiced by Henry).

After Cleveland dispatches Donna's good-for-nothing ex-husband, Robert (voiced by Corey Holcomb), as a romantic rival, the episode—which introduces neighbors Tim (voiced by MacFarlane), who happens to be a bear; redneck Lester (voiced by Richardson); and diminutive Holt (voiced by Jason Sudeikis), who lives with his mother—ends in nuptials between Cleveland and Donna, setting up their blended family. The episode also introduces the bar its core friend group frequents, The Broken Stool, but does not yet feature its owner.

That proprietor would be Gus, voiced by Lynch—and, indeed, very much drawn to look like him. That's a choice cocreator Henry credits to the artist who did the initial design for the character. "It looked just like David, which cracked us up," he said. "So we went with it—all part of the creative collaboration on the show. I give so much credit to the directors and artists for helping the show be great."

A friendly if somewhat clueless small business owner with a mysterious past, Gus provides occasional motivation and support to Cleveland while also serving as a vessel for a bit of weirdness. "He has a great matter-of-factness with the way he delivers lines," said Kevin Biggins, who cowrote the first episode in which Lynch appears. "He had the ability, which is what you want in any side-character voice actor, to make these five lines or whatever 15 percent funnier. It was really effortless, it seemed, for him to do that."

If the writers found a game participant in Lynch, they delighted in feeding him outlandish dialogue that populates YouTube clips and reliably achieves virality on social media, where it's habitually rediscovered by both longtime fans and those unfamiliar with Lynch's acting work outside of *Twin Peaks*.

• • •

While *The Cleveland Show* is kicked off by an abortive road trip to California, the beginning of Mike Henry's own personal creative journey also involves a road trip to California . . . inspired by a film about another abortive road trip to California.

The son of two artists (his dad was a sculptor and his mother an oil painter), Henry consciously aimed for a bit more structure and normalcy out of high school, attending Washington and Lee University. He then took a job at an advertising agency in Richmond, Virginia, in an attempt to blend business and creativity. Several weeks in, he knew it wasn't the path for him.

A screening of *Wild at Heart* changed the trajectory of his life. "I think I went with a date who wasn't really as inspired as I was," recalled Henry. "But I carried it with me, and then I went and saw it again by myself in the theater. And it really caught my spirit at the time . . . and sort of spurred my midlife crisis at twenty-four. So I had to go chase my truth.

"I was like, this is clearly so true to him. And if he can do something like that and be so celebrated and successful and awesome and inspiring," he continued, "then I'm going to go do my version of this life."

So Henry hopped in his Jetta and drove to Los Angeles. "I came out here and just wasn't sure what I wanted to do other than I wanted to make funny stuff," he said. "Steve Martin and Chevy Chase were my comedy heroes at the time. And then when I saw *Wild at Heart*, David was immediately right up there with those guys. I wanted to do some combination of all of that.

"I actually almost went to AFI [American Film Institute] because [Lynch] had gone there, and I was going to apply to the director's program because I was just writing some little things that I could shoot. But at the time, I didn't see how I was going to be able to sustain that financially. So I just did stand-up and improv and some PA work and waited tables for a few years. That was the beginning of my creative journey."

After three years, Henry did move back east for a bit—a three-year stint in Virginia to gain more production experience on commercials and comedy shorts, then a couple of years in New York, where he was getting close to a *Saturday Night Live* audition—before reconnecting with MacFarlane, whom he'd met as his brother Patrick's college roommate at Rhode Island School of Design and developed a strong rapport with. After assisting MacFarlane on jokes for his *Family Guy* pitch to Fox, Henry returned to LA and joined the show as both a writer and voice artist when it staffed up. From there, *The Cleveland Show* later was birthed.

• • •

For Henry, the green light for *The Cleveland Show* represented a whirlwind of ambitions fulfilled—dreams stretching back more than a decade and a half to that *Wild at Heart* viewing. So when it came time to cast the show, he didn't hesitate to swing big.

"I don't remember how specific I got with [the] casting [department]," Henry said. "I think it was just like, 'I freaking love David Lynch. I know he's got a studio—can you see if he would be up for recurring on this show?' I think that was probably it. And I don't know what she may have mentioned in the call, but I do remember it was surprising how quickly he responded and how game he was. And that actually gave me a great deal of confidence at the time to be able to just make a call to someone like that and have them say yes. . . . I think he just liked the vibe of it. I think he liked my very American name as a stranger to him. I don't know. But he had an instinct on it and was just down from the beginning."

Lynch's assistant at the time, Mindy Ramaker, has a strong memory of why he said yes. "The scripts were really good and funny," she said. "From my perspective, that was always the ultimate decider in what David said yes to in terms of acting. Mike Henry is also a super kind and talented guy who I know David enjoyed. If you could make David laugh, which Mike could,

he really had a special affinity for you."

For the initial meeting, on September 2, 2008, Henry went to Lynch's Hollywood Hills house with Kirker Butler, one of the other producers on the show, and his brother Patrick, a production consultant on the series. "You couldn't have a better encounter with someone that you look up to so much," said Henry. "He immediately made you feel like you were all old friends and was just so cool. And he signed my *Wild at Heart* poster and wrote, 'To Mike, I'm making my lunch, David Lynch,' quoting *Wild at Heart*, of course." [Photo: Mike Henry (left), Lynch, and Patrick Henry]

While Henry's Lynch fandom was most formative, there was no shortage of other admirers on staff at *The Cleveland Show*. "I've been pretty obsessed with David Lynch for decades," said Aaron Lee, a writer across all four seasons and coproducer on seasons there and four, crediting Danny Peary's *Cult Movies* with turning him on to *Eraserhead* and, by extension, the filmmaker's later work. "So just the fact that I was getting to write for David Lynch was incredibly exciting. . . . It really was like dream-come-true stuff."

For Biggins, also a writer on all four seasons, and a coproducer in season four, pitching dialogue for Gus became one of the highlights of the writers' room. "I felt like after my impersonation had been kind of given the green light by Mike, who was able to do a pretty good impression as well, we would just go back and forth, and (other) people would chime in too," he said. "There were a lot of fans of Lynch on that staff. So it was always fun to just all be talking like David Lynch, going around and pitching [jokes]."

• • •

One interesting note is that before landing on Gus, Lynch was slated to portray another character. "At first, he was supposed to play Mr. Waterman, who is this gay Southern gentleman who has a crush on Cleveland's friend Terry [also voiced by Sudeikis]. So he read, and we had him in mind, for that," said Henry. "But then we started writing it just for David's voice or whatever, and I remember talking to David and saying, 'Hey man, how would you feel about playing the bartender?' Because we had pitched a bunch of stuff and sort of rallied around that idea [of him as Gus]. And he was so glad he didn't have to play a homosexual is what he said. So I don't know if you want to include that, or even if I want to be quoted on saying that, but it was just so funny to hear him say that. I don't know, very random.

"He loves the ladies, obviously," continued Henry. "And so it was just funny that he wanted to play someone more like himself, I think, is what he was saying."

In the annals of successful sitcoms, the occupation of bartender is a time-honored character, from drink pourers Sam and Woody of *Cheers* to Moe Szyslak of *The Simpsons*. The pivot to a more archetypal role for Lynch, therefore, helped open up greater pathways of comedic opportunity. "A lot of people look to bartenders for just straight-up advice, and as Gus, [Lynch] was able to do that in a little bit of a different way that was hilarious," noted Biggins. "He was kind of a shoulder to lean on. He could give Cleveland honest, earnest advice that was 10 percent funnier than if it was coming from a guy [speaking gruffly]. It was more optimistic. He had a very positive way of delivering his lines to Cleveland."

With his character solidified, Lynch was no shrinking violet with regard to the show's frequently ribald tone. There was never any joke or dialogue he refused to say. "He said, 'You're in charge of this thing. I'm just a piece of meat,'" said Henry.

After recording the first session in person at Lynch's house, Henry bundled dialogue from subsequent episodes and had Lynch record it from his home studio with assistance from Dean Hurley. For the show's duration, Henry was the one, via remote, who gave notes on performance—surely a surreal experience. "At that point, I had done enough stuff where I could be pretty specific with what I was asking him to do," said Henry. "I think he appreciated the specificity and the direction."

On February 23, two days after his first vocal performance, Lynch tweeted, "Yes, it's true. I play Gus the bartender on *The Cleveland Show*. Mike Henry asked me to do it, so I said yes."

Said Henry: "When I saw that, I was like, I'm done."

• • •

The following is a summary of Lynch's appearances on *The Cleveland Show*:

S1 E14: "The Curious Case of Jr. Working at the Stool"
This episode introduces Gus in prominent fashion and showcases offbeat jokes that establish how the show will lean into Lynch's off-screen persona. After Gus serves beers to the guys and banters good-naturedly with them about their intention to eventually settle up on their tab ("Good, I need

to pay my 'rent,'" says Gus, deploying air quotes), Cleveland laughs and says, "Oh Gus, what a crazy bar owner you are!" before offering a toast to the Stool.

The main narrative thrust finds Cleveland Jr. trying to get a job and ending up at the Broken Stool, where cleaning up seems to help his OCD. In appreciation, Gus offers Junior a coloring book and crayons ("Can you believe that something so fun can be made of paraffin wax?") and then agrees with him that the peach crayon does not in fact taste like a peach ("You're right, it should say wax").

After Junior creates a way for Gus to better track how much money he's owed, an irritated Cleveland conspires to get his son fired. Delivering the bad news to Junior, Gus asks him to first sit down. "You know, I don't think sitting was quite right," he says. "How about if you crouch like a baseball catcher?" After Junior complies, Gus strokes his chin and says, "I was thinking a little less Gary Carter and a little more Tony Peña," and then, after Junior approximates the trademark catching stance of the five-time all-star, says, "Wrong leg, but close enough."

"That was the first episode of television I ever wrote," said Biggins with a laugh. "I remember [writing partner] Travis [Bowe] and I laughing a lot, and having a very fun time thinking about all the weird things that this kind of sweet, fat, innocent boy, [who] has an interesting way of thinking and is very honest, and David Lynch as a bartender could talk about and just what their interaction would be like.

"Hearing him say those lines was hilarious. Travis played baseball in college, and we knew Mike was a huge fan of all things baseball, so those references he added on to. That was all Mike, sticking his leg out and referencing those players from the 1980s."

Indeed, the combination of the specificity of the joke and its delivery by Lynch, who doesn't particularly read as a sports nut, makes for one of the more off-kilter and memorable lines of Gus's dialogue from the show's entire run. "I can pretty much guarantee he had no idea who those people were," said former Lynch assistant Jay Aaseng with a laugh. "But you never know. I mean, growing up my childhood idol was Nolan Ryan, and I remember telling that to David at some point thinking it would mean nothing to him, and he knew who that was. He was like, 'Yeah, Nolan Ryan, feel the heat,' and that just kind of blew my mind."

"Since that was our first episode to air, we had some sort of viewing party," added Biggins. "And to just see people's reactions to it and get that joke that Lynch delivered perfectly was really satisfying. That gave us the confidence to go ahead and know that this was gonna be a show that was gonna be different from *Family Guy*. You know, you wouldn't make that joke in *Family Guy*. It was more up Mike's alley. And that kind of gave us the confidence of like, 'Yeah, even if 80 percent of the country isn't getting this, so what? The other 20 percent really had a treat.'"

S1 E17: "Gone with the Wind"
After Cleveland goes on a high-fiber diet and gets a "fart card" from his doctor, his flatulence intersects with a couples' karaoke contest at the Broken Stool, emceed by Gus.

After Lester and his wife Kendra wash out, Gus intones, "Wow, that really was not very popular," and introduces the next contestants. Cleveland's melodic control of his gassiness proves a hit with the crowd; much later, in the karaoke finals, as Cleveland attempts to control his farting, Gus becomes agitated, yelling out, "Any ass can sing. We want the singing ass!"

This episode is most notable, however, for Cleveland's ex-wife, Loretta, dying in the same bathtub gag frequently used to humiliate Cleveland in *Family Guy*. In a sequence that will surely trigger memories for *Twin Peaks* fans, a confusedly distraught Cleveland (experiencing what he later calls survivor's guilt) jumps on her casket at the funeral.

S1 E21: "You're the Best Man, Cleveland Brown"
The final episode of season one revolves around Cleveland's mother, Cookie, remarrying his philandering father Freight Train, with whom Cleveland has a strained relationship. During an opening segment at the bar, Gus serves drinks to the guys and then, a moment later, after a joke about *Two and a Half Men*, delivers a rimshot from a set of drums in front of "You Must At Least Look 21 To Drink in This Establishment" signage, sporting formal wear and acknowledging Holt's thanks with "You got it kid!" At the end of the episode, Gus appears as a guest at the wedding, without dialogue.

S2 E3: "How Cleveland Got His Groove Back"
Cleveland, who enjoyed baseball success as a youngster, makes a bet with the inexperienced Lester that he can't strike him out. Gus attends the competition and laughs at Cleveland's jokes at Lester's expense. After getting hit with an errant throw, the injured Gus makes an exclamation I like to think would have been a great fit with the commercially offered ringtones from DavidLynch.com: "Oww, doo doo balls!"

S2 E4: "It's the Great Pancake, Junior Brown"
Cleveland attempts to get his fourteen-year-old son to grow up and stop trick-or-treating for Halloween, with unintended consequences. Gus appears only in passing; when Cleveland asks for a beer to go, he says, "Sure thing, favorite patron of mine!" and obliges by pouring the rest of Cleveland's brew in a paper bag.

S2 E6: "Fat and Wet"
Cleveland Jr. and Kendra, both overweight, take up a fight for "fat rights" with a local ballot initiative, engendering embarrassment from the men in their lives. At the Broken Stool, Gus says, "So, Cleveland and Lester, how does it feel to have your son and wife be the laughingstock of our town?" Lester angrily replies, "Shut up, Eraserhead!"

After some more back-and-forth, Gus advises the guys, "You don't wanna be sober when you walk into that booth and see your names associated with the grossest thing on Earth: fat people." When Holt proffers a different idea of what's grossest, Gus smacks him and angrily exclaims, "Hey, prolapsed rectums are *not* funny!"

S2 E9: "Beer Walk!"
Cleveland hatches the idea to raise money for Donna's charity with a self-centered fundraiser at the Broken Stool, which brings his *Family Guy* friends from Quahog to town. After Donna is heckled, Gus intervenes: "Okay, buzzkill terminated—let's get this tax-deductible party started!"

S2 E11: "How Do You Solve a Problem Like Roberta?"
After a fed-up Donna leaves for the weekend, Cleveland grapples with the difficulties of parenting a teenage daughter, but Gus's early-episode appearance comes when he mans a one dollar wish booth at the Stoolbend carnival. When Rallo approaches, Gus mock grants his wish by saying, "Okay, you will be invisible starting now!" and then pretends not to see him after Rallo strips off his clothes and runs around.

S2 E16: "The Way the Cookie Crumbles"

This episode features what is probably the most heavily circulated clip of David Lynch from *The Cleveland Show*. When Cookie and Freight Train get scammed, Cleveland's father has a garage sale for money and Cleveland aims to track down the con man responsible to try to win his father's respect. After picking up some of his childhood stuff and taking it to a self-storage facility, he runs into Gus, who's arranging formaldehyde jars on shelves in his unit.

"Oh, hey Cleveland, I didn't know you stored things," says Gus. After Cleveland replies that he just started, Gus gently strokes Cleveland's head and says, "I'm proud of you man. You're coming along real nice."

Cleveland's wish, in an interior monologue, that Gus was his father feeds a fantasy sequence, complete with a childlike POV, in which Gus lovingly plays with a giggling Cleveland, bouncing him on his knee. As the pair fall to the floor together, Gus tells Cleveland that he loves him, and Cleveland replies, "I love you too, Dad."

As silly as the sequence is, it's rooted in a place of deep feeling. "What's kind of funny is that growing up, my dad wasn't in the house," said Henry. "My parents split up, so it was almost written, as a lot of Cleveland stuff was written, autobiographically—of him wanting a different take on a dad, who might've been more satisfying in some way.

"Cleveland is me, basically. I am not Cleveland, but Cleveland is me . . . not anymore for now, as events dictated. I work for a corporation. But there was so much of me in Cleveland. . . . If you're writing for yourself or from yourself, then you write what you know. So a lot of that spilled over into Cleveland's life. And that notion or that sequence was certainly part of that."

S2 E20: "Back to Cool"

After Junior takes a liking to Donna's ex-husband, Cleveland tries to reconnect with his son via competing in the Coolympics against Robert. Gus serves as emcee, reminding people, "We have absolutely no street permits for this event. So if the cops come, run like hell!" before introducing "the three coolest men alive, who agreed to judge this event because they were misled about the nature of this competition."

Gus presenting cool experts Snoop Dogg and Tony Hawk ("Our next judge takes a lot of credit while gravity does the work . . . the only professional skateboarder in the universe") is an amusing treat, and he also sets up the competition's four categories. The episode births another much-clipped exchange when Snoop says, "The guy gettin' ass always wins," and Gus excitedly concurs, "You got that right, friend!"

S3 E1: "BFFS"

In the opening episode of the third season, while gathered at the Broken Stool, Cleveland finds out Peter Griffin was in town and didn't contact him. Holt mentions that he was picking up his daughter Meg, whom he apparently left when he was in town for the Beer Walk last year. Says Gus: "She'd been in the lost and found box for over a week, so I figured I could have her."

S3 E3: "A Nightmare on Grace Street (That's the Name of Cleveland's Street)"

This Halloween-themed episode opens with Gus in a cemetery addressing viewers directly. "Happy Halloween, I'm Gus, filling in for Vincent Price, because he's dead." He then rips a leg off a corpse and carries it back to what looks like a dirty, antiquated operating room. "Here in Stoolbend, everyone's busy with my annual Broken Stool pumpkin carving contest, sponsored by Harrison Gourds," he continues. "Harrison Gourds: good Lord, that's a good gourd." Gus then cuts a slice off the leg, places it between two dressed slices of bread, walks out, serves Cleveland a "turkey sandwich," and reveals the aforementioned space to be the Broken Stool's back room.

The rest of the episode centers on a haunted house visit and the ostracization of an annoying, pun-happy bar patron, Donny (voiced by Danny Smith). Gus addresses a gathering saying, "And now it's time to announce the winner of the Broken Stool's Day-Before-Halloween Pumpkin Carving Contest! Or what some might call Premature E-Jack-o-Lantern!" When that joke bombs, Gus tells Donny he's going off prompter before giving a disappointed exhalation. Donny snaps and tries to kill Cleveland and his family but meets his untimely demise after falling from a window; the episode ends with Gus dragging Donny's body to the trunk of his car (presumably for more sandwiches) and winking at the camera—another wink and nod, both figurative and literal, at the darkness in Lynch's work.

S3 E7: "Die Semi-Hard"

Family Guy remains well-known for its parodies, most notably involving the *Star Wars* franchise. In this episode sending up *Die Hard*, Cleveland is on a plane sitting next to Gus, who says, "What's wrong, fellow traveler? You look nervous." After Cleveland replies, "This is our first parody," Gus says, "Ahh, you want to know the secret to a good parody? When you get to your destination, take off your shoes and socks and make fists with your toes. Now you can help me: Am I allowed to call it a sandwich if I eat three pieces of bread stacked together?" Part of the blow to the scene involves Gus explaining his frequent bathroom trips: "I have a too-small colostomy bag."

S3 E9: "There Goes El Neighborhood"

When Choni (voiced by Rosie Perez) moves into a McMansion across the street and steals Cleveland's friends for a Super Bowl party, a frustrated Cleveland trips headlong into a bunch of insensitive behavior and cultural misunderstandings, and Choni accuses him of being racist. Gus gets in a dig, saying, "Not to pile on, Cleveland, but you never listened to that Enrique Iglesias CD I burned for you."

S3 E10: "Dancing with the Stools"

Gus pulls more emcee duty in this episode, which includes 1991, 1998 ("Close but no cigar—ha ha, that sure is topical for this period in history"), and 2002 flashbacks to Stoolbend's dance contest, which Donna has lost each year. Back in the present day, other choice Gus lines include "Next up: please let it be magic. Nope: more dancing" and, in what feels like it should absolutely be interpolated into an upbeat club mix by Moby, "Are you gonna dance or what?"

S3 E20: "Flush of Genius"

After Cleveland Jr. shadows his father during a workday for a social studies report, his brutally honest assessment causes Cleveland shame. When Junior then pivots to instead writing a report on Gus ("And that's just one of the uses for formaldehyde . . . "), Cleveland is shocked. "He's a very accomplished bartender and filmmaker," explains Junior.

"A little bit of fourth wall is okay," Henry said about this wink at Lynch's film work, reminiscent of the *Eraserhead* putdown in season two. "I'm sure if we had gone for another few years, we would've had some pretty deep Gus diving."

The sequence ends with Junior inviting Gus upstairs to finish his interview with him. "Unfortunately, I can't handle stairs, for I have the knees of a cow," says Gus. "But if you'd agree to carry me, Carlton . . . " A bit later, as Junior does indeed carry Gus on his shoulders past Rallo's room, there's a slice of whimsy from Gus that reads as pure Lynch: "Wheee, this is wonderful!"

"He really became kind of a crutch" said Lee, the writer of this episode. "We really relied on him for blows to scenes, to just walk in and say something outrageous and destroy. We all really depended on David Lynch, and it was his fun to pitch in his voice, as you can imagine."

S4 E1: "Escape from Goochland"

Much in the mold of Springfield/Shelbyville from *The Simpsons* and Pawnee/Eagleton from *Parks & Recreation*, Stoolbend's rival city is Goochland (named after a real county in Virginia). After a football game against their longtime nemesis ends with Cleveland and the gang fleeing an antagonized mob, they hole up at the Broken Stool with the stolen wooden wife, Eunice, of President William Henry Harrison, which serves as the totem of Goochland's superiority.

There, Gus explains Eunice actually belongs to Stoolbend: "Goochland borrowed it from us for the aught-three World Fair and never returned it." Asked how he knows this, Gus replies that he's 117 years old. When those assembled are whipped into a fervor and start to vocalize various calls to action, Gus twice exclaims, "Intern the Japanese!" In the show's tag, after Stoolbend citizenry has defeated encroaching Goochlanders, Gus puts Eunice in his trunk (that's two bodies, for those keeping score) and says, "By the time I'm done with you, you're going to be a canoe!"

S4 E4: "Turkey Pot Die"

If you want a clip of Lynch shouting "No más curly fries!" this is your episode. Upset that Junior wouldn't shoot a turkey for Thanksgiving, Cleveland is sulking at the Broken Stool when Lester mentions the curly fries are only for bonding fathers and sons. An agitated Cleveland vetoes them for the entire bar, and Gus enforces the ban, calling out to his unseen line cook, "¿Por qué? Cleveland called it, that's por qué!"

S4 E9: "Here Comes the Bribe"

Donna pitches a renewal of wedding vows, but after Cleveland botches things at the ceremony, the pair lands in marriage counseling. Gus appears as a guest at the service, with no dialogue in the broadcast episode.

S4 E14: "Hangover: Part Tubbs"

When Donna runs for the school board, Cleveland's shortcomings as a husband are cast into such stark relief that Donna hires a fake husband to make her campaign look better. Gus has an early line of dialogue informing the gang that their hot wings order is ready at a particularly awkward moment, but the bigger clip-worthy bit comes when Gus thanks Donna for coming to Gustavo's, a classy upstairs restaurant, and then, immediately after she walks downstairs to the Broken Stool, greets her again. "Sorry, no time for your weirdness, Gus," says Donna, walking past him. Gus somehow suddenly appears in front of her and snaps back, "Make time!" While not explicitly referential, this in some ways feels like an acknowledgement of the singularity of Lynch's body of work.

S4 E16: "Who Done Did It?"

While the bulk of this episode is framed as an *Alfred Hitchcock Presents*-style mystery centered on the revelation that Freight Train writes whodunit novels under a female pseudonym, the opening scene at a silent auction features another standout bit, with Gus selling copies of what he deems his new exercise video. When he clicks play to show Cleveland, we get a POV shot of a terrified blonde fleeing Gus as he exhorts, "Run faster! You don't want me to catch you!"

At episode's end, after a "One Year Later" card, Gus toasts Freight Train's success: "What a night it's been! Whodunit? You done it, Freight Train. Once again!" For those wondering, no, Gus doesn't preface the last exclamation with "It's a Friday."

S4 E17: "Fist & The Furious"

Cleveland finds out his physician is actually in witness protection after serving as a mob doctor in New York, and they end up at the Broken Stool, where Gus says, "You're welcome to lay low as long as you need. And remember: all the decorative guns on the wall are loaded. As is a random urinal."

What viewers hear next depends on their platform of choice, as the sound of a shotgun blast and the exclamation "Oww, dammit, Gus!" are both excised from the episode's streaming iteration, leaving a pregnant pause before Gus's reply: "Ha! Sorry friend!"

For Henry, the moment stands out as one of Lynch's most memorable lines. "It's the most dismissive, kidding line, juxtaposed to the most horrible thing that you could do to somebody. That's the beauty of animation too — you can just kind of say and do anything. His read on it, just the deadpan of it all, was so funny to me."

S4 E22: "Crazy Train"

In the show's penultimate episode, Cleveland bonds with Freight Train as the latter finally opens up while experiencing off-brand, prescription-drug-induced lunacy. At a lowrider convention the pair attend, Gus is introduced in front of a bouncing hearse. "I don't have hydraulics," a wide-eyed Gus says. "Those were ghosts in there!"

• • •

On May 13, 2013, *The Cleveland Show* was canceled, bringing to an end the intermittent delight of silly and sometimes profane non sequiturs emanating from the mouth of an animated David Lynch stand-in. For those wondering, the original, broadcast episodes of the series sometimes differ slightly from what is currently streaming. *The Cleveland Show*'s full-season DVDs, meanwhile, contain extra material trimmed both for time and content considerations.

Some of those extended or excised scenes (with additional lines from Gus) are occasionally uploaded to YouTube. Among this material is a monologue in which Gus reveals that his parents died in a murder-suicide and he was relocated to Stoolbend by the federal government, plus a sequence in which Gus strolls into a laundromat, unzips a flesh suit with Roberta watching, puts it in washing machine, greets her, and says, "You know, I saw Eric Clapton in here once." For those pondering where Gus lives, there's a montage of him walking out of a mausoleum in a bathrobe, coffee cup in hand, to pick up a newspaper.

Other bits include a reference to Gus's outstanding Columbia House Record and Tape Club balance (a deep cut that Generation X will appreciate), plus a sequence with Freight Train in which an incredulous Gus says, "Shut the front door! You're saying you were with *two* girls?" Told yes and that if you add their ages together, they were almost age appropriate, Gus inquires, "Say blood, where you get these bitches?"

For those looking for a *Twin Peaks* reference, there's a scene in which Gus, standing indoors with a llama, says, "Sorry, guys, I've got all the llamas I need. What majestic creatures, yes you are! Who's majestic? You! You are—good, majestic llama," before pausing, offering the llama a nuzzled kiss, and intoning, "I feed them garbage."

No garbage, though, was fed to Lynch as a vocal performer on *The Cleveland Show*—Henry and the other writers honed in on the distinctiveness of his voice and found a way, with Gus, to bring a pinch of Lynch's uniqueness to their twisted little animated world. "I feel like he has a very homespun, direct, logical way of speaking, where it's a little bit comforting, and therefore he can be funny just about saying anything," said Biggins.

For Lynch, the series provided the first and most direct showcase of his robust sense of humor outside of material of his own creation. For some fans, his participation might have been eyebrow raising. For others, though, it made a certain amount of sense, confirming both a sincere if less seen side of Lynch's personality and his idiosyncratic authenticity.

"I'll tell you, numerous times over the past couple years I've stopped by YouTube and [typed] in 'David Lynch Cleveland Show,' where people make supercuts of just his scenes," said Lee, "and to see those back-to-back-to-back is one of the funniest things, just hilarious."

−*CHAPTER 30*−

DAVID LYNCH SIGNATURE CUP COFFEE (2011)

Perhaps Lynch's experience on *The Cleveland Show*, and getting to step into a character that certainly wasn't him but at least shared his physical appearance, was freeing or even inspiring in a way. Or maybe Lynch was pondering the riptide currents of American consumerism. Insert "Why Not Both?" Old El Paso meme here.

Either way, in the homestretch of his second season of voice work as Gus on the aforementioned series, Lynch in May 2011 released a commercial for his David Lynch Signature Cup Coffee brand (which had launched in 2006 and enjoyed a good run before being wound down by roaster Allegro Coffee in November 2021, after Amazon's purchase of distribution partner Whole Foods several years earlier). The ad caught the attention of Lynch fans as well as lawyers for Mattel, Inc., the toy manufacturing and entertainment behemoth. The reason for the latter? It featured their iconic Barbie doll.

Framed as a meet-cute conversation with this smiling, inanimate (and quite possibly disembodied) doll head, the four-minute video finds Lynch taking on the dual voice roles of Barbie and a rib-nudging version of himself, modulating his tone not so much by register or pitch but by injecting overwhelming wonderment into Barbie's line readings. It was met with a cease-and-desist order, and for a while scrubbed from all the websites that had embedded videos in their articles about it. Naturally, it now lives on YouTube.

"He really loved using those Barbie dolls, but since Mattel wrote that letter, it was very curtailed, and he was really mad about that because he felt he personified this head—he didn't say it was the Barbie doll or anything," said Sabrina Sutherland, Lynch's longtime producer. "It was just this great doll, and they should quite honestly be happy that he used it. I mean it was a cool commercial. It was actually very high praise."

Shot almost entirely in extreme close-up of a classic blonde, blue-eyed Barbie head cradled (and occasionally squeezed) in Lynch's left hand, the short conveys a dreaminess not uncharacteristic of some of his work but perhaps surprising given the nature of the content itself. It achieves this by way of both its tranquil, almost fairy-tale score ("Romantic Strings," performed on an Optigan, a 1970s-era keyboard instrument, in three-quarters time and played on a loop throughout) and Lynch's mellow, solicitous tone.

The dialogue is a slightly flirty back-and-forth between an awestruck, somewhat nervous admirer and this version of Lynch as rock star. Greetings are exchanged (and re-exchanged) before an announcement arrives via intercom with some slight feedback: "Mr. Lynch to the autograph stage, Mr. Lynch to the autograph stage." This is followed by the sound of a door opening, the din of screaming fans, and police sirens wailing in the distance. "Hurry, there's 10 million people out here!" someone off-screen yells.

"Jeez, what's goin' on?" Barbie inquires. "Just, ya know, working on some stuff," Lynch says. After a long pause, Barbie haltingly asks Lynch what he's drinking. "Just taking a coffee," he says. When she asks what kind, the pitch arrives: "I'm drinking, uh, David Lynch Signature Cup Coffee, espresso."

Affirming its quality ("Yeah, it's really good"), Lynch also confirms that it's organic and fairly traded, with he and Barbie exchanging mutual compliments on their respective attractiveness squeezed in between. When Lynch tells her that he's going to get her a cup, Barbie swoons. "Whoa . . . so great," she says. "Jeez, Dave, thanks. Thanks, it's really beautiful. I feel dreamy just thinking about it." Before the video fades to a shot of the branded coffee bag and "Real Good" in red vertical letters, Lynch aims to seal the deal, saying, "Let's go get that cup of coffee, baby."

In 2023, a Barbie movie starring Margot Robbie and crammed to the rafters with product placement from General Motors, Chanel, Prada, Moschino, and many more brands grossed almost $1.5 billion in theaters. Among a certain set of cinephiles, it also reboosted the profile of this curio.

Certainly, no fan of product placement in movies (see his famous 2007 AFI Dallas International Film Festival interview, where he called it "bullshit, total fucking bullshit"), Lynch here delivers a piece of work that playfully comments on the relationship between art and commerce. While its layers of commentary may not run as deep as Todd Haynes's Barbie-starring "Superstar: The Karen Carpenter Story," it undoubtedly plays on multiple levels.

In repurposing an iconic brand that itself is given product placement in numerous programs aimed at young girls—by showing Barbie as almost literal putty in Lynch's hands, unable to resist the allure of his personality, handsomeness, and delicious coffee—the commodification is cannily and amusingly redirected.

Lynch used the Optigan in music for other projects as well, including "Slow 30's Room," which was first part of his 2007 *The Air Is on Fire* art exhibition in Paris before appearing again in season three of *Twin Peaks*. Its use here (as well as other aural background details) speaks to a very specific vision. One is lulled into a larger world where an ad like this makes perfect sense, such that it's not difficult to imagine this as an intended series rather than a humorous one-off.

"He really wanted to experiment more with the dolls, so I think it would've been much more had he been allowed to use them," Sutherland confirmed.

Never fear. While momentarily stalled in his efforts, Lynch would eventually find his way back to Barbie.

—CHAPTER 31—

LOUIE (2012)

If Lynch, throughout his filmmaking career, confounded some critics with his juggling of disparate tonalities and juxtaposition of comedic bits with serious and frequently unsettling ideas, scenes, and images, Louis C.K. qualifies in a certain way as a kindred spirit. While C.K. cut his teeth as a successful staffer for late night comedy shows and later emerged as a well-regarded touring comedian, a good bit of his most trenchant material, as both a writer and stand-up, edges into darker territory.

While some of his routines are shot through with the sort of pessimism and self-deprecation (even loathing) not uncommon among comedians, there is an underlying provocativeness that audiences either appreciate or find too steep a hill to climb. It isn't merely shrewdly observational humor processed through a highly individualized lens—a significantly high bar, but one that plenty of comedians clear. There is thought behind it—smart, deep, and frequently conflicted.

This is especially true of his on-screen breakthrough, *Louie*, which ran for five seasons on FX, from 2010 to 2015, racking up twenty-two Emmy Award nods (and three wins) and two Golden Globe Best Actor-Television Series Musical or Comedy nominations for its multihyphenate creator. Starring C.K. as Louie, a slightly fictionalized version of himself, the series also found him wielding absolute creative control, serving as its executive producer, writer, sole director, and chief editor.

C.K. had honed his directorial skills throughout the 1990s on a series of little-known short films and feature, *Tomorrow Night*, and this difficult-to-pin-down series represented the apex of his screen-captured vision of life as a confusing and sometimes indistinguishable blend of the awkward and heartbreaking, hilarious and humiliating, thought-provoking and bittersweet.

For the most part eschewing a regular fixed cast, the hybrid comedy-drama made use of recurring players and utilized C.K.'s relationships with other comedians, who made occasional cameo appearances, to round out an ensemble. The series unfolded mostly as a series of vignettes (sometimes thematically connected, sometimes not) detailing Louie's career struggles and life as a divorced father of two while also incorporating bits of his stand-up routine. Its episodes were typically standalone, and while some characters provided continuity, the show ignored strict consistency even within seasons, occasionally deploying different actors in the same role or the same performers in different roles.

The show's thirteen-episode third season debuted on June 28, 2012. Lynch appeared in "Late Show Part 2" and "Late Show Part 3." These were the last two episodes of a rare three-episode arc, positioned just before the season's finale, which unpacked Louie's complex relationship with the industry that both sustains and frustrates him. Leaning into melancholy and a deeply observed soul-searching, these episodes were ambitious and also a searing vivisection of the long-run fruitlessness inherently married to show business ambition.

On the heels of a successful appearance in Los Angeles on *The Tonight Show* by Louie, and with David Letterman considering retirement, CBS approaches Louie about serving as the more affordable backup plan to Jerry Seinfeld in taking over *The Late Show*. The West Coast executive who floats this idea (Garry Marshall) sends Louie to see his "main city man" back in New York, Jack Dall (Lynch).

Upon returning home, Louie is thrown into an even greater state of disequilibrium and confusion by dealing with Dall, an enigmatic, withholding figure and supposed comedy whisperer who critiques his weight, forces Louie to read outdated monologue jokes in practice sessions, and lectures him about the importance of comic timing in mannered fashion.

• • •

Jack Dall was conceived of as an instrument of ultimate authority and tremendous tension, a vessel through which further anxiety and uncertainty is heaped upon Louie. Lynch delivers such a distinctive performance that it feels totally hand in glove, and it's hard to imagine anyone else in the part. But he wasn't the first choice—even though he eventually became the *only* choice.

Originally, C.K. thought of Ben Gazzara for the role. But, as he has recounted in interviews, when his team reached out to him, they discovered Gazzara had just passed away. Jerry Lewis, Martin Scorsese, and Al Pacino, among others, were then contacted, and all said no. Lynch's films were enormously meaningful to C.K., but he wasn't top of mind as a performer. When C.K. landed on a picture of Lynch after googling another possibility for the role, however, he thought back to two memorable pieces of footage.

"One was I think I saw him on David Letterman's show when *Twin Peaks* was big, and I remember that—in a sort of fun way, contrary to the tone of some of his films, or actually not really, because if you really know his films, you see this—he was a very cheerful, joyful and humorous guy," said C.K. "He didn't take himself very seriously even though he took his work very seriously, in a sense. And so I always liked the way he sounded."

The other memory involved a preshow trailer shown frequently at the IFC Center on Sixth Avenue in New York, where C.K. saw many movies. In it, Lynch talked briefly about his films, followed by a behind-the-scenes excerpt of him giving direction. "In his shouting, he had the pipes of a working director," recalled C.K., "but you could tell he wanted everyone to be enjoying it. And so I just always had this affection for him. I never expected to meet him my whole life. He would've been a guy I would say, 'Yeah, that's somebody who's on a coin or something—I don't meet people like that.'"

The big clincher for C.K., though, was a heavily viral clip, originally featured on *Inland Empire*'s DVD release, in which Lynch is asked about audiovisual presentation and segues into his thoughts about people watching movies on their phones. He talks about it being "such a sadness" before ending with punchy profanity and an exhortation to "get real."

Seeing this solidified the idea, already in the script, that a late-night comedy guru within a large corporate entity would rise to that hallowed level precisely because of his eccentricity. "I saw the passion in his anger," said C.K. of the snippet, "and it made me fucking *need* it to be him. It *had* to be him. And it inserted into the character this toughness, this certitude—he's the seer."

C.K. was now convinced he'd found his Dall. In a March email to Lynch, he wrote in part: "If you read the scripts that I'm sending to you, you might think that it's not a part that would come naturally to you because you're not the typical choice. And I want you to know while reading it that I'm not hoping for you to play it as a 'character' outside of your own nature. The idea that excites me is that you would take what's written here and read it as yourself, away from what's expected."

Lynch, however, still wasn't sure. The process of landing him became a bit of a dance, with the New York-based multihyphenate trying to convince the Los Angeles-based filmmaker to come east. "I think it was a couple of months, and I think it was about four or five emails," recalled C.K. "And the thing that kept giving me hope was that he was giving me reasons for saying no. And you learn this in show businesses—if you don't want to do a gig you just say no, and you just use a reason like 'It doesn't work for me, I don't want it.' Because otherwise they'll keep asking. And he wasn't doing that. He was saying, 'I don't want to travel, and I feel there are a million people who could do this better than I could.' And so to me that was like, well, all I have to do is convince them of two things. Number one, I can make his trip as short as possible and as easy as possible. And number two, I can convince him that it has to be him.

"And so I got quite intimate with him and his assistant in saying the reasons that I thought it had to be him, and they were all true. And also I wanted him to fucking do it," he continued. "Our show had a very flexible structure to it so that I was able to say, 'We're not shooting this until we get David Lynch.' So we just kept moving the dates for the shoot. And I know that the passionate is only helped by the practical, so I got my line producer, Blair [Breard], to really work on that schedule and really find a way to shoot out Jack Dall [as quickly as possible]. It was a lot of material, but we had to get it done."

Lynch's hesitance tamed and conditions satisfied, he opted in. On April 18, Lynch emailed C.K. and said, simply and directly, "I'll be your guy for Jack Dall." The episodes shot on May 30 and 31, 2012, in New York City—days forty-one and forty-two of a forty-nine-day cross-boarded production schedule. The first day, consisting of three TV studio scenes spread across both episodes, took place at one of the show's usual locations, NEP Studios. The second day, with two scenes set in Dall's office, was filmed at DH Blair, an investment firm on Wall Street.

S3 E11: "Late Show Part 2" (Airdate: September 13, 2012)

Louie meets with his ex-wife, Janet (Susan Kelechi Watson), but attempts to use split custody of his daughters, Lilly (Hadley Delany) and Jane (Ursula Parker), as an excuse for why he can't pursue the opportunity. Janet bluntly says to "forget the kids" and tells Louie to get the job in order to be a better role model for them.

When Louie goes with his agent, Doug (Edward Gelbinovich), to see Dall, a secretary corrects him on the pronunciation of Dall's name. When a call comes giving the nervous party the go-ahead to enter Dall's office (an encounter that will share much in common with one that would come a decade later in *The Fabelmans*), a different secretary is shown answering the phone before the master shot reverts back to the first secretary (more on this in a moment).

Dall is introduced at the 6:25 mark with an over-the-shoulder shot of him rubbing his left ear with his index and middle fingers, a low background thrum interrupted when Louie opens his office door and Doug enters behind him. As Louie awkwardly introduces himself, Dall doesn't look up but says, "Sent here? What are you, a letter? Nobody sent you." As Dall reaches into his desk drawer and pulls out a stopwatch, an overhead shot reveals other items: a Remington shaver, some monogrammed stationery, foreign currency, a microcassette tape, and a pearl-handled gun.

As Louie nervously rambles on, Dall issues a series of blunt directives, instructing Doug to pick up a cue card and each of them to stand in a certain spot. Dall clicks the stopwatch and looks expectantly at Louie, finally instructing him to read the card, which contains a joke about President Nixon. When Louie finally finishes and says, "We'll be right back," Dall clicks his stopwatch and makes an entry in a small notebook. "It took you one minute and twelve seconds to tell one joke. It's too long," he admonishes Louie. "Comedy is about timing, son." Advising Louie to work on his speed, he tells him to come back on Wednesday. The aforementioned thrum returns as Dall starts absentmindedly rubbing his ear and dismisses Louie and Doug by no longer looking at them.

Lynch's next scene, running four and a half minutes, takes place on a stage in front of a curtained backdrop. From a control room, Dall barks at Louie to begin his next test, and as Louie struggles to meet his expectation, a frustrated Dall says, "I'm comin' in."

Dall enters from behind the curtain (not red, mind you) and schools Louie on how things operate. "You come out, you say hello, you start the show," he says. "What's the mystery?" Deciding he needs to show Louie, Dall exits and re-enters from behind the curtain, adjusting his jacket and revealing two gaffer's glasses on thin lanyards around his neck—something Lynch frequently wears on set. As Dall plays to an imaginary crowd, an astonished Louie watches through the monitor and hears applause from the nonexistent audience.

As Doug again stands holding cue cards, Louie asks Dall if he can have more modern references for his practice monologue jokes, and the latter replies, "You're not ready." After he finishes, Dall returns and says, "Let's talk about this," pointing at Louie up and down. "Body, face, beard, hair, clothes: you. Let's talk about it." The pair argue about Louie wearing a suit, at the end of which Dall writes down an address on a piece of paper and instructs Louie to go there. Asked if they're done, Dall mutters, "Dear God, I hope so," while walking back through the curtain.

• • •

While Dall is a finely sketched character, his introduction subtly leans into elements of Lynch's persona, and even work, in a way that delighted fans. That actually began before shooting, with Lynch getting a chance to weigh in on the items in Dall's desk. "We came up with some objects, and we asked David to pick them," said C.K. "Everybody on the show was extremely excited to be working with him. So with another character I wouldn't have gotten that kind of variety, but I asked the prop people to come up with a bunch of props, and then we asked him to handpick what's in the drawer."

While C.K. demurred when asked if certain bits were metatextual nods to Lynch's casting ("Well, they were just more opportunities that came up"), he admitted some editorial choices might have been different without Lynch there.

With respect to the decision to use two secretaries, C.K. said, "Being with David just loosened those things up. I also knew that there were a lot of people watching the episode who know who he is. I wasn't looking for stuff to match with him [necessarily], but I had two very different women read for the part, and I loved them both very much. And I get more attached to scenes like that than I do a scene of great dramatic consequence—just the texture of this woman saying his name over and over again. I had these two terrific actors doing it and I just thought, *Fuck it, let's just get 'em both. Why not?* Having David there gave it a little bit of that freedom."

The droning sound effect was something C.K. married in postproduction to an idea Lynch had shared. "There were very few things that he [asked] to do, but one of them was this gesture with his hand over his ear while he's waiting for me to come in the office," he said. "I wish I could remember what it contained. The sound design was largely stuff that I found, and that was definitely chosen to suit him and . . . bring a little bit of who David is into the character."

While C.K. found inspiration in working opposite Lynch, his other partner in the two scenes was along for the ride, not driving the dialogue, largely silently taking everything in.

Gelbinovich came on in *Louie*'s second season as agent Doug (the joke being, as he explained, that he "looks young, really young, to the point where it almost doesn't even make sense") and ended up appearing in seven episodes across three seasons, including all three in the "Late Show" arc. He said he didn't know he would be acting opposite Lynch until the morning he showed up on set. "I know [Louis] kind of liked to keep things as closed up as possible in terms of who knows what," said Gelbinovich. "They'll do that with a lot of different projects. But in a way, maybe it was even better here, because we aren't really supposed to know what's going on, so then when we meet [Dall], we're even more confused."

C.K., always one to convey exactitude in his dialogue, also worked to maximize the discomfort Louie and Doug feel in their initial encounter with Dall, Gelbinovich noted. Specifically with regard to the blocking for the cue card sequence, "it was about capturing all that awkwardness, where he's like, 'What are we supposed to do?' That's kind of what we were going for," he said. "And I think it worked out really well, where both [our characters] in our own way had no idea what was really happening."

• • •

Lynch not only got to choose the items in Dall's desk, he also brought his own prop to set in the form of the gaffer's glasses. "First thing he said to me when I met him was 'Is it okay if I wear this around my neck?" recalled C.K. "I said, 'Yeah, don't worry about it, of course. It's fine.' I don't think it was that important to him. He just was asking can this character wear this. It's a bit of [added] mystery."

For Gelbinovich, Lynch was a revelation. "He is a force. He was extremely professional," he said. "You can see right away that he's very comfortable with himself. He knew who he was, and he knew he prepared and just said, 'This is what I'm going to do.' And he didn't stray from that. Of course, if there was some direction or something [he would adjust], but it was also so easy to direct him because he didn't really need it."

His initial impressions were solidified in the sequence where Dall puts Louie through the paces, confidently owning the stage as he mock hosts and argues with Louie about a suit. "You put him in a part, whether it's a cameo or something that's a little bit more in-depth, and right away, because he's in it, you just feel the impact of it," said Gelbinovich. "We went through it on both ends, working with him there and then seeing the finished product."

"He just remembered everything so perfectly, the lines," he continued. "But he knew what everyone else was going to say too, to the point that if something was happening, he would [be able to] help out also."

C.K. echoed such descriptions of Lynch's preparation and performance. "He was extremely consistent. He memorized his lines like nobody's business and nailed it. He was very precise. But at the same time, his own little version of saying hello in *The Tonight Show*, it was kind of astonishing. I had written that he was really natural and that it's easy to imagine him as a host, but seeing David do it, I was like, 'I can't believe this is actually taking place.' Him saying hello, good evening—he was perfect. David could have hosted *The Tonight Show*. He would've been a viable and excellent late-night host."

That said, C.K. admitted the production was difficult—but not for reasons one might assume. "I was frustrated I couldn't talk to him about his work or how much I loved him, because that was not an appropriate rapport for us in what we were accomplishing," he said. "When you're working with somebody and you're directing them and shooting scenes with them, you need to have a little quiet between you. And also, I wanted to be respectful of him. I didn't want to trap him into a fan situation, because he was so nice to do the show. We did share a few cigarettes, because he smoked every five or ten minutes during the shoot."

S3 E12: "Late Show Part 3" (Airdate: September 20, 2012)

Dall's first two scenes, as he makes a final push in helping Louie prep for a test show, run about seven minutes in total and come early in the episode, back-to-back. After a half minute during which Louie sits in silence as Dall barks out a series of responses on a phone call, Dall hangs up and starts talking to Louie about taking over for Letterman. This segment includes a humorous explanation of a piece of obvious conversational shorthand, heavily celebrated online, that may have been among the clinchers for Lynch tackling the role (more on this shortly).

"If you wanna be a talk show host, it's better if you're funny," Dall points out, before listing some exceptions to the rule and asking Louie if he's ever had any experience with being funny. Told that he does, Dall responds, "You're a comedian? Well, I've known you for a week and you haven't made me laugh once. I had no idea you were a comedian. I thought you were a newsman."

Dall orders Louie to make him laugh, but Louie can't rise to the challenge. "You're just scared, like a rookie—you're like some kid at a talent show with a number pinned to your shirt," Dall tells him and gives him a series of increasingly stern countdowns. After Louie makes a heartfelt plea ("This is either a door or a wall for me") and eventually has a breakthrough, an expressionless Dall tells him, "You just bought yourself another week." The sequence ends with a great button ("Please leave this room," says Dall to Doug) in which it is revealed that Louie's agent has been sitting just off-screen the entire time, witnessing this debacle.

This scene flows directly into the next, set back on the studio stage, this time on a mock set for a practice session. Dall, seated in the deep background, berates Louie for sitting in the wrong spot ("No, genius, sit in the host chair, for cryin' in a cup!"), then orders him to conduct an interview. After a befuddled Louie points out there's no guest, Dall exits, muttering to himself, and returns, gently shepherding a diminutive cleaning lady, introducing her as Elaine (Polina Nikiforova).

Louie's attempts at small talk turn uncomfortable when he accidentally elicits painful memories from Elaine about her mother. From the wing, Dall fumes: "Oh, this is terrific, just wonderful—tune in every night folks. It's the crying cleaning lady show!"

In Dall's final scene (which was actually the first thing Lynch shot), he visits Louie and Doug in the former's dressing room before Louie tapes his test show and brings him a tailored suit. Dall sits on the armrest of Doug's chair (mirroring an earlier scene with Garry Marshall) and tells Louie this will be the last time they see each other. "If you get the show, they'll bring in some young producer. If you don't, well then that'll be that," he says. "In any case, I told you what I know, and the rest is up to you. It's just if you can do it."

As Doug stares up at him from an awkward angle, Dall says he's going to impart the three rules of show business. As the camera pushes in, Dall says, "Number one: look 'em in the eye and speak from the heart. Number two: you gotta go away to come back. And number three: if someone asks you to keep a secret, their secret is a lie." Louie takes in the advice (a portion of which turns out to be especially valuable), thanks Dall for everything, and stands to shake his hand. Dall stares at Louie, leaves his hand unshaken, and wishes him good luck before exiting.

• • •

When asked if there's a particular line he's happiest with having put in Lynch's mouth, C.K. pondered the bountiful array of potential responses. "I don't know, it might be him in front of the curtain just saying 'Good evening.' And it also might've been 'You've got to go away to come back,' that little speech. And also his monologue about 'You better get that belly moving.' I think there's a lot of truth in it, and he said that with conviction. I love the way he did it."

C.K. had no doubts about what Lynch's favorite line was, however. "When he was first brought in the studio and I was introduced to him, I was a little nervous," he said. "And he was not formal. He was just a regular guy, but I told him we were going to shoot this [first] scene in this little room. And he said, 'Okay, champ. That's short for champion,' and he had a big grin on his face. So I knew that was his favorite line, and he was excited to say it. So that was a lovely thing."

Louie's second office scene with Dall lands so well because it builds to a place of sincere emotional resonance, flowing from Louie finally overcoming some of the blockage that has been crippling him with self-doubt. It also works because while viewers have seen Doug and Louie together in all of the previous scenes, Louie's intense personal humiliation tricks the mind into forgetting the former's absence. It's a master stroke of conceptualization, camera placement, and editing—even when Louie stands, before he leaves, we never see Doug—and Lynch's flattened line reading is the cherry (or perhaps just its twisted stem) on top of the sundae.

The practice interview, meanwhile, represents the classic "two-steps-back" idiom, finding Louie once again getting Nancy Kerrigan-ed by the monsters of uncertainty in his head just as much as by Dall's verbal onslaughts.

"I think probably my favorite thing in the whole arc was him with Elaine," said C.K. "I think that was the best because . . . I worked at NBC, and I know this culture. There actually is a cleaning woman named Elaine. Every time I would go back to 30 Rock she was there, and we'd give each other a big hug. And there's a kind of relationship between the quiet, mousy, light-blue-wearing cleaning women and [TV] executives. There's a weird connection there [in that] both [have] been around for a while. And he was the right guy to play that because he is a great artist and a very down-to-earth, American, apple pie boy at the same moment. And I know that's saying a lot about a small thing, but I think his gentleness with her in the scene, and then his contempt for my inability to just be a fucking human being and talk to somebody, [is fantastic]."

For Nikiforova, the audition for *Louie* hit close to home. "Sorry to say it, but it was a very sad time. My mom passed away in 2009, and 2012 is not much time for me," she said. "Plus, because I'm talking about my mom as well in this episode it was very close to my heart."

That same sorrowful connection to the material that helped her book the role helped during rehearsal, when she refused artificial tear assistance, and then during shooting as well. "I said, 'No, I can cry, no worries,'" said Nikiforova. "And every time we do this, again and again, I always cry, and David [would give] two thumbs up."

Maybe there is something to C.K.'s description of the cross-class bond between custodial services and career corporate managers. "David, God bless his memory, he was around me all day during shooting," said Nikiforova. "We just met, but he was taking care of me like I don't even know [who]. My phone wasn't working inside, and he showed me a place where I can call somebody and talk to my son on the phone. And when I was walking around in the hallway like crazy [during a delay], he said, 'That's what we do. Sometimes we have to wait a very long time.' All shooting day, he was around me. I don't know why he was so kind—just a very real person."

For all the notable laugh lines present in his four other scenes (and there are many of them), it's probably the final scene that certifies the depth and deftness of Lynch's performance—again, all the more remarkable given that it was filmed first. Dall, softened and reflective, for the first time makes an effort to connect with Louie on his terms. And Gelbinovich had a close-up, if imperfect, view of the whole sequence. "His timing was just perfect. And because his timing was perfect I feel like, from my perspective, I worked off of him," reflected Gelbinovich. "The way that he just presented himself in that scene, it was like, 'This is him, this is his part, he *is* this character.'"

While Dall exits Louie's life without a handshake, in real life C.K. was able to reconnect with Lynch and finally have a more personal moment of the sort that he had scrupulously avoided during shooting. "Later, I got to visit him in his home, and I saw where he worked, and that was really special," said C.K. "I think it was a couple of years afterward. I was going to LA, and we had corresponded a little. We always kept up with each other up until only a few years ago. I would always get emails from him in all caps for some reason.

"As a hang, he was just kind of quiet, and he would just want to sit and keep company a little," he continued. "I was always comfortable with him. I always felt like I was with a nice person, a kind person, and he was a little lost in his head in a way that was very charming."

Looking back with gratitude, C.K. reflected on some of the lessons he absorbed, as well as firsthand perspective gained on Lynch as an artist. "I think the thing that David and I have in common and that I learned from him is the idea that if you're going to make a story about something that's really not in reality, something that doesn't follow the rules of regular reality, or the obvious rules of fiction and building of tension and three-act structure—if you're going to walk away from that stuff—you should be dedicated to it," C.K. said.

"David, because he's an artist, a visual artist, deals in material," he continued. "He's like, 'I'm going to make a painting with a piece of cotton fluff coming out of it, so I need to know something about how that material behaves.' He's not just some weirdo with a cigarette telling people 'Be weird.' He's fucking *dedicated*, and he's executing—just in a world of strange ideas."

• • •

In addition to offering a wonderful role and showcase for Lynch's comedic instincts, *Louie* taught him something valuable that he carried forth with him into other acting endeavors. "When he did *Louie*, he was given lines [in advance]," said Sabrina Sutherland. "And I think doing voice-over, you can read the lines as you're going, but actually being on camera, David had either had small parts in the past or he wrote the parts, so he would know what to say. But with the Louis C.K. show, he'd memorized everything, but he hadn't said it out loud. And when he went to say it out loud, he realized that it's a whole different thing, and he had to relearn it by speaking it out loud. That was his epiphany—that he had to actually voice it. You can't just memorize the lines and kind of mouth stuff. You actually have to talk and hear yourself and repeat that in order to get it right. So definitely that was what he learned from *Louie* . . . and it was something that he did always reference afterward as well."

If the show taught Lynch a lesson, it also was an instructive experience for others. Unpacking the two-day shoot offers a compelling case study on the power that Lynch had to connect deeply with folks whose lives intersected with his own only very briefly.

Nikiforova, much like her character, seems like someone quite often looked through or past, but possessing a rich interior life many choose not to see. She was a traveling performer who first came to the United States in 1989 with the Moscow Circus, touring for two years. During that time, she met George Carlin in Las Vegas, and he advised her on the importance of performing artists always having multiple streams of income—what we'd call a side hustle, in today's parlance.

When Nikiforova returned to New York in 1993 to start a family, she went to school for *ashiatsu* massage ("They need petite women like me, forty-seven kilograms") and started a job at a Manhattan spa, where today she still works one day a week while enjoying time with her two grandchildren. In between, she also resurrected a vaudevillian-style, costumed musical act in which she portrayed different gendered characters while playing the piano, trombone, and more. She auditioned for *America's Got Talent* in 2008 as a novelty act with her beloved mother. And, yes, she wrote a screenplay about her adventurous existence. She lived a full life, even as many artistic dreams went unfulfilled.

That she felt extraordinarily seen by Lynch, even in their portion of one day together, is a little thing that feels telling. "David was, like, perfect. He was all day with me, nobody else. I couldn't believe it," recalled Nikiforova with a wide smile. "I think we could be friends maybe. He was a big dreamer, and I like that. He is a surrealist. It's hard for people to understand his movies—they're not for a wide audience. I like that. He's like nobody else, right? And I'm a big dreamer also, all my life."

Gelbinovich also felt greatly impacted by his brief time with Lynch. "I never forgot that experience, because I feel like I took so much from it in such a short time. I'll never forget how unique it was. And I am so grateful for it. It's very emotional, because when you work with someone like that and then they're not . . .." Here he paused, trailing off for a moment and composing himself. "In as short of a time frame as it might have been, it's still an impact. And for someone to have an impact like that, it doesn't happen often."

Listening to both Gelbinovich and Nikiforova describe the strength of their interactions with Lynch now, many years later and knowing more about his work, it's easy to fall into the trap of assigning an almost shamanistic quality to Lynch's presence. But it's worth noting they had not been fans of Lynch's work in the same way as Louis C.K.

Gelbinovich had seen some of *Twin Peaks* and was familiar enough with Lynch's major works to know who he was. Nikiforova, however, had not even that frame of reference. "To be honest, no, I didn't even know it's David Lynch," admitted Nikiforova. "I spoke to my son, and he said, 'What's the cast?' And I said, 'I don't know, David Lynch.' He said, 'Polina! David Lynch!?'"

Lynch's personal impact seems to be not so much, if at all, about wow-factor celebrity and more the combined result of sincere kindness and a preternatural ability to simply be present. That the latter quality is frequently remarked upon as a hallmark of good actors seems not to be a coincidence.

−CHAPTER 32−

"MEMORY FILM" (2012)

Coming out of his experience on *Louie*, Lynch was presumably meeting with Mark Frost—the first inkling that a return of *Twin Peaks* was being kicked around by the pair. In the fall, Swiss art curator Hans Ulrich Obrist, whom Lynch knew personally and met with many times throughout the years, requested a short-form video contribution for a gathering dubbed the Memory Marathon. Lynch balked at the initially suggested length of ten to twenty minutes and instead created "Memory Film," running just over four minutes.

The seventh in an acclaimed series of themed art events held at the Serpentine Galleries—a pair of affiliated contemporary art museums in Kensington Gardens, Greater London—the three-day weekend featured contributions and in-person presentations from a wide-ranging collection of artists, scientists, theorists, musicians, and others. The event was billed as a minifestival investigating the "problem" of memory, including anything and everything under that umbrella, from personal and collective histories to trauma, forgetting, and embodied remembrances. It took place October 12-14, 2012.

Lynch had long been interested in memory. And issues of recollection, perspective and fractured identity figure prominently in a good deal of his work, from Fred Madison's comment in *Lost Highway* ("I like to remember things my own way. How I remembered them, not necessarily the way they happened") and Rita's amnesia in *Mulholland Drive* to even the unusual two-part structure of Lynch's memoir *Room to Dream*, in which Kristine McKenna's researched biographical segments are intercut with his reminiscences on the same topics.

In a 2018 interview with Lynch, I touched on the subject, because in portions of the memoir he displays an almost eidetic memory—recalling not just mood, but also names and places with incredible clarity dating back to his childhood. Other times, when someone is describing a major creative choice on his part, he insists he is unable to recall it. When I asked Lynch whether there are particular *types* of things, moments, or people that he is more likely to recall, he paused and took a long beat. "That's a very good question, but no," he said. "I don't know why some things are, like you say, very, very clear in the memory bank. My first wife, Peggy, was telling me just the other day that one night we drove to this place, and she told me that we were there with this other person. But I don't remember that *at* all. She remembers it, but that other person is not in my memory. I remember us alone. So this is just the way it is—selective memory."

Lynch's "Memory Film," then, is interesting to ponder as a subconscious excavation of remembrance, creativity, and their intersection with mental health. It opens against the backdrop of an accordion-forward score, with Lynch's right hand clasped over his eyes and nose. A cut-out paper eye floats across the screen and over his face. This is interrupted by the assaultive sounds of a battle and a shaky-camera view of one of his artworks featuring a plane, which is then X-ed out three times.

Next, two eyes float across the screen, their shadows falling across Lynch's (still covered) face and body, which are flush right. Back to planes and warfare. A close-up of Lynch, then a wider shot in which what at first looks like an oval potato drifts across the screen, lingering on its lefthand side before it disappears. Then a handcrafted Santa Claus (complete with the sound of jingles) floats across the screen and stops, before that too is X-ed out.

The plane returns and again is X-ed. More component parts (lips, nose) float by, haphazardly arranged before eventually coalescing on the left side of the screen, forming a figure we recognize as the face of Vincent van Gogh. This is followed by a slicing sound effect and small, animated blood droplets bursting forth from the side of his head. Clothes and background elements fade into focus, and as the profile snaps into a proper, bordered likeness, Lynch removes his hand and looks at van Gogh.

The image is modeled after a fairly well-known self-portrait of the artist, one of several painted in January 1889, in which van Gogh appears with his bandaged ear, wearing a heavy jacket and hat, smoking a pipe. Lynch was assisted with the special animated effects on the piece by Noriko Miyakawa, who worked in various editorial capacities for him dating back to some 2010 commercials and would go on to serve as a visual effects and editing compositor on the third season of *Twin Peaks*. Dean Hurley handled the piece's mixing.

Lynch presents here as a seeker, but one self-restricted by blindness. The juxtaposition with van Gogh, whose self-torment Lynch was convinced hindered rather than aided his artistic genius, is quite intentional. "I like to think that van Gogh would have been even more prolific and even greater if he wasn't so restricted by the things tormenting him," Lynch said in *Catching the Big Fish*. "I don't think it was pain that made him so great. I think his painting brought him whatever happiness he had."

In finally aligning their visages and gazes, Lynch seems to be trying to speak across time to a fellow creative visionary—one who was never able to escape the war zone inside his head and was so troubled that he eventually took his own life.

—CHAPTER 33—

LAFORET MUSEUM EXHIBITION (2012)

Lynch was no stranger to retrospectives, awards, and various other honorifics, particularly as his career wound on. And for these events, he often liked to craft bespoke short-form pieces.

"He liked having an idea first, before accepting something, but if he had to accept something before an idea, then that was something that really kind of stressed him," said Sabrina Sutherland, Lynch's longtime producer.

Perhaps a somewhat low-key example of this stress arrives in this seventy-second video touting a November 10, 2012, exhibition of his work at

Tokyo's Laforet Museum in the Harajuku commercial district.

In it, Lynch stands in front of the familiar red-curtained backdrop in his home studio, clad in a black coat and white button-down shirt. Various animated objects, including ladders and the swirling logo from his *DumbLand* days, free float around him. After offering a brief phonetic greeting to everyone in Japanese, he forthrightly introduces the planned presentation of his artwork.

In the exhibition, he says, there will be paintings, watercolors, drawings, and photographs. Upon his enunciation of "painting," an image of his 2010 mixed-media piece *Boy Lights Fire* covers the entire screen. After three seconds, Lynch lifts it up above his head, out of frame. A box, animated in primary colors, briefly covers his face before Lynch pops it off his head, and it remains floating, a set of chattering white keys representing teeth protruding from its right side.

As Lynch mentions each of the other categories of his work, an example, accompanied by the sound of a bell, pops on the screen (one to his left, one to his right, the last over his chest), which he indicates with his hands before guiding them off-screen, set to the sound effect of a slide whistle. After Lynch says, "Please come to the Laforet Museum and enjoy the show," the hovering colored box snaps back down over Lynch's head. In a muffled voice, he then says, "Thank you. *Arigatō*."

A wonderful example of Lynch's longtime affinity for his personal workspace ("a pretty good deal," as he said to me and plenty of other reporters over the years), his frequent commingling of media, and his playful sense of self-presentation, this work richly embodies light-lift, air-quote performance as a way to remain connected to the essentiality of his restless, ever-present creative spirit.

—CHAPTER 34—

"DAVID LYNCH: BETWEEN TWO WORLDS" (2015)

As his producer on *The Return* and all sorts of other content, Sabrina Sutherland rode shotgun on a multitude of Lynch's creative endeavors over the last fifteen-plus years of his career. So for something to rank as her favorite in the short-form/commercial performative realm (Gordon Cole remains her overall favorite role from Lynch) is no small matter.

Crafted in support of Lynch's first Australian multimedia exhibition, at the Gallery of Modern Art in Brisbane, "David Lynch: Between Two Worlds" (not to be confused with the same-named *Twin Peaks* home video extra, in which Lynch interviews the assembled Palmer family) is a two-minute audiovisual piece, with an emphasis on audio, that basically serves as a teaser for the show, which took place March 14 to June 7, 2015.

Its animated tableaux, taken from his 2004 mixed-media piece *Well . . . I Can Dream, Can't I?*, centers on a mustard-colored female figure sprawled out on a yellow couch, legs splayed open, nude except for buckled Mary Jane shoes and a pair of panties gathered around one knee. In her left hand she clutches the receiver of a pink rotary-dial phone. The animation consists of mouth and occasional head movements as Lynch provides the voices for a dialogue between two women, Marge and an unnamed friend.

After briefly commiserating with her friend about the state of the world, Marge tries to relay that her husband tried to kill her again that morning and instead shot their dog in the living room, but the friend replies, "The only bright spot I see is the David Lynch show at the Queensland Art Gallery, Gallery of Modern Art."

When an agitated Marge interrupts and repeats herself, her friend exclaims, "Well, take a couple of Xanax and call the cops. He can't get away with treating you like this. Firing a weapon in the house?! D-I-V-O-R-C-E is what I'm thinking." Upon confirming details of the show (which also appear on screen), Marge determines that she wants to attend and begins laughing hysterically. "Yeah, settle down, Marge," her friend advises before adding, "I hope [Lynch is] there. He's such a dreamboat."

"Oh my God, you're not kidding," says Marge. "But the girls say he's calmed down some." Her friend considers this and says, "Yeah, I guess he is getting on in years. Aren't we all?"

No word on whether Marge and her friend made it, but Lynch did indeed attend the event in person and sat for a moderated conversation in front of around fifteen hundred people the night before its opening, discussing his upbringing, inspirations, and some of his work. The showcase itself, comprising two hundred-plus works, from photographs, large mixed-media pieces, and drawings to lamps and sketches on table napkins and matchbooks, even included one room built fully to scale as a 3-D replica of one of his pictures.

This occurred in the period leading up to Lynch's brief withdrawal from the third season of *Twin Peaks*, a fact to which he alluded in a number of contemporaneous interviews, laying down a marker by speaking about negotiations for the show and the fact that he hadn't officially returned yet.

"Every time I hear it, it makes me at least smile, if not laugh," said Sutherland, when asked why it is her favorite short-form performance piece from Lynch. "It's just his sense of humor. He would always say to people, 'Settle down.' If I was going on about something, he'd say, 'Settle down, Sabrina.' So, I mean, it was really kind of him." Here she paused briefly. "And he liked to say he was a dreamboat," she added with a laugh.

Lynch recorded the audio and edited "Between Two Worlds" with Noriko Miyakawa. While giving a nod to the swirling darkness of the real world (and perhaps winking at the type of bizarre true crime programming that Lynch professed to enjoy), this work both showcases Lynch's sense of humor by good-naturedly tweaking his self-image as a Casanova and also serves as another example of his correlative belief that the art life's creativity shouldn't be restricted to specific mediums. That it might also have served as a release, however slight, from the ongoing uncertainty surrounding his participation in *Twin Peaks* is an interesting thing to ponder.

–CHAPTER 35–

TRIBECA DISRUPTIVE INNOVATION AWARD (2015)

The 2013 cancellation of *The Cleveland Show*, along with the deep-dive nature of Lynch's collaboration with Mark Frost on the scripting of *The Return*, explains a gap in Lynch's performative work.

On April 24, 2015, however, Lynch dipped back into acting by way of the premiere of a new short video offering. While Mattel's intervention over his 2011 David Lynch Signature Cup Coffee ad put a temporary end to Lynch's experimentation with what might have become an ongoing series of dialogues with Barbie, he returned to the doll with this quasisequel, which gave the character the cover of a different proper name and seemed to limn a world in which the pair had become a couple.

Running four minutes and twenty-five seconds, the piece served as the video acceptance for Lynch's Tribeca Disruptive Innovation Award—celebrating innovators who broke with tradition to help foster positive change in different industries—honoring his advocacy of Transcendental Meditation through his eponymous foundation. It uses the same Optigan "Romantic Strings" score, in three-quarter time, but finds Barbie's head swaddled in a soft purple cloth instead of Lynch's bare hand.

"Hi, Dave isn't here right now. But he asked me to thank you all on his behalf. Actually, all of them asked me to thank you," says Trixie, this time definitively disembodied. "I was telling Dave that my form of meditation is taking all my clothes off and laying in the sun at the beach. That's what I like."

A phone rings, and she answers. "Trixie, it's Dave. I'm down at the store. I can't find that nail polish you asked me to get. Are you sure about the name of that stuff?" After some back-and-forth about this purchase, Trixie shares what she told viewers about her form of meditation.

"Trixie, how many times have I gotta tell you—laying in the sun isn't meditation," says Lynch. "Going for a jog or reading a book, that's not meditation. Transcendental Meditation is a technique that allows any human being to dive within and experience the deepest level of life, that ocean of pure consciousness within every human being."

Following some further joyful promulgation of meditation's benefits, Lynch ends by saying, "It's such a blessing for the human being." After affirmation from Trixie ("Gee, Dave, it sounds so good"), Lynch asks if she told the audience about her surprise. She says no and then reminds Lynch about shampoo she asked him to get. "Oh, right," says Lynch. "Blast! Shampoo and nail polish. Okay, Trixie, I'll see ya later." After a brief introduction by Trixie and an accompanying drumroll, we cut to three little plastic birds of the same sort glimpsed garnering applause from Lynch in *The Art Life*. Arranged in a row in front of a branded Tribeca Disruptive Innovation Awards sledgehammer, they chirp out a brief melody before "Thank you" flashes on the screen.

At this point, Lynch's daughter Lula with then-wife Emily Stofle would have been about two and a half years old, so it's certainly possible that Barbie dolls were part of her life and thus reintroduced into Lynch's day-to-day routine. But clearly there is also thought put into advancing the "narrative" of the pair's relationship, which is amusing to consider.

Taken in tandem with "Between Two Worlds" before it, this short leans into both high absurdity and rib-nudging notions of public-image massaging. When one further considers some of Gordon Cole's scenes in *The Return*—delivered in its final scripted form to Showtime only three months earlier—it seems cheekily affirming his heartthrob status was very much on Lynch's mind at the time.

Unfortunately, footage showing the reaction of the awards show audience, particularly during the portion where Barbie talks about her predilection for nude sunbathing, doesn't seem to exist. Nevertheless, this short-form effort confirms that for Lynch, it's a Barbie world.

–CHAPTER 36–

FAMILY GUY (2010, 2016)

After making his first appearance in *The Cleveland Show* on February 21, 2010, and then appearing in two more episodes that season, Lynch made his debut on the "mothership" of the extended *Family Guy* universe in "The Splendid Source," falling chronologically between those later two episodes of *The Cleveland Show*.

Airing on May 16, 2010, the nineteenth episode of *Family Guy*'s eighth season marks the first official crossover between the two series. In it, Peter Griffin and his friends Quagmire and Joe attempt to find the origin of the world's dirtiest joke. After tracking its journey through a chain of possible sources, including REO Speedwagon ("Heard it from a friend, who heard it from a friend . . . "), they're told it came from a Virginia bartender.

Hijacking a road trip vacation planned by their wives, the gang detours and heads south, ending up at The Broken Stool. "Hi there, what can I do for you gentlemen?" Gus, the establishment's bartender (voiced by Lynch), asks. Handed an index card by Quagmire and told that they've traveled a long way to find out where he heard this joke, Gus exclaims "oh!" and lets out a raspy laugh. "I remember that! I heard it from that guy!" Gus says, pointing to Cleveland and sending the group in furtherance of their quest. Gus's narrative obligation thus fulfilled, Lynch's *Family Guy* initiation is complete.

• • •

Lynch's most famous appearance on *Family Guy*, however, came years later, when he voiced himself in an irreverent, self-referential cameo in "How the

Griffin Stole Christmas," which aired on December 11, 2016.

The fifteenth-season episode centers on Peter getting hired as a mall Santa Claus and falling in love with all the freebies the job offers while Brian and Stewie crash office holiday parties and the latter accidentally lands a job. "I think that was maybe my third or fourth season at *Family Guy*," said Aaron Lee, the credited writer on the episode. "I had done a couple seasons, and I just remember . . . being happy because the Christmas episodes get rerun a lot, and that means more money."

The twenty-five-second Lynch bit, arriving in the cold open, kicks off the episode after the opening-credits theme song. In the Griffin den, Brian, Chris, Meg, and Stewie are all gathered watching a TV program that an announcer, coming back from a commercial break, reintroduces as *How David Lynch Stole Christmas*.

As a child shakes a gift under a Christmas tree, Lynch—dressed in a black blazer with a white dress shirt buttoned up to the collar—slithers down a chimney decorated with stockings. "Hello, I got you a present," he says, producing a gift-wrapped box from behind his back and opening it. "It's a thumb."

The child recoils in terror. "Don't look away. Let the fear wash over you," says Lynch. "I don't understand," the confused child replies. "That's the whole point," Lynch says. "Now did you leave a plate of black coffee out for me?" After Lynch is told no, his eyebrows and voice fall slightly in uniform disappointment, and he gently admonishes the child: "In the future, please leave a plate of black coffee out for me. Also in the past."

As much as anything he ever did performancewise for a project initiated by an outside party, this beloved *Family Guy* cameo reflects Lynch's refusal to take himself seriously, even while still taking his work seriously. It's a series of pitch-perfect line readings—straightforward and sincere, then tinted with a soupçon of sadness when he realizes there is no delicious coffee to be had. Naturally, Lynch had no control over the actual animation of the episode. But there's a subtle moment at the end of the scene—the lids of his eyes lowering with the delivery of the punchline—that seems to indicate a level of in-on-the-joke knowingness with regard to Lynch's participation, even within the series itself.

This type of TV-show-within-a-show riff is a regular feature of animated programs in which characters consume in-world media, but also a particularly popular staple of *Family Guy*. These would get pitched in group sessions; the jokes that achieved consensus support would then get fleshed out a bit more. Sometimes, though, less refinement was needed.

"You would get sent into rooms [to] just come up with ten TV gags," recalled Lee. "So basically we were in a room where the assignment was just to pitch an opening TV gag for the Christmas episode I was writing, and Kevin Biggins pitched that whole thing, almost top to bottom verbatim . . . [and] we were dying laughing. And at *Family Guy*, you then go and kind of perform your own bits at the end of the day for all the other writers who weren't in your room, to see what gets laughs. Kevin performed it there, it got huge laughs, everybody loved it, and it went straight in the show. I think maybe the punchline got changed a little bit at some point, but I have to say that is a Kevin Biggins piece from start to finish. My name is on the episode and I love that I get the credit, but the truth is it was entirely Kevin."

"I remember thinking what's the most absurd thing, and I think it just started with the rhyme of Grinch and Lynch," laughed Biggins, who confirmed the inclusion of a thumb was a coded *Blue Velvet* reference. "I just enjoyed him so much from my experience with him on *The Cleveland Show*. I knew, or at least thought, he would be game to acknowledge his absurdity, or his love of the absurd rather, in that gag. And I knew there would be a chance we could get him because he'd already done all the episodes of *The Cleveland Show*. Those are some things [you think about], and all those things that I was checking off were green lights to go ahead and pitch this— because if it got a good response, then logistically it would work out."

For Biggins, the Lynch-as-Grinch bit was not a random one-off either. The *Family Guy* writing staff at the time was populated with fans of Lynch. Mike Henry—who'd been a writer on the first seven seasons and continued to do voice work on the show—helped seed that ground before launching *The Cleveland Show*, but many, many others deeply appreciated both Lynch's work and his unique persona. "I myself usually would pitch two or three David Lynch TV gags a year," said Biggins, sharing the example of a pitch involving an exploding grenade after its David Lynch pin is pulled. "And I'm very happy that one made it all the way to TV, because I just think his cadence and delivery is so humorous."

Of those pitches that didn't make it to air, Biggins has one particular favorite. "It was gonna be called 'David Lynch on Ice,'" he said. "I think it was he comes out, and there's a blue curtain [behind him]. It was all of his movies set to [ice skating]. That was in a script of mine, and it was in a few versions. . . . I was thinking, *What's the most absurd Ice Capades that could be?* and I thought we'd maybe have bits about *Mulholland Drive* and *Blue Velvet* and *Lost Highway*. I was just trying to get all the [iconic] imagery I actually remember from his movies, like the dumpster monster [from *Mulholland Drive*], the scary guy by the end of the bed in *Twin Peaks*. They were all in there, and I think with Laura Palmer, somebody slid her across [the ice, wrapped in plastic]. It was kind of morbid.

"But again, the great thing about David Lynch is that you would assume that he's probably game for just about anything and seemed to have a good sense of humor about himself. As dark as some of his stuff was, he always seemed to kind of have a little wink and a nod where he could see the humor in it."

−CHAPTER 37−

GIRLFRIEND'S DAY (2017)

During my career as an entertainment journalist, I've had the good fortune to travel to many film festivals, both internationally and domestically. These experiences have always been special because I find "film people" are overwhelmingly curious and empathetic, and the events serve as living reminders that one's tribe has nothing to do with geographical proximity or race or gender or so many other popular classifications and actually everything to do with how one sees the world, chooses to interact with it, and treats the people around them.

Once upon a time, at a smaller, regional festival, in the context of a conversation about some of the challenges it faced, I was asked about programming ideas. For whatever reason, my mind immediately jumped to the fact that for reasons both understandable and vexing, law enforcement, doctors, lawyers, and the military are overrepresented in on-screen entertainment—even in the independent realm. My idea, then, was a prize-awarded film section (or even an entire festival) throwing a spotlight on underrepresented and/or unusual occupations, the idea being that in time it could potentially spur not only new creative thought patterns with respect to character and storytelling, but also new cinematic voices.

For many reasons, this half pitch never came to fruition, but I still think about the idea occasionally, and an example of something that could have found welcome reception within this concept is director Michael Paul Stephenson's *Girlfriend's Day*, a dark comedy cowritten over a period of fifteen years by Bob Odenkirk (who also stars) and Philip Zlotorynski. The movie is set in the world of greeting card writers (novels, it's said, are for people who can't edit themselves), and it's a surprisingly ambitious, genre-straddling affair (a pinch of noir seasoning, a bit of a *The Big Lebowski* vibe at times) that unfolds in a stylized, effectively budget-managed Los Angeles.

While wrapped around a love story, *Girlfriend's Day* also dips into 1970s conspiracy thrillers, with a modern, absurdist bent. At its center is Ray Wentworth (Odenkirk), an award-winning card writer whose best days may be behind him. Fired from his job and weighed down by a recent divorce that saddles him with writer's block, Ray finds himself pulled into a high-stakes contest to produce the best card submission for the newly created titular holiday.

How exactly, you might be wondering, does *Girlfriend's Day*—shot in the fall of 2015, at the same time as *Twin Peaks*'s third season—intersect with a performance from Lynch? His contribution comes by way of a three-sentence voice-over narration to open the film, authoritatively setting up its vocational backdrop. "His [Odenkirk's] production company reached out to our office and pitched the idea of David just recording the intro, and David was a huge fan of *Breaking Bad* and *Better Call Saul*," said Michael Barile, Lynch's assistant at the time. "He loved Bob Odenkirk's character, and he was happy to do it."

Lynch recorded his voice-over on June 20, 2016, and Netflix, in an understandable but misbegotten attempt to attach some relevance to its premiere date, released the movie on Valentine's Day 2017.

Lynch's twenty-five-second narration unfolds under a montage of cards on their way from a printing press and assembly line to loading pallets and stores and finally to the hand of a purchaser picking it off the rack. "Last year Americans purchased upwards of $3 billion in greeting cards. Weddings, romance, thank-yous, and birthdays are all sales leaders, with major holidays providing steady profits. It's a thriving industry where it's often said the right card can make the day," says Lynch, punching the word "said."

Lynch's delivery here—sincere and straightforward—provides no preview of the movie's offbeat tone, nor its twists and turns. Instead, it credibly sets the table for the eccentric exploration of a most unconventional occupation—another already damaged by digital technology and, sadly, possibly awaiting AI-driven decimation. While Lynch's participation seems mostly rooted in his Saul Goodman fandom, one fun connection to Lynchland is *Girlfriend's Day* costar Amber Tamblyn—the wife of frequent Odenkirk collaborator David Cross, and the daughter of Russ Tamblyn.

Given the distinctiveness of Lynch's voice, this type of work was an alternate, light-lift creative path he could have easily carved out for himself if he desired. That he didn't opt for considerable or even just steady cash-in—in a space virtually no one would have batted an eye at or held against him—suggests that each voice-over choice held for Lynch some significance, however small or unapparent at the time. Here, it seems a "game-recognizes-game" act of piqued curiosity, rooted in the belief that if multihyphenate Odenkirk was telling a story set against this unusual backdrop, it would be a *Day* worth lending his voice to.

—CHAPTER 38—

LUCKY (2017)

David Lynch and Harry Dean Stanton were close friends for almost three decades. The latter costarred in Lynch's 1988 short "The Cowboy and the Frenchman," playing a character whose difficulty hearing and the comedic value mined from said impairment could, without too much squinting, be seen as an inspiration for Gordon Cole.

Stanton would go on to appear in six more of the director's projects, including scene-stealing work as exasperated trailer park manager Carl Rodd in *Fire Walk With Me*, a role he reprised nearly a quarter century later in the third season of *Twin Peaks*. After Stanton had finished shooting the latter project, but before it aired, he shot what would be his penultimate film credit and final starring role, in the lovingly crafted and criminally underseen drama *Lucky*.

Directed by veteran character actor John Carroll Lynch (no relation to David), the movie is coscripted by Drago Sumonja and Logan Sparks, who worked as Stanton's assistant on *Big Love* and became close friends with him despite their age gap. The title character of the film, which draws extensively from Stanton's own life experiences and philosophy ("Harry Dean Stanton is . . . Lucky" reads the title card), is a chain-smoking, curmudgeonly atheist who lives in a small California desert town, does morning yoga in his underwear, and enjoys a simple life of routines as he grapples over the course of several days with questions of mortality after suffering a fall at home.

Upon receiving a clean bill of health from his doctor (Ed Begley Jr.) and having a frank conversation about aging, Lucky seems to soften, just by degrees, in his behavior toward Loretta (Yvonne Huff) and Joe (Barry Shabaka Henley), the waitress and owner of the diner he frequents; Paulie

(James Darren), the husband of the owner of the bar he visits; and Howard (David Lynch), who counts Lucky as perhaps his closest human friend, behind only his beloved pet tortoise, President Roosevelt.

Elegiac but still coursing with a surprising vitality, *Lucky* is very much a character study, as its title suggests. But it pushes well past the unambitious shape and plotting of numerous similar films, touching both the profound and the mystical with its moving blend of small, just-so moments; artful symbolism; and intriguing ambiguity.

• • •

John Carroll Lynch was initially approached to appear in *Lucky* as an actor, and with Stanton's involvement it was a quick, easy yes. When Begley Jr. vacated the director's chair in August 2015 (he would remain as an actor), Sumonja phoned Lynch, who by that time was in Atlanta shooting *The Founder*, to gauge his interest in stepping in. "We had a long conversation about what the movie from the directing chair looks like," said Lynch, "because it's a very different commitment—two days is a very different commitment to a year, essentially. Also, you ask the question 'What is the movie about?' Not what your scenes are about, but what the movie is about."

Lynch found his response to the screenplay heavily colored by his diagnosis with prostate cancer less than four years earlier, when he was only fifty. Being forced to confront his own mortality cast his life's priorities into starker relief. Consequently, he found *Lucky*'s story particularly resonant, if also fraught with challenges.

"It's a very tricky piece of material because it's Harry's life, fictionalized," said Lynch. "So the pieces were always extraordinarily strong—the language, the dialogue. It was 'What's the story we're telling?' The thing we [Sumonja, Sparks and Lynch] talked about a lot was that even though it's Harry's biography, it's Lucky's story. So how is Lucky different than Harry? And what's Lucky going through? How do you follow an entirely interior journey and where Lucky is at any individual moment? That was entirely the work that we did on the film over about three months of back-and-forth and noting and arguments and agreements and all that.

"So we worked to get it on page," he continued. "I'm a big believer [in working] on the script, because that's the cheapest way to make the movie. Then you'll know what you really need." Further refinements came by way of Ira Steven Behr (*Star Trek: Deep Space Nine, Outlander*) and Richard Kahan, who came on board as producers and helped strengthen some of the supporting characters.

Influence on the film's final sequence also flowed from an unexpected source, as the team arrived at what they felt was a workable final draft early in the new year. "Drago called Logan . . . and said, 'This is gonna sound crazy, but I want to end the movie the way Burt Reynolds looked at us in *Smokey and the Bandit*. I want Harry to have that moment where he just looks at us,'" said Lynch. "And the day of shooting it, we're out in the desert. Harry's just exhausted, and he's doing that shot and lights his cigarette and turns and looks at us and smiles." Here Lynch pauses. "I still get choked up about it. It was so beautiful to see on that little clamshell monitor, and it felt so right for that movie. But the inspiration being *Smokey and the Bandit* makes me laugh."

With the script suitably sharpened, the filmmakers started looking in earnest for financing in January 2016. "When you have an eighty-nine-year-old lead, a quick no is really good; a quick yes is better," quipped Lynch with a smile.

A little family money from Sparks and John Carroll Lynch got things rolling ("I approached a cousin of mine who is a photographer and loves filmmaking, and he agreed to help finance a portion of the film," said the director), and the group got its first outside commitment in the spring from Superlative, a microfinancing organization run by Danielle Renfrew Behrens. Greg Gilreath and Adam Hendricks at Divide/Conquer liked the screenplay, signed on, and invited other potential investors to a script reading with Stanton. Lagralane Group then came on board with the final third of funding.

Sam Shepard originally agreed to play the part of Howard (the role David Lynch wound up playing) but ended up not being able to travel out of state due to a pending DUI charge. Later, on the set of *The Return* in the early spring of 2016, Sparks mentioned to his friend Michael Barile, Lynch's assistant, that he was working on *Lucky* and there was a part for Lynch if he wanted it.

"I mentioned the idea to David, and he was open to it because he liked the thought of working with Harry," said Barile. "So Logan sent over the pages for Howard, and I read them to David in his trailer on set. David liked the writing and agreed to the part if the schedule worked out, which we arranged so that it would."

For the *Lucky* team, the conditional yes was thrilling news but not the end of the road. Relationships had helped open the door to the casting, and David Lynch's affection for Stanton and the material had sealed the deal. But still lurking was one of the great Hollywood bugaboos: the possibility of scheduling conflicts.

Financing for *Lucky* ended up being contingent upon four participants included in the final contracts: Stanton, John Carroll Lynch, Begley Jr. (as an actor), and David Lynch. "If any one of those pieces had fallen out, we would have had to search for somebody of commensurate value or scuttled the picture," said the director.

"It was primarily Logan's relationship with Harry and Logan's relationship with David's assistant and Logan's relationship with David that allowed us to facilitate David's participation in the movie," John Carroll Lynch continued. "He was the one who managed to boat that marlin. We had to simply be patient as the bureaucracy unfolded. It was at times quite tense while we waited for dates."

• • •

Lucky's shoot was never going to be normal. To accommodate the age of its lead, the production team staggered its eighteen shooting days, choosing to film three or at most four days per week.

For *Lucky*'s sun-drenched walking scenes throughout town and certain key exteriors, producers chose Piru, a small unincorporated historic town with a population of a couple of thousand roughly fifty miles northwest of Los Angeles. One and a half days in Arizona were added, not far from Sparks's family home, for the real desert scenes, set among saguaros. Interiors for Lucky's house, the diner, and Elaine's (the bar frequented by Lucky and his friends) were shot in the San Fernando Valley, with the VFW Post in Van Nuys standing in for Elaine's.

David Lynch was busy editing *The Return* at this time. The needle to thread, then, was finding a window outside of his editing that would also work for the *Lucky* team. Those dates turned out to be Saturday, July 2, and Sunday, July 3.

Sabrina Sutherland and Barile accompanied Lynch to the shoot, along with his then-wife Emily Stofle and their young daughter, Lula. For Lynch, this provided a break from the detail-oriented pressure-cooker of postproduction on *Twin Peaks*. He showed up all systems go, wholly ready to embody a character who—in the hands of a lesser actor, and if not imbued with the proper emotional sincerity—could have come across as an empty eccentric.

The two Lynches met in David's trailer upon his arrival to go over the material. "I wanted a bow tie for his character," said John Carroll Lynch. "And he said, 'I'd like to tie it like this,' which was basically just a circle with a bow tie short. And I said, you know, fine." Here he laughed. "I wasn't worried too much about that. Then we started to work. And he was extraordinarily giving to me as a director, a first-time director particularly. He was there fully prepared to do the work—as I would imagine he would expect of his own actors."

This approach of individual preparation rather than structured run-throughs mirrored the director's tack with Stanton. "With Harry, I wouldn't say what we did was rehearse," said Lynch. "We would read parts, and sometimes Harry would say, 'I would never say that.' And Logan would say, 'You said that last week. I mean literally, word for word, that's what you said last week.' And Harry would go, 'Eh, I don't know.'"

Among Lynch's scenes is an important one with Stanton and Ron Livingston, who portrays Bobby, a lawyer attempting to assist Howard in setting up a will. Like many participants, Livingston signed on for a chance to appear opposite Stanton: "I kind of said yes right there. And then David Lynch [too] was like, 'That's gravy!'"

While unfamiliar with Lynch as a performer and thus unsure of what to expect showing up on set, Livingston was acquainted with Lynch's directorial work.

"I had seen a lot of his stuff. The first moment I'd become aware of him was *Twin Peaks*," said Livingston. "It was the episode where Kyle MacLachlan has the big chalkboard out in the field and is throwing rocks at the bottle. And it's one of those things that I didn't sit down to watch. I just stumbled upon it. I'm clicking around and it was on, and I couldn't turn away from it.

"*Blue Velvet* I think was the next thing that I was aware of, and that is such a strong thing, with its own flavor. I think I only learned later that *The Elephant Man* was his," he continued. "It took me a while to get back to *Eraserhead*. I'd seen *Wild at Heart*. Also, I grew up in Eastern Iowa, and *The Straight Story* gets Iowa right better than any movie I've ever seen that references Iowa. I was like, 'Yeah, that's us. That's the people; that's the affect. Those are the relationships, and that's how you solve a problem.'"

Livingston also had read Lynch's *Catching the Big Fish*. "That was really interesting. And it's funny, because in the last maybe fifteen years I've gotten into using dreamscapes and Jungian stuff in my acting and creative work," he said. "But before that, I was reading about David Lynch's version of doing it, and it seemed both crazy and amazing. So I think his was probably the first exposure I had to that being a way into the subconscious. And I feel like that's what I would say about him as a director anyway—that he very much let the subconscious be the star of the movie and didn't stick it in a supporting role. He let subconscious [elements] be front and center and didn't apologize for the moments where it didn't seem to add up or make sense. That was just part of the mystery."

• • •

Lynch's Howard appears in three scenes, all at the bar *Lucky*'s main characters frequent, totaling a bit over eleven minutes of screen time.

At the 15:06 mark, as Lucky enjoys a Bloody Maria at Elaine's, a bothered Howard enters (orange bow tie askew) wearing a cream-colored, slightly too-roomy suit and a white fedora. "President Roosevelt escaped," he says, the surname pronounced with a U. "I saw him eyeing that gate the other day—he had to have timed it out perfectly." Other patrons rib him about the notion of a tortoise being able to slip away, but Lucky sticks up for his friend. "I'm gonna miss him," Howard says of his tortoise before exiting to the bathroom. "He's outlived two of my wives."

At the 34:50 mark, Howard meets with Bobby to discuss an end-of-life plan that will leave his assets to President Roosevelt. This time he sports a dark suit, his hat sitting nearby on the booth table. Lucky ambles over, and after some back-and-forth becomes increasingly agitated, feeling that Bobby is taking advantage of his friend. "The tortoise is an amazing creature, Lucky," says Howard. "They're as noble as a king and as kindhearted as a grandmother. I miss my friend, his company. I miss his personality." When Lucky inadvertently misidentifies Roosevelt as a turtle, Howard explodes, giving Lynch responsibility for one of the movie's big emotional releases. "You all think of a tortoise as something slow. But I think about the burden he has to carry around on his back," says an impassioned Howard. "Yeah, it's for protection, but ultimately it's the coffin he's gonna get buried in. And he has to drag that thing around his entire life? Go ahead and laugh, but he affected me, you know what I'm saying? He affected me. There are some things in this universe, ladies and gentlemen, that are bigger than all of us, and a tortoise is one of them!"

Seventy-three minutes into the film, in a scene lasting more than five minutes, Howard appears again sporting his fedora, in a third suit with a green bow tie. Lucky assumes his well-worn seat next to him at the bar, and Howard reflects on the still-missing Roosevelt with newfound serenity. "I kept thinking about how much time he spent planning his escape and how much care he took in making sure I couldn't find him," he says. "And then I started to realize that he wasn't leaving me, he was just going off someplace else to do something he thought was important. I even felt guilty for standing in his way for so long. So I stopped looking for him. If it's meant to be, I'll see him again. He knows where I am, and I'm leaving the gate open."

This sequence ends with Lucky attempting to light a cigarette indoors and being ordered not to do so by Elaine (Beth Grant). After delivering what could be viewed as a characteristically pessimistic view of both the afterlife and the present, Lucky is then queried about the meaning of life. His rejoinder engenders thoughtful reflection from all present and indicates an awakening of sorts on Lucky's part.

• • •

Lynch's arrival on set, coming later in the shoot, was hotly anticipated by crew and cast alike. "I'd say because both he and Harry Dean are such luminous personages, there was a certain amount of everybody on set just [wanting] to hear them tell stories," said Livingston with a smile.

"So I just did a lot of listening," he continued. "I was a little bit of a fly on the wall trying to just hear the stories that he was talking about. People [would] come up with questions, and they want to kiss the ring a little bit. And he was lovely about, 'Okay, well, I'm going to tell a little bit about the thing that they have come up saying they're interested in, I'm going to give a little nugget.' He was very gracious about doing that [between scenes]."

While everyone else may have been eager to hear the pair reminisce, Lynch and Stanton's bond transcended the need for a lot of conversational patter. "The warmth between them, the love between them, was as clear then as it was in the documentary [*Harry Dean Stanton: Partly Fiction*]," said director Lynch. "The two of them could have sat on that couch with a cup of coffee and like two children just smiled at each other for an hour or so. There would have been no problem. They [didn't] really need to talk, in my brief experience with the two of them."

When it came time to shoot, though, Lynch the actor was dialed in, all business. "On *Lucky*, he was one of the most prepared actors there, and there was a lot of great talent," said Barile. "And that's not to say anything against any of the other actors. But I feel like on a set, there's a lot going on and people are getting direction and there's time between takes and stuff, and David just nailed the mark every single time."

"Once the scene started with him, it was really cool because I kind of compare it to when you go see outsider art a little bit," added Livingston, "where it's really compelling and dropped in and grounded, but it doesn't follow any of the rules they teach you in drama school about what to do with your voice and how to modulate [it]. So it was really unique and individual. And also, he didn't seem to have any nervousness. There was no sign that this wasn't the thing that he does for a living, and I just remember marveling at that."

Stanton and Lynch's friendship of nearly thirty years did come with some side effects, however. "There was a moment where Harry was struggling with this one beat that we ended up cutting from the film because Harry was actually right," John Carroll Lynch recalled. "It was just a beat with Beth Grant, and he said, 'Why am I even turning to her right now? Why is that happening?' And I said, 'Well, Harry, this is kind of why.' And as with every actor in the world I've ever worked with, looking for allies for a moment they want to get out of, he turned to David and said, 'Well, what do you think?' And David looked at me and I said, 'Jump in. I'm happy to have this conversation, because as an actor I don't want to be shut out of these conversations.' And he turned back to Harry. 'Do you understand the moment?' Harry said, and David said, 'Yes.' And Harry said, 'Well, what is it?' And David said, 'It's not my place to say, Harry.'

"So David took notes. He played with everyone in the piece," the director continued, implicitly praising Lynch's respect for boundaries and the separation of responsibilities. The sole exception to this came during the filming of the climactic bar scene, the third and final shared sequence between these two old friends. While Stanton felt his character was experiencing a moment of heretofore unrealized clarity, there was disagreement about how to present the dialogue, and Lynch the actor finally asked if he might make a suggestion. Told yes, Lynch opined, "Harry, you aren't having a revelation— you've known this secret your entire life. You're just now finding the words to manifest the idea." The viewpoint helped unlock something special, resulting in what is seen in the finished scene.

"[David's] gift to the picture was not only his love of Harry," said John Carroll Lynch, "but his love of the craft of acting and actors, and his love and dedication to filmmaking in general."

• • •

While it's been clipped and bandied about on social media in a way that frames it differently, Lynch's aforementioned monologue—which includes an uninterrupted shot of nearly forty seconds—lends *Lucky* a moment of unexpected emotional power. It works so totally owing in part to the fact that it's a marriage of slightly offbeat material and like-minded performer, yes, but also because it rings true as a moment of someone blowing their top over something that matters deeply and sincerely to them even if no one else had ever stopped to consider things from that perspective.

"The structure and energy of that scene is that I'm kind of a hanger-on," said Livingston. "I'm the one [who] keeps trying to bring it back to the practical, and I don't really understand 100 percent what they're talking about. So I didn't have to do a lot. His monologue, talking about the tortoise, is its own shape. It's its own tone. It's so completely kind of him. It also is so completely of the movie that we're doing. It's a set-piece monologue that's not delivered as a set piece. It kind of feels like it's pouring out of him. I was really struck by that.

"It didn't feel like it was copied from anything that anyone else had ever done before," Livingston continued. "And that was the kind of comparison that had me draw back to thinking of him as a director, [because] I don't remember ever seeing him do something that felt like it was derivative of something else."

"I just remember [the monologue] being very emotional," Sutherland concurred. "I thought he hit it really well, he did such a great job."

There were significant struggles during the production—though not because of Lynch. "The real challenge of the job, and it's the reason I signed onto it, is I said, 'This is probably Harry Dean Stanton's last movie. I'm coming in service of that,'" said Livingston. "And when I got there I think is when I realized, 'Oh, and that's going to require a lot.' Because he couldn't really hear what you were saying unless you were shouting it at him. At that point, his short-term working memory for lines was not there. He couldn't really see the sides to read them. So a lot of it was like, 'Alright, what do we need to do to help Harry, to set Harry up to succeed in this and so that he can bring his magic?' It was a lot of stop-start takes and aborted takes and calling for lines. And I really had to go, 'Oh, I'm going to be yelling all my lines in this scene, even the ones that are not necessarily to him.'" Here Livingston laughed in fond recollection. "I'm going to be yelling them so that he can hear the cues and know when to talk, and that's going to be okay. That's what I'm here for."

"Ron, I'm always beholden to him for saying yes to the film, but also for his magnanimity and willingness to play in frustrating circumstances, because Harry was quite frustrated," said John Carroll Lynch. "He was struggling with lines. And mostly he was struggling with lines—in my opinion, I never really got to ask him this—but because he was nervous in front of David. He really wanted to be good, and I think he was nervous. There were other reasons—it was at the end of the shoot, and he had been through a lot. And it was very dense material. So all of that was the case. But Ron was quite patient with everything and played with whatever was there. He never lost concentration. And neither did David when things were frustrating. There's an energy or an atmosphere on a set that the director has to maintain, which is a kind of quiet serenity . . . a confidence that we're going to get the scene. And there were times that Harry certainly felt like he was letting us down. I did not feel that way, and no one else around felt that way. But as an actor you start to feel fearful, and the door that you're walking through to get your performance gets narrow. There were moments where that happened."

"That bit would be way above my pay grade," said Livingston when asked if he felt Stanton was additionally on edge due to acting opposite his longtime friend. "I would never have put that together. But again, I didn't have the lead-in. I didn't know what their [full] relationship was.

"I feel like so much of acting is about overcoming nervousness, walking in nervous and then letting it go," he added. "So Harry Dean's stuff . . . it didn't seem novel to me. I've seen actors do that a lot, and that's a lot of people's process sometimes. They're hard on themselves, and they want it to go well—sometimes that's just how people do it. And then some people feel that way inside, but they're blithe and pretend like they don't care, and they kind of mask it all. That's a different style too, and I don't think necessarily either of them leads to any better results than the other.

"I think however you get to the part where you're saying the line and it's coming from down deep and you're a conduit for it . . . I feel like, for me anyway, that's what I'm always chasing," Livingston continued. "And that's the thing: I saw Harry Dean do that. It might take us fourteen times, but then when it came, it's like, 'Oh, *that's* Harry Dean Stanton.' It's dropped in, it's inhabited."

• • •

After production was complete, the filmmakers pushed for a cut to submit to Sundance, but the movie was not accepted. South by Southwest was targeted as the next logical domestic festival destination, and a test screening at Vidiots in Santa Monica helped John Carroll Lynch hone the picture.

"That was extremely helpful. A lot of filmmakers came and had thoughts or questions about the movie," he said. "And many of those things put to rest some of the arguments that were going on in the production in terms of 'How can we afford this song, or is there some other way to do it?'

"There were a couple of scenes that were tricky," Lynch continued. "They just didn't work. I misshot them, frankly, and Frank [Reynolds, credited with additional editing] helped wrangle those into the movie."

The film was accepted into South by Southwest and made its world premiere on March 11, 2017. Stanton, whose health was in decline, didn't attend; John Carroll Lynch attended but didn't watch the movie. "I couldn't," he said, likening the experience to that of a theater director who doesn't go to the first show. "You're finished; your job is over. But it was received very well."

Reviews were indeed glowing, and within three weeks Magnolia Pictures acquired the film's worldwide distribution rights and slated it for a fall release. The movie opened in theaters on September 29, 2017—exactly two weeks after Stanton passed away at the age of ninety-one.

In that interregnum period, during which director Lynch was back on the East Coast working, he didn't personally speak with Stanton, instead connecting when he could through Sparks. "Harry didn't want to watch the movie on an iPad; he wanted to watch it in a theater," Lynch said. "And I don't think he ever saw [the full film]." As Stanton at this time was experiencing ups and downs, and would eventually land in hospice care, not only was a theatrical viewing experience infeasible, but even finding several consecutive hours for Stanton to intently focus on *Lucky* in its entirety was difficult. Sparks did, however, share with Stanton several of the movie's key scenes, including those with his old friend David Lynch.

A week before its theatrical release and a week after Stanton died, the film premiered in Los Angeles. "One of the people who came was Dabney [Coleman]. At the time he was losing his eyesight to macular degeneration, so he had to sit in the front row and look at the movie from the side of his eyes. And he was a rag at the end of the film," said Lynch. "It was emotional for him, as it was for all of us, in different degrees. I had an odd feeling about it. I loved Harry. I loved him as a person before I met him, really. And then when I met him, I thought he was a tremendously interesting, very difficult man in so many ways. And our relationship was almost entirely professional. But I think more about Harry today than I did at the time. I think about *him* now. The older I get, the more I think about him."

Lucky and Stanton's performance were each lauded at several festivals. But director Lynch can't help but think what if Stanton had been alive to bask in the response. "It would've been my belief that had he lived, I think there would have been an opportunity for the Academy [of Motion Picture Arts and Sciences] to laud him, if not for that film then for his career. But it didn't happen," he said. "But it's a stupendous piece of work. And like *Birdman* in a lot of ways, it's an actor revealing themselves so fully—of using their own emotional lives so transparently—that I don't think people understand how raw that is. There were many times in production that Harry was really confused about 'How much am I really revealing of myself?' And I'm not sure he was always comfortable with it. Like with the mockingbird story, I'm sure he was most definitely not comfortable. And like Lucky, he felt his failing abilities in the course of the film. But all of that is part of what the makeup of the movie is."

Despite the sadness of Stanton not getting to bear witness to the full final version of the film and feel the embrace of its reception, there is a nice moment of kismet that brought the two Lynches together again and put a bow on the special collaboration.

Among a number of European festivals to which *Lucky* traveled in the fall of 2017 was Camerimage, held annually in November in Toruń, Poland. John Carroll Lynch went, and David Lynch, who had a longstanding relationship with the festival, was invited as well, showing the first two episodes of *Twin Peaks: The Return* and christening the grand opening of *Silence and Dynamism*, a multidisciplinary exhibition featuring over four hundred works of his art.

"He did a talk back, and he had a great gift of not answering anybody's questions," said John Carroll Lynch with a smile. "People would ask him specifics about all kinds of movies and he would say, 'Well, that's in the movie. I already said it.' And a woman stood up, was called on. She asked about *Elephant Man*. She said it's her favorite David Lynch film and she loves it because it's so different from all the others and why did David think that? And he said, 'Well, it's a different story, so I needed to do it differently. And I love that story. And it's really love that steers the boat.'"

That answer made John Carroll Lynch reflect upon the other Lynch in his movie. "David was in *Lucky* because he loved Harry, because he was asked, and because he read it. And you know, I have no illusions about the fact that he wouldn't have done it if he thought the script sucked or he was at all uncomfortable with me in the directing chair. He would have figured out a way to get out of it, I imagine. But he was there exclusively because he loved Harry."

—CHAPTER 39—

"THE BLACK GHIANDOLA" (2017)

Depending on a perspective informed largely by one's age, it's either a bit odd or not at all unusual that Johnny Depp and David Lynch never worked together. To some, Depp is Captain Jack Sparrow—and perhaps the perfect on-screen conduit for the imagination of Tim Burton, with whom he worked across eight movies.

But before he became a globe-straddling superstar, throughout much of the 1990s Depp was largely devoted to channeling eccentric characters while also leaning into commercially risky projects. His penchant for offbeat fare and mixed tonalities would seem to align, on a certain level, with Lynch's sensibilities. Alas, it never worked out. (There was an offer out to Depp, and serious consideration, on *Lost Highway*, but that's another story.)

But wait, Lynch and Depp actually *did* share a screen credit—just not in the manner and defined roles one might expect. The pair's collaboration comes not in the form of a feature film, but by way of "The Black Ghiandola," a 2017 short cowritten by and starring terminally ill teenager Anthony Conti.

The Make a Film Foundation, a nonprofit organization founded in 2006 by filmmaker and arts advocate Tamika Lamison, helps children with serious medical conditions create short films by teaming them up with Hollywood professionals, and of course all the institutional knowledge that comes with that experience. While all cast and crew donate their time, budgets can still land in the mid-to-high-five-figure range, funded almost entirely by donations. The nature of the organization's work means that production is both fast-paced and chaotic, with many details often being finalized last minute.

Children frequently choose to make short documentaries dealing directly with their illnesses. But of course that's not dictated. And Conti had strong ideas about what his dream of a Hollywood production would be. Born in 2000, and growing up in Walpole, Massachusetts, about twenty miles south of Boston, Conti had long loved films, particularly the horror genre, as well as the TV show *The Walking Dead*. From the time he was ten years old, he was intrigued by acting and then even making short movies. In 2016, he was enrolled in a summer film course when he learned of his shocking diagnosis—stage four adrenocortical carcinoma, a rare cancer attacking the adrenal glands inside the upper abdomen, on top of each kidney. Conti reached out to MAFF, which at first wasn't sure there would be enough time to grant his wish. He wanted to make a zombie movie.

• • •

Adele Jones came to be involved with MAFF by way of chance attendance of a 2011 taping of the syndicated daytime talk show *The Doctors*. "I said to myself, 'Wow, I am going to get involved in this foundation.' And I really believed that this was a day that was going to change the rest of my life," said Jones, who was in large measure so moved because she was very familiar with disability and caregiving through her family, with one of her brothers having suffered a spinal cord injury and becoming quadriplegic after being shot when she was still quite young.

Jones, an actress who also worked as a casting director and an operations manager at historic Los Angeles venues the Wiltern Theatre and Palladium, met up with Lamison, and immediately hit it off. "[Tamika] and I both realized she'd be great at bringing in all the crew, and I'd be exactly who she needed to bring in all of the A-list talent," said Jones, whose first film with the organization was 2012's "The Magic Bracelet," which she cast with Hailee Steinfeld, J. K. Simmons, and James Van Der Beek.

"The thing that's so crazy about Make a Film Foundation, which makes it very hard on the casting side, is that number one, it's free," Jones said. "So you're asking people to take off a day a week in exchange for the high-dollar amounts they get paid, because we're asking A-listers to block that out [in advance]. And that's hard. So a lot of times it gets booked last minute. You might be working on this thing for six months, but the reality of who's going to fit into what role is who's available two weeks before [or less] for that date. So it's a whirlwind."

MAFF's commitment to top talent is with good reason, though. "Number one, which is the least obvious I think to the public, is that generally speaking these are the people that do the job," Jones noted. "They're the best. And if I've got one take with my sick kid, I need the A-team. Number two, the light it can bring to a child's illness and that story. And number three, well, the excitement of course, that it would bring to the child."

"The Black Ghiandola," which would come to be shot over five nonconsecutive days by a trio of directors (Catherine Hardwicke, Sam Raimi, and Ted Melfi), is in certain ways a good old-fashioned, postapocalyptic reanimated-undead flick. But it's also deeply rooted in its lead's off-screen condition (*ghiandola* is Italian for gland, a nod to the site of Conti's cancer) and a philosophical grappling with the inexplicable randomness and basic unfairness of it. Scott Kosar (*The Texas Chainsaw Massacre* and *The Amityville Horror* remakes) and Wash Westmoreland (*Still Alice*) helped mentor Conti on the scripting of his idea, giving shape to his vision.

In the sixteen-minute short, Conti stars as Jacob. After returning to an abandoned house and discovering a panicked video left by his trapped father (Simmons), Jacob makes his way to a hospital. There, an oddly positive-minded doctor (Richard Chamberlain) gives him a good bill of health before a mysterious med tech (Depp) advises Jacob of his course of treatment just prior to meeting a bloody end. Later, Jacob shelters a girl, Bri (Jade Pettyjohn), from her abusive stepfather (Chad Coleman), before the security of his house is breached, leading to a final standoff.

In late October 2016, Hardwicke shot a day with just Simmons for his recorded monologue that opens the movie. Melfi shot day two, which was the other side of that scene, on Friday, November 11, with Conti. That left three days of production, which were planned to shoot in sequential order over a long weekend.

When Conti told Jones that *The Elephant Man* was one of his favorite movies, she got to work. She reached out to Anthony Hopkins in early November; he wanted to participate, but his schedule was booked up, and he asked to instead donate to the organization. Jones got Bruce Davison, who played John Merrick on Broadway, to help provide mentorship to Conti. Unrelatedly, Trent Reznor and Atticus Ross came on board to do the short film's music. Directors like Spike Jonze connected with Conti too.

Jones reached out to Lynch on Wednesday, November 16, which

happened to be one year to the day after her last shooting day in the role of Lieutenant Knox in *The Return*. She'd been hesitant but was encouraged by one of her mentors, Lynch's longtime casting director Johanna Ray. "I felt so intimidated to reach out to him. But Johanna said to me, 'Adele, I could help you if you wanted. However, better yet, why don't you just reach out to him yourself and go ahead and copy me on the email so he knows who gave you his personal email address?'"

Jones swallowed hard and took the plunge. "I remember writing to David: 'Anthony, although he's a young spirit, is still fighting, and he has an affinity for the arts and also the grotesque,'" said Jones with a smile. She explained that Conti's health was deteriorating quickly, so the nature of the project was that it was moving forward quickly and she needed an answer, whether yea or nay.

Jones gave Lynch the option of three possible days for filming—that Friday, Saturday, or Sunday, with the first two days in Burbank and the latter being in Simi Valley. "I said Sam Raimi has some ideas and we will take you in any capacity that you can be there—if you can be there for thirty minutes, if you can be there for one hour. If you can be there for four [hours], I might put you in special effects makeup," she said. "I gave a lot of options, [because] if David said yes, I wanted him to do whatever he wants to do."

Additionally, taking Ray's advice to her to heart, Jones mentioned to Conti that it would be more impactful if he also made an appeal to Lynch directly. So she had Conti record a short video and sent it along as well.

Lynch came back with an answer: he had thirty minutes on Friday, because he was heading to another commitment that evening that happened to also be in Burbank. Jones then explained that Raimi's schedule had shifted, so Hardwicke would be directing him instead, and sent Lynch his lines.

Four hours prior to emailing Lynch, while she was still working up the courage, Jones had also emailed Laura Dern in an entirely separate ask. When Dern came back with a yes as well, after Lynch, the fluidity of the situation—not necessarily atypical for a MAFF project—required a rewrite. "We added stuff into the script that wasn't there, because originally David was actually going to walk through and talk to [Anthony] and ask him about a crinkled candy bar wrapper that was lavender," said Jones.

"Anthony was like, 'Yeah, I just want David to walk in as himself. I just want him to show up in the film,'" Jones continued. "So he called him the Man in Black, which is so funny. He reminds me in a way [of one of the woodsmen] in *Twin Peaks*, but without all the makeup."

For Hardwicke—ebullient in her recollections, and prone to wide eyes and wider smiles that read as relived, can-you-believe-this? joyfulness—

her week had begun with work on other projects, believing her MAFF commitment over. When Raimi's schedule changed and Jones reached out, Hardwicke agreed to pick up a half-day Friday shoot with Chamberlain. "I'm in the middle of other projects or TV or development or something," she said, "and I remember (thinking), *Okay, I'm directing a nice little scene with Anthony and Dr. Kildare tomorrow. Love it.*"

Around four o'clock on Thursday, Hardwicke received a phone call informing her of Lynch and Dern's participation the next day. "They're going to come by the set, and they're going to have thirty minutes," she recalled. "He's going to wear what he always wears, that's going to be his costume. He's going to walk in and say a couple lines and leave. That's all you got.

"I'm like, 'Great, what's he going to say?' 'Well, you need to write something for him.' I literally stop whatever project I was on and go online and watch him in a couple little podcasts and interviews. I'm like, 'Okay, how can I integrate that to the scene?' I write up a scene in twenty minutes. I send it back to them. They send it to David. He approves it. He's in. He and Laura are in."

Hardwicke's capacity for adaptability wasn't through being tested, however. "One hour later they call up, and Johnny Depp wants to be in the movie tomorrow. I'm like, what? 'And he's got two hours, but not the same as theirs—he's coming first, and then they're going to come in.' I'm like, okay. I mean, is this real?" recalled Hardwicke with a laugh.

"So I'm trying to expand the scene to fit Johnny in [but instead] make a whole new scene for Johnny. . . .I just kind of made up stuff on the spot and just reacted. Sitting right here," she said, pointing at her stylish home worktable. "I send it out, and Johnny's people approve his scene. I'm like, 'Great, okay, but are these people really going to show?'"

Just two days after Jones's initial email to Lynch, on the afternoon of Friday, November 18, he shot his scene with Dern at Providence Saint Joseph Medical Center in Burbank, a working hospital with an empty wing it loaned out. (Raimi would end up directing both weekend days of production.) Hardwicke's dizzying day, though, would begin in the morning, with Depp and Chamberlain.

Walking in to meet them, she heard Depp rehearsing the wrong lines. "I've never met either of 'em before," Hardwicke noted. "So I've got to be diplomatic. And I walk in there: 'Johnny, hey, by the way, those aren't the lines you're going to say. Richard Chamberlain's going to say that. And he's, like, in his seventies, I think we should let him do his lines. . . . You would be this med tech. I wrote a different scene. I thought you'd gotten it, sorry.'" After defusing the momentary confusion, Hardwicke broached another subject that hadn't been passed along to Depp. "I said, 'And do you mind being attacked by a zombie?' And he goes, 'Well, I've been attacked by worse, haven't I?'"

Since Depp's dialogue was studded with medical jargon, they wrote it out on cue cards and coffee cups, but "he just started going way off book at one point, and saying all this crazy-ass shit," recalled Hardwicke with a laugh. "And Anthony just rolled with it. He just improvised with him. [Johnny] said this and this, but Anthony skillfully brought it back to the script [by] himself. He steered it back. We finished the scene and at the end, Johnny wanted to go out and get a cigarette. He ran away, and I looked at Anthony and go, 'Do you realize you just did an incredible improv with Johnny Depp, and you were right there with him the whole time, you were spot-on? You were amazing, and you were the one that brought it back.' He was like, 'Cool!'"

• • •

After a bit of cleanup on set in between scenes (spoiler: there's some blood involved), Lynch and Dern arrived, right on schedule.

Lynch's scene comes at the front end of the sequence at the hospital, which includes infected people in various stages of sickness, and before Jacob's interaction with Chamberlain's doctor. Just past the movie's three-minute mark, as Jacob looks on, Lynch enters in the deep background, while Dern, also portraying a doctor, reacts with puzzlement over Jacob's completely normal test readings. Lynch's so-called Man in Black crosses behind the nameless doctor and grabs her by the left arm. Their twenty-five-second exchange is as follows, after which they hurriedly exit:

Lynch: "How long has it been since you've had a home-cooked meal?"
Dern: "Sir, can't you see what's happening here?"
Lynch: "How long?!"
Dern: "Well, actually I've been eating from the vending machine for over a week, and there's nothing left."
Lynch: (menacingly) "I'd like to cook for you."
Dern: "You would? That's lovely."
Lynch: (grabbing her neck) "Lasagna."
Dern: (nervous) "I like lasagna."

Removing the stage direction, this could read as a touching moment of humanity amidst a rising tide of societal unraveling. And in fact that was the intention. Lynch, however, had other ideas. By injecting his line readings with an ambiguous but charged sense of intimidation, a whole new, darkly funny, and yet even more unsettling world opens up—what exactly is going on in this guy's mind, and what meaning or significance does lasagna have to him?

"I heard from Johanna that David and Laura were talking a lot about how they were going to do these lines and that David ultimately decided he was going to threaten her with lasagna. And I just love it," said Jones with a laugh. "It's genius, and he really thought about it. I was told he thought of several different ways to approach it and that when he decided that he was going to threaten her with lasagna, that was it."

For Hardwicke, the moment provided her with a story she'll never forget. "David and Laura come in, and I'm like, 'Ticktock, man, thirty minutes, I've got to be on my game,'" she said. "So I walk in, and boom, we do the scene, and David delivers his lines. I go, 'You know what? I never thought that that was meant to be so sinister. Do you want to try one . . . a different way?' He goes, 'No, I don't. Basically, the way I did it is the way I'm doing it.' And I was kind of shocked—no actor's ever said that to me before, but this is David Lynch! I was like, 'Okay, cool, then that's the way it's going to be. Awesome.' And you know what? I love it."

"He said the lines I wrote, but not in the way I thought he would say it, and he wasn't going to say it any other way," Hardwicke continued. "And it's pretty great the way he said it. I was just going for some variation, but he was not into that. So that's cool." Here she laughed again. "I mean, to me, it couldn't have been more perfect and amazing. Hilarious! I mean, just so unique—there's no human being ever on any planet like this person."

Once their scene was done and the day officially complete, there was time for just a bit of chitchat. Some photos were taken, and then Lynch went on his way, off to his other engagement.

Depp, however, lingered longer. "Johnny was having so much fun that he didn't leave after his two hours. He stayed and played steel-pedal guitar for everybody. We couldn't even get rid of him," said Hardwicke.

"He was there when we were closing down the set, and he was having so much fun," she continued. "He goes, 'I want to run around right now in this outfit and go to 7-Eleven. I'm going to keep this bloody outfit.' And I go, 'Johnny, this is a charity. Are you really going to steal the wardrobe from a charity?' And he goes, 'You're right, that's not cool, is it? Okay, I won't steal it.' He was hysterical, and lovely to Anthony, just lovely."

• • •

After filming, MAFF typically tries to organize both a special Hollywood event as well as a premiere in the filmmaker child's hometown. But with Conti, Jones worried about how the realities of his health situation intersected with their more typical timeline. "I remember knowing, or I should say expecting, that we wouldn't see Anthony again, and that it was a miracle he flew here from Boston as it was," she said. "They were changing his medicine one day that we were on set. The boy had such incredible strength. He was dizzy and his body was regulating to new meds. It was horrible. I said, 'I don't think this kid's going to be back.' I had actually just helped my brother die of ALS, so I'm very good at seeing things, and I just felt like Anthony wasn't doing well."

Still, Jones wanted Conti to have a red-carpet moment. The Media Access Awards, which highlight and promote the representation of disability in film and television, were happening that same night, so Jones contacted them and asked if she could get Conti on the red carpet. They said yes, and Conti attended with Coleman and Simmons at his side.

After Conti returned home, postproduction work on "The Black Ghiandola" began. "I had to call him to do a couple ADR lines we wanted off-camera, lines that weren't clear," said Hardwicke. "He's in the hospital, last days. [I asked how he] was feeling, and he said, 'I can't really chitchat Catherine, because I've got Trent Reznor on the other line. He did the score.' I'm like, okay, you're on your deathbed, but you just worked with Johnny Depp, Laura Dern, David Lynch, and Trent Reznor's on the line too. They said it probably kept him alive another two months.

"What a wild experience—just beautiful for him. They put him with incredible mentors, getting to work with these writers and hear about that process, getting to act with different directors—because we directed him as an actor. So he got multiple experiences like that."

While each director pitched in finishing the segments they shot, Raimi and Jones pulled things forward on the calendar over December's holiday break, working with editor Lisa Robison via Zoom to put together a cut so Conti could see it. "That was sooner than we expected to do it, but we knew how important that was," said Jones. "It got sent to Boston, where he was in the hospital,

and shown with his whole team of nurses. They all got to see it, which was great. And he loved it."

Jones's instincts regarding both the red-carpet experience and the movie's expedited postproduction schedule proved prescient. On January 29, 2017, around a month before what would've been his seventeenth birthday, Conti succumbed to adrenocortical carcinoma.

For many who watch "The Black Ghiandola," their enduring memory will likely be Lynch's singular line delivery, or Depp's eccentric ad-libbing (an extended portion of which, with apologies to the city of Cleveland, pops up in the movie's credits). For Jones, though, among the many remembrances she'll hold dear is one that occurred off-screen between Lynch and Conti.

"I'll never forget this moment. This moment has informed my decisions since I saw it—just in life, in terms of how I go about creatively always doing what I want to do and not worrying about whether or not anybody likes it, because the most important thing is whether or not I feel settled," said Jones. "When David came to set, and I was bringing him to see Catherine and to meet Anthony, David puts his arm on his shoulder and Anthony says, 'Do you like my script?' And David says, 'I do. Do *you* like your script?' And Anthony's like, 'Yeah.' And he's like, 'That's the most important thing.' And that just always resonated with me, because David was like, 'It doesn't matter. I'm here to make your movie. I showed up for you today.' In that way, just, it really doesn't matter," said Jones, her voice catching slightly with emotion and trailing off.

"To see David say that to him, it was like, 'Oh my God, David, everybody dreams about you being in their presence and being in one of your projects,' and you're here showing up for this kid right now and you're saying, 'I'm here for you, and let's do this.'"

—CHAPTER 40—

TWIN PEAKS: THE RETURN (2017)

When I first experienced *Twin Peaks*, I wasn't solely preoccupied with the identity of Laura Palmer's killer. Even upon initial release, I was drawn to its abundance. It was a show that acknowledged secrets and the corrosive power they can hold, even perhaps the biggest secret kept from young people—that some things in life don't have tidy, comforting answers. Its heady expression of mood showed there's more than one way to communicate meaning—a powerful lesson that I would carry forth into a lifetime of plying words.

To a kid absorbed in his own head, the show's ambiguousness felt far more inviting than impenetrable. Its framing as a procedural was a wonderful peg on which to hang narrative, but also expansive mysteries and thoughts about life and our society.

This is all to say that while I don't begrudge theory hounds their fun, which is often quite interesting, to me the notion that there's a single "correct" reading to *Twin Peaks* feels a bit silly. That idea ignores the care and deep emotionality that Lynch and Mark Frost infuse into their characters and their various plights, which seem hardly in service of only one rigid, highly intellectualized artistic statement.

That said, FBI Deputy Director Gordon Cole's expanded role in season three feels noteworthy. And while Lynch and Frost cocreated the character and wrote season three together, I think Cole represents something different for Lynch. The character's evolution from voice cameo to colorful on-screen appearances to someone connected to the show's deepening mysteries and finally a major figure driving its investigatory thread speaks powerfully to a mature artist's evolving relationship with his own work. That *Twin Peaks* represented both Lynch's greatest mainstream success and likely the source of his biggest professional heartache other than *Dune* is additionally significant.

There was a time, older fans can confirm, when references within the series were seen as weighty clues to the show's mysteries—an idea that Frost, at a September 8, 1990, Hollywood Foreign Press Association press conference, parried, describing them instead as "more sort of decorative than they are substantial." Nowadays, parsing metatextual elements (of which there are many) is one way to assign definition to *Twin Peaks*. Because Lynch and Frost trade in dense storytelling and aren't afraid of the figurative and abstract, there are also myriad explanations that unpack the narrative in almost entirely mythic terms.

I enjoy many of these interpretations. They're rich and endlessly fascinating because they reflect different levels of engagement with the material. And with almost every conversation one has with another fan, they're likely to come away with something new to consider. But to view such theories in absolute, concrete terms is a disservice. That tack flattens the spiky and frequently unsettling contradictions, as well as commingled tonalities, that are a large part of what makes Lynch's work so uniquely enthralling. Attempting to examine season three solely through Cole, then, is just another fun exercise—not a planted flag.

The character appears in roughly thirty-two scenes (counting continuations) spread across eleven of the eighteen episodes, or "parts," as Lynch preferred to call them. With principal photography spanning 142 shooting days, from September 2015, to April 14, 2016, not counting the second-unit Parisian shoot, season three of *Twin Peaks* represents the culmination of a life's work, and not merely because it ended up being Lynch's last major directorial effort. I'll proceed with details, impressions, and recollections from collaborators in Lynch's scenes, but end things by zooming out and examining Lynch's re-formed relationship with the character of Cole. As a brief note, while I have incredible love for them, supplemental material like *The Secret History of Twin Peaks* and *Twin Peaks: The Final Dossier* are not factored into character discussion here.

. . .

Lynch appeared as Gordon Cole in the following eleven third-season episodes:

Part 3

Cole's season-three introduction takes place in the Philadelphia FBI office, where he, Tammy Preston (Chrystabell), and Albert Rosenfield (Miguel Ferrer) sit around a table with five other agents. Rosenfield sets the scene, a classic Frost and Lynch subversion of authoritative investigation that serves as a wonderful reminder of the series's embrace of absurdity. A politician stands suspected of murdering his wife, but he's provided a collection of six objects he says serve as clues to the real killer. Surveying the odd assortment, Cole quips, "The congressman's dilemma," before dismissing the team to get to work on the case. Preston then shows Cole and Rosenfield footage from the glass box murders in New York City, prompting by far the most viral of Cole's eight hell-based exclamations (a terse "What the hell?!") in all of *Twin Peaks*. The scene ends with Cole receiving a call regarding the discovery and detention of the long-lost Dale Cooper (Kyle MacLachlan), setting up the trio's travel to South Dakota.

Both Jose Rosete and Heaven Stellar (credited as Kate Romero), two of the aforementioned FBI agents, recall their shooting day, December 12, 2015, being shrouded in mystery.

"I was not told what role I would play or the show I would be working on in advance. Everything was top, top secret," said Stellar.

"I didn't know what I was showing up for. It was super hush-hush. I've never signed so much NDA-type paper work in my life," added Rosete.

After being shuttled to the set at a downtown Los Angeles location in an unmarked black van, they discovered the nature of their work. "My impression of David Lynch as an actor was his extreme intensity in everything he did—his confidence and his authority," recalled Stellar. "His childlike playfulness and extreme commitment were surreal to me, and when I spoke to him he made me feel as though I was the only person in the room."

"I had a goatee he wanted me to shave, and I refused," said Rosete. "Looking back, that was pretty silly of me, but we compromised and I had it trimmed a bit. He was stern and demanding of his crew, but there's nothing wrong with that—he was definitely very much respected. At the end of the night, I couldn't stop thinking what a *great* voice he had. He was smooth and cool, and he made it look easy."

Rosete scored an additional benefit from his work. "I remember going straight to a bar in my suit afterward and telling my bartender actor buddy what I just experienced, and he totally went crazy because he was a *huge* fan," he said. "Free drinks for me that night!"

Part 4

Cole's first appearance here is a scene with Denise Bryson (David Duchovny), and is explored separately in a chapter following this one. The six other scenes find Cole, Rosenfield, and Preston making their way to see the imprisoned Cooper and that visit's aftermath. After an airport pickup and some wordplay shenanigans playing off of Cole's deafness, the FBI trio meet up with Warden Murphy (James Morrison) and Randy Hollister (Karl Makinen), the latter of whom fills them in on the unusual circumstances of Cooper's detainment and the items found in his trunk: cocaine, a machine gun, and a dog leg. Shown Cooper's booking photograph, a stunned Cole says, "Holy jumpin' George. Let's go talk to him."

The third of four brothers whose father was a police detective, the New York-born Makinen was no stranger to being cast as a figure of authority (fun fact: he grew up on Long Island with Moira Kelly, who portrayed Donna Hayward in *Fire Walk With Me*, performing in plays with her in high school). When he met with Johanna Ray, Makinen told the story of an early-career guest-star booking as a murderer on *NYPD Blue*, his father's favorite show. "It was a cop killer in every sense—my father finally gave up on [pestering me about becoming a police officer]," he said.

Cast roughly three weeks before shooting, Makinen was told only that he was going to be working for three days, playing a detective. From the facial hair files, he elected not to shave, noting it's always easier to take off than add on. "I had kind of a handlebar thing, and I thought for sure they were going to tell me to get rid of it," Makinen said. "But David liked it and went with it. It wasn't very typical, but then again there's nothing typical about what he does."

The big walk-and-talk portion of the scene was shot first. "I did hear that sometimes he would work scenes really hard, but we didn't. I'd say we only did three takes maybe for each setup. It wasn't very intricate or a lot," said Makinen. Regarding Lynch's acting, Makinen was struck by his confidence. "There was no switch, no preparing," he said. "He just walked into it, and he was it. He lived it. He knew what it was, which totally makes sense." Here Makinen smiled. "His cadence was really what threw me. I didn't understand the backstory of that. But I didn't know or understand why I had a dog leg either," he added with a laugh.

Cole's next scene, in which he employs a bit of showmanship ("Ladies and gentlemen, I am going to speak now to Special Agent Dale Cooper"), is incredibly tense, as he tries to interpret the creepy automaton behavior of this strange figure behind glass. Leaving, Cole says, "Warden Murphy, I suggest you give him his *private* phone call, and I expect to hear all about it." Outside, Cole and Rosenfield have a postmortem. "Albert, I hate to admit this, but I don't understand this situation at all," says Cole before they land on two certainties: this is a Blue Rose case, and they need to connect with Diane (Laura Dern). The first time we see Cole dial up his hearing aids and speak quietly, this is one of Lynch's finest scenes as an actor, as he injects both deep unease and melancholy into the proceedings.

"The energy was thick," said Chrystabell of the Mr. C interrogation scene. "Tammy is meticulously attuned to Gordon's expressions, his energetic shifts, his emotional changes, because I know Tammy sees that as really a big part of her role in Gordon's life. She's watching the exchange . . . and as Mr. C, Kyle's just got such charisma and gravitas, but Tammy is far more interested in what's happening with Gordon. She's paying attention to Gordon and to Albert [because] their history with the person they're seeing is immense, and its intensity is giving me a lot of information, and I like to have information."

Part 6

Lynch phones it in as (an unseen) Cole here, chatting with Rosenfield as the latter braves a rainstorm while heading to meet up with Diane in a scene shot on December 2, 2015. "Thank you, Albert, and let me remind you that this work you are doing tonight is very, very important. And I will be thinking of you as I drink this fine Bordeaux," says Cole. An interposed "Thank you sweetheart" establishes Cole is not alone and reaffirms his playboy status.

Part 7

Cole appears in five scenes here, the first of which finds him in his office whistling what sounds like Rammstein's "Engel" when Rosenfield knocks and reports on his unsuccessful rendezvous with Diane. The pair then make a house (well, apartment) call. "FBI, champ—friends of Diane," says Cole to Diane's presumed paramour (Jesse Johnson) when the latter answers her door. Unlike some actors cast by way of a conversational tape with Johanna Ray, Johnson knew he was meeting for *Twin Peaks*. But he had no familiarity with the series, and no information was given to him about the character prior to shooting. "I didn't know David was in the scene until I stepped onto the set," said Johnson, who described Lynch's screen persona as "effortless, calm, aware of everything—incredible command of his voice." Lynch's attention to detail as a director, Johnson said, was unmatched.

The trio's meeting, shot at a private residence on Wilshire Boulevard in the Koreatown area of LA, establishes Diane's profane thorniness ("Fuck you, Gordon"), which necessitates cajoling by Cole: "Diane, this may require a slight change of attitude on your part." She relents and joins Cole, Rosenfield, and Preston on a flight back to South Dakota. En route, Cole tells Preston the left ring finger "is the spiritual mound" and says, "You think about that, Tammy." Upon arrival, Cole reassures Diane before her private visit with "Cooper." Then, after her fraught meeting, he advises Warden Murphy to keep Mr. C detained, and attempts to comfort Diane outside, though with a halting embrace.

James Morrison describes being struck by Lynch's work ever since he first caught *Eraserhead* at Waverly Place Theater in New York. "I saw a kindred spirit, weirdly, and I sort of felt violated in that way because I thought, *Oh my God, this guy's seen into my head and he sees how I see the world,*" he said. From then on, Lynch was one of his favorite filmmakers. That made for a little nervousness, however, after he got his scene sides and saw the characters' names, knowing who had played Cole previously. "I went, 'Oh boy,'" said Morrison with a laugh. "And I'll tell you this because there's just no use in trying to hide it. When I was in the scenes with him, all I could think was *Oh my God, I'm standing toe-to-toe with David Lynch and the cameras are rolling.* And that was for the first maybe thirty seconds, and then I settled down. But it was every take. It wasn't just that I got that out of my system. It was *every* scene. But he made it easy because he just made you feel welcome and that you were a peer, you were a collaborator . . . even though he was a visionary." His apprehensiveness could be channeled into Murphy's interactions with Cole. "He's unique, to say the least. And I was acutely aware of not reacting to him because of my professional relationship in law enforcement," said Morrison.

Lynch's one piece of direction for Morrison was that every time Murphy was around Mr. C, he felt queasy. But Morrison made the point that all the mystery surrounding the production helped create an on-set atmosphere that fed into the finished product. "It worked. I didn't need to go beyond that," he noted. Morrison also said Lynch's multihyphenate skill set was always readily apparent. "One part of you takes precedence over the other, but the other part is always still very active and observant and contributive. So I sensed that in him when I was working with him. . . . And I remember every moment with him, because I really was present," said Morrison, noting the emotional response he had walking back to his trailer after shooting his final scene and Lynch wrapping him out, as the director did with all cast members.

Part 9

Following the brain-melting Part 8, viewers are treated to another Cole-packed episode. Picking up on the plane after the above-described prison visit from Part 7, Cole receives two phone calls, learning first about the discovery of the body of Major Briggs in another part of the state and then that "Cooper flew the coop," as he exclaims. Arriving in Buckhorn, South Dakota, the group meets up with Detective Macklay (Brent Briscoe) and Lieutenant Knox (Adele Jones) to view Briggs's body. Diane hangs back while Macklay, in a walk-and-talk, briefs the group on case particulars before they meet with coroner Constance Talbot (Jane Adams). Cole and Rosenfield, the former's right hand resting on the latter's shoulder throughout, have a hallway discussion about Cooper's years-ago connection to Briggs before returning to the morgue.

Jones, who viewed Lieutenant Knox as "a woman who has been through a lot in life, but glides," felt a kinship with her character's strong sense of duty. This makes sense, given that Jones's own life of robust advocacy and volunteer work (inclusive of "The Black Ghiandola") was shaped in no small part by the experience of having one quadriplegic brother, who suffered a spinal cord injury after being shot, and another diagnosed with ALS.

Knox's military uniform was, in Jones's mind, close enough to politicians' suits to cause her to reflect deeply on her time lobbying in Washington, D.C., on behalf of the ALS Association just six months prior to shooting. "That's why I loved it when [David] called me Lieutenant Knox [off-screen]," said Jones. "I said, I *feel* like Lieutenant Knox. I'm that girl. And I just felt early on that Lieutenant Knox was [somehow] related to Major Briggs, like that he's my uncle. I always felt that way. I'm sure David would never say that or never feel that, I don't know. One way or another, it's open for interpretation."

Her scenes with Lynch were shot in Highland Park on November 14, 2015, and Jones recalled one hiccup during the first take of the walk-and-talk hallway sequence. "David stops and goes, 'Cut, we got to do it again—I was looking into the lens,'" she said with a laugh. Things got a bit more difficult in the morgue. "Filming that scene, I was next to Jane and next to the body, and there were cow intestines—like real cow intestines—in there that smelled so bad," Jones said. Five and a half months pregnant at the time, a queasy Jones asked for a safety bag to be placed just to the right of the camera but ultimately finished shooting and made it back to her trailer before vomiting. "It's funny," she said, "because just being an actor, I didn't want to throw up, I didn't want to mess up my makeup."

Noise was another issue in the morgue setting's confined space. "When David started talking, I knew that he talked loudly, but unless you're in that room, you don't realize how it really feels. Like, he's yelling. You're standing there, and you're like, *My God*. It's not a bad thing, but I'm jarred by this because he would say 'rolling' and start, and then he turned up the level of volume ten times. And rather than thinking about what we're doing there, I am so distracted by the volume of his voice. It was funny."

The episode ends with Cole and others watching Preston question William Hastings (Matthew Lillard) about his search for "the Zone." Sandwiched between that and the morgue sequence, however, is an interesting scene: Cole and Preston join Diane on the steps outside, where she's smoking. After greeting Diane, Preston stands uncomfortably while Cole silently eyes Diane's cigarette for exactly one minute, his eyes darting back and forth to her face more than two dozen times before he removes his hand from his pocket and motions, fingers open, for her to share.

"David is not the director interested in really anyone improvising," said Chrystabell, recounting the genesis of this scene. "He wants things read and executed as the script details. But David and Laura and I were on the Buckhorn [set], and it was the first time David and Laura and I had ever shared time and space. They were supertight, and they loved working together and they had such a lovely repartee. And really I was just basking in the enjoyment of watching them talk. It was so lovely. And David very graciously always was trying to weave me into their conversation.

"So that happened multiple times, where the three of us are sitting there and they drift off into historical references or whatever, and then David brings me back in the conversation. But really, I'm just so happy, and I'm just maybe slightly awkwardly looking over at them in enjoyment. And David picked up on something from our exchange in that moment. So if you can think about the parallel to Tammy, a new person in Cole's life, relatively, to Diane, it was mirroring what was happening in this conversation. The little idea fairy dropped in, and David was like, 'Okay, ladies, we're about to do a scene that's not in the script, and this is what it's going to be.' . . . And it was precisely bringing forth all the elements of this conversation that we were having together and putting it into this scene, which has Tammy kind of awkwardly witnessing this deep connection that goes beyond her with Gordon and Diane. It ends up being a very fertile moment with very little conversation.

"That was one inkling of all of the magic, because there's not really a better word. It was super-, superspecial. And there was many of those in *Twin Peaks*. . . . You can have the best production, the best team, but it can't create the elements that *Twin Peaks* possesses. There is an otherness that is a part of the equation that is undeniable, and it can't be manufactured. You can't plan it, and you can't certainly can't buy it. And somehow David really magnetizes those othernesses, because of probably the people he chooses to work with and [the fact] just that he's available."

Part 10

In between Las Vegas scenes that sketch out imperiled circumstances for Dougie Jones (MacLachlan) is a short, heartwarming beat where Cole and Preston watch Rosenfield enjoying dinner with Buckhorn coroner Talbot. Later, alone in his hotel room, Cole is drawing an antlered creature when he answers a knock at his door and sees a vision of a stricken Laura Palmer, with Sarah faintly calling out for her. As it fades away, Cole invites in a confused Rosenfield, who shares with him intercepted text messages to and from Diane that indicate an at-odds alliance. "I felt it when she hugged me, but this confirms it," says Cole. Preston joins and shares with the men a photo recovered from the site of the New York City glass box murders, showing Mr. C. "Damn! This is something," says Cole. "This is really something."

Part 11

In a seven-and-a-half-minute scene, shot mostly on November 30, 2015, a half dozen folks pull up in two cars to a rundown area with several dilapidated structures, including one next to two shipping containers. Remaining in the backseat of Macklay's car, a rattled Hastings points out where he encountered Briggs. Rosenfield and Cole spot one of the woodsmen before passing through an opening in a chainlink fence; Preston and Diane hang back. As electricity crackles, Cole spots a vortex and reaches up toward it. This eventually manifests a vision of three woodsmen on a set of stairs. As Cole seems to flicker, Rosenfield pulls him away, noting, "Well, I guess we found out." Replies Cole, "We sure did, Albert."

The pair spot the headless body of Ruth Davenport, and Rosenfield takes a photo of coordinates written on her arm. A woodsman sneaks up on Macklay's car, and makes Hastings's day a lot worse, startling everyone.

"He's dead," says Cole matter-of-factly. Later, back at the police station, Cole, Rosenfield and Diane sit decompressing, the latter on a stool that affords her an angled perch. "Cat on a hot tin roof," says Cole, looking at his shaking right hand. "It's never done that before." In dialogue that could be read as comedic mishearing, coded communication, or a combination of both, Cole and Rosenfield engage, with the latter finally pulling out a printed photo of Ruth's arm. Diane looks down and clocks the coordinates, slowly mouthing them. Preston and Macklay enter with coffee and donuts, prompting Cole's proclamation, "The policeman's dream." The conversation turns to Hastings's death, for which Macklay says there are no suspects. Cole says that he saw someone, whom Rosenfield describes. Others chime in, and Cole recollects seeing the group of three dirty, bearded men.

Part 12

Back at the hotel, after Cole turns up his hearing aids so that they can speak more quietly, Rosenfield briefs Preston and invites her to join the Blue Rose task force. Honored, she quickly says yes. The trio toasts with wine, and when Diane joins they deputize her to assist in the Cooper investigation. Later, in one of the season's more commented upon scenes, Cole's evening with a French woman (Bérénice Marlohe, see below) is interrupted by Rosenfield. After he asks to speak to Cole alone, the woman spends more than two minutes gathering herself as a stone-faced Rosenfield stands silently. Upon her exit, wordplay from Cole does little to change his disposition, and eventually he gets to reveal the reason for his visit: another pair of incriminating text messages to and from Diane. Expressing concern but also wanting to pivot back to his suspended evening plans, Cole says, "Albert, sometimes I really worry about you."

Part 14

This episode opens with Cole returning a call from the Twin Peaks sheriff's office, where Lucy (Kimmy Robertson) answers. After some chitchat, she patches him through to Sheriff Frank Truman (Robert Forster), who shares with Cole that Deputy Hawk (Michael Horse) found pages from Laura's diary suggesting the existence of two Coopers. Naturally, when Cole is first connected he believes he's speaking with Harry S. Truman (played by Michael Ontkean in the first two seasons). Frank explains that he's Harry's brother and that Harry is sick and "in the doctor's care." Cole expresses his sympathies and says, "Thank you very much, Frank. Although I can't comment on this information, I want you to know I really appreciate it. And all the best to you and all the best to Harry."

In the absence of any definitive statement at the time, misinformation about Ontkean's nonparticipation in season three spread, something Ontkean, who lives in Hawaii, cleared up. "I wasn't able to come to the mainland for season three. My wife, Susan, was battling a terminal illness, and I was her main caregiver. It was reported that Ontkean had retired: true. However, I would have paddled a boat to the West Coast in full support of David if my wife wasn't in need of round-the-clock care. Being a beautifully private person, Susan did not wish her situation to be known."

In Cole's next scene, he joins Rosenfield and Preston in their hotel workroom, announcing that it's coffee time. Diane joins them. Pressed by Cole for details about the last night she saw Cooper, she confirms that he mentioned Briggs. When Rosenfield describes the inscription on a ring found in Briggs's stomach, Diane reacts with surprise, noting the names match her estranged half-sister and her husband, Janey-E (Naomi Watts) and Dougie. Cole calls the Las Vegas FBI office and advises them to "put caution in the shotgun seat" but find Douglas Jones.

After Diane leaves, Cole relates his phone conversation with Sheriff Truman indicating the possibility of two Coopers. "And last night I had another Monica Bellucci dream," Cole then says to Rosenfield and Preston. "I was in Paris on a case. Monica called and asked me to meet her at a certain café."

Here the scene shifts to another heavily discussed and dissected sequence, intercut with black-and-white footage of Cole, Bellucci, and a friend as Cole recounts his dream with intense concentration. "She said she needed to talk to me. When we met at the café, Cooper was there, but I couldn't see his face. Monica was very pleasant. She had brought friends. We all had a coffee. And then she said the ancient phrase." We cut to Bellucci: "We're like the dreamer who dreams and then lives inside the dream," she says, which

Cole repeats, followed by "I told her I understood." The same mirrored-cut structure follows with the question "But who is the dreamer?" The camera cuts back to Cole, who says, "A very powerful, uneasy feeling came over me. Monica looked past me and indicated to me to look back at something that was happening there. I turned and looked. I saw myself."

From here, Cole's story is intercut with footage from the unsettling *Fire Walk With Me* Philadelphia FBI office sequence in which Phillip Jeffries (David Bowie) first reappears and then quickly disappears again. Recollecting Jeffries's pointed query about Cooper, Cole exclaims, "Damn, I hadn't remembered that. Now this is really something interesting to think about."

While Bellucci understandably gets most of the attention in this scene, her female friend, who shares an on-screen coffee with the pair, is Mélita Toscan du Plantier, who has known Lynch since the late 1990s. The director of the Marrakech International Film Festival, she brokered the connection with Bellucci, another personal friend, roughly two months before the scene was shot in April 2016. Both her inclusion and the location—it was shot next door to Idem Paris, a gallery in the Montparnasse district where Lynch practiced lithography—hint at the degree to which Lynch spotlighted personal connections in the third season.

"When he called me, he wanted me to sign a NDA because it was all very secret," recalled Toscan du Plantier, saying that Lynch had briefly crossed paths with Bellucci at a cocktail but had no other relationship with her. "I didn't want to, and I said, 'I can help you, and I will not say anything.' So then he told me, 'I want Monica for a scene, and if she says yes, we'll come to Paris.' And I said, 'That's easy.' So I called Monica and called him back twenty minutes later, and I said, 'It's done.' He said, 'Great, so I will send you the [NDA] for both of you.' And I said, 'What do you mean both of you?' And he said, 'Yeah, because I want you in the scene too.' I'm like, 'I never do that.' He said, 'Yeah, but I want you to do it for me.'

"It was fun," continued Toscan du Plantier, who has no recollection of the gentleman who walks up with them in the scene, incidentally. "[David] gave the dialogue to Monica just when we arrived. It was quite simple, but she was very excited to just work with him. For me, it's cinema. Just to have seen the first episodes on a big screen at Cannes was kind of magical. And I know that this scene is important because so many people—even still today, sometimes I receive texts from people who say, 'Oh my God, I saw you.' But at the time it came out, I received so many, and people really were amazed that he got Monica Bellucci—because it's a fantasy in the film, and she's a fantasy for many men. So he loved the idea that she did it. And she did it for nothing."

Part 16

Cole's first appearance is brief but striking, running just over thirty seconds and sandwiched between two scenes of a comatose Dougie in the hospital. Cole stands in the Buckhorn hotel workroom surveying the whirring high-tech equipment around him, with a slightly worried expression. Cole's other, much bigger scene comes later. In an installment in which viewers receive colorful farewells for Richard Horne (Eamon Farren), Hutch (Tim Roth), and Chantal (Jennifer Jason Leigh), another character's fate proves even more shocking. As a seemingly remote-activated Diane approaches the FBI workroom under the Muddy Magnolias' "American Woman" remix, Cole senses her outside and says, "Come in, Diane." She enters, joining Cole, Preston, and Rosenfield. As Rosenfield gets her a drink and Cole sizes her up, Diane proceeds to tell the dark story of the night Cooper last visited her. At the end, she begins to unravel, thrice saying "I'm in the sheriff's station" and stammering, "I'm not me." Reaching into her purse for a handgun, Diane takes aim at Cole—who evidences no panic or other reaction—but Rosenfield and Preston shoot Diane first, and she flies backward against her chair for a moment before being pulled away and vanishing, revealing herself to actually be a tulpa. Despite the shock of the moment, Cole, more focused than nonplussed, simply says, "Sheriff's station?"

Part 17

Cole, Rosenfield and Preston kick off this episode, unsurprising given the events that transpired when last we saw them. Staring down at his gun, Cole says, "I couldn't do it, Albert. I couldn't do it." Told he's gone soft in his old age, Cole smashes the beachball-sized setup high and deep: "Not where it counts, buddy."

After toasting the bureau with red wine (as one does midday after witnessing a tulpa violently disappear), Cole settles in for a 200-plus-word monologue interweaving various secrets and a plan he's kept private for twenty-five years. Part confessional, part evocative snapshot of an aged character, the monologue is also duty-bound plot service and reminiscent of the heavy expositional lifts of Cole's season-two appearances. What helps get it over the hump is that there's also a pinch of humor ("Phillip Jeffries, who doesn't really exist anymore, at least not in the normal sense . . . ") and poignance over Cole's decision not to share the plan earlier ("I know you understand, Albert, and I'm still sorry"). After confessing his uncertainty as to whether his withheld scheme is now unfolding, Cole receives a phone call from the Las Vegas FBI, who tell him they've (nominally) located Dougie; it's Bushnell Mullins (Don Murray), however, who ends up delivering a message from Dougie to Cole: "I am headed for Sheriff Truman's. It is 2:53 in Las Vegas, and that adds up to a ten, the number of completion." Cole exclaims, "Dougie is Cooper? How the hell is this?"

Cole, Rosenfield, and Preston head to Twin Peaks, where they join a motley assortment of new and legacy characters at the sheriff's station—a group that, in a moment of symmetry, eventually totals seventeen people in the seventeenth episode. They arrive after the defeat of the Bob orb by Freddie Sykes (Jake Wardle), during a monologue by Cooper, and just before Naido (Nae Yuuki) rushes over to Cooper, touching hands with him and transforming into the real Diane. (As a side note, for those wondering, Lynch's penchant for secrecy does have moments of respite. "I once asked him about the meaning of Naido," said Yuuki. "She was a very elusive character, and I wanted to know what her role was in the story. He said, 'Don't tell anyone,' and explained it to me.") A distorted voice says, "We live inside a dream," and Cooper says, "I hope I see all of you again . . . every one of you."

Darkness and confusion descend on the group, but the intensely ominous whooshing resolves with Cooper, Diane, and Cole walking forward in the basement of the Great Northern Hotel. Enacting his two-birds-one-stone plan, Cooper states, "Now listen, I'm going through this door. Don't try to follow me, either of you." In his last line, Cole replies, "Be thinking of you, Coop."

If the convergence of these characters in the penultimate installment was an eye-opener for viewers, it was for the cast as well—bringing together disparate narrative strands and serving as a send-off for a lot of performers. For many, it was the first knowledge or confirmation that Lynch was also acting in the project, and for almost everyone it was a chance to wonder about the story events that had brought this group together. "I assumed he would reprise his role as Gordon Cole, but it wasn't until I got the script, some time before the day of the shoot, that I found out we actually had a scene together," said Yuuki.

"I had my big long monologue story, so I'd already learned that all by heart. But I didn't know about the Bob fight or anything," said Wardle, who was given his dialogue on a Post-It note, and stunned to learn the full nature of his pivotal role. "The fact that Gordon Cole was in the scene with me as well at the end, that was incredible."

It was the second favorite day of filming, behind only a conga-line dance, for Andrea Watrouse (credited as Andrea Leal), who appears as one of the Mitchum brothers' trio of personal assistants, Mandie. Part of the reason was that it dovetailed perfectly with the experience of watching original-run *Twin Peaks* while shooting, being given a full primer by castmate Giselle

DaMier. "I'd started to know and love these characters and David's character and the world of *Twin Peaks*," she said. "And I showed up that morning and I saw everyone there, no context. Usually we would show up and it would be only me, the girls, Jim [Belushi], and Robert [Knepper]. So this day everyone was there, and it was extremely exciting, and I could tell something was happening. We were in a little holding area with a bunch of chairs until the set was ready, and then we walked into the sheriff's office, and that's when I saw David in his costume and everyone else. It was a really beautiful moment where we finally got to join the actual world of *Twin Peaks* instead of just the periphery. And it was like I was watching the TV show in real time and also in it."

According to nearly a dozen participants, all the day's scenes were shot without many takes and had a buzzy energy. "Even though I couldn't see it during the actual shoot because of the makeup, I could feel the energy and importance of the moment," said Yuuki. Recalling Lynch's personal application of creamed corn around a hole in the floor before Freddie's battle with Bob, Wardle said, "*Twin Peaks* was his canvas, and he really wanted to [be] hands-on with everything and craft it in a certain way, which was so cool."

"We had just shot something, and there was smoke, a lot of smoke," recalled Chrystabell. "And David came on and he was about to share something, and he was like, 'Holy smokes!' and everybody just lost it. I mean, there was so much excitement for that particular scene that everybody was in, but with his tone and just having such a great read on people he could really make you feel all kinds of ways—calm, tense, exuberant, buoyant, or just really joyful."

While everyone else was getting a dose of that exuberance from Lynch, Robertson was the recipient also of at least one moment of tension. "I was around the set, and I heard David calling for Lucy," recalled Robertson on learning that she would actually be the one responsible for taking out Mr. C. "I walked into that hallway and he came and got me, and he had a gun in his hand. And he said, 'Have you ever shot a gun before?'"

After the first take, Lynch wanted an adjustment. "He yelled cut louder than I've ever heard him yell it before," Robertson continued. "He put his headphones down, took a breath, and started walking towards me. And I went, 'Uh-oh.' He said, 'Lucy, you just shot dead what may have been Agent Cooper,' and then he also explained about the phone call before. He said, 'Is that how Lucy would act if she may have shot Agent Cooper or she may have shot a bad guy?' I said no. And he goes, 'Okay, can we do it again where you actually do that?' And I said, 'I'm sorry, I forgot to act.'"

"So that was the closest I've ever seen to him actually being angry at anything on any set that I have been on with him. That was really awful," Robertson added with a laugh.

• • •

When one talks to folks involved in *Twin Peaks: The Return* you're bound, at some point, to get a story that illustrates Lynch's unique, preternatural combination of vivid imagination and utter surety. Sometimes it involves casting. Sometimes it intersects with directing, where Lynch had a strong and specific sense for staging scenes while still allowing for the flexibility to discover and incorporate accidents, happy and otherwise, along the way. Sometimes it has to do with plaster of paris most assuredly *not* being the same thing as Fix-It-All.

The first two are relevant with respect to analyzing performance by way of comparison. As Lynch stepped further into the world of *Twin Peaks* at this point in his life and career, one could reasonably assume he might have had a different enough relationship with the material that he would want to do things just a bit differently—that in crafting something so definitively his vision, he might aim to center, ever so slightly, his performance. This was, however, not the case. Creativity and raw instinct coexisted, as always.

In 2010, Wardle was an eighteen-year-old who'd uploaded a video of himself doing accents to YouTube, where it became a viral sensation, eventually pulling in over thirty-four million views. Lynch was among those who saw it, and producer Sabrina Sutherland reached out to Wardle on his behalf in 2012, setting up a video chat. "It was so informal, casual, friendly, just like, 'Hey Jake, how are you doing, buddy?'" said Wardle, yes, doing a Lynch impression of course. "And then he basically, in a nutshell, said how much he loved my accents video and asked me if I'd considered getting into acting. I said not really, but I was starting to think about it. So he [told] me he had an idea for a project, and he didn't tell me much about it, but he said he had an idea of potentially how I might be able to fit into that project."

The pair would continue to connect via video chat every several months as Lynch worked to secure funding. "Maybe around late 2013, he said, 'Unfortunately, we're going to have to shelve it for now because it's just not getting off the ground,'" said Wardle. "But I remember this: He said, 'Don't worry, I won't forget about you. I do want to use you for something.' And he kept his word. Then, sometime in 2014, he Skyped me again and said, 'Have you ever heard of *Twin Peaks*?'

"I can still remember it like it was yesterday. It's very surreal, the whole experience, especially all these years later. Some days I'm just living my normal life, working my flexible day job around my performance work, and everything's ordinary. And sometimes I think, *Did all of that really happen?*

Did David really reach out to me, and I went and did Twin Peaks?"

Meanwhile, Watrouse was perhaps an even more unlikely casting story. "I wasn't an actress and I wasn't pursuing anything, but a person I had met casually through mutual friends was helping cast, and they were looking for blondes of a certain height, and he thought he'd pitch me," she said. "So I got asked to do a self-tape talking about myself and my hobbies—but as not an actor. I didn't really know what that meant, so I just grabbed my phone, and I did an actual selfie video. And that's what I sent in, and I never thought about it again, never expected to hear back."

Watrouse was visiting a friend in Nashville who had just been cast—small-world alert, and in a moment of *Mulholland Drive* "This is the girl" parallelism—in a Billy Ray Cyrus television show, and was on set with her when she got a call. "They were being very vague, [but] they told me the director wanted me, and that this is what we were going to be filming," Watrouse recollected. "I tried to decline it because I was in Nashville, and they were like, 'No, no, this is a really, really cool opportunity—trust me, you have to do this.' And so I flew the next day and did the fitting."

Told nothing about her scenes with Candie (Amy Shiels) and Sandie (DaMier) other than they served in some capacity with the Mitchums, Watrouse would receive day-of instruction for her scenes. "As someone who had never acted before, that was really terrifying for me on the first day," she said. "But I got to know pretty early on that I didn't need to think that hard about it because David's vision was so specific. He already knew how much my index finger should be lifted. He had every detail down. I didn't need to worry about the fact that I didn't know what we were doing. I just needed to trust the process and it was all going to work out."

For another role, Lynch would tap a performer with whom he had great familiarity, but not as an actress. "First of all, he never mentioned the words *Twin Peaks*," said Chrystabell. "We were in the midst of doing a recording session for *Somewhere in the Nowhere*, and it was one of our final sessions. . . . All he said was 'Chrystabell, I think there's a role for you in my new project.' And of course at that time we all know what the new project is; that information had been made clear. But I had zero expectation that I would be a part of it."

Curiosity and suspense hung in the air for weeks or perhaps even months, Chrystabell said. Finally, when they had another album session after a break, the subject came up again. "I thought clearly I'd be doing music," she said. "I would be singing—naturally, right? And then he said, 'No, you'll be acting.' And I was like, 'David, are you sure, darling? Are you quite positive about this?' But when someone like David imbues confidence in you, you just believe that you can do it, even if you're utterly terrified. But even then,

I didn't know what the part was. All he said was, supercheeky, 'She's not like you at all, Chrystabell. She's very professional.'"

Chrystabell drove down from Oakland to read a script at Rancho Rosa headquarters in Van Nuys, knowing nothing about the character, nature, or size of her role. She was astounded when given a bulky stack of pages with just her scenes. "I read the script and saw how Tammy and Gordon were peas in a pod, just like me and David . . . and then how much Gordon believed in Tammy and how it reflected so just beautifully and tenderly how David had believed in me," she said. "Then I saw that Tammy was initiated in the Blue Rose task force and [says in] the script, without hesitation, 'I'm in.' It was at that moment that it was like . . . " Here Chrystabell trailed off. "I don't think there's anything else like that moment in my life. Even performing it on set was different, and magnificent in its own way. But reading the words in the script when I had no idea that Tammy would have this trajectory, it was a significant life moment. It was astounding, honestly. It was life transformative."

For Knepper, a veteran actor with more than 150 credits who's perhaps best known for *Prison Break*, the story of Lynch's vision arrives by way of an on-set accident during a scene in which his character, crooked but complicated casino owner Rodney Mitchum, and his brother, Bradley (Belushi), are in a security room angrily reviewing footage of Dougie winning $425,000. "Right before we're ready to shoot the close-up for that, I'm over standing next to David, kind of chumming around with him a little bit. I'm about to go back, and David turns to Sabrina and says, 'Robert has such a beautiful face. Don't you think he has such a beautiful face?' And Sabrina says, 'Yeah, I think he does.' So I go onto the set. There's Jim on my right. I'm about to point out something on the monitor, and all of a sudden, out of nowhere, this huge lamp standing in front of me comes down onto my face.

"It's on a tree, and it's got sandbags at the bottom. Well, unfortunately, there was not enough sandbags on the thing, and it toppled over and hit me—thank God, right there," continued Knepper, pointing to a spot next to his left eye. "I still have a little bit of a scar from it. The blood—it was like a [Sam] Peckinpah movie. It was just all over everything. I saw white light, I went down onto the ground, and then I heard a cacophony of sound and I get up and sit on the bench. And I'm like, 'David, David, what are we going to do? We've shot half the movie and now I got this big cut.' And I could hear David shouting, 'Shut up, shut up! You're in a state of, of . . . whatever that is.' And somebody shouts out, 'Shock—he's in a state of shock.' David was in a state of shock! But ever since I can remember in acting, if there was a mishap, I'm always like, 'Oh no, what about opening night?' It was always about trying to save the day. Somebody said, 'If anybody can fix it, it's David—you give David lemons and he makes lemonade.'"

Production found a plastic surgeon, and plans were made for Knepper to go on his lunch break. "He's like, 'Ooh, that's a deep cut. Thank God it didn't take your eye out,'" recalled Knepper. "It was only an inch long, but it was right on the cheekbone of my beautiful face. So he opens me up, puts two or three stitches on the inside muscle tissue and then two or three on the outside and puts a butterfly Band-Aid on it."

"While we still had him, we rehearsed the next scene, which was sort of this wider shot in that room with the girls and all the people," recollected script supervisor Cori Glazer. "So when he came back, we figured he would stand in a position where we were only seeing [one] side of his face. He went off. We went to lunch. We came back from lunch. He wasn't back yet. We had a stand-in over his shoulder, but we were able to shoot out [the scene], and then he came back. He had this Band-Aid on his face, and he said, 'The surgeon said I cannot take this Band-Aid off. You can put makeup on it, but you cannot take this Band-Aid off.'"

"I wanted to go back to work," said Knepper with a laugh and a shrug. "So we continue with the scene, and David's like, 'I don't know how I'm going to fix it, but I'll fix it.' Then he came up with this great idea that Jim's character and I are watching television, and Candie is trying to get this fly. David said, 'I'm going to shoot it from behind. You're just looking at the TV over there.' And David's coaching her through the whole thing: 'Then you pick up the remote control, and you're trying to find it. And finally, you get this moment. Don't hit him. Don't hit Robert. But at that moment you're going to hit him right across the face and make it *look* like you hit [him].'" The shooting of this scene, running two and a half minutes, is the inciting incident for the aforementioned viral behind-the-scenes clip in which Lynch agitatedly asks, "Who gives a fucking shit how long a scene is?"

Knepper grappled with headaches for the four or five weeks of shooting that remained, but the show went on. In that time, lo and behold, the wound mostly resolved and could be covered with just a little bit of makeup, according to Knepper, which inspired the limousine scene in which Bradley rips off Rodney's Band-Aid on their way to meet Dougie. "I never skipped a beat. I mean, we just kept shooting, and I love it because I know I basically took one for the team," said Knepper. "I didn't say anything about it, and the way David was able to solve that problem, it was so typical of *Twin Peaks*'s style—like, somehow, some little miracle."

The common thread among these aforementioned elements, from casting to troubleshooting, is that Lynch viewed each through a lens of certainty. While he was always open to small serendipities, once he had his mind set on something, he was dogged in his pursuit. These assorted anecdotes—and dozens of others similar in theme—all connect associatively to performance because, while shooting the equivalent of nine feature films over 142 days, Lynch was also acting in a not inconsiderable role. And yet these castings, adjustments, and other elements were all a part of his vision for the world of *Twin Peaks*, every bit as much as Gordon Cole. Despite the increased size (and prominence) of his role, Lynch was not overly precious about the particulars of his performance, and, from beginning to end, it received no prioritization compared with any other elements of production.

There were no special accommodations or allowances carved out for Lynch's acting work in the shoot's complex scheduling, according to Sutherland. "It would just be what we needed to do more so for the other actors. David was always there, but other actors weren't always available, so we had to accommodate them," she said. "And David was willing to do that to have the actors. So he never voiced anything about not being either prepared or that it wasn't a good day to do [scene] X, Y, and Z because of his acting."

Through early-morning calls and long days shooting, this tack continued. On set, as glimpsed in the superlative "Behind the Curtain" making-of material on the project's "From Z to A" Blu-ray release, sometimes Lynch would run lines with Glazer before performing in a scene. Other times, though, he would not. "I think because he'd written a lot of these Gordon Cole lines that he remembered what they were," said Sutherland. "He remembered the script better than most people. He could tell everybody what their lines were."

The same approach extended to postproduction. Asked if he recalled any moments when Lynch was either reflective or self-critical about his performance or even wanted to fine-tune the character of Cole, editor Duwayne Dunham said, "No, not in the sense that you're asking. David was pretty spot-on with the character in his performance, and it was just a matter of picking the right pieces. And probably, in my mind, I'm just thinking Gordon Cole is David Lynch. When I would talk to him, I would try and refer to Gordon Cole as opposed to 'you, David.'"

• • •

Given these facts, what does Lynch's stepping back into the world of *Twin Peaks* mean to him as an artist? The uncertain yet symbolically rich relationship between the watcher and watched is a component of many Lynch works. Sometimes this element takes on a sense of danger, and sometimes it's framed more for amusement. There's Jeffrey hiding in Dorothy's closet in *Blue Velvet*; the in-universe soap opera of *Invitation to Love* within *Twin Peaks*; delivered videotapes and the Mystery Man's menacing recording activities in *Lost Highway*; and Betty and Rita's viewing of Rebekah Del Rio's "Llorando" at Club Silencio in *Mulholland Drive*, to name several examples.

Here, this same notion is explored with the glass box in New York City. It's also filtered through the question "But who is the dreamer?" in the Bellucci sequence. A lot of people focus on "who" in that query in relation to identity. Without disappearing down a rabbit hole, I've always tended to think of it more as a broader prompt of self-inquiry, reflecting essential thought—with all of the spiritual and moral considerations, both individually and collectively, that implies—more deeply inward. In presenting this scene as Cole's dream and having him see a younger version of himself from *Fire Walk With Me*, Lynch plays with multiple meanings in a highly stimulating manner, but one that would seem to certainly not preclude (and perhaps even embrace) a wider interpretation.

In the uncut "A Slice of Lynch" featurette, originally filmed in 2007 and available across a number of the franchise's home video releases, Lynch chooses very consciously at the end to distill his reflection upon the series to "I love Twin Peaks and its world." He says he's making this statement in seven words to reflect his fondness for that digit, his lucky number. But it also nods to the existence of an almost extradimensional space and, perhaps subconsciously as it pertains to season three, the magnetic pull of that field upon his own creative vision. His work on *Twin Peaks* was, after all, when he first fell in love with continuing stories. Over time, this would lead to both a larger role for Cole and a larger canvas overall as the scope of the franchise grew to plumb enormous philosophical questions.

To some viewers, the size of that third season frame—and the more methodical pace it indulged—pulled them a bit out of the show. To others, it deepened their appreciation of the work. For some, it was a bit of both. "Just talking as a fan, I watched it every week and started getting impatient," said Harley Peyton. "I mean, David's relationship to time was always so weird. And by the way, a lot of times it was genius, right? Like, a mother who's just found out her daughter has died is going to have a reaction much bigger and longer than you might expect, and you'll find yourself being surprised by that and moved by it at the same time. David also was willing to have someone sweep up in a bar for an endless amount of time." Here Peyton laughed. "But I always appreciated that. I think that's part of its charm in a weird way. I mean, I can't imagine what they were thinking at Showtime, but I was all in on it. Like a lot of audience members, I was frustrated waiting for Cooper to come back, but there was a value in being made to wait like that. And also Kyle was doing such extraordinary work that it wasn't like that was hard to watch. And I loved the new characters.

"I would say that I think there was a little too much Gordon Cole, but part of that was just because there ended up being eighteen episodes and not ten," Peyton added. "I always thought that Gordon was a character who worked better in small measures. And look, I completely respect his desire to revisit that character, because I think he did deepen it in some ways—the emotions of that character, who that character was. And again, I was not on the set [or involved], but it was a very emotional time [with Catherine Coulson being ill and other] people who were having problems that way. I think that maybe that factored into a little bit of the way Gordon Cole operated. It was both a reunion and in some cases a farewell. And that's not insignificant."

"The Soul Detective"'s Davi de Oliveira Pinheiro too cites the "goodbye factor" as a compelling lens through which to explore the passage of time. But he also views Cole specifically as representing a counterbalancing virtuousness in an even more complex metaphor. "I think he fills the space Dale Cooper leaves behind, [and] as Kyle MacLachlan already said, he was imitating David Lynch [some in his performance]. That becomes kind of a new layer of meta. I think there's an inherent goodness to a character who can't be good in real life. Gordon Cole is not going to be a good person, the real Gordon Cole, if you meet him, because there's not the kind of space for that. But he brings this goodness [to the show] on a planet that's much worse than when *Twin Peaks* first [debuted]. It's a worse world, and [Lynch's] view is darker because in those twenty-five years, I think how he sees the nuclear bomb changed. It's become a very urgent subject for him even if he doesn't express it in interviews. I remember after watching Episode 8, I went to a bar with friends and I thought we just saw *The Silmarillion* of *Twin Peaks*. It's a codifier of everything that *Twin Peaks* is now about—the evil that was born in the moment we discovered we can kill people and not have to clean it. Violence became very cosmetic because of the nuclear bomb—the moment you can kill someone and it's only ashes, violence takes on a new path. I think it changes everything about the way we behave."

• • •

While Lynch was never the type of performer to get lost in live-action characterizations that blurred the line of his off-screen persona, there was certainly a single-mindedness to some of the acting he did in self-generated projects. The manner in which he approached playing Cole, though, seems to indicate that while there was some weighted significance to Lynch's on-screen prominence in *The Return*, in the end there was not a lot of front-of-brain rationalization. One can read this several ways. First, as Lynch being comfortable in both his own skin and the suit of his character, each of which seems undoubtedly true. In parallel, though, one could argue that this bolsters the interpretation of Cole as an authorial stand-in. By relying more heavily on elements of his own personality, Lynch is further imprinting his identity on the series.

A fair number of collaborators don't have a strong opinion on this question, feeling it's just a part that works and fits for him, a piece of the overall tapestry. Others, however, see more of a sense of ownership. Watching the season upon its broadcast, Yuuki reflected, "He looked more dashing than ever, like a character from a French noir film. His presence was striking and refined [and his] expanded role fascinating. He seems more self-assured and content in this season, savoring life with fine wine and beautiful women. Gordon feels like David himself appearing in the story."

Horse sees significance in the larger role for Cole too. "Yes, because David is driving this time," the actor said. "He even says he kind of missed it a little bit when he left in the second season to do other things. But this time he says, 'I'm in the driver's seat, I'm going to do this.' I would say David's in control and so's Gordon Cole, and he's going to take this where he wants it to go."

"I think Gordon Cole was his most comfortable role because he just got to be sort of his absurdist self," reflected Jennifer Lynch. "[But] I think it was also obvious it was nourishing him to be playing Gordon and to be looking for a way to help his friend and solve a mystery—which was always a very big thing for Dad. Again, to reach out to someone who was somehow in another place or lost in some way or inaccessible in a way they used to be greatly accessible and to showcase missing someone and using every tool you have to try and find them [was important]. . . . Gordon got to look for his buddy Cooper and try to make things what he considered right with the world."

In that quest, the third season version of Cole incorporates so many things Lynch did and/or enjoyed: red wine, sketching, smoking, etcetera. Would these traits have meshed with an audience's view of the character twenty-five years earlier? Probably not. But they reflect Lynch at the time—a powerful statement on his ownership of the character. (Other tidbits, meanwhile, get doled out to different figures—Lynch's affinity for Cheetos, to cite one example, is passed off to Chantal.)

Chrystabell, meanwhile, sees full-spectrum artistic representation in the third season and describes it in a holistic way that summons to mind a performance art piece. "Every artwork, every sculpture, every piece of furniture, every film, every TV scene, every script, every poem, every meditation, it's all in *The Return*. It's all represented, every music composition—it's all there," she said. "That's why *The Return* is . . . I mean, the word 'miracle' honestly isn't big enough. I'm biased, perhaps, but the fact that it even happened is kind of unbelievable."

Cole's increased relevance and Lynch fusing the character with more personal elements are, again, not some skeleton key for the third season. We don't really know—can't really know—their full meaning. There are a multiplicity of answers and a beautiful imponderability to it all. How deep into the ground one wants to run with a "unified theory" of Cole is a matter of personal preference. (I'm sure eventually a YouTube video will pop up.) For me, his screen time attaches itself to both narrative and reasons outside of that frame. And that's fine. Cole is in the world of *Twin Peaks*, helping to drive it and show us things, and that's enough.

–CHAPTER 41–

"FIX [YOUR] HEARTS OR DIE . . ."

Five words. If you're reading this book, you likely already know them, from Gordon Cole's conversation with transgender FBI Chief of Staff Denise Bryson (David Duchovny) in Part 4 of *The Return* (the actual quote is "fix their hearts or die," but it has been popularly appropriated as "fix your hearts . . ."). In a series filled with quotable lines, there may be nothing, at least in its return incarnation, that has captured the mainstream zeitgeist quite like the (adjusted) title of this chapter.

If the recent American rise of celebrated cruelty, boisterous ignorance, and incipient fascism has been aided by the embrace of short, often meaningless slogans that do little except demonize other persons or groups, then perhaps pushback against dehumanizing tropes needs its own rallying cry. Both in and out of the context in which they appear, these five words from Lynch and Mark Frost stand in defiant opposition to the bigotry of the times, or indifference to the same. It's a rebuke, a challenge, a line in the sand.

That the words are delivered in character on camera by one of the show's cocreators offers a credible, direct endorsement of their message.

I gasped audibly when I first heard it in 2017, and on any rewatch it still lands with an affecting incisiveness. As a straight white male, I've not personally experienced even a sliver of the discrimination of so many marginalized groups. And yet here was a phrase that spoke in a principled but incandescent way to the frustration of watching prejudice and injustice visited regularly upon others.

That it would be picked up as a rallying cry by so many in the trans community (and beyond) is not surprising. While it's not Cole's most noteworthy scene or even the apex of Lynch's acting in season three, it might in some ways be his most impactful scene, so it felt worthwhile to spotlight this sequence. Let's unpack, then, the character, the scene, and its power—and share some insights about Lynch's connection to it.

• • •

As presented in the original series, Bryson is a FBI agent on loan to the DEA, assigned to investigate Agent Cooper after he's accused of the theft of cocaine being used in a sting operation by the Royal Canadian Mounted Police, stemming from Cooper and Truman's across-the-border rescue of Audrey Horne (Sherilyn Fenn). By the third season, Bryson has risen to FBI chief of staff. According to Duchovny in a March 2022 interview with *Vanity Fair*, James Spader (who starred for Frost in *Storyville*) not only was originally set to portray Bryson, but actually conceived of her; when his appearance didn't work out, it opened the door for Duchovny to step into the role.

I won't dissect the character in full detail here, but certainly part of the reason that, in 2017 and beyond, the "Fix their hearts or die" line resonates was because Bryson was treated with openheartedness back in 1990. And of course a significant part of that was rooted in a performance that is respectful and fully lived-in. Duwayne Dunham, the director of the eleventh episode of season two, in which Bryson is introduced, recalled much of that flowing from the comfort of the actor himself. "David Duchovny was so fantastic, and I don't mean just his performance was fantastic—he just embraced it. It was no big deal when he showed up on set and there he is dressed like a female," Dunham said. "He was smiling and laughing and carrying on, and it was just another day at the office. David made it very, very easy—he was not one bit hesitant or intimidated by the role. He totally embraced it and had a lot of fun."

In the episode, Cole places a phone call checking in on Cooper and setting up Bryson's arrival (though not indicating anything about her transition), positioning the character in a positive light. It's also worth noting that the writing (the script is credited to Barry Pullman) goes out of its way to present Bryson with both the opportunity to tell Cooper a personal story of the awakening that led to her transition ("No, I like talking about it," she prefaces) and to show grace—the appellation "Dennis" is gently corrected by Denise, leading to an apology by Cooper. It's a no-big-deal slipup, and they continue their conversation. Cooper's comment to FBI Agent Roger Hardy (Clarence Williams III) in the same episode that "I'm talking about seeing beyond fear—about looking at the world with love," while occurring in a different context, feels relevant too.

All this background gives the Bryson character both professional and personal credibility heading into her season three appearance. Shot at the downtown Los Angeles City Hall building on the afternoon of December 12, 2015 (with Frost also on set, as behind-the-scenes footage shows), the scene, running just over four minutes, opens with some small talk between Cole and Bill Kennedy (Richard Chamberlain), who escorts Cole into Bryson's office. Cole sits quietly for a beat, eyeing a bouquet of roses and orchids in the chair to his right. After twenty seconds, Bryson enters. Their exchange is as follows:

Cole: (standing) Denise.
Bryson: Gordon, thank you for coming in. What've you got?
Cole: It's Cooper. We found him.
Bryson: Where?
Cole: South Dakota, Denise. He's in a federal prison in South Dakota. We're going out to see him tomorrow.
Bryson: I heard.
Cole: Yes? How's that?
Bryson: You're taking Agent Preston with you?
Cole: Yes.
Bryson: Really, Gordon?
Cole: What are you gettin' at, Denise?
Bryson: Well, I know your profile Gordon. Beautiful agent, barely thirty.
Cole: I'm old school Denise, you know that. (Beat.) Before you were Denise, when you were Dennis, and I was your boss, when I had you working undercover at the DEA, you were a confused and wild thing sometimes. I had enough dirt on you to fill the Grand Canyon, and I never used a spoonful because you were and are a great agent. And when you became Denise, I told all of your colleagues, those clown comics, to fix their hearts or die.
Bryson: Yes, and as I've said many times before Gordon, I can never repay you enough for that kindness.
Cole: Agent Tammy Preston has the stuff, Denise.
Bryson: I know, I know. I'm speaking more as a woman now than as the chief of staff of the entire Federal Bureau of Investigation. Don't you just love sometimes saying Federal Bureau of Investigation like that, all at once? Unabbreviated. It just gives me such a thrill.
Cole: It is thrilling, Denise.
Bryson: Tammy . . . Tammy is so beautiful.
Cole: There's room, in this Federal Bureau of Investigation, for more than one beautiful woman.
Bryson: Oh Gordon, that is so sweet. You know normally I can't think like this, I have to forgo all that and grow balls of steel to do this job, and it's a bitch, let me tell you, sometimes. Not to mention the screaming hormones.
(Gordon winces.)
Bryson: Oh I know. I'm sorry, Gordon. I know. Gordon, I trust you. You know that. And I believe you're on the trail of something big.
Cole: Big.
Bryson: Will Albert be with you?
Cole: Do birds fly?
Bryson: (rising) Good luck.

Cole: (rising) Ten-four, good buddy.
(They exchange a handshake and Gordon exits as Bill opens the door; Denise stands silently for a moment, then fans herself.)

Lynch's performance here is fantastic, and the scene is studded with small moments, both verbal and nonverbal, that connect, deepening the emotional punch of Cole's testimonial. There's Cole's terse shake of his head at Bryson's mention of his "profile." There's Cole's use of Denise's former name as an on-ramp to his story. There's Cole parrying Bryson yet sincerely complimenting her in an attempt to lay to rest her qualms about Preston. The one I appreciate most, though, is Cole's discomfort and wincing at Bryson's mention of hormones. Individually or in aggregate, these elements might, in the view of some, transgress boundaries. But they ring so true to character and the way these two colleagues—of different generations and a relationship spanning decades, with their power dynamic now flipped—would interact. It shows that acceptance isn't impossible, that all it takes is listening to the experiences of others and meeting them where they are.

"I think that's why Gordon Cole telling people to fix their hearts or die was of such importance, because Gordon was an old school, grandfather-aged American man, and most of those people did not know what to do with the trans community," said Jennifer Lynch. "And Dad was able to see very clearly that the trans community had been around forever. We were just now empowering them enough to do something about being here. And he knows what it's like to want to be yourself and be afraid to do that. So I think that it was important that Gordon Cole say 'Fix your hearts or die,' not Cooper, not Lucy. It was this old-school man set in his ways, and his ability to see that these people were being discriminated against when they already suffer the greatest wound, which is to not be in the body you think you should be in—what an absolute nightmare. And then to be hated for it, or ridiculed for it—what an absolute devastation."

The comment works in universe as a direct shot at transphobes, with Cole also defending his relationship with Preston by reminding Bryson that appearances often don't tell a complete story. Additionally, it serves as a nice bookend, bringing symmetry to Cole's (off-screen) introduction of the character so long ago. Of course, a large part of the line's cultural power stems from the dialogue being delivered by Lynch himself—something not lost on his collaborators at the time.

"I could totally see him saying that in real life, definitely," said Sabrina Sutherland. "I thought it was a very powerful statement, and David was always all inclusive. It was a matter of pride for him in a way—he didn't care about race, religion, sexual orientation. He did not care. He embraced everybody."

To Kimmy Robertson, there was an undeniable metatextuality to the proceedings, even at the time. "When he's having that whole conversation, that's the longest I can remember Gordon Cole was ever on camera. And I found that *really* fascinating because in some ways I could see David Lynch talking to David Duchovny like in code, and then in other ways it was Gordon Cole and Denise. Every other time it was Gordon Cole it was not David Lynch, and there was nothing about it other than the fastidiousness of information that was David Lynch. It's a little more information than I should be giving you, but I felt that was David talking to David. It was really powerful."

The layered nature of this scene isn't just a shiny coat of critical theory. While varied interpretations are part of *Twin Peaks*'s appeal, Lynch's connection to his dialogue's message is grounded in verifiable personal details, beyond the parameters of the scene.

"My father and I both had things about our bodies that were either visibly broken or wrong . . . so we understood hating a body that we were in, or thinking less of it," said Jennifer Lynch. "And yet we weren't ridiculed for it. I'll tell you that I had a best friend and was married to a trans person. And it is because of Gordon, I think, that my ex-partner was able to exist more comfortably in the world, knowing that the man who made *Eraserhead*, their favorite movie, also said 'Fix your hearts or die.' So Dad knew that what he was saying was the clearest version of 'It is not on these people to feel bad. It is on you to understand.'

"I think that Dad had a real empathy for (those who) suffered because he believed suffering was totally unnecessary, and yet he knew it happened to everybody. And he himself suffered, and he himself felt at times that he was in a body he wished he could change, and that for at least as long as I was with my partner . . . Dad was not only somebody they could admire, but somebody who treated them in a gentle enough way that they felt they could have a voice."

Asked about those feelings attached to dysmorphia, Lynch continued. "I was born with really severely clubbed feet, and my dad had one bad foot," she shared. "He had a very upsetting memory of being a child running up a hill in the snow with his friends, and he got to the top, towards the end of the group, and everybody was pointing and laughing at the footprints he left in the snow because one of his feet didn't look like the other."

When Jennifer was young, the pair would go to Bob's Big Boy, where her father's feelings would manifest. "He would draw on napkins this leg, this below-the-knee attachment he wanted to build for himself that he thought was much better than the one he had—he just wanted to cut it the fuck off and build a new one," she said. "He also used to say he would do my club feet surgery, since I likely need another one. He'd say, 'I'll do it for you.' I was close to letting him a few times." Here Lynch laughed in reflection.

"It's the same thing with *Boxing Helena* and the Venus de Milo," she continued. "As a toddler, I never crawled, and they would sit me under the Venus de Milo, and I would see people look at her as if she was beautiful, even though she was broken. And I'd think, *Someday, maybe somebody will think I'm beautiful even though I'm broken.* And when I was born with the club feet, Dad instantly asked the doctor, 'Does this have anything to do with my foot?' And they said not one bit. But Dad and I used to always say we had previous lives together, and that the foot thing was a connection we had. We'd ponder what we might have done on our feet or with our feet that would cause us to be so upset about them in this life.

"It always used to shock me that he felt the way he did about it, except that I felt the way I do about my ankles. So I related to it, but I wasn't wanting to cut my ankles off. What makes it so endearing is that it isn't a big deal, but that in his mind, that foot was busted. As he'd say, 'It's fucking *busted*, and I'd like to do something about it.' But I think it is one of the reasons he had such compassion for people who felt that maybe they were in the wrong body. . . . I think that's one of the reasons he was so able to tap into John Merrick—that he had a part of himself he thought was wrong or monstrous. And it really wasn't, it's just how he saw it. It didn't impede his life. If he wore good shoes, he was fine."

• • •

If Lynch's relationship to Cole's feelings is somewhat clear, there's still the interesting question of how the line caught on even outside of *Twin Peaks* fandom. It's widely embraced in the trans community, yes, but also among a broader swath of allies and individuals repulsed by the demagoguery of our time. Canadian author, philosopher, and media studies pioneer Marshall McLuhan is famous for the idea that "the medium is the message," which posits that the characteristics of media greatly influence how messages are perceived and that new forms of communication and interaction can shape society in profound ways. The internet most robustly illustrates this principle—especially social media, which has fundamentally transformed how most people consume and share information, notionally "democratizing" things (but in fact signal boosting the most terminally online) and placing facts alongside opinion and disinformation in an always-open, all-you-can-eat buffet.

This cuts both ways. The bad is quite bad. In just a little over a generation, the internet has assisted many unprincipled people with arguably no drive other than the accumulation of money and raw power in manipulating credulous and/or broken-brained folks into believing that anything and everything wrong or lacking in their own lives (or indeed the whole world) is simultaneously the fault of others—immigrants, the LGBTQ population, minorities, feminists, and/or mysterious "elites," people who happen to have dedicated themselves to amassing a base of expertise in any field, whether it be academia, science, or medicine. It can be disorienting, this near-ceaseless assault on objective truth and basic human decency.

But then there is the inverse. And in a world in which sloganeering is more and more important and people are inundated on social media by a barrage of information (much of it negative) that the human brain as currently evolved is ill equipped to handle, the phrase "Fix your hearts or die" is perhaps the ultimate shorthand response. It's assaultive and bracing, yes. It espouses a radical empathy, placing the onus of correcting bigotry or backward thinking on the people who have that thinking, not on the people they hate or want to control and not on society to accommodate their prejudices. There's a moral clarity to it: fundamental decency isn't up for debate. You can adjust and join society in a better shared future or . . . well, take a long walk off a short pier.

It's my belief that Cole's line fits hand in glove with Lynch's off-screen persona, which contributes to its currency. "I do love that he's a bit of a hero to those who feel so vulnerable," said Jennifer Lynch. However much some might describe Lynch as enigmatic or fixate on apparent contradictions between his mien and the content of his films, there's a forthrightness to his personality that (especially younger) people immediately grasp. He's a remarkably direct (and consistently positive) communicator. And, for that reason, I believe the phrase itself, in all its clipped virality, will continue to serve as a magnet, drawing new viewers both to *Twin Peaks* and Lynch's other work more broadly.

Occasionally one will see bad-faith actors take a swing at the line. Knowing not a thing about *Twin Peaks* and understanding nothing about art in general except their instinct to suppress it and tear it down—lest it plant any seed of personal reflection, growth, or even change of which they do not approve—they try to frame "Fix your hearts or die" as what it most assuredly is not: an endorsement of violence. In fact, it's no different in its sentiment than a verse from Bob Dylan's "The Times They Are a-Changin'": "Come senators, congressmen, please heed the call/Don't stand in the doorway, don't block up the hall/For he that gets hurt will be who has stalled."

Within *Twin Peaks*, the line speaks to transphobes. More broadly, "Fix your hearts or die" cuts, with a startling efficiency, through the din of assorted bigotry and narrow-mindedness. Against the modern backdrop of incivility and cruelty, both actual and performative, there may be no more profound individual act than empathetic identification, but also—and this is crucial—the righteous (and indeed sometimes angry) promulgation of the same.

Professing intolerance of intolerance is no great sin. Just as the question "But who is the dreamer?" is at least in part an open summons to look within, this phrase uttered by Cole is a solicitation to consider the better angels of our nature—an invitation to love, if you will.

–CHAPTER 42–

"MAYBE I'M OMAZE-D . . ." (2017-2018)

Coming off the grueling production experience of *Twin Peaks* but still locked in postproduction, Lynch also plotted and launched his Festival of Disruption, an immersive multiday concert, art, talk, and multimedia experience with 100 percent of its proceeds going to the David Lynch Foundation, funding Transcendental Meditation programs with a special focus on assisting children and trauma survivors. The first event took place on October 8-9, 2016, at the Theatre at Ace Hotel in Los Angeles, a former movie palace built in 1927 and since placed on the National Register of Historic Places.

In the ensuing years, the festival would enjoy a dozen incarnations, usually as a bicoastal affair, with an October event at Ace Hotel and a May weekend at Brooklyn Steel in New York. For these events, Lynch's foundation teamed up with the online fundraising platform Omaze to raffle off special experiences. Former assistant Mindy Ramaker, who by now had moved on to the role of creative director at DLF, would hit up her old boss to record greetings. If he had availability, which he typically did, Lynch would oblige.

Frequently these videos were straightforward, as with the first-year pitch, in which a sunglasses-sporting Lynch solicits ten-dollar donations ("or more, if you feel it") for a chance to win VIP tickets, or a 2020 video pitch for a virtual coffee to benefit a "Heal the Healers" initiative, in which Lynch would sketch the winner and send them the drawing as a keepsake. If inspiration and additional free time aligned, however, Lynch would sometimes craft a short playacted piece. The two most inarguably performative of these Omaze efforts are the Festival of Disruption's 2017 and 2018 presentations.

Running 1:49, "No One Can Understand David Lynch" was released in early September—either ironically or quite strategically the same week the finale of *Twin Peaks* season three aired—for the October 14-15, 2017, event in Los Angeles. It opens on a small female porcelain figure in a bathing suit, shot in handheld fashion by Lynch. A medium establishing shot, filmed by Lynch's assistant Michael Barile, reveals our subject (in a rare blue shirt!) sitting and looking at the figure while holding a funnel-like object in his right hand. Gazing down, he speaks into it in garbled, unintelligible fashion before a burst of electricity sends a small white flash of animation flying up and off the screen, leaving Lynch with a confused look on his face. Invitational promotional text floats down from the top of the screen, and this process repeats four more times ("You'll meet me and you'll meet Sheryl Lee over cherry pie and doughnuts"), providing more details of the event. It ends with Lynch's gaze returning to the figurine followed by more handheld

footage pushing in closer on it before "Click the link sweethearts" appears on-screen.

Its title a nod to the free-form ominousness of the owls in *Twin Peaks*, "This Video of David Lynch Is Not What It Seems" [Photo to side] was released the second week of April to promote the NYC Festival of Disruption, held May 19-20, 2018. Filmed by Barile and running just over four minutes, this backward-shot piece is captured mostly in black-and-white and features Lynch from the shoulders up splayed out as if on the floor under a desk. Raising his hands on either side of what looks like a gauze-wrapped light fixture, he conjures a small, color-animated figure who sways to Hawaiian music for thirty seconds before returning from whence she came. As Lynch stares intently, the words "five golden rings" manifest and float upward from the fixture, matched by distorted music.

In backward speech, Lynch intones a word and slowly touches all five fingers on his right hand, then presses a button and blows through a tube, creating a gray orb that gets bigger until it fills the screen. Text appears soliciting entries for VIP admission, then violently disappears; the process repeats, this time more slowly, with a second text card noting that Lynch and Kyle MacLachlan want to meet you there. The piece ends with some screen-titled backward speech as Lynch says, "Art. Music. Fun. Meditation," and the letters D, L, and F. This is followed by a flash of light. Lynch's hands flutter, the screen flickers like a glitchy video game, and the soundtrack swells, sounding like Lynch has just won a bunch of tickets playing Skee-Ball.

Individually and in tandem, these videos serve as a reflection of Lynch's belief that value and meaning is found just as frequently in intuitive communication as in concretely expressed words. Ergo, the text blocks handle the necessary lift of specific event details; this then leaves Lynch free to play around the narrative edges in both structure and performance, courting connection through mystery and engendered curiosity. Sound design and background ambience also features prominently in each video.

Is deep consideration given to character in either of these pieces? Not likely, but there's still straight-faced playfulness in each. The 2018 video—unsurprisingly the more ambitious and deeply conceived of the two, given the more relaxed demands on his time relative to the previous summer—finds Lynch leaning a bit into a shamanistic persona while simultaneously having fun again with backward speech, further solidifying a uniquely personal creative ownership of this technique. In both of these short-form works, Lynch displays his passion for the core "art life" principle of simply *doing*, and expressing himself however felt truest in the moment.

—CHAPTER 43—

"WHAT DID JACK DO?" (2017)

David Lynch as a homicide detective grilling a talking monkey seems, as a concept, like a perfect "cabin fever dream." And for many people hunkering down during the COVID pandemic, that's exactly what "What Did Jack Do?" was. More than five years elapsed from gestation to final, wide-platform release, though, and the seventeen-minute film's date of attribution is somewhat a matter of preference; we're going here with when it made its premiere.

The project's origin actually traces back to 2014 and an inquiry from the Fondation Cartier in Paris, with whom Lynch enjoyed a lengthy relationship. "I think they were doing an animal series where they had different artists each month, or at different times they were having these animal experiences, and you created something for that event," said Sabrina Sutherland, who produced "What Did Jack Do?" and wore several other hats during its shoot. "He was asked, and David says, 'I'm going to have a talking monkey.' And that was it. He started formulating it at that time."

"It was an idea that came long before it became what it was," said Lynch's longtime assistant Michael Barile, "and I think a lot of projects for David were that way. He was constantly dreaming and constantly doodling, and I think fragments of ideas would come—or even whole ideas that he would just sort of set aside in a physical drawer or a mental drawer. And then an opportunity would come, and he wouldn't need to search for a new idea. It was already sort of there waiting. This was that sort of thing."

Shot at Lynch's home by Scott Ressler and a small crew in 2014, just before Christmas, the black-and-white short is mostly a two-hander (Emily Stofle makes a brief appearance as a waitress) that finds Lynch leaning once again into lawman mode, but this time as a hard-boiled detective. The film is set at a locked-down train station, and its premise is simple: Lynch's unnamed investigator puts the squeeze on monkey Jack Cruz (also voiced by Lynch), attempting to extract a confession for the murder of Max Clegg, the suspected new boyfriend of chicken Toototabon, Jack's former lover.

Jack is by turns evasive ("Look at me—are my pupils dilated?") and combative ("You can burn in hell!") but also quietly reflective. Asked if he doesn't ever wonder about anything, he replies, "The wonder was in my heart—but you wouldn't understand something like that." There's a selection of amusingly punchy non sequiturs dropped into the mix (echoing the rhetoric of Joseph McCarthy, the detective asks Jack about any Communist Party affiliation, to which Jack replies, "Let me tell you a story") as well as some characteristically Lynchian wordplay ("There's an elephant in the room—I'd like you to start talking turkey," says Lynch . . . to a monkey, about a murder case tied to a chicken, for those keeping score).

For much of its running time, the detective rope-a-dopes Jack, attempting various gambits to elicit an admission of guilt. Lynch long favored blending tones and genres, and while the short's conceit presents as comedic (and it is), there's a good amount of pathos sprinkled in—sometimes even in the same line, as when Jack begins a winding monologue by saying, "For argument's sake, let's say I was a horse. Even so, it'd be hard to imagine how hard my first wife rode my ass." The piece builds to a reverie that crescendos with a performance of "True Love's Flame." It's not quite "In Heaven," and Jack certainly isn't the Lady in the Radiator, but emotionally, it feels like a callback to *Eraserhead* in a small way. Lynch edited the short and worked on its visual effects with assistant editor Noriko Miyakawa; he also cowrote and arranged the aforementioned pining song with Dean Hurley, in addition to performing the tune.

The completed work wouldn't premiere until November 8, 2017, at Fondation Cartier, which held two-year exclusivity rights with an exemption carved out for a stateside premiere on May 20, 2018, at Lynch's Festival of Disruption in New York City. While these screenings were written about, more casual fans had no idea of the short's existence until January 20, 2020 (Lynch's seventy-fourth birthday), when it premiered on Netflix. From there, as the quarantine spread, so did the short's legend, by word of mouth. According to a Netflix source not authorized to speak about viewership data, per its internal metrics "What Did Jack Do?" ranked in the top five of all nonepisodic short-form content for seven of the eight quarters following its release.

"I was contacted about the project pretty shortly before it filmed, and I wasn't given a great deal of information," recalled Ressler. "I think I was told that David would be interviewing a monkey, and maybe a detective was mentioned. So I drew from that that it was either noir or at least had a hard-boiled fiction quality to it. And when I got there, I realized or was told quickly that it was black-and-white, but I wasn't told explicitly that it was noir. They just assumed I would get that because the set was somewhat that way. So I lit it in a more neo-noir way, and then immediately David said, 'No, what are you doing?' So I had to just strip out what I had done really quickly.

"I didn't have a lot of hard lights with me, [but] luckily David had a kit of small lights somewhere else in the house, and we grabbed those and started tacking them up. And so it was a very small shoot and done relatively quickly. I know it was less than five hours, but I don't remember exactly how long. David likes to finish things quickly and I think maintain the energy of it, so definitely there was no sitting around. It was move, move, move."

Shooting with a borrowed Sony Alpha 7S Mark 1, and in standard high-def, not 4K, Ressler faced some monkey-related challenges that helped shape the final look of the film, which embraces video anomalies and added grain to give the piece an additionally aged feeling. "The notable feature of that camera is that it can shoot in very low light," said Ressler. "And so what happened was I didn't realize how small the monkey was. It's tiny—I mean, it was probably ten inches tall or something. And [David] wanted a close-up shot, a head and shoulders, to match the one we filmed of him. And the depth of field, the ability to keep that monkey in focus, was very limited.

"It occurred to me that if I boosted the ISO, the lowlight sensitivity of the camera, to a really high level, then I could stop the lens down, which would give more area in front and behind the monkey in focus," Ressler continued. "And so that's what I did, but that naturally increases the noise. It became a much grainier shot."

Ressler wasn't part of the postproduction process, but he told Miyakawa that shots would have to be treated in post with some noise reduction. "So David probably or to some degree liked it," noted Ressler. "My guess is they probably did a little bit of noise reduction for that and then added noise to the rest of it to match because they just liked it, or he liked it. Those scenes were 42,000 ISO, which is enormously high. And then I think the f-stop was an 11 so that we could have more depth of field, more area and focus."

It's easy to envision Lynch getting most excited—in both preproduction and editing—about some of these types of technical challenges in executing his vision. Performancewise, though, given when it was actually shot, it's amusing to think of "What Did Jack Do?" as a dry run for slipping back into law enforcement as Cole.

Through these two characters—one on-screen, one voiced—Lynch gets to embody both stern authority and rascally defiance, performing against himself and exercising a creative muscle not indulged since his first Barbie coffee commercial (and, before that, *DumbLand*). That Lynch would, in the months immediately after "What Did Jack Do?" was shot, go on to create at least two more short-form works ("David Lynch: Between Two Worlds" and the Tribeca Disruption Innovation Award acceptance video) in which he voiced interacting characters would seem to indicate a headspace in which he was preoccupied with mirrored or conflicted identities at the same time he and Mark Frost had just finished writing *The Return* and Lynch was turning his attention toward preparing to shoot it.

After its release on Netflix, "What Did Jack Do?" began its march toward buzzy cultural reception, enrapturing Lynch devotees but also causing no small amount of befuddlement among folks who stumbled across it on their streaming home page. "I just remember saying, 'Oh, a brand-new David Lynch series,'" said Seth Green. "I turned it on and I'm maybe six minutes in before I just started laughing.

"I was like, 'This is the craziest thing I have ever tried to watch,'" added Green, likening the feeling of its editorial suturing to *Space Ghost Coast to Coast*. "Then I started thinking about how did this get shot? It just felt like madness, like a little bit of crazy. And every time something like that comes out on a major platform, I feel like we've won just a little bit."

"I remember watching that and just laughing at every single thing," said

Adele Jones, who produced "The Black Ghiandola" and appeared in season three of *Twin Peaks*. "I love it when nothing makes sense, because it takes you out of your element. Our crazy human brains that are always trying to calculate and know what to expect and have things be cohesive—David threw that shit out the window."

"I really love 'What Did Jack Do?'" added *Twin Peaks* actress Andrea Watrouse. "We had a screening—me and some of the other cast got together right after he passed and rewatched that. I loved his acting in that, how serious and comedic it was all at the same time."

Meanwhile, Ressler received feedback from both poles of reaction. "I told my mom about it, and I got this call back saying that it was the dumbest thing she had ever seen in her life. But she had a conservative boyfriend at the time, and they watched it together, so I think that influenced her opinion," he said with a laugh. "The former head of the [American Society of Cinematographers], Shelly Johnson, contacted me a couple days after Lynch passed away . . . he'd watched 'What Did Jack Do?' and was blown away. He thought it was one of the most brilliant things he'd ever seen in his life. So it's interesting how radically different the reactions are to that film."

—CHAPTER 44—

"WAITING FOR MR. LYNCH" (2018)

Lynch's history with the Lisbon & Estoril Film Festival, also known as LEFFEST, has deep roots. Its first incarnation, in 2007, hosted a full retrospective of Lynch's work, and he appeared alongside producer and festival founder Paulo Branco (who had spearheaded *Inland Empire*'s theatrical release in Portugal) for a public Q&A session. In 2014, the festival included an exhibition, *Here &Now*, which brought together lithographs by Lynch and French artist Jean-Michel Alberola.

In 2017, the festival moved from Estoril, along the Portuguese Riviera, about a dozen miles north to Sintra, and the following year it chose to again honor Lynch. Held November 16-25, LEFFEST 2018 screened many of his films, plus created a multidisciplinary program centered on two exhibitions:

Psychogenic Fugue, Sandro Miller's 2016 collaboration with John Malkovich, who portrayed iconic characters from Lynch's screen work, and the debut of *Small Stories*, an exhibition of fifty-five large-format photographs from Lynch.

Chrystabell (who served as a member of the festival's jury) and *Room to Dream* author Kristine McKenna also appeared for separate special events, discussing their collaborations with Lynch. In support of the festival, he created "Waiting for Mr. Lynch," a black-and-white one-and-a-half-minute video short that made its world premiere at the gathering.

Presented mostly as a tableau, the animated photo-illustration features a beat-up, bowlegged one-armed baby doll sitting in a small chair slightly to the left of screen on the trash-strewn ground of a dingy room. Slightly to the right is an open window. "Hey," the doll says with a slight wave before its left leg moves, and then its right leg—each of the latter movements accompanied by the sound of an old-timey cash register. There's a flash of lightning and the roll of thunder outdoors, followed by the sound of rain. "I cut my arm off, and I'm waiting for the ambulance to arrive," the doll says, followed by seven seconds of silence, then, "I don't know where Mr. Lynch is. He was here a little while ago and made a real mess of this place." After a dozen more seconds, the doll delivers its final line of dialogue: "My name is Betty. What's yours?" Another roll of thunder is chased by the slowly approaching siren of an emergency responder.

While Lynch's previous Barbie short-form efforts each exuded a mostly pleasant, dreamy vibe, the presentation of this doll gives off an entirely different mood. There's a sense of foreboding, in no small measure owing to the sound design, which elicits unease even prior to the arrival of the thunder and rain.

Like "Between Two Worlds" and even *DumbLand*, this work reflects Lynch's enjoyment with tweaking the timbre of his voice, as the doll (even before revealing her name) has a higher-than-normal register for a female. Also, the piece's conclusion recalls, at least a little bit, another simple six-word query: "Hello Johnny, how are you today?" This leaves a viewer to ponder the significance of Betty revealing her name and its relationship to the unfolding horror.

Overall, "Waiting For Mr. Lynch" is a simple and in some respects slight work—an audiovisual display of gratitude for another honorific, of which there were many—but one that cheekily invites multiple interpretations while also checking the box of expressing Lynch's sense of humor.

—CHAPTER 45—

"FIRE IS COMING" (2019)

The Festival of Disruption, celebrating not only Lynch's films and art but also the music and creative endeavors of others, bore its own Lynch-performance-related fruits when Flying Lotus, a versatile music producer, artist, and filmmaker, performed a DJ set at the event's May 19-20, 2018, New York program. He'd been kicking around for a while the idea of a thematic album centered somehow on fire. When he heard Lynch speak, reciting an ambiguous short piece he'd written touching on the sudden encroachment of the classical element, something clicked and Flying Lotus knew he wanted to use those exact words.

"I didn't know exactly how I would convey the concept of fire at the time, but I just kept thinking about [how] obviously we had wildfires here [in California], plenty of those, but [I was] also just thinking about culture and society and seeing things collapse," he said. "And I had been writing a screenplay about some strange things that happened with a fire in the distance. When I heard that speech at the party, there were some things in there kind of close to the screenplay idea—just really, *really* close—and I loved it."

Thus came into sharper focus the electronic jazz-funk hip-hop hybrid *Flamagra*, featuring a diverse roster of collaborators including George Clinton, Anderson .Paak, Solange, Thundercat, and Little Dragon. For the lead single of his first album in five years, Flying Lotus selected the piece that helped inspire him: "Fire Is Coming," featuring Lynch. Released alongside the single on April 17, 2019, the expressive interlude's music video stands on its own as an arresting piece of short-form art.

Codirected by Flying Lotus and David Firth, the three-and-a-half-minute video for "Fire Is Coming" opens on an animated dystopian landscape as the camera pushes in on a room in a high tower. There, a group of children dressed in wolf costumes engage in room-trashing mayhem. As a siren sounds, they obediently gather and sit on the floor. Emitting a low growl, a wheelchair-bound wolf figure—resembling a demented Wes Anderson-like stop-motion animation creature come to life, half whimsical and half terrifying—wheels itself out. After a flash of light and rumble of noise, the figure's mouth opens, revealing Lynch's face. As a phone in the background rings, Lynch's contribution unfolds: a 258-word spoken piece, pregnant with subtext, in which a (presumably young) boy, Tommy, answers the kitchen phone, his father being downstairs in the basement woodshop and his mother outside tending to her troubled flower garden. When Tommy tells his mother about the call and relates the message from the man on the phone ("He said you would know what it's about"), he sees lines of worry race across her face. As the story winds toward its conclusion, echo and distortion are applied to some of Lynch's words, the sound of crackling fire is introduced, and a percussive beat rises to meet the unsettling mood.

Flying Lotus first got into Lynch's work through *Lost Highway* and his teenage appreciation for Nine Inch Nails and Trent Reznor. Delving further into Lynch's movies (which he knew by reputation), and later his subsequent works, he discovered valuable lessons for his own artistic endeavors. "I found some kinship in his process because when I made my film *Kuso*, that was my *Eraserhead*," said Flying Lotus, like Lynch a multidisciplinary artist with widely varied interests. "That was the movie I was working on with me and two other people, and it was a movie made with friends and favors and all that stuff. So it reminded me of that, the ambition. And it was just also really inspiring. But for me, I think an important thing I'm trying to always keep in mind and consider [as] inspiration from him is he only did things that he was super passionate about. I don't think he's done anything in his career where he was lukewarm about it—except for *Dune*. But I think it's important for someone to go through that and come back and be more true to themself anyway."

While they'd met at Festival of Disruption, Flying Lotus stopped by Lynch's house to play him some music and so that the two could get to know each other a bit better. "I think before we even knew what was going to happen, he let me stop by for a coffee," Flying Lotus said. A rapport established, he made his pitch to Lynch and found a welcome reception. "Part of the reason why it all worked out was because he didn't have to think of anything or come up with anything new, because he's really grumpy," said Flying Lotus with a laugh. "He was like, 'Hey, I'm doing my own thing, leave me alone.' So I was like, 'Look, you got it done—it's done already. Just record it and then lemme use it.'" Here Flying Lotus laughed again at the memory. "So that was the vibe.

"It sounded great. It was what I wanted," he continued, regarding the audio recorded at Lynch's home on Friday, August 3, 2018. "I didn't know how the delivery of that would be, but it's not like I had a specific vision yet [for the music]. I just had to hear what it was and then craft the thing around it, which is what I did."

For the short-form video piece, Flying Lotus also wanted to lean into a unique visual representation of Lynch that embodied a certain amount of mystery. "I initially was going to work with a 3-D animator on it because, again, I wanted to get him in this video, but I didn't want to have him have to leave the compound. So I had to think of a thing that we could do and I could say, 'He doesn't have to go out.' How do I make it super easy to have him say yes?" recalled Flying Lotus, yet again with a laugh. "That was kind of the attitude. So it was like, 'Well, let's put his face on a puppet or something.' But I went myself over there and had him sit, and I took a whole shit ton of pictures of him at every angle for my friend to scan. And we tried some stuff; we tried some tests. But I also, in that time, filmed him saying the speech, and that ended up producing better results—just using his actual face as video and then stitching it onto the puppet.

"As soon as we were done, he was like, 'Can I go back to work now?' It was like, 'Yes, yes, yes you can.'"

Looking back now, there's a prophetic sadness to the piece given the nature of Lynch's passing, which was precipitated by his evacuation from his home during the devastating 2025 Los Angeles wildfires. Its ending is particularly powerful: "Something else scrambled into Tommy's awareness," says the Wolf Lynch. "He saw that the sky was noticeably darker than usual, and he saw a huge red-orange glow moving on the horizon. Just then a man appeared, running frantically in the street, the man yelling, 'Fire is coming.'" The last three words are repeated seven more times.

Taking Flying Lotus's words to heart, Lynch didn't really collaborate on the creation of the wolf character. Rather, it's an example of a performance crafted largely after audiovisual capture by its directors. Still, this is no different from voice work, and the fact that Lynch's prose was self-written gives it extra relevance and resonance. The rooting of his monologue in a specific name (Tommy), his evocative use of key colors, an economic linking of threats both established and unknown—all of these scripted elements combine to serve Flying Lotus's grander musical vision and breathe life into Lynch's first performance outside of his own work for the first time in several years. Additionally, there's a full-circle, smile-inducing sense of kismet that comes from Lynch's art-life-promulgating festival providing unifying clarity for someone else's long-gestating creative work, and that art then featuring a performance from Lynch himself.

"He's an icon. He's got that iconic face and voice, and the hair," said Flying Lotus. "He's a character. In terms of Hollywood and the movie business, I think he really enjoyed those aspects of it just as well when it made sense. He didn't seem like a person who was like, 'I hate being a celebrity, I hate being this person that people imagine.' I think he reveled in the David Lynch-ness that he created. It's like you spend your whole life people telling you you're weird and stuff, and then you make it your success. You make your obsession reality, and you have validation that your dreams mean something." A uniquely shared dream in the case of "Fire Is Coming."

—CHAPTER 46—
ROBOT CHICKEN (2020, 2022)

It would be difficult to come up with an acting role for which David Lynch and renowned rapper and music producer Dr. Dre would be the top two choices. But *Robot Chicken* is not your ordinary show.

Cocreated by Seth Green and Matthew Senreich, the Emmy Award-winning series is a popular stop-motion animated sketch comedy show that has since 2005 made its television home in the United States as part of Cartoon Network's Adult Swim nighttime programming block.

With deep roots in the worlds of comics and cartoons, *Robot Chicken* is like a Gatling gun of farcical humor for in-the-know pop culture fans. Employing action figures, Claymation and other techniques, episodes run around eleven or twelve minutes and consist of mostly unrelated skits varying from a few minutes to mere seconds in length.

Over the course of eleven seasons, the show's opening credits feature a framing device with a white-haired, maniacally smiling character. For the first five seasons this Mad Scientist, as he's known, is presented as the chief antagonist, taking a dead chicken from the road, reanimating him, restraining him in front of a bank of televisions, and making him watch the sketches that make up the episode.

At the end of the fifth season, the chicken kills the scientist, so in the credits for the next two seasons the chicken revives him as a cyborg and returns the forced-viewing favor. A descendant of the Mad Scientist appears in the introductions for seasons eight and nine, which find the chicken taken from a frozen ice block and subjected once again to tortured viewing. There are further credit iterations and some other episodic appearances that shape the character and leave him looking a bit mangled (the Mad Scientist's son plucks out his remaining good eye, to bypass an optical scanner; his name is also revealed to be Fritz Huhnmörder, which translates from German as "chicken murderer"), but this is the most germane buildup and backstory.

Throughout all of this, the Mad Scientist never speaks. The decision to finally give him a voice, therefore, was a significant creative choice. The idea arose in conjunction with the two hundredth episode of the series. "Every season we joke about being canceled, and it gives us an out in case the show doesn't get picked up," said Green with a laugh. "But this time, because we hit such a milestone, we were like, 'God, we should really have a point. Why is the Mad Scientist doing this? Why has he strapped this chicken to a chair for ten seasons and forced him to watch television? It's obviously some kind of great experiment.'"

Since it's the first and potentially only time viewers were going to hear this character, the decision of whom to cast was something *Robot Chicken*'s key creatives took quite seriously, despite the show's wackiness. "For a while we were like, 'Well, let's get a real doctor, like Dr. Dre. Let's get Dr. Dre to do it. That would be very, very funny,'" recalled Green during a shared interview with Tom Sheppard, the director on *Robot Chicken* since its eighth season. "And then the more we started thinking about going out to Dr. Dre, I can't remember who said it first—I mean, it might've been me—but I feel like the second it was even an idea, the second there was a *possibility* that we could go to David Lynch, [Tom] and I became obsessed with the idea. We're like, 'There's no one else. We *have* to have him.'"

"Yeah, I remember the Dr. Dre thing, and then one of us said David Lynch," agreed Sheppard. "I remember you and I locking eyes and just nodding. It was just one of those moments where you just were like, yep, that's it."

The show's casting department reached out. "I was definitely familiar with [the show] and David wasn't," said Lynch's longtime assistant Michael Barile. "I think I sent him a link to clips on YouTube." A yes came quickly, and Green and Sheppard swung into action. "Tom and I were both in shock, so we [said], 'Let's not waste any time. Let's just get out there and record it,'" Green recalled. "And this was the best part—they're like, 'Hey, we have plenty of recording equipment at David's studio, so if you guys would come to us, we'll just give you the tracks.' And Tom and I were like, yeah, *obviously* we'll go to David Lynch's home studio. 'Sure, alright—should I bring him some wine? What's appropriate?'"

So it was that on Tuesday, May 28, 2019, Green and Sheppard made their trek up to Lynch's house. "They were kind of funny, and David's hilarious, so they had a lot of back and forth," said Barile. "It was a lot of laughing that day." At least one attempted spearfished reaction was not successfully elicited, however. "I wore a specific T-shirt just in hopes that he would notice. And I don't remember what I wore now, but I do remember that he didn't notice," said Green with a laugh. "It was awesome, though. We got brought into his screening room and I just thought about the fact that this is where this guy works. He cuts stuff here; he makes changes here. They've got an ISO booth right off the side to do ADR. He just brings everybody to him, and I loved it. It felt so crazy."

"And then the big red curtains," exclaimed Sheppard in addition. "I remember I was so nervous. Seth, you know my favorite thing on the show is working with actors, and I am rarely stressed out about it, but I could almost not talk. I was so glad that you were there with me for the first five minutes. I was just like, 'I can't believe this.' I'm sure you were too, but you were better at covering."

"I've acquired a skill over my career to turn off the part of my brain that knows anything about this person beyond the fact that they're going to be good at the job they're tasked with in the moment," replied Green. "And so if I can do my job well, which is communicating usually in those instances, then whoever I'm working with, whether it's George Lucas or David Lynch, I still gotta get the tracks no matter what. I need to leave with these tracks. So that's the thing that I focus on, how to get that person to give it to us. And he was so game, that's the best part."

Far from simply diving into a cold-reading interpretation of the material, and despite his lines being more of a monologue than dialogue with another character, Lynch wanted some backstory on the Mad Scientist. So the pair gave him a rundown. "I remember thinking, *Is this too much information for him?* But I watched him listen," said Sheppard. "He was really attentive and soaking it in. I think on some level, as with any actor, he just wanted to do a great job. I could see it on his face that he was trying to get as much information as possible to play the part."

The pair also explained their preferred process of recording three takes in a row and making adjustments from there, stopping once they knew they had what they needed. "I remember he did the lines, three takes of it, and I said something. I gave him a note, like, 'Hey, just a little more.' Or maybe, 'Hey, just a little louder,'" said Green. "Whatever it was, it was such a mechanical direction—it was like, 'Just emphasize this, or come in a little bit quicker.' And then at the end, after we got all of it—and Tom can attest to this, my heart almost stopped—he steps out of the booth and he points at me real casually and he goes, 'You're a good director.' I said [haltingly], 'Thanks. Thank you.' And I still haven't quite caught my breath from that moment."

• • •

Lynch made his debut in season ten's final episode, "Endgame," which aired July 27, 2020. For the sharp-eared, Lynch actually makes a small, foreshadowing vocal cameo in the show's opening credits, shouting "Robot Chicken!" toward the end of the theme song by Les Claypool of Primus. This replaces the normal, Frankenstein-echoing exclamation of "It's alive!"

At the end of the episode—which includes a Play-Doh/Plato sketch but is chiefly built around a quest involving the Nerd, a tritagonist character voiced by Green—the Mad Scientist has called a press conference regarding his long-running experiment. "And with that sketch my ten seasons of research has concluded," he says. "Ten seasons of injecting pure streams of pop culture into a captive viewer—what has that done to their brain, what has that done to their mind? All of my data has been plugged into this computer, which will now spit out the answer: what is the perfect joke?" Here the Mad Scientist punches a button, examines the result, and waits a beat before delivering the punchline: "*La La Land*. Thank you for your time."

A nod to the long-lingering fallout (especially on social media) from the wrong-envelope snafu at the 89th Academy Awards in 2017, *La La Land* was always the intended quip and not selected from a deep list of alternate jokes from Lynch's recording session. "It's, like, a good movie . . . but pop takes on its own shape. And pop over time turns things into other things," Green said, laughing again. "And we just felt like *La La Land* really represented, in the Mad Scientist, the culmination of all of his scientific study. *La La Land* really did represent the perfect joke."

After the credits, the Mad Scientist unstraps the Nerd from a chair in front of the TV bank and mutters, "Here we go, buddy," before putting the Nerd in a wooden crate, and then, "Sleep tight, pal," as he nails shut and padlocks the container. Vocalizing to himself in singsong fashion, the Mad Scientist then wheels the box off into a deep warehouse full of other crates, à la *Raiders of the Lost Ark*.

For the eleventh-season finale, meanwhile, "May Cause Season 11 To End," which aired April 11, 2022, Green and Sheppard chose to pull the trigger on another humorous notion that they'd been holding in reserve for a while. Naturally, they wanted Lynch to make an appearance in the assembled ensemble as the Mad Scientist.

"[We'd] had an idea to make one of the episodes end like the end of *SNL* and to have all the cast under the music saying things to each other while they fake hugged or walked around listlessly on the set as the camera caught them," said Green. "And so we put together a whole list of [insults] for him to say, like, 'Fuck you' or 'Yeah, you just try it, asshole.' So funny! And we sent it, and we were like, 'Hey man, at your leisure, three in a row of each of these lines.' And I'm still laughing about it because his takes . . . Oh my God. I still have the file on my personal computer, and I've shared it with other friends of mine who are obsessed with him in the same way, love him in the same way, because you just hear David going [with slight variations in tone], 'Get the fuck out of here! Get the fuck out of here! Get the fuck out of here!' It's unlike any other piece of recorded information."

The episode itself includes jokes about fornicating American cheese slices, a branded cereal named after the Zodiac Killer, and Cookie Monster misunderstanding cookie acceptance on websites before ending with two profane outbursts from Lynch. In the end credits, when a guy tells him he can't wait to not see him for six months, the Mad Scientist replies, "Fuck you, fuckface!" Later, when two purple and pink blobs (ostensibly the episode's musical guest, the Boobahs) surround the Mad Scientist, he exclaims, "I've had just about enough of your bullshit!"

Those pondering, through their laughter, that treasure trove of other vulgar Lynch eruptions are not alone. And there's at least a small chance they could even pop up on *Robot Chicken* somewhere down the line in the form of a gag reel. "We have *a lot* of dialogue from him," admitted Green. "We have *a lot* of takes, and there's an easy way to put it all together as if [the Mad Scientist is] coming through a door or trying to shoot a scene in a kitchen. You could really wrap this dialogue in a way where we could say the greatest highlights of his on-camera career and then cut it into gag lines of him just missing a line and being like, 'Fuck you!' I don't know, we dream about it."

"It's going to click for one or both of us at the same time," agreed Sheppard, "and then we'll go, 'Oh, this is it!'"

"It would have to be its own thing. But the fact that neither one of us has adequately shot it down says we'll probably do it," added Green, laughing again. "It might be a personal project, though. It might be the kind of thing that we couldn't actually release, but [if so] we'll figure it out."

• • •

With all apologies to Dr. Dre, it's incredibly appropriate that Lynch would be cast in a role to bring clarity to a long-running *experiment* given his effusive love for that word itself—and of course all the trial-and-error, free-form creativity it encompassed in his pursuit of the art life. Even in the capacity of his small role, it's hard to see and hear the Mad Scientist and imagine anyone else embodying him. That the character also performs, in so many of *Robot Chicken*'s opening-credits sequences, reanimating fowl surgery that would put Lynch's old "chicken kits" to shame is an amusing, if unintended, meta twist.

Overall, the series was a great way for Lynch to indulge and showcase his sense of humor as well as breathe life into an iconic character—all without leaving the comfort of his own home. In the process, he left a lasting impression on Green and Sheppard, even if their paths crossed in person for a little less than an hour. "I think because he's such a skilled and studied director, he knows things instinctively that other actors may not," said Green, summing up Lynch's talents as a performer. "And one thing that he always uses to his advantage is stillness. It's an economy of movement; it's an economy of facial expressions—everything is targeted and exactly intentional."

The beautiful mystery of some of those intentions in the selection of performative roles, meanwhile, only adds to Lynch's appeal and stature, bringing together disparate fandoms and creating the opportunity for wonderful mash-ups.

—CHAPTER 47—

PANDEMIC LIFELINES (2020-2022)

Just as the events of 9/11 spurred Lynch to lean into a more public-facing persona and talk more openly about his embrace of Transcendental Meditation, there's ample evidence to suggest the COVID pandemic and its attendant quarantine measures sparked a concerted program of artistic outreach.

On the one hand, for someone who enjoyed both set routines and the pleasures of work, there was likely some relief. (Indeed, in an October 2020 interview with *PCS Literary Magazine* he said, "I love isolation.") On the other hand, the pandemic likely separated Lynch from family. Plus, arriving as it did at a time when he was attempting to move forward on casting for a long-form project, real-world slowdown and industry retrenchment forced his creative energies in a certain direction.

Even if he enjoyed isolation, Lynch seemed immediately and acutely aware of the mental stresses it caused many others, and felt some small measure of if not responsibility then at least inclination to reach out and connect with fans of his work, by way of increased posting to his YouTube channel, David Lynch Theater. Are the return of weather reports and other videos in which Lynch appears sharing some whimsy but mainly documenting quotidian behaviors conceptual performance art? Again, I return to the idea that publicly presented routinized acts force interpretation upon a viewer.

These videos also gave Lynch the opportunity, when he so chose, to comment on outside events. In aggregate, several series and stand-alone works served as a balm, both personally and collectively. For some viewers they were an amusement or escape, but for others they helped to provide a sense of normalcy in a world drowning in unpredictability.

Weather Reports Redux (2020-2022)

On Monday, May 11, 2020, Lynch would return to the weather reports he pioneered for his website. The first couple of weeks of his reboot tended to be a bit shorter, in the forty-second range, with some exceptions; on June 6, he would share a lengthy dream he once had about being killed (as a German soldier) on the beaches of Normandy during D-Day. Eventually, the typical length of the videos would stretch back out to around one minute. In November, Lynch would move from close to his outdoor painting workspace to an interior location. These videos eschewed the old pull-down rig. "This was new [and shot] on his phone. He built a kind of contraption to hold it," said Lynch's longtime producer Sabrina Sutherland.

"For the most part David was shooting himself, or I shot him," she continued. "He would set it up first thing in the morning. He had a certain regimen of what he did. He'd set the alarm, he checked the weather, he kept this little sheet of paper where everything was [written] really small—the day and the time and the weather for that day."

Speaking to *ArtReview* in January 2021 and asked directly if he saw these as an ongoing performance, Lynch replied, "I see it as a torment. I have to do this every day. The good news is there's a lot of great people on my site. They're just a good bunch, and they like the weather report and the number each day. And I want to give it to them." It's a classic artist's dodge, dressed up in a sardonicism infrequently but no less amusingly deployed by Lynch in interviews.

In 2021, Lynch would grow a beard, and as it and his hair grew out, the internet took notice. Peak length was achieved on June 1, his usual trademark upswept 'do falling forward in a fashionable emo look; the next day he was shorn and clean-shaven, recommending John Lee Hooker's "Boom Boom." Sometimes Lynch would dip a toe into the melancholic ("Today I feel like just sitting here with you for a while if that's okay"), and sometimes he would acknowledge the psychological toll of simply existing ("Today I'm making a list of all the good things that are happening in the world," and then, holding up a blank pad, "I'm still thinking"). There would be times he weighed in on current events, as on June 3, 2020, when he gave the weather report in front of a sign that read "Black Lives Matter. Peace, Justice. No Fear" and then walked off, leaving it on-screen for a full minute. Or on February 5, 2022, when he condemned Russia's invasion and ongoing war against Ukraine in a stirring direct address to Vladimir Putin.

Mostly, though, there were music recommendations and other ephemeral musings, sprinkled with staple bits of wholesomeness—talking about riding on "the fun work train," and advising folks to take time to enjoy the dining and observation cars—plus ending each workweek with "If youuuuu can belieeeeeve it, it's a Friday once again!" Along the way, Lynch would also settle on a typical sign-off that bent the usual California weather into a sort of nondenominational benediction, with either an affirmed forecast of or a wish for "Blue skies and golden sunshine, all along the way," followed by a hearty held wave paired with the exclamation "Everyone, have a great day!"

On December 16, 2022, after 950 consecutive days, Lynch would bring his weather reports to an end. "I think he felt kind of pressured," said Sutherland. "I mean, that's why we really stopped—he kind of felt like it was a job. Now he had to get up at a certain time. He had to do this because the weather report was something he wanted to get up for [local radio station] KCRW. He wanted to have it before I think nine o'clock, when they do the weather. So it was something where he had to have it done, I had to have it edited, [uploaded and] sent to them. And he was thinking of what songs [to mention], and it became a thing [where] he just didn't want to feel that pressure."

For thousands of viewers, though, Lynch's daily check-in provided value for a long time. "I really enjoyed his YouTube weather reports," said Nae Yuuki, who appeared as Naido in *The Return*. "During the isolating times of COVID, imagining the golden California sun and blue skies he described was comforting."

As an ongoing performance exercise, this incarnation of weather reports seems to check a lot of different boxes—giving Lynch moments to express his sense of humor and indulge an art life routine, not to mention returning to something familiar (an act of importance for everyone in those times). But it also seemed to affirm and even bolster a personal connection to those who appreciated his work. If it was, in some small sense, an incrementally increasing obligation Lynch grew to tolerate more than enjoy, its duration speaks volumes about him as a person.

What Is David Working on Today? (2020, 2022)

A series consisting of eighteen short videos, most between May 28 and August 23, 2020, two more later that same year, and a final entry in 2022 (showing Lynch excitedly building a small, to-scale barn for, as he puts it, "a course on farm" that he's teaching for his young daughter Lula's school), *What Is David Working on Today?* connects as performative salve—a themed program extolling the benefits of workaday projects and simple tasks, an active mind and body.

"I'd said, 'Well, let's do some other content. Let's create some other videos,'" said Sutherland. "He wanted to put some of the old stuff up [online], and I said, 'That's great, but let's do some new stuff. Everybody loves watching what you do, so let me just shoot.' So I was shooting some stuff of him, and then . . . he says no. I don't know if it was he didn't get the attraction of himself—whereas everybody else, just watching him work, it's very interesting. To me, I could sit and just watch him working. For him, it was like 'No one wants to see that.' I'm like, 'But yes, they do, I think. I know I do.'"

In short order, Lynch came around, particularly when his work could be framed in a more active fashion, with him talking to the camera as opposed to just being documented. In his mind that clicked, making it more relatable.

Spotlighted work in these videos includes Lynch replacing the bottom on his beloved workplace wooden sink; patching holes in the knees of his pants; showing off a microphone stand and protective box he built to house the instrument he used each day making weather reports; and presenting a special checking stick ("Wood is such a blessing for humanity"), used in tongue-in-cheek fashion for helping to intuit how to proceed with a piece of artwork. Several entries here would also take on a teasingly artistic bent, showcasing a half-painted glass jar and ping-pong balls, whose raison d'être would be revealed in another series—yes, Lynch's performance art even gave us discrete spinoffs.

Sutherland was right about people finding worth in just watching Lynch talk through whatever project he was working on. The performative aspect here, though, as often as not came from the juxtaposition of Lynch's deep sincerity or some other captured element presented in matter-of-fact fashion with incongruity over the project's value proposition. At the conclusion of a lengthy monologue discussing his design for a wooden iPhone holder, Lynch says, "It's so much fun to build our own things and solve the problems and figure out a way to do it on our own," before pulling out a store-bought version for comparison and cheerfully acknowledging that it works even better.

Other times there's a straight-faced earnestness and enthusiasm that feels designed to pull viewers into a more positive state of mind. When showcasing a rubber mold he uses to cast resin, Lynch details his solution for preventing leaks from his pattern by ardently stating, "I've developed this poor man's mother mold—paper towel impregnated with wood glue," a definitionally accurate description that still can't help but feel like a joke.

Lynch would frequently wish viewers well on their own projects, whatever they were, reinforcing *What Is David Working on Today?* as a series that through both action and framing communicates simple but valuable messages about small moments of perseverance. It held lessons of extra importance to many during the pandemic lockdown and continues to do so today.

Today's Number Is . . . (2020-2022)

On Sunday, August 16, 2020, in a *What Is David Working on Today?* video titled "Jar Final," Lynch revealed the grander purpose of his jar: to randomly select a ping-pong ball from among ten numbered balls, with the winning number then deemed the "number of the day." Beginning outdoors before moving indoors, this series—filmed separately from his weather reports—also ran through December 16, 2022.

As with his other short-form YouTube efforts, Lynch would soon establish a certain soothing uniformity of action and language in his selection ("Swirl the numbers . . ."), each video running just under a minute with a simple text introductory title card that floated gently toward the screen. As things unfolded, a poster on YouTube each day commented, "Man, if tomorrow isn't a seven, I'm gonna lose it." As that digit's drought dragged on and on, the running joke took on a life of its own among habitual commenters. Then, finally, one day: a seven. Lynch, cracking a smile, broke the good news while singling out the commenter by name.

"David would look at comments for sure," said Sutherland. "He didn't pore over them, but every once in a while he'd look and read through and see what people were saying—especially at the beginning, just to make sure that it was still something that was relevant to people. And of course it was still during COVID, so we were shut down and that was something that he could look at and see how people were. And there were some people who said that they were struggling, and David would reach out to them. And obviously all of that's very private, but he was somebody who really cared about his fans and really cared about what people would say. A lot of the time I would go through and pull out [comments] and say, 'Hey, this person wrote this . . . What do you think about it?' So I also was kind of selecting things for him to look at."

While suiting Lynch's established affinity for routine, *Today's Number Is . . .* edges into an ongoing act of performance art by asking viewers to contemplate the pieces' similarities and small differences as well as the meaning—individually and communally—of each day's randomly selected number. There would be a couple of small hiccups here and there (on December 10, 2022, for example, Lynch confessed a camera screwup resulting in a failed recording and announced the number manually, saying, "I can't do it again. You have to take my word for it"), but for 851 straight days viewers had a lucky number to ponder if they so chose.

"The Story of a Small Bug" (2020)

Making its premiere on David Lynch Theater on June 12, 2020, the two-and-a-half- minute "The Story of a Small Bug" showcases another of Lynch's lifelong fascinations—the smaller forms of nature that we often choose to ignore.

A cursive title card on a black screen gives way to a matted composition featuring Lynch standing outside on his property near a retainer wall. "This bug was on the hill here, I think in topsoil," Lynch says, positing that it was "maybe nibbling on a small root when it poked through and came up and found itself coming out of the ground cover up there." The camera at this point pans up. Faced with a steep slope and the consequences of gravity, the bug "started falling down, and it kept catching itself and crawling back up," says Lynch, his fingers waving in animated fashion while describing the action. He ends his introduction at the one-minute mark with a simple declarative sentence that carries surprising emotional heft: "It was desperately trying to get home."

For twenty-five seconds, a small caterpillar-like creature struggles upward against a thrumming aural backdrop, the loosening of soil conveyed with the deeper rumble of a rockslide. Then the bug tumbles out of frame, and in a flash cut we see its new home—in the mouth of a lizard. For the next minute, against an ever-present windswept soundtrack, we watch the lizard attempt to consume its lunch while intercut sounds of digestion, choking, and a light trilling come and go.

It's a model of economic storytelling, and one could easily argue (and indeed be correct) that this is another example of Lynch, creative antennae up, locating narrative in almost anything that surrounds him. Assistant Michael Barile shot the footage of Lynch, while Lynch captured the bug footage himself. What lends the piece a certain performative quality, though, is the opening narration. While plainspoken and inarguably delivered in Lynch's usual speaking voice, it sets an expectation. I don't imagine it was scripted, but it's delivered with an intent that lifts it from the incidental. This editorial hinge, along with the sophisticated sound design, makes for a compelling short-form work, with Lynch's passion for sharing this dark story clearly expressing a desire to connect with his art life roots.

"The Adventures of Alan R." (2020)

An animated piece released during the first week of July 2020, "The Adventures of Alan R." most assuredly offers, in its title, a nod to the Oscar-winning sound designer and sound editor who helped Lynch craft dense and compelling aural landscapes dating all the way back to "The Grandmother," Alan R. Splet.

Running just under ninety seconds, this black-and-white work opens under a percussive and slightly menacing beat with an echoing effect. [Photo to the side. Courtesy David Lynch Theater] At the thirty-five-second mark, under the sounds of a ticking clock and perhaps interpolated swirling wind and labored breathing, the title card gives way to a disembodied head—teeth gritted but not quite touching—lying on a chevron floor whose style will surely look familiar. The head's pronounced ears and open eye sockets also bear a more than passing similarity to Lynch's "Clay Head With Turkey, Cheese and Ants" (1991), which served double duty as the album cover for Julee Cruise's *The Voice of Love*.

In the top righthand corner of the frame is the bottom of a couch or chair, its upholstered curtain fringe (a style popular in older home furnishing of the sort when Lynch was much younger) split open, offering an upside-down "V." Through clenched jaw, the figure voiced by Lynch speaks, saying, "I am not going fishing, Mom." Then, again, after a five-second pause, "Mom, I am not going fishing." (Perhaps there was a fish in the percolator?) Each word is declaratively stated, almost its own sentence. As the piece fades to black, the ticking clock likewise powers down.

It's hard not to view this little pandemic-era curio, shot through with anxiety, as rumination on both aging and acts in which we have no interest that are nonetheless foisted upon us as children. Lynch's line readings communicate both a rising panic and an asserted independence, locating a crucial adolescent pivot point. The similarities in form and style to previous works reflect not so much any grander thematic preoccupation as likely just a connection to Splet and *Eraserhead*, given that his collaboration on exacting sound design was so crucial to that picture's style and mood. As we age, it's common to look back on past relationships, especially when a person with whom we shared an important event or defining success is no longer with us. This work can't help but in a way seem like Lynch reaching out through time and space to a friend with whom he shared a special relationship; the performative component here again feels pronouncedly personal, even as a solo work.

—CHAPTER 48—

THE FABELMANS (2022)

Other than Gordon Cole, of all the Lynch performances discussed with people for this book, none elicited more praise than his turn as director John Ford in Steven Spielberg's *The Fabelmans*. Outside of *Twin Peaks*, it's his most widely known long-form work as an actor. Perhaps that's not terribly surprising. There's some recency bias, true, but a pivotal role in a coming-of-age tale rooted in personal biography from the most acclaimed and prolific American populist filmmaker of the last half-century is going to rightly garner attention. Add in the fact that the cameo arrives in the movie's penultimate scene, serving as a thematic summation and moment of catharsis for our young protagonist, and it's easy to understand why this performance has achieved the profile it has.

Heavily inspired by Spielberg's own adolescence and family dynamics, *The Fabelmans* is a moving portrait of an understandably confused teenager, already falling in love with movies, who finds himself further driven to cinematic storytelling as a way to make sense of his crumbling domestic life.

The movie centers on Sammy (Gabriel LaBelle) and his three younger sisters, computer engineer father Burt (Paul Dano), and artistically inclined mother Mitzi (Michelle Williams). As the close-knit family first moves from New Jersey to Arizona and then settles in California, their bonds fray when Burt and Mitzi struggle with their relationship and eventually decide to divorce.

Toward the end of the movie, Sammy is living in Hollywood with his father, consumed by his passion for filmmaking but struggling with his path forward when a contact lands him a meeting with one of his biggest heroes—John Ford, the award-winning director of *Stagecoach*, *The Grapes of Wrath*, *How Green Was My Valley*, *The Searchers*, and *The Man Who Shot Liberty Valance*. In suit and tie, a nervous Sammy shows up at Ford's studio-lot office and marvels at the posters of his idol's work. When Ford returns from lunch and wordlessly heads to his inner sanctum, his doting secretary, Nona (Jan Hoag), rushes to tend to Ford and then suggests Sammy ditch the tie before sending him in for his chat.

Spielberg spends a full minute ratcheting up the anticipation, focusing on Ford preparing, lighting, and then puffing on a cigar. Finally, he speaks: "They tell me you wanna be a picture maker." Told yes, Ford asks, "Why? This business, it'll rip you apart." As a flustered Sammy struggles with how to respond, Ford asks him, "So, what do you know about art, kid?" When Sammy starts sputtering about how much he loves Ford's movies, the director interrupts him and spits out, "No. *Art.*"

What follows—based on Spielberg's recollection of this real-life meeting—is Ford, with increasing agitation, quizzing Sammy on what the kid sees in several of the paintings on his office wall, pressing him to answer the question "Where's the goddamn horizon?" Drawing answers out of him, Ford then imparts a simple, three-sentence piece of advice ("When the horizon's at the bottom, it's interesting. When the horizon's at the top, it's interesting. When the horizon's in the middle, it's boring as shit!") before gruffly dismissing Sammy. As soon as the youngster scrambles out, he ducks back in to offer his thanks. Puffing on his cigar, Ford replies, "My pleasure."

As Spielberg noted in several interviews, the idea for Lynch's casting came by way of journalist Mark Harris, the husband of frequent collaborator and *The Fabelmans* coscreenwriter Tony Kushner. In a March 6, 2023, interview on *The Late Show with Stephen Colbert*, Spielberg recounted the moment: "The lightbulbs went off—the second I heard that name, I went, 'Oh my God, that's so right.'" For Lynch, however, it wasn't quite the same "eureka" moment. In fact, it took a bit of convincing before he accepted the role.

"David had a coffee with Laura Dern, and she mentioned that Steven wanted to have a chat with him," recalled assistant Michael Barile. "And honestly, I don't know if she told him what it was about or if it was a legitimate surprise, but Spielberg called the office one day and I put him on with David. I didn't often sit in on calls with David, but I would check in with him after the fact. And he just said that Spielberg was working on a picture and wanted him to play a role, and he said that he committed to doing it. I was a little surprised [because] he wasn't interested in acting at all, really. The voice work stuff he didn't mind—he could do it from home. But the idea of being on somebody else's big set, I thought it was kind of interesting."

Other sources recall a more drawn-out process—akin to Lynch's back-and-forth with Louis C.K., in which he first suggested others might be better suited for the *Louie* role—involving a couple of phone calls from Dern and/or Spielberg to seal the deal. But the outcome was the same: Lynch accepted the part, with a couple of small asks (some Cheetos, famously) more than demands. "He requested the wardrobe in advance," said Barile, "to sort of wear it with the eye patch and get a feel for the character in that way." Lynch's producer Sabrina Sutherland helped Lynch with his preparation, and would end up accompanying him to filming.

"So we had I think two weeks with the script before going to the shooting, and I think he didn't really start looking at the lines until maybe the week before. He finally said he had to memorize them," Sutherland said. "We started going through them, and it took maybe two days where he would say the lines and I would correct him, actually, because even though he thought he had them memorized, he didn't have them exact—there would be words that would be missing or whatever.

"And I'm like, 'Well, do you want to say it exactly as in the script?' And he said, 'Yeah, every word, exact.' So any time there were those changes, we had to work on that so he had it exactly as it was written. And then the other issue was the way he delivered lines and what they meant. He worked on that for a while."

The Fabelmans was shot from mid-July through mid-September 2021, and Lynch's scene was filmed at the Wilshire Ebell Theatre, a historic structure in midcity Los Angeles, on Friday, August 6. "I was already reeling from being hired by Steven Spielberg," said Hoag, a bright, amiable personality with a boisterous voice that recalls the enthusiasm of Gordon Cole. "Then I get to work—and you know everything is protected by NDAs these days; they don't want you to know when someone goes to the bathroom—and I think one of the makeup people said to me, 'You know that David Lynch is playing your boss, don't you?' And I looked at her. I couldn't believe it. I said, 'Oh my God, what parallel universe is this?' I'm surprised I didn't go screaming from the building."

The sequence was shot in order, allowing even more natural tension to build, and while Hoag didn't share much screen time with Lynch, he still made an impression. "I personally thought he was adorable, the cutest guy," she said.

"He and I didn't really have any dialogue together. Everything was implied on how well I knew him and that he was in trouble again. But we would be sitting in the same room where his office was, so I'd be in there sitting with him, and he was just so pleasant. What I really remember about him is that he was always grinning—either he was having the best time or he was just really nice. . . . We'd be trying to be quiet, because we couldn't talk then either. I just got a really good vibe off of him. And then at the end, when we wrapped, he hugged me."

"We hadn't rehearsed on that at all, and so David just showed up," said LaBelle, his face lighting up with a smile at the memory. "What was great about that scene was I just spent the entire morning making myself as nervous as possible, for Sammy, because he's seeing a god. So it's like, 'I'm not worthy, and you're a god.' And that's easy to do when you've been spending time with Steven Spielberg. It's easy to do when David Lynch, the guy who made fucking *Blue Velvet*, is about to walk in. And so by the time he showed up, I was just like . . . " Here LaBelle pantomimed standing back, his eyes wide as saucers, and laughed. "As a performer, he was so intimidating, because he was just so good and so precise every single time. And Steven was so excited. Like, I think we ran it once before we shot it, and Steven is running around the room, like, 'Oh!' You know, he was so happy. And I just remember thinking, *I can't mess up.*"

For Hoag, there was a genuine sense of anticipation to the scene with Sammy and Ford, even though she wasn't directly part of it. "So I'm sitting up in the green room, knowing it's going to go on any minute," she said. "One of the crew people . . . came and got me, and I got to watch the whole thing on their iPad with them. I was right above and could actually hear it some. And what a job he did in that scene!"

"One of the things with actors which is difficult, I think—and which David was able to do because he had [the lines] down so well—was you do a master and you might do the whole scene, but then you might come in for a particular piece [in close-up] so you have to know where you are in the script," said Sutherland. "He was really good at that, to be able to just jump to wherever something needed to be repeated, whatever he needed to do. I don't think he had—in fact, I can almost say with certainty that he didn't make—one mistake in terms of the script while he was shooting. I think the hardest thing was maybe doing the lighting of that stupid cigar. He did that a few times."

For Lynch's scene partner, it was an out-of-body experience. "David and I only really communicated between action and cut," recalled LaBelle. "And what I love about that scene is as an actor you have certain moments where you kind of lose yourself and you are only the character—it feels like this superpower control over your emotions, where you're not doing anything but you're doing everything, and at the same time you're kind of floating above yourself. And you can have that in a look, a take, or in one line. But I don't know what happened, whether it was my prep or that David Lynch is just on another frequency. For some reason every time the camera was on me in that scene, I really felt like I wasn't me. And that's a wicked experience to have—that's a very life-changing thing of like, 'Oh wow, I just want to recreate *that* again.' I don't know what it was. But at the end of it, David stands up and says, 'Sammy, come here.' He gives me a hug and then he walks away, and that was it. And I slept really well that night, knowing that I did what I was supposed to do."

• • •

One can analyze both Lynch's performance and his reticence in accepting the role and find lessons in the evolution of his relationship with acting. Here, more than in any other major production since *Louie*, Lynch's performance unfolds on a professional set on which he had no real personal connection. Regardless of his tremendous respect for Spielberg, Lynch had to consider whether or not to take the role. His decision finally to accept was a reflection not only of his positive response to the writing itself, but also his friendship with Dern. One can also reasonably hypothesize that opting in had a lot to do with the curiosity of being involved in a personal project (something with which he was certainly familiar) from someone who had achieved phenomenal commercial success, something that had eluded Lynch.

The performance itself suggests a celebrated figure understanding their impact on a nervous party and calibrating their response accordingly. This is seen both in Lynch's delivery of Ford's second line (waving his hands around when saying "This business—it'll rip you apart") and at scene's end with the half-chortle attached to his reply of "My pleasure." In the 110 seconds between these lines, there is a shrewdly crafted performance-within-performance. Ford was said to sometimes display a temper (most frequently with studio executives) as a show—a way to maintain power through reputational erraticism. Here he's doing it to illustrate to Sammy that he will need a thick skin to survive in a tough business. But Ford's irascibility (per Spielberg's articulated recollections) also forcefully conveys an underlying element of his advice—that in order to find and hone one's own voice and succeed as a director, one needs to look at a broader spectrum of art outside of simply other movies, and to experience the real world, with all its attendant beauty and misery.

It's a fascinating, layered turn—Lynch cantankerously embodying the spirit of another filmmaking legend, but also giving advice rooted in artistic composition and commenting on the moviemaking industry in a trenchant way. These elements can't help but feel metatextual given Lynch's fine arts background and the somewhat at-arm's-length nature of Hollywood respect accorded Lynch—acknowledging his greatness, but frequently unwilling to attach dollars to that polite esteem.

As mentioned, the praise for Lynch's performance was wide-ranging. Lynch was singled out in many reviews, and among the seven credited actors nominated for Outstanding Performance by a Cast in a Motion Picture as part of the Screen Actors Guild Awards. I can attest he also received strong consideration from numerous respected critics groups in Best Supporting Actor voting. It's a showcase role, undoubtedly, but the vigor and intelligence with which Lynch tackled it are its elevating factors.

"John Ford . . . is certainly one of my favorites, someone who I know quite a bit about, and I kept thinking *I don't really see him as John fucking Ford*," said *Twin Peaks* writer-producer Harley Peyton. "But that was really underestimating his acting ability, quite frankly. I love that scene, and I don't know anyone who didn't. He was just great in it. It's funny, but David was a really accomplished actor—as if he needed another skill set, for God's sake. But there's something really nice about that."

"Oh my God, he was a revelation," added *Twin Peaks* actor James Morrison. "Because you can't really tell—and this is said with all the love and respect I have for him—what kind of an actor he is from Gordon Cole, [where] he's so broad and absurd, really. But you truly see it in *The Fabelmans*. He was a formidable actor. I mean, that was a wonderful performance— layered and thoughtful, and drawn with a great reverence you could see. And it was a brilliant idea to cast him in that role too, using one of the greatest film directors ever to play one of the greatest film directors ever, by one of the greatest film directors ever."

"The Soul Detective" director Davi de Oliveira Pinheiro had an interesting international perspective. "I would say that maybe because of what happens in *The Fabelmans*, it may be the last great American film, that mythological beast, in terms of what it is," said the Brazilian-born filmmaker. "[If] D. W. Griffith was the father of the classical language, John Ford is the one who perfected it. So you have this figure who is the perfecter of the classical language (of cinema), where even the experimentation of David Lynch can only exist because John Ford created a plateau [whereby] if this is normal, [then] this is abnormal. You have this filmmaker that is such an experimental filmmaker, maybe the greatest North American filmmaker who ever lived— and that's very, very confusing to say about this film, because you're talking about Ford, Spielberg, and Lynch, and I'm not going to say who of those three I'm talking about.

"You have this axis where you have this classical language, and this conduit of the unconscious [portraying] this classical language author in the film of a guy who is the most classical experimentalist who ever lived. And that is Spielberg, because he's always experimenting but he's just so good you never notice—he's so accessible and in control of his communication skills that even when he goes to dark places, he is very clear about his intention. Because for him cinema is a lingua franca, while for David Lynch cinema may be just another language.

"He likes to work on different canvases, and this canvas is really cool. It's just cool to make films: 'I can paint, and my paintings can get movement. I can make music, and my music can be expressed in separated sounds.' So it feels like that for Lynch, [cinema] was just another instrument for him. But for Spielberg, it feels like the only way he could live."

"[For] me, the best part of *The Fabelmans* was David," said longtime editor Duwayne Dunham. "When I saw it, it was like, that is *so* David, that I asked him when I saw him, 'David, did Steven give you any notes or did he just let you do that?' And he said, 'He just let me do that,'" Dunham added with a laugh. "He did a great job."

"I thought it was one of the most brilliant, hilarious pieces of acting—quite apart from David—that I'd ever seen," said *Zelly and Me* director Tina Rathborne. "I don't know whether it's how much I love David or how much like him it is, but I found it hysterical and brilliant." *The Elephant Man* producer Jonathan Sanger agreed. "I thought the work he did was amazing," he said. "It may have been [Ford], but it was certainly *so* David too. There was a duality there."

For former assistants of Lynch, *The Fabelmans* may have connected on yet another (and is that third, or fourth?) level. "I remember talking to Erik [Crary] and others about this when it came out," said Jay Aaseng. "We were just like, 'Oh my gosh, did you see that?' And we thought there was a lot of David in that. It feels like he's playing a very ornery version of himself. We wouldn't see him get mad that often, but he would get frustrated, just like anybody, and sometimes when he would get really frustrated . . . we're like, 'Yeah, that's basically him just getting really pissed off right now, that character.'"

For script supervisor Cori Glazer, meanwhile, the scene summoned specific memories. "He took on that character so well, I thought. But also I felt like there was . . . " Here she paused, before referring to the well-circulated behind-the-scenes clip from *Twin Peaks: The Return* of Lynch becoming agitated over the offhand mention that a scene could be trimmed. [Photo below] "Not everybody knows it's me that he's yelling at," she said, with a shrug and a laugh. "He did apologize and tell me he loved me, but of course *that* never made it to the clip."

—CHAPTER 49—

CELLOPHANE MEMORIES (2024)

The last publicly known entries in Lynch's performative canon are a series of imaginative promotional videos he created for *Cellophane Memories*, his third and final full-length musical collaboration with Chrystabell. In advance of the album's August 2, 2024, release, Lynch scripted new dialogue exchanges that were then laid over footage of various public domain movies by way of voice-over.

The first of three efforts, "We'll Deliver 'Em," released June 12, is the most straightforward of the bunch. Running just over a minute, it finds two trainmen on a locomotive. As one eyes a superimposed promo block showing the album's cover, the pair (both voiced by Lynch) discuss the lengthy wait for new music by Chrystabell and Lynch and their commitment to getting it to the people, with the more grizzled of the two opining, "I think this one's goin' all the way to the top!"

With "The Moon's Glow," Lynch affirmed the status of one of his most viral tweets—a June 18, 2010 post that "This weekend I'm going to try to find out if I'm connected to the moon" (which he updated three days later, saying "I'm pretty sure I'm connected to the moon"). Released July 19 and running just under three minutes, this short features an ornery old coot (voiced by Lynch) and his secretary (voiced by Chrystabell), beginning with a bit of a spat about music ("You weren't on the list 'cause you didn't buy their last album—you just kept listening to mine!") before the latter starts taking dictation. The man gets testy at the secretary's suggestion to hydrate ("I don't like drinkin' water!") before two men (also voiced by Lynch) enter, and the conversation eventually lands on the notion of a dead mule eating an apple.

Running just over four minutes and released July 26, "Will There Be Anything Else?" centers on two men in a diner, each beset by crisis. One bemoans "a big boil the size of a big red apple" on his rear end, while the other is enduring a much more existential crisis, eventually pondering the date of August 2 and a curious act from his dream that would unlock its meaning. "Those were always fun to do," said Lynch's producer Sabrina Sutherland, who lends her voice here to a waitress on the receiving end of a hilariously unexpected rejoinder. "He has a great sense of humor, and that was his chosen thing to do. He wrote out lines for it matching what was there, so he had to really work at it to make it fit what they were talking about."

"David had an idea and he said, 'Chrystabell, I need you to set me up with all of the latest films in the public domain,'" recalled his *Cellophane Memories* collaborator. Swinging into action, she located a healthy slate of such movies, with 1945 noir *Detour* (used for "Will There Be Anything Else?") being the best known. From there, however, it was no quick task; in fact, Lynch could watch for hours until one of the movies spoke to him in a certain way. "Of course, in between all of these things, he's doing work on Photoshop," continued Chrystabell. "There's always some creative endeavor that's being explored. That's what life is for David. And when he got the inclination to go watch some public domain films and work on promos, then that's what he does. If he's going to go on his computer and watch videos of Maharishi just to feed his spirit, then he does that. Everything is very exactly as he feels inclined."

The shorts ended up being crafted over roughly a five-week period, Chrystabell estimated, and when inspiration finally struck, the resultant work would flow fairly quickly. "When he found the one that's talking to him, all of the voices, all of the words come out, and he's got everything going," she said. "Then I cut up the part that he wants, and we upload it into Premiere Pro, and then from there with the same little recorder that we used for all of *Cellophane Memories*, he does the voices."

A director to the end, Lynch didn't inattentively outsource the particulars of the work after the voice-over recording was complete, instead giving Chrystabell detailed feedback on subtitle placement and the like. "He wants it very specific—how the words look, the spelling, where the apostrophes go," she said. "He's like, 'That's great, but this needs to last a little longer,' because he knows how it looks in his mind.

"I'm so grateful we got to work together in that way, which was so much fun. We had the first promo, and he just loved doing it so much. He was like, 'Well, let's make some more,'" Chrystabell continued. "He would go through many, many more hours of public domain [footage], and there was never a manufacturer of the spark. It was always either it was there or it wasn't, but then he found some more. I think during one of them I was back in Texas, and we were doing that remotely and Sabrina was helping. [Assistant] Michael [Barile]'s the glue that holds everything together, and Sabrina is the lubrication that keeps everything going. But between the two of them, David was so beautifully cared for, and then I got to come in and make music and create art and share time—it was a beautiful, beautiful time."

As for any special insights into the rumination that "a washed butt never boils" or the inclusion of a bit of animation of a singing ant being electrocuted, the particulars of those "Will There Be Anything Else?" inspirations remain with Lynch alone. "Those things come to him, and he's so tickled. It's like it was a little special delivery: boop," said Chrystabell with a smile. "It's something that got in his mind, and he's just like, 'Ah, there it is. It's something that didn't exist, and now it will always exist.' And for me, it was like opening presents—what is it going to be? Sometimes I'm there when those things are happening, and sometimes I'm not, or I'm there for part of it, and then he finishes it and I'm like, 'Oh, wow, I didn't see that one coming. I couldn't have predicted that.' And then you're like, of course—I mean, anyone who thinks that they can predict what David Lynch will do clearly doesn't know David Lynch."

The *Cellophane Memories* promos reflect multiple avenues of performative fulfillment for Lynch—the personal, obviously, given the closeness of his relationships with Chrystabell and Sutherland; his sense of humor; and then also the added experiential/curiosity factor of applying a creative lens to already existent material. In this respect they serve as interesting expressive experiments, and perhaps in their very lack of a grand, unifying statement (other than "Hey, we've got an album coming out!"), there's actually an artistic lesson underscored.

Indulging Lynch's general playfulness, his affinity for wordplay, and his fascination with old Hollywood, these shorts reflect Lynch being seized by, and surrendering to, the lure of an idea—something Lynch evangelized about for years. That they ended up being his last performance is quite sad, but in a way poetic, given the robustness with which they embodied so many things that prompted him over the years to step into some of his own art.

−CHAPTER 50−

A FALL FROM GRACE

Readers who visit IMDb (at least as of the time of this writing) will see a project listed in Lynch's acting credits as "upcoming," in which he was to play a character named William Tabb. Titled *A Fall from Grace*, the project has existed in this same state of mysterious suspension for more than a decade (long before the 2020 Tyler Perry movie of the same name), and throughout the years one would occasionally hear various rumors about its re-formation or start-up. Given Lynch's fondness for secrecy, sometimes one would even encounter word from an aspiring clout farmer that it in fact had already been shot.

This is not true. While there might be an alternate timeline in which the project exists in actualized form, in our current realm it is unrealized, and will remain so. Jennifer Lynch, however, provided some information about what could have been an intriguing daughter-father collaboration and notable entry in Lynch's acting filmography.

"It was always meant to be a feature," she said. "But I did a short teaser for it. We were trying to raise money and interest, and I was fortunate enough to have my daughter in it and have Bill Pullman narrate it, which was fun. It was a little teaser about kidnapped girls, and it was nice and dark, and we had a blast making it for five bucks."

The idea for *A Fall from Grace* originated with Eric Wilkinson (credited in some projects as Eric Charles), a St. Louis native struck by the unusual history and creepy vibe of the abandoned Old Chain of Rocks Bridge over the Mississippi River. His detective thriller script didn't quite click with Jennifer, so she passed on it. Wilkinson was persistent, however, and gave his blessing for her to completely rewrite it. After she did, the project came together with Wilkinson and fellow producer David Michaels, with whom Jennifer Lynch had just worked on *Surveillance*, teaming up to secure funding. In early 2012, she was touted in a press release as the film's director.

"The script was one that Dad really liked, and there was a role in it that the gentleman I was working with at the time said, 'You know who'd be great at this?' And I instantly knew they were talking about Dad, and I said, 'Yes, he would. He'd be fantastic,'" said Lynch. "At the time, we were in cahoots with Tim Roth to play the lead male, and so he would've been playing Tim Roth's father. And William Tabb was not a well man, but he was a gentle man and had a great and dark history. And I was talking to Dad about the role, which he agreed to once I told him he could have a sore. He wanted a sore on his face." Here Lynch laughed, the memory clearly tickling her. "And I said, 'Yes, nothing [pustular], but you can have a raw red spot.' He goes, 'Great, great, great, great.' That was his big request—that I allowed him to have a sore. And he just gets more and more fucking charming the more words he speaks, so even if he'd said, 'It has to be [pustular],' I probably would've given in."

In late February 2013, news broke in the Hollywood trades about the senior Lynch's casting in the project, with Roth starring as a homicide detective on the trail of a serial killer. (Other names mentioned in the prospective cast included Vincent D'Onofrio and Paz Vega.) It was this iteration of the movie—which was always meant to shoot on location in St. Louis and make prominent use of notable locations that Lynch had scouted and soaked up while shooting the aforementioned teaser—that got closest to filming.

While *A Fall from Grace* was very much more an investigatory thriller than a domestic drama, Lynch's proposed role was no stunt cameo. The father-son relationship connected substantively to the film's plotting, and the idea of David Lynch sharing the screen with Roth is a fascinating one. (Their potential pairing lends an extra dimension of relatability to the warmth of the greeting between the two in the behind-the-scenes material from *The Return* in the "From Z to A" release.)

"There were two very important scenes in the film that would've included Dad, and I think he would've done a masterful job at it," said Lynch. "As you know from his own work, and from his own acting, there is both an incredible boldness and an incredible gentleness about him. And those were the two greatest ways I would've described William Tabb. William wasn't all here anymore when we met him. He'd lost a bit of his mental capacity; he saw things a certain way from a certain time and wasn't always in the present moment as it actually was. And Dad would've done a beautiful job at that as a man who had done not always the right thing in his life but found himself in a very vulnerable and gentle space today. It was also a big coup—everybody was very excited that he said yes. And of course when people found out we had attached him to the film, the film got even more attention."

Financing independent films is extremely difficult to navigate ("Such an incredible fight, and so delicate—like one wrong move and there's no money for anything," Lynch aptly noted), and the public announcement of movies that then end up unraveling is more common than a layperson might think. Actors commit to projects in which they have a genuine interest but tend to have more than one job a year. As windows of availability shift, casting commitments change, and sometimes pledged money walks out the door too.

"I moved on when it was starting to look like we were not going to get financed in time to make things work with the people we wanted to make it work with," said Lynch. "I've been several times involved in projects, whether *Boxing Helena* or *Surveillance* or what have you, where at a certain point it's just time to either rethink the whole piece with new people in a new way or it's time to let it go. And there were some personalities involved in the project that I just felt, when things got to be their most bleak, I didn't necessarily think people stepped up the way they could have stepped up. And I just thought that was a sign about who I should be working with and who I shouldn't be working with. So I made a very gentle decision to just accept the fact that we weren't going to get financing. And because it was a movie, in essence, about a detective who breaks a pedophile ring, there were some very dark, delicate moments in the script, and I didn't want to do that with the wrong people."

It seems odd, this phantom credit lingering on ostensibly reputable film databases for more than a decade. One supposes it can't last forever—at least not with David Lynch's attachment still listed. But even Jennifer Lynch doesn't necessarily know if *A Fall from Grace* (whether her script or another iteration) will ever see the light of day. "It's kind of floating around somewhere. I don't know if it's with anybody else," she said with no bitterness, only serenity. "I know that the two producers I was working with are now well into different lives. One is directing, and the other I believe is married and doing something else entirely."

"I don't even think it should still be on IMDb," she continued, "but I think some people involved in it are still using that as somewhat of a calling card, even though years and years have gone by. And I don't fault anybody for maintaining whatever credit they can maintain for things. I get it. I have a good sweater I pull out every now and then." Here Lynch let loose with another laugh. "I look good in that sweater, and I'll pull that out if I need to look good," she said. "But I was very touched that Dad said yes and was very excited to be directed by me. And all he wanted was a sore—that was his toughest negotiation."

• • •

As our conversation wound down, I related to Lynch a personal detail that's connected, in its own way, to the character of William Tabb, and it's telling that her first reaction was one of openheartedness and compassion.

During the time I spent working on this book, my father had been struggling with dementia. There are good days and bad days, with the balance, over time, tipping slowly over into the latter category. He understood I was working on this project, and then, at a certain point, he kind of didn't. Not really.

Even before this, though, David Lynch's work was not my father's cup of tea. It just never connected; he didn't respond to it. While a dedicated movie buff (back in the days before streaming, when these things called VHS tapes existed, he would set timers to record the "free weekend" promotions HBO occasionally ran, religiously switching out tapes every six hours, then labeling index cards to create his own home video library), my dad preferred what I call meat-and-potatoes filmmaking—conventionally plotted dramas told in straightforward fashion.

When my father first heard of Lynch's death, though, despite it being a day he was struggling considerably, he immediately snapped out of it and said, "Oh, I'm really sorry to hear that, because I know you liked his movies and his work." This one detail then became a conversational touchstone for a very long time, because he connected Lynch's passing to my work, and it worried him greatly.

To Jennifer Lynch, there's a poetic loveliness in that sentiment. "I love that he was a channel for a connection and a coherent moment," she said of her father. "William Tabb had a bit of dementia, and I think it's beautiful that your dad, although not capable of appreciating him and his work the way you did, knew so much that you did, and loved you, and that you two shared a moment of great clarity, where it was like 'Well, he's gone. Well, does that mean your joy is gone? Are you going to still get to do what you love to do?' That's a beautiful thing.

"*A Fall from Grace* has a very special place in my heart because of the writing that I did for it, the subject matter, and the fact that I was going to be working with Dad," she continued. "And it was not in a fit of joy that I backed away. It was with great gratitude that it almost happened, because I wanted to make sure the film had the budget and the cast it deserved so that it didn't become something that either made a mockery of or less of the subject matter. But we never saw it to fruition, which still makes me sad."

—CHAPTER 51—

"I'LL CATCH YOU WITH MY

GRAB BAG . . ."

David Lynch lived a full life, existing in the public eye for quite a long time. When attempting to tackle a career-spanning project like this with, ahem, an atypical frame, one finds themself sifting through no small amount of informational shards—chasing down rumors of a voice role in a Swedish animated short, say, or participation in a Canadian student film from the 1980s. Once compiled and ordered, some projects are inevitably going to be left on the outside looking in. Still, it's worth touching on these titles.

First, in the spirit of myth-busting, there are a couple of "almost" performances that turned out in the end not to be. At the top of this list is probably the animated mystery comedy *Gravity Falls*, which debuted in 2012. Creator Alex Hirsch has been vocal about wanting Lynch to voice Bill Cipher, an interdimensional demon who served as the show's chief antagonist. "David received the scripts and read them, but didn't feel the part was right for him," said Mindy Ramaker, his assistant at the time. "But he did consider it." (Hirsch would end up voicing the role himself.)

There's also 2004's *Jiminy Glick in Lalawood*. David Lynch, as a character, appeared in this movie quite substantially, smoking up a storm, providing opening narration, rhapsodizing about his fondnesses ("I like the idea of a dark road—darkness is like a magnet to madness"), and helping frame, drive, and resolve the comedy's murder mystery. Lynch was offered the role, and despite both his affinity for detectives and his previous relationship with multihyphenate Martin Short (who was at one point set to topline *One Saliva Bubble* with Steve Martin), he ultimately passed. Short himself would portray Lynch in heavy makeup, delivering an impression that misses the mark.

On the other hand, Lynch was in fact never approached about a cameo in Denis Villeneuve's *Dune*, six sources on both sides of the equation confirmed; Warner Bros. and producers knew better than to kick that hornet's nest.

In terms of things that do exist, there's the 2012 music video for "Crazy Clown Time," which is certainly a vibe. Recollections of this piece came up with several interviewees, typically followed by laughs of disbelief. Lynch directed the video—a backyard nighttime party in which a collection of intense and/or boozed-out characters provide an in-unison percussive beat and descend into madness while Lynch's falsetto-delivered lyrics describe in forthright detail their clothes and destructive actions. His on-screen participation, however, is limited to musical performance inserts shot separately and put on a monitor. "David actually camera operated most if not all of that," said cameraman Scott Ressler. "We had two cameras going, but of course he got the good spot first, and then I squeezed in wherever I could."

Also on the music side, Lynch directed the 2011 concert *Duran Duran: Unstaged*, shot with Peter Deming. Initial plans were to include intensive, completely live in-camera special effects; some of those fell away, but it's still a visually ambitious work. Lynch pops up to kick off the whole affair as a gleeful emcee. Sporting sunglasses and holding forth for just over a minute in staticky black-and-white footage with lots of camera movement, Lynch says, "Welcome everyone, to [the] March 23 Duran Duran live cyberspace concert! This is not your normal concert. This will be an experiment—a kind of live conjuring of spontaneous musical images and today's concert. I'm hoping for some happy accidents." When he ends the bit by saying, "When I snap my fingers, the concert will begin," one can't help but feel it's Lynch trying on the persona of a TV host, if only for a moment.

Lynch inspired so many other artists that it's not particularly surprising to see interviews with him spun off into acts of artistic repurposing, embracing a variety of modes, moods, and techniques. At the top of this list is Jonas Hollerup Helle's hilarious, exquisitely edited mash-up of separate interviews with Lynch and Cher; part of the Danish artist's *The Talk* series, made entirely of appropriated clips from *Charlie Rose*, it imagines an odd conversation between the pair. One probably wouldn't choose to tally as a performance Agnieszka Jurek's "Does That Hurt You?," a twenty-six-minute short on the making of *DumbLand* in which some of her animation is intercut with overlays from Lynch's cartoon series and video of a warm transcontinental interview between the pair. But what about Sascha Ciezata's animated two-minute short "When Lynch Met Lucas," which imaginatively adapts the edited audio of a 2010 interview in which Lynch tells the famous story of flying up to Skywalker Ranch to take a meeting with George Lucas about directing *Star Wars: Return of the Jedi*? Here a director pulls a performance from other material but assigns it meaning with much thought and care.

While not available online, single-word answers by Lynch from a 2001 interview during *Mulholland Drive*'s Cannes presentation are spliced with moments of silence and preconversation tranquility in Claudette Bernini's meditative, ninety-second "Impressions from Another Plane." An even shorter but far less interesting apparent interview grab comes in *Rocksteppy*, a (quite tiresome) 2017 comedy in which a five-second Lynch clip expressing unfamiliarity with the movie's fictional music duo is thrown into the mix.

Much stronger cases for performance can be made for material in which Lynch either had a hand in creating or more actively opted in to. One such example is Raymond Depardon's "The 8th Floor," a 2014 short-form, Cartier-exclusive, nonfiction art installation piece with Lynch, Agnès Varda, Takeshi Kitano, Patti Smith, and others, each individually featured sitting in a minute of silence.

Stretching back further, there are several offerings from Lynch's website, from the aforementioned "panties-in-mouth" bit to a trumpet-led announcement of a special "Lunch with Lynch" promotional contest winner.

The most intriguing of this batch is "Pierre and Sonny Jim," one of the first pieces of DavidLynch.com content. Running three and a half minutes, the short centers on a pair of inflated white rubber gloves with rudimentary faces (two eyes, two nostrils, agape mouths), with puffed-up digits lending the appearance of spiky hair. Each balloon-head is in turn perched upon a small, short-sleeve dress shirt, one white and one patterned (but both buttoned up to the "neck," naturally).

The title provides a nod to Lynch's belief that names can carry inherent significance, something he's mentioned in interviews. Sonny Jim (perhaps a reference to the imaginary child in *Who's Afraid of Virginia Woolf?*) makes a reappearance as the name of Dougie and Janey-E's son in *The Return*; Pierre, meanwhile, dates back to "The Cowboy and the Frenchman" and Mrs. Tremond's grandson in *Twin Peaks* and additionally pops up in *DumbLand*.

The short unfolds as a minimaster class in sound design, with what sounds, variously, like air escaping from balloons being rubbed together, a whistling teakettle, squealing pig, a whinnying horse, an agitated monkey, and a whining child. This renders our titular characters Minions predecessors, as they communicate with increasing distress in a "language" entirely their own. Lynch collaborated on the short with director Eli Roth, who at the time worked as one of his assistants. "We did the voices and the sound effects," Roth said, noting their use of a children's novelty fart machine. "We puppeteered them and I helped make costumes and David of course drew the faces. We were very committed. It was just experimenting and laughing and having fun."

The number of other short-form videos Lynch recorded, especially over the last ten to twelve years of his life, is considerable, according to assistant Michael Barile. Occasionally these involved animation, but they seemed to have mostly leaned toward live action with effects, which Lynch could turn around quickly. "David generally waited until the last minute to shoot these kinds of things," said Barile. "If we had a deadline, he'd shoot it the day before, cut it, mix it, and turn it in on the day. He definitely did procrastinate, but he also definitely liked to wait in case he got more ideas or another, better idea, which sometimes happened."

Everyone who was in Lynch's professional orbit has their own personal favorite of these pieces of ephemera. For me, one of the funnest and most striking may be "David Lynch: The Unified Field," a sixty-five-second mixed-format concept produced in advance of Lynch's same-named, first major museum exhibition in the United States, held September 13, 2014-January 11, 2015, at the Pennsylvania Academy of Fine Arts. Opening with the sound of a struck match, it features Lynch in repose from the torso down, a smaller shot of his head featured in tight close-up and shadow at an impossible angle. As text touting the show unfolds, Lynch serves up nonsubtitled gibberish, an oddly soothing cross between backward speech and baby talk. As a performance, it endorses feelings' supremacy over language—a thematic staple of his oeuvre. At the end, as the slightest smile from Lynch acknowledges both the honorific and the piece itself, five words appear on screen: "Thank you, my neck hurts."

Another amusing standout is a two-minute welcome video Lynch recorded for 2017 Comic-Con, shown in advance of the convention's panel with cast members from season three of *Twin Peaks*. Under the strains of the show's iconic opening credits song, it unfolds as three discrete absurd direct-address comic vignettes ("I gotta show you something," says Lynch, wresting an object from a clenched fist he pulls into frame from below. "This supposedly is the last golf ball O. J. Simpson hit before going into prison in Nevada"), each interrupted by off-screen noise and eventually static.

More short-form videos have popped up recently, especially in the months after Lynch's passing. But these pieces were frequently intended for small audiences—special event introductions, festival benedictions, symposium acknowledgements, and the like—with no complementary online component. As such, many have still not surfaced, and perhaps never will.

Among the most interesting quick-hit performative one-offs, in my opinion, are a quartet of offerings in which Lynch inarguably presents as himself but also casts forth a persona that either advances or sustains his public image.

"David approaches things like a performance artist would in that he's brave and kind of fearless," said Ressler. "He doesn't care what you think of him in that respect. A lot of this is supposition, but I just think . . . the way his mind works is often to try to figure out a way that hasn't been done before. So his character in *Twin Peaks* with the double hearing aids and so forth—I mean, when have you ever seen that before? I just feel like [his is] less of an actor's approach and more of an artist's approach."

Early in his career, before that identity was more firmly set, Lynch made a thank you video, shot by Frederick Elmes, for the Nuart Theatre in Los Angeles, a beloved, three hundred-seat art house that for years played *Eraserhead* as a midnight show. In a minute-plus piece that played before 1982 screenings of his reissued film, Lynch sits on a couch between five Woody Woodpecker dolls, whom he introduces in sincere fashion as Chuck-O, Buster, Pete, Bob, and Dan. After expressing brief appreciation for all the support for *Eraserhead*, Lynch says, "The boys wanted me to wish you peace and happiness. These guys aren't just a bunch of goofballs. They know that there's plenty of suffering in the world, and they spent many years with little iron hooks in their backs up on Sunset Boulevard. But they tell me there's this all-pervading happiness underneath everything, and the more time I spend with them, the more I believe it. So we wish you peace and happiness."

For me, watching this decades later, and paying particular attention to the words Lynch uses, it reads quite clearly and remarkably as a cryptoperformance, a way to stump for Transcendental Meditation without naming it. In this controlled environment (working in short form, and with a close friend), Lynch is telegraphing traits that would anchor his burgeoning public persona as a genial eccentric. As for the dolls themselves, in an interview with the Hollywood Foreign Press Association on May 22, 2017, at the Four Seasons Hotel in Beverly Hills, Lynch reminisced about rescuing them and shared an update on their fate. "They were my dear friends for a while, but certain traits started coming out, and they became not so nice," he said with a small laugh. "They are not in my life anymore."

A very close second for me in the performance art category is Lynch sitting with a rented cow stumping for *Inland Empire* awards consideration for Laura Dern on Wednesday, November 15, 2006. It's a beautiful, full-hearted gesture if ever there was one, and a savvy way to leverage personal celebrity in the attention economy. But it's also an act that embraces his well-documented eccentricity.

Lynch ended up sending news editors scrambling, spending roughly four hours at the intersection of Hollywood Boulevard and La Brea Avenue with said bovine and another four hours at the now-shuttered Tower Records, two and a half miles west on the Sunset Strip, with *Polish Night Music* collaborator Marek Zebrowski providing accompaniment on keyboards.

"The night before, he told me he was going to spend a couple days with a cow," said Jennifer Lynch with a laugh. "I didn't know exactly what that meant, and I think I'd grown so accustomed to hearing absurdities that I didn't say 'What the hell are you talking about?' But of course the next morning at 10:00 a.m. I knew what he was talking about. It was all over the news, and he really enjoyed spending time with that cow. He was worried at first that the cow was going to be unhappy amidst all the traffic and everything, but he claims that the cow and he had a great time together."

"It was some sort of inside moment or joke with he and Laura about cheese," said Erik Crary, who was on the scene for part of the day with fellow assistant Jay Aaseng, shooting video and providing support. "I can't remember everything now. Somehow that led to him renting a cow." Speaking three days later to the Hollywood Foreign Press Association at a press conference at the Beverly Wilshire Hotel on November 18, Lynch talked about the event in characteristically amiable but oblique fashion. "Necessity is the mother of invention. I got this idea to go out for Laura Dern on the street," he said. "I like cows and I say that I love cheese, and cheese is made from milk and I ate a lot of cheese during the shooting [of the movie], so it seemed to make sense to me. And people loved the cow. . . . It was really beautiful."

"It was a performative thing," said Aaseng. "Except that he was pretty much just being himself on that one from what I remember. Looking back on it, I wonder what he thought was going to happen. I mean, he clearly went out there, and it's not his personality to do something like that whatsoever. So he clearly had to get into some sort of different headspace.

"Somehow, maybe just because it was so sporadic and people didn't have warning, even though there were a lot of people that were coming out to say hi, it was a pretty respectful thing. A lot of fans came over, shook his hand, and took a selfie with him and stuff. But it was like he was just there and open to the universe at that moment. He was very gracious with whoever approached him [yet] he wasn't in any kind of a schmoozing, glad-handing mode. He was just willing to sit there and kind of be himself. He wasn't even making a point to be like, 'Oh, yeah, thanks for coming out—see the film.'"

Years later, Lynch would again win the daily internet by taking part in the ALS Ice Bucket Challenge on Tuesday, August 26, 2014. After being nominated in this viral fundraising/awareness campaign by both Dern and Justin Theroux, Lynch added a double shot of espresso to a bucket of water and then pulled out a trumpet (of which he owned several) to play a snippet of "Over the Rainbow" before getting doused. Ramaker, who filmed the bit (and can be heard trying to suppress a laugh), acknowledges that if there was a performance here, it wasn't when that water hit him, as that was in her view one of the most raw reactions Lynch ever had on-screen—a fact underscored by his involuntary gasp when his son Riley dumps the second bucket of cold water on him. Instead, Lynch's performance is rooted in his fifteen-second trumpet solo, connecting back to his lifelong embrace of *The Wizard of Oz* and frequent implementation and transmutation of its filmic vocabulary. It's also present in the back-end plot twist when Lynch, as was characteristic of the challenge, passes it on by nominating another person— in this case, Vladimir Putin . . . who, in yet another demerit on his soul, did *not* accept Lynch's challenge.

One of the last acts of performance art from Lynch was his 2024 Super Bowl commercial. "Wait . . . *what?*" It's true. Lynch voiced a thirty-second spot that year for Noteworthy Paper & Press. The commercial's roots stretch to Maximum Effort, a film production company and digital marketing agency cofounded in 2018 by George Dewey and actor Ryan Reynolds. Their marketing arm was acquired in 2021 by MNTN, an advertising software platform that focuses on performative metrics to help brands optimize ad spends, and under that banner it devises and implements campaigns. The idea was born for a case study: to run a local business ad in a small market during the most-watched TV event of the year and also on streaming networks using targeted-consumer software to see which performed better. Lynch's hometown of Missoula, Montana, was selected for its high concentration of small businesses (you can see where this is going), and Noteworthy was identified as a good fit.

Creative team Kathleen Swanson and Pierce Thiot, who would also end up writing the narration Lynch provided, had the initial idea for the piece, and things moved quickly. Maximum Effort first reached out to Noteworthy on Monday, January 22; virtual meetings ensued, and by Thursday a film crew was in Missoula shooting stylish B-roll.

Lynch recorded his voice-over from home on Friday, January 26, in advance of the game on February 11. The script: "Hello, I'm David Lynch with a word on paper. In the world of screens and pixels, Noteworthy Paper and Press is a sanctuary where stories unfold on paper. Rediscover the tangible: postcards, paper gifts, messengers of sentiment in a digital era. Order online at NoteworthyStore.com, or come on in."

"Lynch's roots in Missoula added resonance, but the fit goes deeper," explained Dewey. "His voice brings an unmistakable tone of surreal nostalgia and reflective calm, perfectly complementing Noteworthy's handshake between tactile tradition and modern storytelling. The pairing elevated what could have been a purely local spot into something poetic.

"His work has always captured the uncanny texture of small-town life, which made him a natural fit to highlight a small shop with an outsized sense of character. Creatively, it was the perfect juxtaposition: one of the biggest names in cinema on the biggest stage in advertising lending his sensibility to a tiny Montana business."

This voice-over represents an incredible and unforeseeable full-circle moment. If *The Return*, jam-packed with details and memories from Lynch's artistic and personal life, didn't make clear his belief of art as life and life as art, there's a symmetry here that underscores that view. Lynch's participation summons to mind numerous points of reference, from Leland Palmer's shouted line of return delivery to Maddie Ferguson in *Twin Peaks* to his own early, four-word press kit biography: "Eagle Scout: Missoula, Montana." It's easy to see why Lynch grabbed the opportunity of this commercial—which reached more than seven million viewers—and what the act of its performance, far more than its words, likely meant to him.

—CHAPTER 52—

DAVID LYNCH: COMEDY ICON

Lynch's Valentine's Day 1997 interview on *Charlie Rose* featured an exchange regarding his interest in humor that in hindsight comes across as revelatory. "An out-and-out comedy, even though I've written them," said Lynch, "I somehow keep myself from following through and doing it."

Lynch's website became a wonderful repository for his sense of humor. And it's true that he made multiple, sincere runs at more comedically oriented film projects, like *One Saliva Bubble* and *Dream of the Bovine*, that never came to fruition. But if, eventually, Lynch's sense of his own public persona might have caused those aforementioned feelings of trepidation to calcify, that didn't stop so many writers, performers, and other artists from absorbing the uncanniness and absurdity in his work and redirecting that stimulated imagination into work of their own.

Indeed, one of the interesting things in talking to so many people for this project was the number who spoke—numerous times unprompted—about Lynch's influence on American humor.

"I can't help but see him as honestly having had a huge influence on modern comedy," said writer Aaron Lee. "Really, you wouldn't have [comedy duo] Tim and Eric and that whole kind of school of Adult Swim surreal humor without him. So in some ways, I never really thought about this, but it's completely appropriate that he ended up in *The Cleveland Show* and *Family Guy*—it's really not such a non sequitur. In a way, this whole school of comedy I really do think came out of David Lynch.

"I'll tell you the moment in totally silly, goofy, mainstream comedy that I first saw that I went, 'Oh, that's David Lynch jumping into the mainstream,' his sensibility and his sense of humor," Lee continued. "And it comes to mind because my daughter's on an Adam Sandler kick recently. She rewatched *Billy Madison*, and there's a scene where Steve Buscemi was bullied by Billy as a kid and Billy [as a young adult] calls and apologizes. And Steve Buscemi says, 'Oh, that's okay,' hangs up the phone, and he [has] a list on his wall that says, 'People to kill,' and he crosses out [Billy's name] and starts putting lipstick on his mouth and then all over his face like Diane Ladd in *Wild at Heart*. And it's a total Lynch moment, just now played for mainstream comedy laughs, you know? So I honestly think there's so many places you could say he had enormous [comedic] influence here or there, but I don't feel like I see that spoken to as much. I don't know that people always got the humor of his work at the time."

"That lipstick gag is a straight pull from *Wild at Heart*," agreed *Robot Chicken*'s Seth Green. "It's an easy line to draw between all that because David Lynch is like the subversive punk rock of filmmaking. He's on the side of your John Waters and your other cinematic rebels. And so it's not hard to see all of the influence that he as a filmmaker and as a performer has had . . . [So many viewers] long for something that feels sincere but also feels just a little extra rough around the edges, because that *is* sincere. Some people live in the fringes, and it's much more comfortable."

In discussing Lynch's comedic influence, many people cited examples from his movies, with Frank Booth's enthusiastically profane endorsement of Pabst Blue Ribbon over Heineken in *Blue Velvet*, Cousin Dell's exclamation of "I'm making my lunch!" from *Wild at Heart*, and both the "Have you ever done this before?"/"I don't know" exchange and hitman sequence from *Mulholland Drive* all rating multiple mentions.

But others talked about his off-screen personality, with its amiable earnestness (as with Louis C.K. noting his belief that Lynch would've been a good late night TV talk show host) and coexistence alongside the darker themes explored in his work. Additionally, many cited his acting. "I always loved Gordon Cole," said *Robot Chicken* director Tom Sheppard, "partly because one of the things I loved about *Twin Peaks* that he did is that he's got so many tones he's balancing in the show constantly, [and often] within the same scenes, because Gordon Cole is this over-the-top, almost cartoonish caricature of a crazy FBI agent, and he's playing off of Dale Cooper, who is very understated. And he makes it work. It's like he's not afraid to try anything, even in his own performance. Whereas an actor directing themselves is very often self-conscious, he's just owning it."

Several interviewees cited Lynch's website acting work, which gleefully undercut the stereotype of a serious, intellectual, brooding auteur. That many people would find their way to this material through its later dissemination via YouTube clips and—absent any context regarding its original presentation—still respond enthusiastically to it reinforces the unique nature of his performative connection. As Lynch's identity as a cinematic trailblazer began—for a generation who never really got to experience his films in theaters—to recede a bit, his ascendence as a feisty and offbeat internet personality took off. It's ironic: Lynch, despite his preference for buttoned-up work shirts, destroyed this buttoned-up archetype, almost instinctively viewing it as self-limiting.

For assistant Jay Aaseng, it's a connection that "100 percent" makes sense. "He had an amazing sense of humor. We would joke around all the time, and I wish I'd been around when he was doing *On the Air*," he said. "It was a show that just didn't work out at that time, for whatever reason. But I remember watching that—he did a screening of the pilot at his place at one point, and we were just dying laughing—and it was like, 'Man, this is so different, so from another time, but also just incredible.'"

"He had such a humorous side to him, and he wasn't sarcastic," added producer Sabrina Sutherland. "It was almost like good, clean comedy, but he had that straight-man delivery of something that was so ludicrous that you just had to laugh because of the way he'd say it."

"His sense of humor was sort of old-fashioned, but with a twinkle of mischief," said assistant Mindy Ramaker. "I remember telling him I was going to Seattle, and he'd say, 'Who's Attle?' Or when I'd say, 'I'm running to the store,' he'd say, 'You should drive.'"

"I think there was a part of him that wanted to do more comedy, but I think he also was aware of the difficulty in doing that," Aaseng continued. "I think a lot of people really want their comedies to be very defined in a certain way . . . and David's such his own, singular thing that it sort of works better for him to incorporate comedy into the world of whatever he's doing rather than to do something that is a quote-unquote comedy. But I think he had a lot of respect for comedy, and he's got hilariously funny scenes in pretty much everything that he's done."

Still other interview subjects noted Lynch's embrace of "happy accidents" in filming and how that aspect of his work was extremely resonant, if underdiscussed, among writers—that in comedy writing especially, there is often a surface joke and then ways to plumb that initial idea more deeply. It's here, in addition to his indulgence of commingled tonalities, that many most readily see Lynch's influence.

"I really just respected his steadfastness to stay with whatever idea he had. He knew it evoked an emotion in him and in other people, and that's why I think he ended up switching from painting to film—that film had it all," said writer Kevin Biggins. "I think he definitely had a great sense of humor and knew, I think, a lot of the time that if people could just kind of laugh at this absurd situation, then great, one way or the other. Without knowing for sure, I think probably if some people took [a scene] as humorous, I think he'd be fine with that, and if some people took it as terrifying, then that's fine, as long as it's creating a visceral emotion in someone. I think that was a lot of his goal with some of his stuff—he's making you feel. And definitely one of the things was humor."

In the end, it was perhaps the full spectrum of Lynch's oeuvre, behind the camera and on-screen, that informed comedians' appreciation of him. "I think that in his work he was able to be close to other people and empower them to be funny in ways that maybe they otherwise wouldn't have admitted they felt funny," said Jennifer Lynch. "I know that a lot of the things he did gave other people permission to be more authentically themselves. I think that was one of his great gifts—and the way he saw the world and the way he showcased how close joy and horror are to each other."

"My view may be different, because to me he *was* eccentric and quirky, but so what? It wasn't an affectation," said an actor who worked with Lynch but requested anonymity so as to speak more freely. "He was really direct but always friendly and kind of never not himself, and the simpleness of [that act] in his art and life I think helped a lot of other creative people indulge weird thoughts, odd characters, weird stories, just through the simple acknowledgement of the idea that 'Yeah, weirdness exists—people in the world act strangely *all the time.*' So to me it's a combination of his work and his performances and the way he just existed in the world that was influential. I see him having mainstreamed absurdity in comedy far more than so many stand-ups or well-known actors."

—CHAPTER 53—

"IT'S ALWAYS JUST PRETTY MUCH FELT RIGHT"

The question of whether acting scratched a particular creative itch for Lynch is complicated and a subject on which there is considerable diversity of opinion. Some folks who knew and worked with him across decades say yes. Some qualify their answers. Others, meanwhile, reject the notion.

Nadja director Michael Almereyda, whose career intersected with Lynch briefly but in a meaningful fashion, has an interesting perspective, having coaxed out of Lynch his second speaking role in a film project outside of his own creation. "Despite his countless interviews and public appearances, the sweet sincerity conveyed in *The Art Life* documentary, and of course his weather reports, I still hold on to my impression, from when I first met him, that David was actually very shy," said Almereyda. "No one was more fun than Lynch in party mode, a glass of red wine in one hand and a cigarette in the other, but he wasn't always comfortable around people, and the ease he projected publicly was in fact a skill and probably came at a cost. He built a compound for himself, after all—a domestic space fused with multiple studios and workspaces, and it wasn't an easy thing for him to venture outside of it. His celebrity played a part in this, but it was hardly the whole of it. There's no need for me to guess or project—he gave plenty of testimony on the subject. David was someone very comfortable operating by strict rules and routines and living largely in his head."

Almereyda's point underscores the fact that Lynch, while an artistic polyglot, was not driven by any grand urge to be seen or heard on-screen—and certainly not to challenge himself in the ways an actor more traditionally might, tackling a wide variety of parts across periods or genres. If acting added another credit to his multihyphenate label, that seems more incidental rather than intentional. And yet, the fact that Lynch continued to dip in and out of performance for well over three decades—despite his occasional unease—seems to indicate that acting did fulfill *some* type of desire or artistic compulsion.

I posited that Lynch's motivational impulses belonged to four basic buckets, not mutually exclusive. Many projects, including some over which Lynch didn't have creative control, were deeply rooted in personal relationships with his collaborators. Some performance was driven by curiosity—over learning and playing around with Adobe Flash for *DumbLand*, for example, or working with Steven Spielberg, whom he admired. Some roles can be viewed as a way for Lynch to reconnect with or advance the essential spirit of the art life, in both himself and/or others. Finally, a great many of Lynch's performative choices served as an outlet for his sense of humor, clearly.

To some, this last classification was less a mere extension of Lynch's personality (after all, offbeat humor was a consistent part of his work) and more an important pressure-release valve. As previously articulated by assistant Jay Aaseng, Billy the Groper afforded Lynch the chance to embody an unruly and profane persona. The same held true for a good bit of his voice work.

"The characters you hear in the 'Between Two Worlds' video make me think of *DumbLand*," said Mindy Ramaker, Lynch's assistant from 2007 to 2015. "These characters are all really silly and extreme. They feel id driven and share a primitive kind of humor. You can see this in some of his paintings too, like *Change the Fuckin' Channel Fuckface*. There's some of

David in there, for sure—he had a great sense of humor, and I think he felt a lot of these things but of course wouldn't express them in real life that way."

By exercising this instinct and channeling it through silly (and occasionally outrageous or assaultive) characters, Lynch found a way to playfully tweak (and perhaps at times quietly rage against?) a public identity that was useful but also reductive. I'd advance the argument that some of these flashes of outré pique or oddness are a significant part of his appeal to younger generations, at least in terms of first capturing their awareness. They're not equal to the staggering artistic heights of his best work, of course, but many Lynch performances—his unexpected voice work on *The Cleveland Show*, *Family Guy* or *Robot Chicken*, his weather reports, or even stumping for his lead actress with a cow—have an element of surprise. They're acts that catch attention individually but also come across as wholly authentic. Ergo, when viewers see *Twin Peaks* or Lynch's films, their idiosyncrasies, tonal complexities, and absurdities ring true. And if they come to these other pieces later, it's part of a self-reinforcing loop that tells us the world is wild at heart and weird on top.

Some interviewees viewed acting as if not a crucial creative indulgence for Lynch then at least an obvious extension of his same gifts behind the camera. "His characters that he plays as a performer are not acting, strictly," said Louis C.K. "He's not listening to the other actor and trying to live in the moment—he's playing a part, he's being something else. It's almost like a superhero or something, do you know what I mean? He's got a comic book kind of acting style, and he's the same as his storytelling—that it's a crazy thing that would never happen, but he's going to show you how if it did happen it really would happen. . . . His acting is similar. He's not playing a normal human being. He's not playing a person with an ego who's trying emotionally to achieve something in a scene—which is what a lot of acting is. He's being a fucking strange person who operates on a different principle socially, but boy is he being that guy. He's playing that better than anybody else could."

• • •

For nearly the last two decades of his life, Lynch did not have an agent, according to multiple sources. This meant that outreach regarding acting projects was made through his entertainment lawyer and passed along that way, made directly to one of his assistants, or required people to find some other creative way of reaching him—as with Spielberg's strategic deployment of Laura Dern to prep Lynch for a direct phone call. "He preferred it this way," said Ramaker. "I remember him saying something like, 'It'll be fun for people to have to be detectives.'"

While that approach perhaps dissuaded a few folks, plenty of pitches still came Lynch's way. "There were all kinds of offers that would come in, but I think at a certain point maybe the word got out or whatever that he just wasn't interested in acting," said Aaseng, who started with Lynch in 2001 and continued through 2008. "They started to die down at a certain point while I was there. Then, for whatever reason, they started to pick up a bit towards the end of my time." Added Ramaker, "There was always a steady stream of acting and voice work requests, maybe a couple a month. David was always flattered, but he really loved working on his own projects and knew that these things would take him away from that. So the answer was usually no."

Given his profile and the sense of anticipation attached to his creative endeavors, Lynch could have, with minimal effort, "eventized" his acting. But as evidence has shown, his performance work wasn't the result of proactively seeking out material—or even just letting it be known that he had an open window and was receptive to an appearance. Things came up, and occasionally he would say yes to people's pitches. When asked if perhaps acting satisfied a particular creative urge in Lynch, Toscan du Plantier, a friend of more than two decades, said, "I think so. And it was kind of very natural for him when he decided to be an actor. It was easy for him. I asked him, 'Do you stress when you [act]?' and he said no."

"There's a bit of a rush, and I'm sure David got that," said onset-dresser Mike Malone, who knows of what he speaks by way of cameos in *Fire Walk With Me*, *The Return*, and several Steven Soderbergh projects. "Because again, everybody on a film set has to be quiet. It's cameras rolling. There's a little bit of pressure. I can't imagine why anybody wouldn't get a little bit of a rush out of it."

"I never had the conversation (with him), but I would imagine it put him inside the story in a different way that I think he would find interesting," said *Twin Peaks* helmer Lesli Linka Glatter. "It's not like as a director you're outside the story—you have to be inside of it to direct it. But literally, acting is a totally different thing. You are in the world with the characters, and I could imagine for him that that would be fascinating."

"I think he enjoyed it most in his own projects, obviously," said the aforementioned actor who worked multiple times with Lynch and asked not to be named. "And that makes sense, because he always had this DIY mentality. But that makes the other acting he did more interesting in a way, because you're trying to figure out the connection or what he actually derived from the experience. The voice work stuff I understand, and almost discount as their own thing. So I think those [projects from other people] absolutely did give him something, though it was probably highly personal. Maybe it was as simple as reminding him of the difficulty of acting sometimes. Or maybe he didn't even know."

To Jennifer Lynch, her father's embrace of performance had roots in his appreciation for curious and colorful personalities. "Dad just loved acting," she said. "Dad loved a good character no matter what, and he got such joy from doing it. He was always so nervous—so nervous! It was so endearing. He would rehearse and rehearse and rehearse and study his lines, but he was giddy about the idea of doing it. The nervousness was because he cared so much."

Others tend to see Lynch's acting as more of an oddity than anything else. "I don't think [it fulfilled a particular function]," said Duwayne Dunham. "Acting was an anomaly. His film work, his painting, his photography, his music, his woodworking, TM, all of that stuff—that's where he spent his time and energy." Eric Bassett, who helped Lynch create DavidLynch.com, the platform for an abundance of his performative work, agreed. "In my opinion, he liked performing music way more than acting," he said. "He would get excited about that. I don't know if he was just being bashful or what—it just seemed like it was a bit more of a chore, the acting part."

Unsurprisingly, a lot of responses fall somewhere in the middle. "I think he was always happy to do it once it was done," said Sabrina Sutherland of Lynch's acting. "He was never happy about having to do something. But if he wanted to do it and he did it, then he'd be good about it."

"I never got the impression that he had a burning desire to do it, even though he clearly had an aptitude for [acting]," said Aaseng, "because he was very self-aware and because he's always been very honest about how he wants to cast the right person in the right role. . . . I imagine he wouldn't use himself unless he really saw a way for that to also really bring something out in the story that he was trying to bring out. That's always the impression I got. And so I think that's why it was maybe a little trickier for him to act in projects that weren't his own. If he's going to be in his own thing, I think it's obviously giving service to whatever's going on there. Gordon Cole does a lot to help the plot and story of *Twin Peaks*, for example. [Other things] I think he didn't have natural inclination to do, necessarily. But it's interesting because I guess it's the same for a lot of people in that category. He's just overflowing with so much talent. He could use it in so many different ways, and he was just more interested in using it in other ways."

"I think they all sort of fit into the same giant picture or puzzle," said writer Bob Engels. "I think he loved doing it, but I don't think he ever wanted to be quote-unquote an actor in that sense of the word. I think he was very selective, but once he found something he jumped right in." Added assistant Erik Crary: "He's just such a funny guy, so the idea that he would do these things once in a while doesn't totally shock me. It's just what he's aware of and what he's not aware of are very mysterious to me."

"I feel like David really enjoys acting," said Chrystabell. "I think that David has a palpable excitement for every element of creative expression. And because I think he also has a talent for expression, and timing, and he knows how he wants it to be done, that he gets a kick out of [acting]."

"But as far as going to New York and being on a set, that was torture. And not just torture the day of, but torture the two weeks until, because he's sensitive," Chrystabell continued, touching her hand to her heart for emphasis. "And I don't think people understood that. Maybe they did, I don't know."

"Here's the thing: David wanted to do everything," said first wife Peggy Reavey. She drew a line of distinction and categorized Lynch's acting and other ancillary creative pursuits as mostly "play," however, and thus an entirely different type of expression. "I'm not saying there isn't an element of play in his directing and writing, but . . . when he wanted to make a painting or a film or a scene, he *knows* what he wants that to be. He can already see it. I'm not saying that certain things wouldn't come up in the process, and he would welcome them. But I was always amazed at how there was nothing fragile about his vision. When he imagined something, it was rock solid. It might as well have been real."

This last point is important to consider in unpacking Lynch's performance credits. While ambiguity and mixed tonalities are a staple of his films, there is a proprietary stamp to that work. Acting, by contrast, was a way to let go, by a few degrees, of that sharp certainty of his imagination and exist on a separate creative plane. Even if he was making a strong choice in performance (recall, if you will, "I'd like to cook for you"), it was a distinctly different experience and part of a larger whole that Lynch sometimes shaped but other times did not.

It's also worth pointing out that while it's true Lynch often had some personal connection to projects in which he acted, there were also multiple roles with longtime friends that he turned down—including, to name one example, Dunham's *Legend of the Happy Worker*, which the pair had been connected to since just after *Blue Velvet* and Dunham finally shot in 2018. "He just said, 'No, I don't wanna play that part,'" said Dunham, of a character originally conceived of as being shrunk to three feet tall on-screen via the use of special effects. With Lynch's answer effectively closing the door on his on-screen participation, the script evolved, and that character wasn't included.

Ergo, while it may not always be readily apparent, it seems there was specific intent behind each performative selection, and the aforementioned buckets are as good a way as any to classify the needs they fulfilled. If Lynch liked the writing or a pitch made him laugh (as was especially the case with *The Cleveland Show* and *Louie*), there was perhaps a wider opening of opportunity. Basically, though, he had to have some type of fairly strong response to the material or, in the case of projects like *The Way of Samodelkin* or "The Black Ghiandola," feel like the relatively small outlay of his time had an outsized impact in someone else's pursuit of "the art life" while reconnecting him to that same spirit of creative adventurousness.

My own interviews with Lynch over the years provide some context and clues, but no definitive answers. In a lengthy 2002 interview, in the context of his website acting work, Lynch said, "Being able to step inside a character and into another world is so beautiful," suggesting a personally discovered value. In another extended conversation, in 2018, while casting an eye back on the *Twin Peaks* experience, Lynch reflected on the arduous workload and said, with a laugh, "I said I was a stud before we started, and now I can barely walk." A lot of that exhaustion was simply related to the production schedule, but when asked about the increased workload because of the significantly larger role as Cole, Lynch responded in characteristically opaque fashion. "I'm not really an actor, and I'm not really a musician either, but I've done those things, and I don't know how it's happened except it's always just pretty much felt right." For an artist who so loved secrets and mysteries, it shouldn't come as a surprise that Lynch's relationship with acting remains somewhat hazy, open to dissection and debate, both collectively and across individual projects.

—CHAPTER 54—

GOLDEN SUNSHINE AND THE

DREAMER'S PATH

This is the chapter I never wanted to write—certainly not for this book, but really ever. While the frame for *The Dreamer's Path* was always

Lynch's work as a performer, it feels negligent to not acknowledge that he's left us.

Yet how does one try to define and pin down the legacy of an artist who created so many indelible works?

One lens—indeed, a powerful collective one—is through the internet. The notion of parasocial relationships has gotten much traction over the last decade. The extreme outpouring of online love in the wake of Lynch's passing seemed outsized and a bit curious (in this instance both good things) for a man who, while revered by cineastes and a passionate fanbase, arguably existed on the edge of mainstream pop culture for the majority of his career. But it didn't seem parasocial or malignant to me. That Lynch's death was nonetheless so acutely felt by people who never met him I think speaks to the power of his art and its connection to deeper reservoirs of meaning and intuitive understanding present in all of us (if we choose to listen). I think it actually also speaks to who Lynch was as a person and how he connected with his audience through many of the performances discussed herein.

With extraordinarily rare exceptions, I didn't see people clout posting or claiming false closeness to Lynch, the way one might with other celebrities. Instead, I saw grieving people talking about *feeling* like he was a friend or a family member and sharing stories with fellow fans in order to process the loss. A number described him as an unmet mentor or a creative north star. Some attempted to unpack the reasons for the depth of those feelings. But the sense of attachment was deep, and the fact that a fairly significant portion of these people were not yet born when some of his seminal works were first made is also notable.

My personal interview history, and the fact that it spanned more than twenty years, gives me a unique, informed perspective on Lynch, and perhaps a bit of an inside track on "knowing" him—or at least having a clearer discernment of his essence. I'm quite clear-eyed, though, about the nature of the relationship. He recognized me and maybe knew who I was, but we weren't friends. Asking a mixture of those who did know him quite well along with those whose professional lives intersected with his in the capacity of a performance seems relevant to rounding out a portrait of Lynch as both a performer and a person.

• • •

For many, Lynch's legacy at least begins with the haunting qualities that defined his films and made an adjective out of his surname. Over and over, his marriage of sound and image was discussed, as well as staging and pacing that captured moments of everyday unusualness that often get sanded down in our compartmentalized memories. "He has his own visual style that I think people really responded to," said actress Heather Graham. "He would hold on moments a really, really long time when other people probably would've cut."

Added Nae Yuuki, who portrayed Naido in *The Return*, "His work delighted us by showing us something unknown and inexplicable that actually exists in both our daily lives and in our minds."

"I think David's legacy is just so immense," said *Twin Peaks* episodic director Lesli Linka Glatter. "I think he changed how we perceive what's around us and moved (American) storytelling in a very different direction. I think he brought the unconscious into some kind of consciousness. There are not many filmmakers who do that, and I think his mark is immense as a result of it. And also David was so accessible as a person on an emotional level, so generous."

"He's an artist first, in the sense of his visuals. He denies the normal or patterns," said *Twin Peaks* production designer Richard Hoover. "He had a joyful mind, I think, a satirical mind, and I think his ability to play with it in a mixed serious and humorous way was also fun. That was his spirit. And in his work . . . definitely his pacing and his view of humanity in a wide-angled, slow way that suggests other possibilities I think was very interesting—the mystery of it all and not objectively solving [something because] life is a quest. It's a thing that keeps happening."

Added "Fire is Coming" collaborator Flying Lotus: "I think he'll be known as the great surrealist of film, and everyone will reference Lynchian forever—that term will never go away."

Many of Lynch's *Twin Peaks* collaborators offered thoughts that extended well beyond the parameters of their work with him. "I'm saying something very banal, but the layers of his creativity are just extraordinary," said director Tina Rathborne. "I think it'll be that volume of work" for which he's remembered, added writer Bob Engels. "And his vision was so, in a weird way, consistent. You think it's so avant-garde, if that's the right term for how he approached things, but in one sense his view of things was remarkably consistent."

"David was a carpenter of the soul [who] built elaborate sandboxes for the purpose of abundant playing," said actor Michael Ontkean. "He was an ultrarare songbird who will continue to be heard and seen, continue to be admired, everywhere films are shown—anywhere on this or any other planet."

Calling Lynch an extraordinary visionary, director and editor Duwayne Dunham invoked the memory of Spanish artist Salvador Dalí, whose work was also surreal. "People would ask [Dalí] if he did that while on drugs, and I remember his quote was, 'I don't do drugs; I *am* drugs.' I kind of think of David that way too. His mind just worked in that way . . . that's just his take on things, which is kind of odd to some people but that's what makes him so interesting. His legacy is he's a great artist, visionary, and he's a great human being. And part of his legacy will be his Transcendental Meditation foundation, which hopefully will just keep going on and on. I suspect that it will. He has left his mark for sure."

Mike Henry, whose work with Lynch on *The Cleveland Show* spanned several years, echoed some of those sentiments. "He was just the avant-garde and the completely normal in the same body. To me that's who he is, just the yin and the yang. And he wasn't afraid to throw 'em both on the same canvas—just the wonder of it all. And the meditation too. He got me into TM and just talking about the unified field of consciousness."

"There was nothing he did where you looked at it and you go, 'Someone else could have done that or would've done it in that way,'" added *Lucky*'s Ron Livingston. "His stuff was very, very specific to him while also being radically different."

International interviewees like Mélita Toscan du Plantier, a longtime friend, and "Peixe Vermelho" director Andreia Vigo, meanwhile, cited the reaction of newspapers to Lynch's passing, covering it not just in the arts and entertainment section but topping their regular news.

"*Libération* said we are lucky to have lived in the time of David Lynch," said France's Toscan du Plantier, adding that *Le Monde* put out a special six- to eight-page section on his life and work. Brazilian newspaper *Folha* ran the headline "The Last Inventor of Cinema Has Died," reinforcing Lynch's impact as deep and far-reaching. "Lynch was a complete artist," said Vigo. "Even his early works, 'The Grandmother' and *Eraserhead*, already revealed the creation of a singular art universe. He didn't just make films; he created entire worlds of emotion, imagery, and narrative that will continue to fascinate and influence forever."

In citing and discussing his body of work, many interviewees honed in on Lynch's persistence of vision and how he did things his way. In a world where we're under constant bombardment—by advertising, by work obligations, by friends and family—in ways that frequently and understandably reorder our priorities, Lynch retained an endearing steadfastness in pursuing that which most fascinated him. His iron-fisted grip on his own childlike (not childish) sense of wonderment as well as certain core preoccupations, both visual and thematic, hold a valuable lesson on how to develop an authentic artistic voice and meaningfully explore and reengage with those elements across time and various projects.

And if the fence around his creative interests and impulses wasn't incidental, neither was it accidental. "He told me once there was a time in his life when he had so much going on in his head that he thought he needed to see a psychiatrist, and he went and had one meeting," recalled *The Elephant Man* producer Jonathan Sanger. "And when he talked to the guy, I don't remember exactly what was said, but it was the notion that the guy was going to clear up stuff for him. And as soon as he heard that, David said, 'I don't want you to clear up stuff. I mean, no, that's not what I want. I'm not interested in that.' So he walked out, and that was it. He said, 'I'm not interested in analyzing myself. I'm interested in going with the things that I feel and understanding them for myself, but I don't want to explain them.' He felt that even psychiatry would be trying to explain him to himself, and he didn't need that. I'm extrapolating, and I'm not sure David would say it that way, but certainly I got the sense from him that a lot of the fount of his creativity was something that he didn't want to mess with. He just wanted to explore it; he wanted to use it. He wanted to use his dreams and his thinking, but it was magical thinking—it was something that needed to be allowed to exist. If you analyzed it and took it apart, it would go away, and he didn't want that."

"It's just unbelievable and so inspirational, I think, to see someone who conquered the film industry—not Hollywood, the film industry worldwide, he's considered rightly one of the greatest artists of our lifetimes—and he still just took these chances," said *Robot Chicken* director Tom Sheppard. "He still just did things that were fun for him to do, and whether they got an audience or not didn't matter, or didn't seem to matter, to him. He just wanted to make really cool stuff that tickled him, and God, we're all the better for it."

"He embodied the uncompromising epitome of an artist, [where] you don't really worry about how people are going to react," said assistant Jay Aaseng. "I mean, he would think about those things to a degree—I think he's a natural performer and wants to connect with an audience—but for the most part he was still going to do what he does. He wants to stay true to the ideas. I think he always did that for better or for worse as far as how anything might have turned out. I think that that's probably going to be his legacy—as somebody that absolutely did it his way, and in a way that nobody else ever had before."

"I would say his visionary films and his integrity [are his legacy]. He didn't budge," said Peggy Reavey. "He was doing what he wanted, not what anybody else wanted."

Even to someone who had a fraught relationship with Lynch, like writer Harley Peyton, Lynch's one-of-a-kind artistry, forged in no small way through headstrong insistence, is something to be held in awe and celebrated. "At [the USC *Twin Peaks* retrospective in 2013], I made the joke that the word 'genius' is thrown around far too easily in our business. And what I said, which is sort of mean, is, 'Aaron Sorkin's not a genius, but David Lynch just might be,' right? And I do believe that. I mean, he was so singular, and the journey he took through Hollywood—it wasn't like he was Jim Jarmusch working around the edges his entire career. He somehow managed to bring surreality and all of these amazing things into mainstream moviemaking.

"It was an amazing life, and he was obviously an extraordinarily talented man. *And* we didn't get along," Peyton said with a laugh. "When the show ended, I had my *Twin Peaks* computer, because we all got Macs, and David made it his business to go, 'I want Harley's computer back. Tell him he has to give his computer back.' And I, being completely childish, refused to give my computer back. I held onto it for as long as possible as David got [angrier]. This is David fucking Lynch, and he's becoming obsessed with the fact that I still have my show computer! I mean, I'm laughing now. I was not laughing then.

"But again, he somehow managed to teleport surreality into mainstream Hollywood," Peyton added. "He just *did*. When you look at the guy who did *Eraserhead*, you go, 'Well, yeah, this guy's going to be making art house movies or maybe performance art, like Chris Burden or something.' You just wouldn't think of him as doing anything like [what he accomplished], and yet it is wholly because of who he was. I mean, Bob Dylan always wrote about the Weird America, and David Lynch came right out of that Weird America. People always talked about the Boy Scout stuff, and that's not inaccurate. But there was that weirdness too. And I think there was a little bit of anger and darkness that was hiding beneath that surface, the gee-whiz stuff. So it was almost like Jimmy Stewart collided with Alfred Hitchcock, and you got this weird American archetype who just did amazing work. And I can't think of another director who managed to do that like he did.

"I mean, the fact that he was able to take that same sense of surreality and put a big fucking horse in someone's living room on ABC is just insane—particularly when you look at what network television was like then. I'd already seen it, but I remember watching that first episode [of *Twin Peaks*] at my house when it aired. A bunch of friends came over, and several of them were from the [Steven] Bochco universe. They were all working on *L.A. Law*, I think it was, and sitting there they got angrier and angrier. By the end of it, you could look at them, and it was almost like they felt they got cheated, like, 'How come you get to [get away with that]? That's not TV!'

"David, I think in the fullness of time, or maybe already, should be seen as one of the more significant figures in this era of moviemaking—I mean, *easily*," Peyton went on. "People always talk about—and I love these people: Spielberg, Scorsese—and David belongs in that pantheon, if only because he was weirder than all of them. And there's just something I really respect about that."

As a consequence of this idiosyncrasy, and his successes, Lynch served throughout his lifetime as a source of artistic inspiration to an enormous number of creative-minded individuals across a wide variety of disciplines, from filmmakers to musicians, graphic artists, and more. To many who knew and worked with Lynch, that will be a significant part of his legacy. "I feel everyone I've met since filming has had some story to tell me about how he influenced them wanting to write, wanting to direct, wanting to act," said Andrea Watrouse, who portrayed Mandie in *The Return*. "And because I had not been in the world of entertainment, I hadn't noticed how foundational studying his art has been for people. I think he gives people with eccentric visions a path to follow."

Several interviewees talked about Lynch's commitment to the art life and finding inspiration—in some cases expressly for themselves—in the authenticity of that lived experience. Livingston described what he saw on the set of *Lucky* as a glimpse at the benefits of such an integrated mindset and said he absorbed lessons he learned there into his own work. "I did definitely get the sense of like, 'Oh, I see relation between his artistry here as an actor and his artistry as a director, even though he's not trying to use those [latter] tools for this job. He was bringing the artistry and a connection with the subconscious that I think sort of drove or inspired his [films as a director]. And that's been really a powerful and freeing thought."

For "The Soul Detective" director Davi de Oliveira Pinheiro, Lynch's legacy is simple: "Just be yourself as an artist; don't try to emulate other people. It is a very dark and difficult world to live in, and it is going to only get harder. To be yourself and to try to make the art you want to make is going to be very difficult. But it's totally worth it, because . . . people can feel and distinguish when someone just loves and wants to express what their inner thoughts are through art. And it doesn't come as a judgment upon who is unable to do that. It shouldn't be a judgment. But it's really great that you have people who inspire other people to try to find the truth—to not just survive [or make a living] in filmmaking or the arts but at least leave that piece of what's truthful [to them] about the planet we live on, the way we see stuff, the way we think about our lives."

"To me," said Lynch's assistant Mindy Ramaker, "David is the pure embodiment of creativity, and he really lived the art life. His vision was so singular that it must have taken a huge amount of bravery to be as committed to his ideas as he was. I think that's part of what draws everyone to him— not just his work, but to him. Of course he achieved a ton of 'success,' but he always said he'd be happy with just some art supplies. And I believe that. He would joke that if he were in prison he'd do a lot better than other people because he's happy being left alone with time to think and draw. If for some reason he hadn't achieved the fame and opportunities he did, I don't think his daily life would have changed much—just the conditions around him. He'd still have spent his days drinking coffee, dreaming, and painting or making something.

"This is a roundabout way of saying that he truly loved the doing. And isn't that so rare—any field, not just the arts? He always said you can't control the outcome. You can control action and action alone, so you have to love the doing. It's incredibly difficult to actually do that, but he did. And I think that brought him a lot of peace. So I think beyond his movies and art, people feel his spirit and can always find inspiration in that."

All these streams of influence flow from a single deep spring, and unsurprisingly when pondering his legacy a good number of folks landed on some of the animating personal characteristics that informed his work. "I know that my kids and people in their twenties really love David," said Louis C.K. "And I think the reason his work will carry on is because there's *love* in him. Because when people like David, they love him. It's not just 'That movie's amazing' or 'That scene's incredible.' They go 'I fucking love that guy.' You can feel and understand, underneath the movie, what a soft and strange and beautiful mind and heart this is coming from. It's like if you're a great wine lover and you drink wine from the south of France, you can taste Bordeaux and know where the grapes and soil is from. With David's work, there's nothing like it in the whole world, and no one's ever faithfully imitated it, or even really tried. And his diversity too—the fact that he made *The Elephant Man* and *Blue Velvet* is crazy, but you can feel *his* love in all [his films]. That's how I feel about it, and that's the sense I get from young people too, so that's what I think will last."

For Adele Jones, who portrayed Lieutenant Knox in *The Return*, a crucial part of Lynch's legacy lies in his accepting nature, as a director and off-screen as well. "His legacy is that gift of be who you are," she shared. "When I talk to a lot of the people who are cast members that I now consider my friends, that's how a lot of us feel when we talk to each other. I just say, 'Hey, thanks for accepting my weird.' David really let me come in and be exactly who I am. He saw me on that screen in that [audition] interview, and he's like, 'Okay, you're being you, so you get to come with me.' It was like a reward for just owning who I am and talking truthfully and not running away from the reality of my existence—and that's been a work in progress my whole life. But sometimes you need people to come in and just say, 'You are okay, and I'm okay, and I'm okay with who you are. And not only am I okay with it, but I find it beautiful. Give me more of that!' That's life-changing too. I know it's been life-changing for me."

Kimmy Robertson's big answer when asked about Lynch's legacy comes in the small package of one word: "Love," she said, followed by a pause. "I think later, when people calm down a little and if they start looking for reality, I think they'll notice that he was just a big bag of love. He was a happy love bug. That's not much of a big, legacy-type explanation, but to me it's what he was. And still is. He's still working. He's with Maharishi Mahesh Yogi and a bunch of other people up there working." Going on to note the forty thousand sensory neurites in the human heart (which regulate function and communicate with the brain in ways not yet fully understood), Robertson added, "I always felt like he had two lines of communication—the one he was saying out loud and the one he was saying with his heart."

• • •

If these reminiscences and perspectives help offer a holistic portrait of Lynch's lasting influence as an artist, they also reflect back on his relationship with performance. Lynch's specific reasons for acting are maybe unknowable but also, when one digs into it, kind of evident.

He never stopped leaning into things that interested him, invigorated him, and yes, sometimes even made him uneasy.

As a filmmaker, Lynch traded heavily in dark themes and embraced abstractions and moods. By also frequently spotlighting the coexistence of absurdity alongside the unsettling, Lynch's work demystifies the latter. Rejecting the carefully fenced-in emotional packaging of so much entertainment product, his films (among many, many other things) refute the idea that, for example, suffering can be put in a neat box, where it exists as that one thing alone.

His acting work can be viewed through the same lens. For more than half his life, Lynch had an entirely earned reputation as a serious filmmaker, a capital-A auteur. But he also was a human being, containing the same multitudes we all do. Performing was a way to remind people of that—others, yes, but maybe even himself.

Stepping inside a story from the perspective of an actor rather than a director also connected Lynch to others' creative energies, which he clearly enjoyed. Despite the impression by some of Lynch as a highly idiosyncratic artist who lived in a bubble, he drew inspiration from his own curiosity about the world and the embrace of friends, family, and other collaborators.

When discussing the meaning of his films, Lynch frequently gave gnomic responses. Throughout his career, Lynch endorsed as valid subjective readings of his movies; if someone found value in them, that was in his view wonderful. Lynch's presence, however, as both creator and performer in a significant cross section of his work (especially on his website, which afforded him a more experimental and controllable platform) speaks to his own view of art's holistic nature, its essential integration into his being.

Nowhere do these postulations find more support than in *Twin Peaks*. While both the original run and *The Return* are captivating fusions of Lynch and Mark Frost's overlapping yet distinct sensibilities and interests, it's okay to assign a weighted value to the arc of Gordon Cole. The show is, by design, rich and well crafted enough to accommodate different interpretations.

In regard to the third season, I neither think nor wish to suggest the dominant tides of Lynch's creative choices were dictated by thoughts of personal legacy. Yet I do feel he had a well-considered sense of both the weight and opportunity presented by his persona. Cultural critics (as well as no small amount of social media scolds—an interesting overlap) sometimes refer to this as "the power of one's platform." Does that mean Lynch felt a "responsibility," in the sense that most of us interpret it, to steer viewers' attention or help frame some of *The Return*'s bigger philosophical questions? No. But he perhaps understood that sometimes the man is the message—that he, himself, was a uniquely suited guide, already well situated in the show's plotting, to help take an audience where he and Frost wanted to go. That Lynch also had a pure sense of participatory pleasure in stepping back into the world of *Twin Peaks* can also be considered. Those aren't mutually exclusive.

As mentioned, the interview with Lynch for this project didn't come to fruition, so these thoughts above and many others exist in the realm of speculation, an inner monologue. My last interview with Lynch, which came after his diagnosis with emphysema, was conducted via Zoom. At the end of the conversation, he asked for my address and said he wanted to send me something. A week or so later I received a small package in the mail. Opening it up, I found inside a lime-green coffee mug, inscribed to me and autographed by him. It was an incredibly kind gesture.

When I think of David Lynch, that honestly isn't what I think of first, second, third, or even fiftieth. I think of his art in all its permutations, which is stupendous. So much of it transcends time, and it's not an exaggeration to say it will last as long as there's recorded human history. I think too of little bits of ephemera that enjoy virality in cyclical fashion—Lynch's blistering responses to product placement in movies or watching films on a smartphone, plus his perturbed reaction "What a heavy load Einstein must've had—fuckin' morons, everywhere!" followed by that moment of what real jerks never do, which is step back and cackle at their own anger. I even think of his laugh in general, which when it came in conversation felt like its own little surprising victory and special connection.

Still, especially when enjoying a damn fine cup of coffee, I sometimes reflect upon that single deed as a placeholder—a small, unexpected, and unrequested act that shows the personal kindness of the man. While in his work he frequently explored terrible darkness in the world, Lynch as a person was full of, and consumed by, its opposite nature and the propagation of that goodwill and compassion. Owing to that, the world just seemed a little bit brighter and better knowing he was in it. Because of his films and art as well—and also those occasional performances. The fact that there even existed the possibility of Lynch popping up on-screen somewhere was an utter delight, a forecast of sunshine.

Reflecting on that no longer being possible edges us to a moment of reckoning. In the beginning of this book, I said we'd arrive in due time at the answer to how many projects Lynch acted in. We've substantively plumbed well over fifty, many having multicomponent parts. We've touched on another fourteen or so that could be entertained as performances. We even unpacked phantom credits, projects unrealized, and opportunities passed on. So how many performances as an actor did Lynch give? The real answer is that there isn't a set number, despite what certain databases may say. I hope, among other things, this book has shown Lynch's relationship with performance extended beyond the definition of "actor" in the most traditional sense of the word. Yes, he played recognizable characters in *Twin Peaks*, several other of his own projects, and films and TV shows made by others. He also leaned into performance art and made consistent gestures that playfully nodded at or tweaked his public persona.

Lynch wholeheartedly embraced the art life at a young age. Still, I believe the aperture of his view on what that truly meant widened throughout the years. In the same general spirit of "Everyday, once a day, give yourself a present," performing—whether acting opposite a friend or lending voice to an eccentric animated character, saying yes to an unexpected short film project or delivering a daily weather report—became part of an expansive, integrated tapestry.

In the end, Lynch's life every bit as much as his creative output summons to mind the phrase and question from Gordon Cole's Monica Bellucci dream, the phrase Cole repeats: "We are like the dreamer who dreams, and then lives inside a dream. But who is the dreamer?" The scene (scripted by Lynch, as we see in *The Art Life*) is perhaps a call for reflection, to both like-minded individuals and those not yet awakened to the wonder of life's interrelatedness. Of course, in life David Lynch was also the dreamer. The dreamer of his own singular path—in two definitions of the word, both out of the ordinary and distinguished by superiority—which we were fortunate enough to share. And he will remain as such forevermore.

—ACKNOWLEDGMENTS—

First, the most deeply felt and sincere thank you to all the interviewees (sixty-two quoted herein and another dozen on background or off the record) for sharing their time and perspective. If there's value in this book, it's fundamentally because of your contributions. Your recollections, candor, opinions and generosity of spirit breathed life into everything I hoped to examine and illuminate.

Special thanks to Sabrina Sutherland, whose professionalism and helpfulness unlocked so much of what *The Dreamer's Path* became. I'm beholden to you.

Extra thanks to a quartet of longtime assistants—Jay Aaseng, Michael Barile, Erik Crary, and Mindy Ramaker—for their insights. You're the heroes of this tome.

Directors Catherine Hardwicke, John Carroll Lynch, Tina Rathborne, and Jonathan Sanger were each giving with their time and went above and beyond in various ways. I'll always appreciate Adele Jones, a bona fide "twofer" who was incredibly open from the jump, and feel fortunate to have gained a friend.

To Jennifer Lynch, at a tender and vulnerable time you were so giving, and the emotionality of our conversations owns a place in my heart forever. I so value your trust in helping to explore this rich part of your father's life.

For invaluable assistance in connecting with interviewees, I'd like to thank the following: David Alicandri, Molly Alves, Jamie Arons, Robin Baum, Peggy Sherwin Becker, Margaret Sutherland Brown, Karin Reznack Byrum, Maria Clemente, Houston Costa, Mike Eisenstadt, Yumi Facciolla, Craig Feblowitz, Blake Fronstin, Antonio Gimenez-Palazon, Bradley Glenn, Brian Goldberg, Sarah Goodwin, Emma Taylor Green, Andy Hazel, Andrew Hersh, Beth Holden-Garland, Seth Howard, Keleigh Kaliher, Lesa Kirk, David Koch, Bebe Lerner, Oliver Mahrdt, Brianna Maloney, Molly Mandel, Alex Flores Martinez, Carri McClure, Maitê Mendonça, Madison Murray, Matt Nordsten, Bella Obando, Sydney Olson, Liz Orr, Tim Patricia, Susan Patricola, Theresa Picciallo,

Alla Plotkin, Montana Rispoli, J.B. Roberts, Danielle Robinson, Jillian Roscoe, Kate Rosenbaum, Erin Schuessler, Michelle Schwartz, David Shaul, John Sloss, Daniel Bender Stern, James Suskin, Yuka Swearengin, Natalie Thomas, Alex Weed, Jason Weinberg, and Lea Cohen Zuckerman. A thank you too to all publicists, managers, and agents who engaged for parties with whom a conversation ultimately didn't work out.

For providing miscellaneous assistance, gratefulness goes out to Ashlay Eugenio, Jason Little, Steven Miller, Stefania Rosini, Cassandra Sherwin, and Miriam Spritzer.

A hearty tip of the cap for their belief in this project to Scott Ryan and David Bushman, the latter of whom provided invaluable guidance in snuffing out dumb habits.

To my better half in almost every way, Tamela Lively, thank you for both giving me the room to dream and walking with me a path wonderful but sometimes strange. You're the view from all the windows of my room. I love you so much and appreciate you keeping me around to reach stuff on the top shelves.

Eternal love to my parents, Lawrence and Nancy Simon, for instilling in me a curiosity about the world and putting paper and a pencil in my hand, and to my sister Erica, who long before I ever thought I could tell stories with words ~~requested~~ demanded bedtime tales. I'm proud of you.

I have many incredible friends I've tricked into believing I'm worthy of their time, the common thread among them being they're more interesting and intelligent than me. Among them, Kevin Hanna is an endless booster, sounding board, and talented writer whose singular friendship means the whole world to me. Would I even be a scribe if not for Mac Rogers and all those movies we mainlined as teenagers? Perhaps, but certainly nowhere near as polished without the example of his gifts, of which I remain in awe. I'm wonderstruck by the encyclopedic knowledge and preternatural kindness of Todd Gilchrist, who's also made me a better writer; I'll cherish our *Twin Peaks: The Return* premiere experience as long as there's a light on in my head. It's difficult to recall a time when I didn't know Eric Fossett, whose friendship I treasure. With Eric Layton I toiled in the editorial trenches when free print alt-weeklies were a viable economic model, and his magnanimity and guidance taught me so much at a young age. I'm indebted to each of you, as well as other friends I can't all list here, in ways you can't fully realize.

The warm embrace of my extended family, including the entirety of the Lively clan, is so enriching, and reaffirms the value in leading with love (a lesson this world needs more than ever). Thanks for your support.

A gallon of acknowledgment to the *Twin Peaks* and David Lynch fan communities. It's indescribably wonderful to have a lingua franca with which to engage with life's unnerving and absurd elements. I never regret meeting a fellow fan; they're good people. That finally brings us to David Lynch himself, who has my infinite gratitude for setting fire to my imagination.

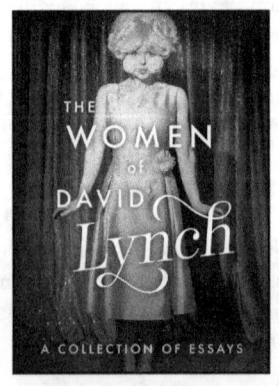